A RHETORICAL CRIME

CENTER FOR THE STUDY OF
GENOCIDE
& HUMAN RIGHTS

Genocide, Political Violence, Human Rights Series

Edited by Alexander Laban Hinton, Stephen Eric Bronner, and Nela Navarro

Nanci Adler, ed., *Understanding the Age of Transitional Justice: Crimes, Courts, Commissions, and Chronicling*

Alan W. Clarke, *Rendition to Torture*

Lawrence Davidson, *Cultural Genocide*

Daniel Feierstein, *Genocide as Social Practice: Reorganizing Society under the Nazis and Argentina's Military Juntas*

Alexander Laban Hinton, ed., *Transitional Justice: Global Mechanisms and Local Realities after Genocide and Mass Violence*

Alexander Laban Hinton, Thomas La Pointe, and Douglas Irvin-Erickson, eds., *Hidden Genocides: Power, Knowledge, Memory*

Douglas A. Kammen, *Three Centuries of Conflict in East Timor*

Walter Richmond, *The Circassian Genocide*

Victoria Sanford, Katerina Stefatos, and Cecilia M. Salvi, eds., *Gender Violence in Peace and War: States of Complicity*

Irina Silber, *Everyday Revolutionaries: Gender, Violence, and Disillusionment in Postwar El Salvador*

Samuel Totten and Rafiki Ubaldo, eds., *We Cannot Forget: Interviews with Survivors of the 1994 Genocide in Rwanda*

Anton Weiss-Wendt, *A Rhetorical Crime: Genocide in the Geopolitical Discourse of the Cold War*

Ronnie Yimsut, *Facing the Khmer Rouge: A Cambodian Journey*

A RHETORICAL CRIME

Genocide in the Geopolitical Discourse of the Cold War

ANTON WEISS-WENDT

RUTGERS UNIVERSITY PRESS
New Brunswick, Camden, and Newark, New Jersey, and London

Library of Congress Cataloging-in-Publication Data

Names: Weiss-Wendt, Anton, 1973– author.
Title: A rhetorical crime : genocide in the geopolitical discourse of the Cold War / Anton Weiss-Wendt.
Description: New Brunswick : Rutgers University Press, [2018] | Series: Genocide, political violence, human rights | Includes bibliographical references and index.
Identifiers: LCCN 2017033842| ISBN 9780813594668 (cloth : alk. paper) | ISBN 9780813594651 (pbk. : alk. paper)
Subjects: LCSH: Convention on the Prevention and Punishment of the Crime of Genocide (1948 December 9) | Genocide (International law) | Genocide intervention—Political aspects. | Cold War. | Soviet Union—Foreign relations—1945–1991. | United States—Foreign relations.
Classification: LCC KZ7180 .W43 2018 | DDC 345/.0251—dc23
LC record available at https://lccn.loc.gov/2017033842

A British Cataloging-in-Publication record for this book is available from the British Library.

⊗ The paper used in this publication meets the requirements of the American National Standard for Information Sciences—Permanence of Paper for Printed Library Materials, ANSI Z39.48–1992.

www.rutgersuniversitypress.org

Manufactured in the United States of America

To Krishna Das

CONTENTS

FOREWORD

DOUGLAS IRVIN-ERICKSON

With the publication of this volume, Anton Weiss-Wendt builds on his long-standing reputation as a leading expert of Soviet legal and political history. *A Rhetorical Crime* offers the most important scholarly consideration to date of the UN Genocide Convention in Soviet law and politics during the Cold War and presents a masterful overview of the position of the convention in US foreign policy. The breadth of the book is built on the author's novel use of new primary sources, including Soviet archives that have been unexplored by scholars in the field of genocide studies, international criminal law, international humanitarian law, and human rights.

The more one studies the history of twentieth-century international law, the more evident it becomes that there was nothing that made our present-day humanitarian laws and institutions inevitable. The great humanitarian treaties and covenants of the twentieth century, such as the UN Genocide Convention and the Declaration of Human Rights, were not self-evident to people living in the wake of the Second World War. Nor were the rights and protections that they ascribed into international law immanent in history. The institutions and laws, and the normative basis for them, had to be imagined, debated, and fought for. Yet, this did not make the UN Genocide Convention a moral document, nor did it alone make the convention a pillar of moral progress. Instead, it reveals that the Genocide Convention and the broader efforts by people around the world to prevent mass murder was (and is) a fundamentally political project. The present book, which picks up the story of genocide in Soviet law and politics around 1953, after the death of Stalin, makes this point perfectly clear.

As I have argued in my own work, *Raphaël Lemkin and the Concept of Genocide* (2017), the delegates at the UN who drafted the convention were career diplomats whose first priority—above the humanitarian impulse that underscored the treaty against genocide and was used to legitimize the need for such a law—was to advance and protect the interests of their governments and states. It is not just that the Soviet Union's delegates attempted to weaken the treaty and bend the text of the convention so that the law could be applied to their geopolitical adversaries but not themselves. The US delegates wanted to outlaw atrocities such as those unleashed by Nazi Germany, but they worried that the United States was also guilty of genocide against "red" and "Negro" Americans, so they fought to weaken the treaty accordingly. Swedish diplomats were instructed to make sure the convention could not be applied to their country's treatment of the Sami; the Canadian delegation was under orders to ensure the convention would suffer death by committee if it seemed the law might criminalize massacres of native peoples and residential schools. The French government attempted to undermine the ability of the treaty to hold individual officials responsible for genocide, and they fought to make the law nonapplicable in colonial territories. The South African delegation generally felt that outlawing genocide would hinder their state's ability to deal with their problem of "backward" peoples. Brazil's delegation believed that genocide against political opponents was part of Latin American culture, and that genocide should be preserved as a right for any government when it needed to deal with threats to the existence of the state. The paradox of this moment, which can seem incongruous at first glance, was that every delegation at the United Nations could agree that the horrors of genocide should be outlawed and atrocities such as the Holocaust should never be repeated—but they also wanted a law that could not be applied to their own grave actions, but still be applied to acts of mass murder that hurt their own national interests. In such a way, Pakistan and India, while accusing each other of genocide and trying to craft a law that could be applied to each other but not themselves, both worked together to support the UN Genocide Convention because they believed it would criminalize the kinds of horrors they suffered under the British.

A look into the archives also reveals alliances and movements that the popular memory of the UN Genocide Convention has conveniently forgotten, such as that the first country that Raphael Lemkin, the originator of the term *genocide*, tried to prosecute for genocide was France. Lemkin, a jurist of Jewish and Polish descent who lost almost his entire family in the Holocaust, believed that a worldwide genocide against Muslims was being prepared in the 1950s, after the European-wide genocide against Jews of the 1930s and 1940s. Lemkin worked tirelessly with delegations from Arab countries to prosecute France for genocide in Algeria and with Pakistan to prosecute genocides stemming from British colonial rule in South Asia. There is more to this history that is inconvenient to our popular narratives. In 1951, for instance, the United Nations was strongly petitioned to investigate whether the United States committed genocide against its citizens of African descent. And, as much as the delegates at the United Nations made reference to the UN Genocide Convention as being necessary for preventing the kinds of horrors committed against Jews by German and Axis-occupied governments, they also contemplated the possibility of Western-backed genocides in the Holy Land. As I have argued elsewhere, all of these movements and complexities of the past are swept aside by reductive popular narratives that find their way into history textbooks and official government accountings. The importance of Weiss-Wendt's book is not only that he grapples with all these conveniently forgotten episodes (and many more), but that for the first time he shows that the Soviet Union (and the country's leaders) was at the center of these events, politically and legally.

The starting point for understanding the politics and history of the UN Genocide Convention is a recognition that the Soviet Union was a party to the drafting of the convention and that Joseph Stalin personally read and annotated every draft, as Anton Weiss-Wendt has demonstrated in his previous scholarship. The final wording of the convention carefully defined genocide so as to avoid criminalizing the kinds of mass violence that had been committed by the powers that won the Second World War—the United States and Canada ensured it could not be applied to native peoples, the United Kingdom and France ensured it could not be applied to the colonies, and the Soviet Union ensured that it could not be applied to political and class conflict and carefully expunged all allusions to starvation as an act of genocide. For this reason and others, the Genocide Convention itself was very much a reflection of the emerging Cold War politics of the postwar world, where the United States and the Soviet Union could agree that the new institutions of the United Nations, such as the Genocide Convention, should be strong enough to constrain the kinds of atrocities that threatened the stability of the international order from which their power derived, but weak enough not to threaten their own sovereignty or jeopardize their national interests. For the Soviets, outlawing genocide was a good thing so long as it did not hurt them geopolitically. If the law could be used to hurt the United States, all the better. For the United States, the calculation was exactly the same.

The geopolitical stakes of the multilateral debates over the Genocide Convention between 1946 and 1948—which was going to be the first humanitarian law of the United Nations and a cornerstone of the new international legal regime of the postwar world—were especially high for the Soviet Union. As Weiss-Wendt has shown previously, the drafting process revealed core beliefs of Stalin's government toward the United Nations, reflected Communist theories of the relationship between the law and political power, and also evinced a particular Soviet approach to international law—that the law was never apolitical, and therefore always an instrument of state policy. International law, it followed, was likewise an instrument of policy wielded by the most powerful actors in international politics. Consequently, in the Soviet view, the law was at once a reflection of the political order and a buttress to it. To risk an oversimplification, it can be said that this practical and political notion of international law flew in the face of liberal, or bourgeois, conceptions that saw the law as just only when it was politically neutral. Criminal law that was used as a political tool, in the liberal view, produced show trials. Likewise, international law that was seen as politically motivated was believed to provoke instability and threaten the foundation for peaceful international relations. In the Soviet conception, all law was political. To pretend otherwise was either delusional or hypocritical.

Lemkin knew this. Never in any of his writings did he waste words pondering the philosophical foundation of the law or worrying about how to create fair international trials. For Lemkin, again as I have argued elsewhere, international law was a pedagogical and political undertaking. He was also well aware that the powerful state actors at the United Nations negotiating the Genocide Convention were pursuing their own self-interests at the expense of their adversaries. Against these forces, Lemkin believed, he had to assemble a coalition of smaller states and former colonies who could vote in large enough numbers to force the United States and the Soviet Union to the negotiating table, while mobilizing a social and civil society movement to lobby Western governments to embrace the humanitarian law. Only with such efforts, Lemkin believed, could worldwide sentiments against genocide be produced and states forced to sign a treaty against genocide—and still it would take real work to convince people that genocide was something that should not be committed. This was the historical crucible in which the Soviet and American Cold War relationship over the UN Genocide Convention was forged, the contentious relationship that very much rests at the center of this book.

One of the great accomplishments of Anton Weiss-Wendt's scholarship is that he exploits previously unused archival sources to reveal, quite clearly, that the Soviet Union was as influential in shaping the institutions of international law as the United Kingdom and the United States, whose efforts are lauded in the scholarly literature on the postwar Nuremberg and Tokyo war crimes tribunals and the United Nations. He is also able to demonstrate, for the first time, that the Soviet Union (and later the Russian Federation) played an equally important role in determining the course of global politics around the UN Genocide Convention. What is also clearly evident in this book is that no government approached the Genocide Convention with purely humanitarian convictions. In fact, the four countries that rushed to claim the credit in the 1990s for leading efforts to outlaw genocide in the 1940s—the United States, United Kingdom, France, and Russia through the Soviet Union—were the four fiercest opponents of efforts to outlaw genocide in the 1940s. During the intervening decades, Weiss-Wendt's book teaches us, genocide and the UN Genocide Convention were little more than moralizing motifs in Soviet and American Cold War discourses. In this, we find that the Soviet legal, political, and social encounter with the UN Genocide Convention has been remarkably similar to that of the United States and other Western countries.

Thanks to Weiss-Wendt's scholarship, we now know that the humanitarian institutions and laws, and the international criminal justice regime in its present form today, are deeply indebted to Soviet legal scholarship and practice. Weiss-Wendt has traced the boundaries between ideology and realpolitik in the Soviet discourse and practice of international criminal law from the 1940s to 1991. As ideology and politics changed after the death of Stalin, Soviet foreign policy priorities changed, which in turn led to changes in the Soviet interpretation of genocide. The present book charts the emergence of a discourse of "Soviet genocide" that took hold in the United States during the late 1940s and 1950s (Chapter 2) and examines how the discourse on Soviet repression in Soviet satellite countries such as Yugoslavia and Hungary changed as these countries sought to switch their allegiances away from the Soviet Union (Chapter 3). In the Third World, we see how accusations of genocide followed the Cold War client lines through the 1950s and 1960s. When Moscow saw genocide in French and English colonies, the West saw genocide in anticolonial violence supported by Moscow (Chapter 4). In domestic US politics toward the Soviet Union, the American far right and the far left OPPOSED AND supported the US ratification of the Genocide Convention, RESPECTIVELY, by making reference to the Soviets (Chapter 6). The left wanted to ratify the convention to avoid moral embarrassment, while the right lambasted the treaty as a deficient instrument to prosecute the spread of world Communism. The Soviets, on the other hand, alleged the United States was guilty of genocide in its treatment of Native Americans and African Americans (Chapter 7). And while the United States and the Soviet Union avoided mentioning the word "genocide" in relation to Armenian and Turkish politics, seeking to strengthen each country's improving relationship with Turkey (Chapter 8), Soviet leaders saw Israel as a client state of the United States and charged Israel with genocide of Palestinians (Chapter 9). The book then turns to the revival of the Genocide Convention in the 1980s in international law and politics (Chapter 10). The 1980s was a decade that began with Soviet war crimes in Afghanistan and US war crimes in Latin America, both committed to back their preferred ideologically motivated actors in each state's perceived sphere of influence, which generated reciprocal claims of genocide. In Weiss-Wendt's own words, "this book is not only about human suffering, but how it was reinterpreted, repackaged, trivialized, and ultimately exploited—all in the name of ideology-colored geopolitics."

The afterword of Weiss-Wendt's book brings us up to the present day, where we find that the political and legal situation has not changed much. The word "genocide" is still being deployed in exaggerated, moralizing, and hyperbolic terms to exploit human suffering for political purposes in the context of geopolitical conflicts. In the summer of 2015, the Russian government labeled Lemkin's 1953 essay on the Soviet genocide in Ukrainian in the 1930s "extremist literature." As Weiss-Wendt writes, censoring Lemkin's essay teaches less about the Soviet Union in the previous century than it tells us about Russian politics today. With the rise of a Ukrainian nationalist movement seeking to end Russian suzerainty in Ukraine, at least since the 2004 Orange Revolution, the Russian government today maintains that the Soviet treatment of Ukraine, and especially the great famine of 1932–1933, was not genocide. The principle underscoring the Russian position today, Weiss-Wendt writes, is simple: geopolitics. Asserting that Stalin orchestrated a genocide in Ukraine in the 1930s has become a powerful statement in Ukrainian nationalist discourse, connecting the direct control of Moscow over Soviet Ukraine in the 1930s to the Russian Federation's influence over the country today.

The "genocide discourse," as I have argued recently, became especially strong after the Russian annexation of Crimea in 2014 and the subsequent Russian occupation of the Donbas region. That the Soviet Union had committed genocide in Ukraine in the 1930s is now asserted to delegitimize Moscow's political control over the country, both in the past and contemporaneously. As Weiss-Wendt discusses in his afterword in this volume, Russian officials responded by opening legal investigations into genocides committed against Russian speakers in southeastern Ukraine, with state TV referring to the prevention of genocide in Ukraine against Russian speakers as a prime reason for Russian involvement in the Donbas. At the same time, after 2014, the Russian Foreign Ministry attacked support among American activists and academics for recognizing the 1930s' Ukrainian genocide as hypocritical given the fact that white police officers in the United States kill so many black citizens. The war of words today is no different from the war of words in the 1950s, with the Soviet Union responding to US accusations by reminding Washington to deal with America's own deplorable record on civil rights before lecturing Moscow on human rights. In the realm of warfare, as well, genocide discourse is deployed for political purposes. Russian scholars and diplomats argue that Russia's military intervention in Georgia and Ukraine did not violate the norms of international law, but instead upheld the norms of the law, because those are efforts to protect vulnerable populations from their own governments' genocides and human rights violations. When challenged, they simply refer to Western interventions in Kosovo, Iraq, and Libya that were legitimized under slogans of genocide prevention and the Responsibility to Protect norm.

The saddest paradox of all is that the phrase the "politics of genocide" no longer refers to the politics surrounding the commission and prevention of mass killing, but to the use of the word "genocide" as a weapon in a self-moralizing war of words. In this, again, the United States and Russia are strikingly consistent even when they spend their energy accusing each other of sponsoring genocide. Any effort by the two governments to prevent mass killing that involves constraining their own national interests is conveniently ignored.

ABBREVIATIONS

ABA: American Bar Association
ADL: Anti-Defamation League
AFL: American Federation of Labor
AIM: American Indian Movement
AJA: American Jewish Archives
AJC: American Jewish Congress
AJHS: American Jewish Historical Society
AJIL: *American Journal of International Law*
AVP RF: Foreign Policy Archives of the Russian Foreign Ministry
BPP: Black Panther Party
CHR: UN Commission on Human Rights
CHRGT: Ad Hoc Committee on the Human Rights and Genocide Treaties
CIA: Central Intelligence Agency
CPSU: Communist Party of the Soviet Union
CPUSA: Communist Party of the United States of America
CRC: Civil Rights Congress
CSCE: Conference on Security and Cooperation in Europe
CWIHP: Cold War International History Project
DK: Democratic Kampuchea
DoS: U.S. Department of State
ECOSOC: UN Economic and Social Council
FMLN: Farabundo Martí National Liberation Front (El Salvador)
FRG: Federal Republic of Germany
GULAG: *Glavnoe upravlenie lagerei* (Soviet forced labor camp system, 1929–1960)
HNC: Hungarian National Council
HUAC: House Un-American Activities Committee
IADL: International Association of Democratic Lawyers
ICC: International Criminal Court
ICJ: International Court of Justice
ILO: International Labor Organization
IMT: International Military Tribunal at Nuremberg
IRD: Information Research Department (counterpropaganda unit within the British Foreign Office, 1948–1978)
KGB: *Komitet gosudarstvennoi bezopasnosti* (Soviet Security Police, 1954–1991)
JLC: Jewish Labor Committee
LAC: Lithuanian American Council
LG: *Literaturnaia Gazeta* (*Literary Newspaper*)

NA: British National Archives
NAACP: National Association for the Advancement of Colored People
NARA: National Archives and Records Administration
NCRAC: National Community Relations Advisory Council
NGO: Nongovernmental organization
NKVD: *Narodnyi kommisariat vnutrennikh del* (Soviet Security Police, 1934–1946)
NNC: National Negro Congress
NSA: National Security Archives
NYPL: New York Public Library
NYT: *New York Times*
OAS: *Organisation de l'armée secrète* (Secret Armed Organization, France)
PLO: Palestine Liberation Organization
RGASPI: Russian State Archives of Social and Political History
SGP: *Sovetskoe gosudarstvo i pravo* (*Soviet State and Law*)
SNCC: Student Nonviolent Coordinating Committee
TASS: *Telegrafnoe agenstvo Sovetskogo Soiuza* (Soviet Telegraph Agency)
UDHR: Universal Declaration of Human Rights
UKDP: United Kurdistan Democratic Party
WAG: Tamiment Library & Robert F. Wagner Labor Archives
WJC: World Jewish Congress
WPC: World Peace Council
YWCA: Young Women's Christian Association

A RHETORICAL CRIME

INTRODUCTION

The legal history of the Genocide Convention features a surprisingly short chronology. It typically begins with a brief discussion of the term *genocide,* as proposed by Raphael Lemkin in 1944, continues with the debates on the draft Genocide Convention in the United Nations in 1947–1948, and then goes straight to the establishment of ad hoc international tribunals for Rwanda and ex-Yugoslavia in 1994 and the Rome Statute of the International Criminal Court in 1998.[1] Another way of narrating the history of the Genocide Convention is by making it essentially into Lemkin's life story. This approach—which generates an enthusiastic public response and therefore is popular among educators—is naturally delimited by the scholar's dates of birth and death, 1900 to 1959. Inevitably, the trajectory of the genocide treaty follows that sketched by Lemkin himself. The romanticized story of the Genocide Convention draws a straight line from Lemkin's earlier ideas all the way to December 9, 1948 when the Genocide Convention was unanimously passed by the UN General Assembly. The subsequent period is usually rendered as the "struggle" for the Genocide Convention, which had lost steam in the 1950s while Lemkin became progressively marginalized (or alternatively maneuvered himself into a corner). The cutoff date for both research perspectives, legal and Lemkin-centric, is usually April 6, 1953. That is when US secretary of state John Foster Dulles declared before the Senate Judiciary Committee that the Eisenhower administration would not push for ratification of the Genocide Convention. Taking into account that the Genocide Convention had only been in existence since 1948, a nearly forty-year gap in its history begs the question. The answer to this question is rather simple: the Cold War rhetoric that reduced the genocide treaty into a tool of ideological warfare. Political casuistry at its worst, it is nonetheless a story to be told.

This book fills the gap by aligning the legal and political history of the Genocide Convention during the Cold War. I take up where the existing scholarship effectively leaves off, that is, following Dulles's announcement and the death of Stalin a year earlier. This self-imposed timeframe is not absolute, of course; the earlier analyses of the Soviet system of repression and the evolution of the legal profession in the USSR—which I discuss in the first two chapters—stretch back to the 1940s. Otherwise, by the mid-1950s the front lines between the Communist bloc and the West have stabilized. The ideological battle waged by the Soviet Union and the United States came to incorporate a legal dimension. Popularized by Charles Dunlop in his 2001 speech at Harvard University, the term *lawfare* denotes the strategic application of law in lieu of military means. Once *lawfare* entered the public domain, the term acquired divergent meanings, including nefarious exploitation of international law for propaganda purposes. Legal experts disagree whether the "academy has lost the initiative and would be fighting a futile cause in trying to recapture the concept as a neutral term."[2] When applied to the Soviet Union—as Christi Scott Bartman has done in her analysis of the Soviet definition of aggressive war—lawfare appears to stand for an entire Communist legal philosophy.[3] Correct as it may be, it unintentionally leaves out other aspects of the Pax Sovietica. After all, the legal discourse constituted just one of many fronts. The Cold War battles raged in the sphere of politics, economy, science, culture, sport, and so on. In that sense, lawfare was one of many examples and simultaneously a reflection of a general trajectory of the postwar world. Conversely, by regarding the factor of international law in isolation one may miss the context and thus overstate the case. This exposition directly relates to the long-term perspective on the Genocide Convention. A part of lawfare no doubt, the struggle over the meaning and application of the genocide treaty cut through the history of the Cold War.

Generally, there is nothing unusual in the fact that political and ideological considerations influence the outcome, in this particular case the Genocide Convention. For that matter, as Lawrence J. LeBlanc has argued, any domestic or international law has a political element to it. The drafters were career diplomats acting in the interests of the states they represented. Insofar as those interests differed, they struggled to find ways to produce an instrument that would be acceptable to the largest possible number of states.[4] Where I disagree with LeBlanc is in his optimistic assessment that the genocide treaty is *not* fundamentally flawed, precisely because it was not just any document of international law. The Genocide Convention was the first humanitarian treaty to emerge from the newly established United Nations—straight into the war of a new kind, the war of words. A casualty of the Cold War, it had generated a cloud of rhetoric that keeps haunting us until today. Sure enough, several convictions on charges of genocide have been meted out after the collapse of international Communism. This, however, occurred in spite of rather than because of the 1948 convention. The Cold War (we want to believe) is over, but the heated debates surrounding the term *genocide* rage on. The question we should be asking ourselves is whether the passionate arguments on display have any objective value attached to them.

I seek to rekindle the discussion along the lines suggested by William A. Schabas. Schabas has argued that the "importance of the Genocide Convention can probably be found not so much in its contemporary potential to address atrocities, something that is largely superseded by more modern texts, as in its historic contribution to the struggle for accountability and the protection of human rights."[5] When looking at history, however, it has been seventy years since the genocide treaty was adopted and, for most of that period, the struggle revolved around geopolitics. Here, history appears to be a deadly weight rather than a path to progress. "The Genocide Convention remains a 'prisoner of the past'," as Mathew Lippman has concluded.[6] Mark Mazower has emerged as the most perceptive commentator on the origins of the United Nations and the postwar human rights regime. Highlighting the pervasive tension between idealism and realism, he pleaded for a better historical understanding of the humanitarian law. In practical terms, it amounts to adding the world of diplomacy to that of intellectual and cultural history. According to Mazower, "it does no service to the cause of human rights to disguise the political struggles and conflicts of interest that accompanied their emergence into the international arena."[7] What Schabas, Lippman, Mazower, and others are essentially emphasizing is the detrimental influence of world politics on international human rights law. In this book I take one step further by gauging the long-term effect of the Cold War on genocide discourse. Insofar as the Genocide Convention became a convenient tool with which to hit the ideological adversary, I ask if the genocide discourse, as it had evolved, perpetuated the divisive rhetoric more than it served the cause of humanity.

The issues raised in this book are most relevant to comparative genocide studies and the history of the Cold War. Scholars working in either field, however, have paid relatively little attention to the ideological significance of the Genocide Convention. While genocide scholars—in the beginning predominantly political and social scientists—tend to dwell on the definition of genocide, historians of the Cold War typically pass over a legal aspect of international politics as a mere illustration of the decisions taken at the highest level. The concept of genocide, unlike the issues of foreign policy, does indeed go beyond current affairs. It had broader legal, historical, social, and even philosophical implications. And that is precisely why it had such an oversize presence in the Cold War rhetoric. The discussions around the crime of genocide never stopped, and indeed intensified during the postwar decades. What we are dealing with here is of course not a detached academic analysis but a geopolitical discourse. In other words, genocide was invoked in pursuit of goals other than humanitarian ones.

Geopolitics is yet another catchword. Geopolitical discourse is essentially the application of power politics to space, or else a pragmatic approach to international politics. Benign as it may sound, the body of knowledge later known as geopolitics handily justified imperialist expansionism. National security state doctrines that geopolitics had engendered later in the twentieth century came to prop up undemocratic regimes. Coincidentally, the future dictator of Chile Augusto Pinochet previously taught geopolitics at the Chilean War Academy.

Despite the valid criticism of geopolitics as an inflated term not unlike lawfare, it effectively stands for balance-of-power politics on a global scale. This is pretty much the definition of geopolitics as provided by US secretary of state Henry Kissinger in the 1970s.[8] In the Soviet Union, it ought to be mentioned, geopolitics was denounced as bourgeois pseudoscience.[9] With regard to the word genocide, the meaning of geopolitics is closer to a "national enterprise of propaganda and teaching," as a French geographer disparagingly described it in the early 1950s.[10]

The story of the Genocide Convention, its intellectual origins and the debates in the United Nations, is fairly well documented by now. The exponential growth of a field of comparative genocide studies from the 1990s onward has generated an unprecedented interest in the life and ideas of Raphael Lemkin. In effect, we may now speak of a new research branch, Lemkinology. As with any scholarly pursuit focusing on a specific individual, a perspective on the Genocide Convention that has emerged from those books, articles, and documentaries is rather one-dimensional.[11] Most recent studies render a more balanced picture that places Lemkin and his intellectual journey in a broader context of the codification of international law during the 1920s and 1930s. As Mark Lewis, Philippe Sands, and Douglas Irvin-Erickson have demonstrated, Lemkin was one of many scholars—some of them hailing from Eastern Europe—who sought international legal deterrence against the most egregious crimes. The path to a UN Genocide Convention was never as straightforward as Lemkin had depicted it and involved more than one dedicated academic.[12]

The dominant perspective on the drafting of the Genocide Convention also tends to be static. This is not a problem of interpretation but rather that of sources. What LeBlanc and Schabas effectively had at their disposal is UN documentation. While official records do give a comprehensive idea of major issues at stake, by definition they cannot provide political background to the genocide treaty on an individual state level. *The Genocide Convention: The Travaux Préparatoires* serves as an extreme example of inadvertent distortion caused by relying on a single documentary source. What the editors basically did was assemble every single document on the Genocide Convention produced by the United Nations in a book format. The result is an unwieldy two-volume publication of 2,200 pages.[13] A. W. Brian Simpson and Frank Chalk have offered a welcome corrective to this unfortunate trend in their research on the British position on the Genocide Convention. A close reading of diplomatic records enabled both scholars to make a viable analysis of specific problems related to genocide facing the United Kingdom.[14] My own research has complemented the British perspective on the drafting of the Genocide Convention with that of the Soviet Union and the United States—three major powers that defined the international postwar order.[15]

None of the former Allies was enthusiastic about a new international treaty to ban genocide, as originally proposed by Lemkin in the fall of 1946. The Soviets, from the get-go, wanted to brand as "genocide" exclusively the mass crimes perpetrated during the Second World War by the Nazis, while the British doubted the very need for such a convention. The Americans proved the most open-minded about legislating against genocide at that point. The US State Department considered the probability of being charged with the genocide of African Americans as remote, yet was forced to change its position under the influence of Soviet antiracist rhetoric in the United Nations. American diplomats were even more concerned about the potential interpretation of the Potsdam Agreement—which effectively sanctioned the mass expulsion of ethnic Germans from Eastern Europe—under the letter of the Genocide Convention. The first comprehensive draft of the Genocide Convention, put together in June 1947 on the behest of the UN secretary-general by Lemkin and two other scholars active in the prewar codification of international criminal law, appeared just as overreaching to any of the UN member states. The United States, the United Kingdom, and the Soviet Union—all had issues with the UN Secretariat draft. The two most significant stumbling blocks during the drafting process proved to be an international criminal court and the protection of political groups. The USSR was opposed to both clauses, the United States was ready to sign up for either of them, and Britain went along—for as long as the treaty in the making did not contravene the judgment passed by the International Criminal Tribunal at Nuremberg.

The conflict of interests nearly derailed the Genocide Convention. The Soviets fought hard against those provisions of the draft convention that could potentially pronounce as criminal the forced labor camp system (the Gulag) and the political subjugation of Eastern Europe. The British felt increasingly apprehensive of their bloody footprint in the colonies—constantly reminded about it by the USSR and its satellites. The Americans, for their part, had second thoughts about such provisions as "inflicting mental harm" and "direct incitement to commit genocide" that might haunt them later. The debates in the Sixth Committee (Legal) and the UN General Assembly during the fall and early winter of 1948 came to resemble more and more shouting matches. The Genocide Convention was adopted unanimously on December 9, 1948, without much faith put into it by the signatories. Contrasted with politicians and diplomats, Lemkin remained one of the few believers in the practical value of the Genocide Convention. Subsequently, the self-described "unofficial man" came to perpetuate the Cold War discourse on genocide in the vain hope of resuscitating the treaty. And herein lies the tragedy of both Lemkin and the instrument of international law that he had conceived and incessantly lobbied for.

Lemkin, who occasionally appears in the first five chapters of this book, came unprepared for the reality of a bipolar world. An academic and humanitarian, he possessed neither the skills of a diplomat nor the art of reading people. He stacked the future of the Genocide Convention on US ratification, without which he correctly presumed the treaty would never become operational. To make that happen, however, Lemkin embraced what he thought was a sure bet—anticommunism. With the few options to choose from, this proved to be a losing proposition. Not only did anticommunist ideology ally Lemkin with East European ethnic organizations that had an agenda of their own, but it also injected a legal element into political rhetoric. By the time the Cold War declared a winner, the Genocide Convention had become just an empty shell.

Cold War dichotomy makes me oscillate between the Soviet and American perspectives on genocide. In rendering these asymmetrical perspectives I am confronted with the issue of sources. When it comes to primary sources, the American governmental records at scholars' disposal are by far more numerous than the Soviet. It has to do not so much with the (restricted) access to Russian archives but with political expedience and remotely with the Soviet system of governance. Moscow was not in a rush to sign the Genocide Convention and delayed ratification. In fact, many a Western observer had believed the USSR would never ratify the treaty. The Soviets showed brief interest in the Genocide Convention in 1951 in anticipation of a decision of the International Court of Justice (ICJ) regarding reservations to international treaties. The Soviet Union signed the Genocide Convention in December 1949, with reservations to Articles IX and XII (settlement of disputes and extension of the application of the convention), and was now nervously watching to see if the ICJ would strike them down. The ICJ's ruling of May 28, 1951 upheld the right to file reservations. Meanwhile Bulgaria, Romania, Poland, Yugoslavia, and later Hungary all ratified the Genocide Convention. The Soviet Union, to everyone's surprise, followed on May 3, 1954, likely as a sign of relief that the just completed UN investigation of forced labor merely slapped the USSR on the wrist. Once the instrument of ratification was deposited, internal discussions around the Genocide Convention at policy level ceased at once. Subsequently Soviet authorities relegated genocide to the arsenal of propaganda, with no particular guidelines attached. To paraphrase: off the negotiation table, out of mind.

The situation was very different in the United States. For one, the American system of checks and balances—as opposed to the hierarchical Soviet model that treated Stalin's every word as a command—accounted for multiple actors engaged in multilevel discussions. The democratic tradition ensured that various interest groups could express themselves on the issue of US ratification. As the ratification was not forthcoming, debates continued, leaving a significant paper trail. Even though the State Department files in the National Archives have only been declassified through the late 1970s at this writing, complementary records from the Department of Justice reach as far back as 1984. The lesser known repository, Tamiment Library & Robert F. Wagner Labor Archives at New York University, contains a wealth of material concerning the public campaign in the United States for and against the Genocide Convention during the 1960s–1980s. The rest of the American, Soviet, and British archives I made use of in this study prove essentially the same: the closer in time, the fewer relevant records are available to researchers.

To compensate, I turned to the academic and popular press. The leading Soviet law journal *Sovetskoe gosudarstvo i pravo* (*Soviet State and Law*) spent considerable time attacking its counterpart, the *American Journal of International Law*, not necessarily in relation to genocide. The verbal exchanges, which proliferated in the early 1950s, testify to the fact of just how different the Soviet and American interpretation of international law was. One probably would not be surprised to find numerous references to genocide in major American newspapers such as the *New York Times* or the *Washington Post*. More unexpected, perhaps, is that *Pravda*, *Izvestia*, or *Literaturnaia Gazeta*, among other Soviet papers, regularly ran stories about genocide starting from the 1960s. Besides mainstream publications, I availed myself of a print source rarely, if at all, used in scholarship, namely American far-right and ultra-conservative publications. These obscure sheets contain an extensive, no doubt vicious, commentary on all things genocide, reserving a share of vitriol for both the United States and the Soviet Union.

When it comes to the rhetorical application of the word *genocide*, the Soviets proved bigger offenders than the Americans. Moscow incorporated genocide into its lexicon of abuse vis-à-vis the West in the early 1950s. Since then, in public statements by USSR representatives in the United Nations and pronouncements by Soviet leaders, articles in newspapers and law journals, book-length publications in Russian or English translations—the message hammered out was one and the same. The absence of a Soviet policy on the Genocide Convention beyond exploiting its letter for propaganda purposes creates a certain misbalance of representation when compared with the United States. Hence, the decision-making process leading up to eventual US accession and the withdrawal of Soviet reservations to the genocide treaty in 1989 can be documented only in the former case and deduced in the latter. Soviet and American proxies took cues from their patrons in throwing around accusations of genocide, with little if any reflection on the instrument of international law dealing with this particular crime.

As with any study of a comparable scope, I try to deal with Cold War hotspots in chronological order. Maintaining a linear narrative works only to a certain degree, though. When considering divergent perspectives on genocide applied to a great many armed conflicts, a temporal overlap is almost unavoidable. For example, the political debate in America on US ratification of the Genocide Convention paralleled the rise of Communist China, which indirectly bore on mass atrocities committed in countries like Bangladesh and Cambodia, which in its turn informed the opposing views in the debate. By the same token, the evolution of Soviet discourse on the Armenian genocide took cues from international current affairs such as the Lebanon War or the invasion of Afghanistan. All these diverse yet interrelated subjects I address in separate chapters.

I begin the book by reflecting on the legal profession in the Soviet Union. Interplay between ideology and realpolitik continued shaping Soviet discourse on international criminal law after the death of Stalin. Deviating from the accepted Communist Party line was inconceivable for both well-established scholars such as Aron Trainin and fresh law school graduates such as Mikhail Andriukhin. Their interpretation of genocide had changed over time, along with the priorities in Soviet foreign policy. On the other side of the ideological divide the opposite tendency took hold, namely viewing Stalin's mass violence as immutable. Chapter 2 maps the discourse on "Soviet genocide" in the United States during the late 1940s and the 1950s. Lemkin served as a liaison of sorts between the many ethnic organizations, trying to rally them around the issue of genocide. Most of the books on ethnic deportations and the forced labor camp system in the Soviet Union were produced by émigrés of East European descent. While some studies proved more analytical than the others, all of them had the Soviet takeover of Eastern Europe as a leitmotif. Chapter 3 examines how the discourse on Soviet repressive policy had changed in those satellite countries that attempted to switch their allegiance, in the case of Yugoslavia successfully and in the case of Hungary unsuccessfully. Yugoslavia launched a blistering attack on Stalin and his policy of terror following the 1948 split, only to tone down its criticism after the program of de-Stalinization in the Soviet Union had ground to a halt under Leonid Brezhnev. An attempt at liberalization in Hungary in 1956 was crushed by the Soviet tanks. Hungary proved the biggest scare for Moscow in terms of potential indictment for genocide by the world organization. The effort to that end in the United Nations fell flat, in no small part thanks to the undetermined position of the United States, which neither ratified the Genocide Convention nor sought direct military confrontation with the Communist bloc.

Chapter 4 moves the discussion into postcolonial Africa and the Middle East. Despite their anticolonial rhetoric, the Soviets exercised a pragmatic, if not cynical, policy vis-à-vis the Third World. The discourse on genocide underlined the status of newly independent countries as mere pawns in the Cold War between the Communist bloc and the West. The accusations of genocide popped up depending on whose client was under fire. Thus, Western capitals ascertained genocide in Biafra while Moscow denied it. In countries like Algeria, Congo, or Angola it was the exact opposite. The biggest hypocrisy of them all was the ever-shifting Soviet position on Kurdish autonomy in Iraq. In the end, building bridges to the nationalist Ba'ath Party proved more important to the Soviets than rallying in support of the Communist Kurds. Occasional claims of genocide proved to be a synonym of duplicity. If in Africa and the Middle East the United States and the Soviet Union competed directly against each other, in Southeast Asia they looked over their shoulder to China. As I discuss in Chapter 5, the rapprochement between Washington and Beijing in the early 1970s influenced the Soviet vs. American position on the episodes of extreme violence that shattered the region, most dramatically Bangladesh in 1971 and Cambodia in 1975–1979. In both those cases, the superpowers remained on the sidelines, watching in silence the Pakistani military in Bangladesh and later the Khmer Rouge in Cambodia killing several million people each. While the Americans, with few exceptions, shied away from using the word *genocide*, the Soviets did not, though only ex post facto, when the emerging strategic alliance came into view.

The following two chapters bring the United States into focus. When lobbying against and for US ratification of the Genocide Convention, respectively, the American far right and the liberal left invariably referred to the Soviet Union. While the left perceived the domestic resistance to ratification as a source of embarrassment and the loss of moral prestige vis-à-vis the Soviet bloc, the right regarded it as a bulwark against world Communism. The ultimate question for both sides was how, or if, potential US ratification would change the status of American-Soviet relations. The Soviets readily exploited the kind of dilemma that only existed in a democracy, inviting the United States to walk its talk on human rights violations. The Soviet attempt to situate the American protest movement within the procrustean bed of Soviet propaganda, however, did not work very well. Moscow was suspicious of the grassroots Vietnam antiwar movement and consequently gave a cold shoulder to the Russell People's Tribunal that indicted the United States, among other crimes, for genocide. Black Panthers, who sought to resuscitate the 1951 "We Charge Genocide" campaign, remained the great unknown for the Soviets. And when Soviet spin doctors picked up the cause of the American Indian Movement, it was already in the process of dissolution.

In Chapter 8 I discuss yet another dilemma, this time one the Soviets had on their hands. The fine line that the US government treaded on the issue of genocide as applied to the treatment of Armenians in Ottoman Turkey is a well-known story. Communist authorities actually faced the exact same problem, trying to balance the growing nationalist sentiment among Soviet Armenians and the gradually improving Soviet-Turkish relations. The half-measures that they had adopted with regard to commemoration of the genocide in Armenia satisfied few but displeased many—a representative illustration of a structural crisis that eventually brought the USSR down. Hesitant to spell out *genocide* in the case of Armenians, the Soviet leadership had no such inhibition with regard to Palestinians, as I recount in Chapter 9. The fact remains that of all the conflicts since the end of the Second World War, the Soviets described most consistently as genocide the Israeli treatment of Palestinians. Here, however, like earlier in the case with the Kurds, words stood for action. The Kremlin questioned many a tactic of the Palestinian Liberation Organization to provide it with full military support. Unwilling to enter the messy, multifactional fight in Lebanon directly, the Soviets chose to draw the Israelis and the Americans in genocide rhetoric. It came across as even more grotesque as they remained tight-lipped when it came to the Nazi genocide of the Jews—with the remarkable perseverance until the last weeks of the Soviet Union's existence.

The final chapter maps the path toward the reactivation of the Genocide Convention in the 1980s. The decade began ominously with the Soviet Union invading Afghanistan and the United States continuously propping up the authoritarian regimes in Latin America. Backing the opposite sides in multiple proxy wars inevitably generated reciprocal claims of genocide. Yet the momentum was on the side of the supporters of the genocide treaty in the United States. Crucially, in 1984 the influential American Bar Association withdrew its long-standing objection to US ratification, also recommended now by the Justice Department. The overall thrust of the proratification argument was that the United States was unlikely ever to be formally indicted for genocide. Electoral politics made President Ronald Reagan pledge his support for ratification, as urged by American Jewish organizations. Beyond US domestic politics, by far the most significant factor was the appointment of Mikhail Gorbachev as the new secretary-general of the Soviet Communist Party and his subsequent decision to extract the USSR from the Cold War. It was now safe to fully embrace the Genocide Convention, forty years after it had been adopted by the UN General Assembly.

What binds the chapters together is the Cold War rhetoric and the genocide hyperbole that it had successfully incorporated. Even though this book does not tell a complete history of the Cold War, it may be the first one to look at it from the prism of a legal treaty, indeed a specific concept derived from a single word—*genocide*. Essentially, *A Rhetorical Crime* is not only about human suffering, but how it was reinterpreted, repackaged, trivialized, and ultimately exploited—all in the name of ideology-colored geopolitics.

1 • SOVIET SCHOLARS OF INTERNATIONAL LAW AS FOOT SOLDIERS IN THE COLD WAR

SOVETSKOE GOSUDARSTVO I PRAVO IN THE WAR OF IDEAS

Propaganda can be rendered as the fight for hearts and minds by means of partisan arguments. Obviously, the superpowers that spread a propaganda message had a more benevolent understanding of their own efforts. Thus the US State Department in 1953 used the example of the United Nations to explicate the relationship between propaganda and substantive policies:

> When our objective is primarily to influence the attitudes of others by communicating to them (through either words or actions) broad ideas or concepts, we speak of propaganda. When our objective is primarily to attain certain diplomatic results, without primary consideration to how these may affect the attitudes of others, we speak of substantive policies. (Most actions in the UN partake of both purposes in varying measure, and obviously in our substantive policies we often undertake propaganda operations to maximize or minimize their popular impact.)[1]

In their own words, from roughly 1946 to 1949 the Americans refrained, for a number of reasons, from frontal attacks on the Soviet Union. Since the beginning of the war in Korea, however, the United States had accelerated its political and psychological offensive in the United Nations, increasing the tempo of anti-Soviet propaganda. Hence the US delegation introduced or encouraged certain UN actions "with the primary purpose of winning Cold War propaganda advantages with little or no expectation that their ostensible purpose would be achieved directly or within a reasonable time." As recent examples, the State

Department listed condemnatory UN resolutions such as "Failure of USSR to Repatriate POWs" (1950), "Observance of Human Rights and Fundamental Freedoms in Bulgaria, Hungary, and Romania" (1950), and the "Report of the Ad Hoc Committee on Forced Labor" (1953). The following quotation from the same document summed up the essence of American propaganda: "In fighting the Cold War in the UN, we are under great pressure to confront the Soviet single-mindedly with sharp attacks, notwithstanding the possibility that such an approach may frighten the timid or alienate the unconvinced." The question remains, though, how effective or ineffective finally was US and Soviet propaganda in the United Nations? To the American diplomats' credit, they had recognized the danger that the preeminence of propaganda might at a minimum obscure and at a maximum derail long-term policy objectives.[2]

Harold D. Lasswell of Yale Law School ascertained in mid-1948 that international politics had frozen into a bipolar mold. The bipolar structure of world power refers to the globe as a military, not a civic arena. Hence, he argued that policies in every sphere of human activity were affected by calculations of the relative strength of the United States and Russia.[3] Insofar as lawfare was just one of many aspects of the Cold War, the Genocide Convention was just one of many treaties that the Soviet Union had deployed in the ideological confrontation with the United States. To put it differently, the argumentation/rhetoric used by the Soviets applied across the specter of international law.

The positions of prominence achieved by Soviet lawyers such as Andrei Vyshinsky, Vladimir Koretsky, and Alexei Pavlov in the United Nations left no doubt that the legal profession had been gaining the respect of the Communist regime. As compared with the situation in the 1920s and 1930s, the status of a lawyer had improved considerably both socially and politically in the immediate postwar years. The Communist Party (CPSU) had expressed its concern for the advancement of legal studies in a resolution of October 1946. The numbers of professionally trained lawyers remained low, however, nothing to compare with an estimated 200,000 lawyers in the United States in 1950. The Soviet Ministry of Justice and the respective ministries of the republics did not have enough qualified judges, prosecutors, and officials. Soviet lawyers were cognizant of their relationship to the state at all times. Among other subjects law school students had to study political theory, which taught them that the court and the lawyer were agents of political power and that the interests of the state were paramount. Under no circumstances should a lawyer conduct a campaign against the state in a spirit of hostility. In short, Soviet lawyers were prepared to become guardians of "socialist legality."[4]

To understand better the concept of *socialist legality*, one may look at how the Soviets interpreted American criminal law. The following summary is derived from a textbook for law schools published in 1948 by the Law Institute of the Soviet Academy of Science. As Serge S. Gorny, an American lawyer of Russian descent, had observed, *Ugolovnoe pravo, obshchaia chast* (*Criminal Law: General Part*) departed markedly from similar texts produced in the Soviet Union during the Second World War. Although the Soviet authors had always written critically of the Western legal system, from the standpoint of a governing political philosophy their analyses tended to be objective. Thus, they might occasionally refer to what they considered to be more acceptable aspects of Anglo-American law. Now they launched a full frontal assault. The attacks went beyond criticism and into a propaganda offensive aiming to distort the fundamentals of American criminal law.[5] Students who entered a Soviet law school in 1948 learned that the US ruling classes had utilized every possible device, including laws, in their war against the revolutionary movement. As an example of the malignant use of law, the textbook referred to the Sacco-Vanzetti trial in Dedham, Massachusetts in 1921.[6] Referring to Andrei Zhdanov's speech at the Cominform founding conference in late September 1947, the textbook authors stated that since the end of the war the US government had adopted an expansionist policy toward the Soviet Union and newly established democracies. The purpose of that policy was to strangle the working-class movement within the United States and anti-imperialist forces elsewhere.[7]

The new textbook kept a detailed record of facts of discrimination on political and racial grounds in the United States. Under the banner of the struggle against Communism, the American justice system went after progressive political organizations, labeling them "subversive." The 1947 Taft-Hartley Act, which prescribed trade unions to expunge Communists from leadership unless they wanted to be officially registered, was clearly an anticommunist bill. Described by some as an organ of "inquisition," the investigative House Un-American Activities Committee (HUAC) was called to life with the purpose of suppressing the Communist movement. A decision from March 1947 required all federal employees to be screened on the matter of their political affiliation. All those deemed disloyal, that is, Communists and their sympathizers, were to be instantly fired. Criminal justice had effectively enshrined racial discrimination in the United States by applying the most grievous criminal laws to black Americans, as for example in the case of the notorious Scottsboro trial in 1931, and by refusing to outlaw lynching. It was not coincidental, Soviet law students were told, that the American justice system had consistently failed to enact a special statute on criminal prosecution for lynching.[8]

Communist witch hunts and racial murder were not the only ills plaguing the United States, according to Soviet criminologists. The textbook painted the United States as a land of organized crime where the gang bosses had maintained close ties to high-level politicians. It even cited Al Capone, who had allegedly said, "Big bankers, industrialists, politicians, and trade union bosses are trying to make me carry on with my activities." Another quotation came from a former chief justice of the US Supreme Court, who had described the situation with regard to the struggle against crime in that country as a "disgrace to our civilization." According to the statistics presented in the textbook, crime rates in the United States were growing exponentially, by 50 percent since the 1930s. In 1937, for every 100,000 persons there were 158 prisoners in America, as compared to 30 in England. The only other country with as high a proportion of the prison population was said to have been Nazi Germany.[9] In short, one would not expect justice in a country where gangsters enjoyed full immunity and crime was rampant!

When analyzing the 1946–1951 Soviet literature on international law, Oliver J. Lissitzyn has noted considerable continuity in Soviet doctrine since the 1938–1941 period. As before, Soviet authors collected and printed passages from Marx, Lenin, and Stalin emphasizing the class nature of international law and its connection to international politics. In a series of lectures delivered at the Hague Academy of International Law in 1947, Sergei Krylov—the first Soviet scholar to do so—essentially advanced the general definition of law as formulated by Vyshinsky in his Twelve Theses on International Law nine years earlier.[10] In a nutshell, the Soviets retained an instrumentalist approach to international law, accepting it insofar as it served the interests of the state, that is, as an instrument of policy.[11]

The legal arena became yet another front in the Soviet-American confrontation. The Soviets surely perceived law publications as weapons and legal scholars as foot soldiers in that global struggle. In June 1951 the director of the Law Institute, Evgeny Korovin, requested permission to quit the Academy of Political Science in New York and the American Society of International Law, in which he had been a member since 1934. The CPSU Foreign Policy Commission supplemented Korovin's request with an explanation, according to which these two academic entities were reactionary organizations that waged a campaign of unbridled slander against the Soviet Union and the people's democracies. Both the academy and the society supposedly argued on behalf of a world government run by the United States—against national sovereignty, yet in support of anti-Soviet political blocs. Needless to say, Korovin was warmly welcomed to renounce his membership. In his nearly identical letters of renunciation, Korovin accused *Political Science Quarterly* and the *American Journal of International Law* of having published false statements concerning Soviet foreign policy and the Soviet approach to international law. The abovementioned journals, insisted Korovin, had become the medium of disinformation vis-à-vis the Soviet Union, the incendiary tool provoking hatred between nations. As a Soviet citizen and scholar of international law aspiring to the ideals of peace and international cooperation, he, Korovin, could no longer regard himself as a member of the organizations that stood behind those publications.[12]

The 1950s engendered a curious exchange between the *American Journal of International Law* (*AJIL*) and *Sovetskoe gosudarstvo i pravo* (*SGP*). Starting in 1951, Polish American political scientist Władysław W. Kulski maintained a regular column in the *AJIL* called "Soviet Comments on International Law and International Relations." His commentary was mainly derived from *SPG*, which occasionally referred to *AJIL* and specifically Kulski, only to be summed up by the latter in the subsequent issue of the journal. Georgy Zadorozhnyi, freshly minted professor of international law, became for a while Kulski's doppelgänger.[13]

First, Kulski patiently explained to his Communist colleagues that the concept of sovereignty did not originate in czarist Russia, contrary to what they had believed. It was indeed remarkable, noted Kulski, that Soviet lawyers had to seek their inspiration in Ivan the Terrible and Peter the Great to avoid the pitfalls of "bourgeois" jurisprudence. Next he engaged with Aron Trainin and his broad interpretation of war propaganda. Expanding the notion of warmongering beyond that of instigation, Trainin ended up arguing that any newspaper article, stump speech, or radio talk show could amount to a crime against humanity. Considering the long Soviet list of Western "warmongers," Kulski speculated, a Communist judge could then convict literally thousands of persons for voicing criticism of Moscow on charges of criminal war propaganda.[14]

In the *SGP* article titled "War Propaganda—the Most Serious Offense Against Peace," Grigory Morozov nailed Quincy Wright, who dared to express the opinion in his respective piece in *AJIL* that war propaganda should also include in its definition propaganda of revolution. Kulski sardonically asked what kind of penalty the Soviets would mete out to the preeminent political scientist and international lawyer for his dissenting views. In the same issue of *SGP* (December 1953), one other author took on Edwin Dickinson, vice president of the American Society of International Law. He accused Dickinson of declaring the primacy of international law and promoting "world government" in order to subject all states to the American dictate.[15]

Along general propaganda lines, the Soviet law journal presented the American Bar Association (ABA) as a reactionary organization servicing the "expansionist aspirations of American imperialism." As a mouthpiece of the association, *AJIL* was known for distortion and apologia, claimed *SGP*. Here is how one of its contributors characterized the bulk of Western scholarship on international law, in a single sentence: "Fascistization of the USA, tightly linked to the aggressive foreign policy of the ruling monopolistic circles of America, engenders the muddy stream of reactionary legal literature, in which American 'scholars,' who have sold their soul to Wall Street, are trying to rationalize and justify the policy of reaction and fascism, to ensnare peoples in a web of lies, to draw them into a new war."[16]

By 1951 *SGP* spoke without qualms of "fascistization" (*fashizatsia*) of the United States, citing as examples the Mutual Security Act, the McCarran Internal Security Act, the war in Korea, and the alleged advocacy for a world government.[17] The methods of the FBI were reportedly no different from those of the Gestapo, and the 1949 trial of the Communist Party USA (CPUSA) comparable to the 1933 Reichstag fire trial.[18] The main element that linked the United States to the Nazi Germany was racial discrimination, especially against blacks and Americans of Slavic origin.[19]

Even without Kulski's overview, the perusal of *SGP* reveals a sharp increase of strictly ideological treatises over legal analyses from 1949/1950 onward. No scruple held Soviets from "attacking the enemy on the ideological front with its own weapon." Thus, in the spring of 1951 *SGP* published a review of the Russian-language edition of Charles Ch. Hyde's *International Law: Chiefly as Interpreted and Applied by the United States*. In typical fashion, the reviewers condemned the author for justifying the expansionist policy of the United States, undermining the idea of sovereignty, perpetuating colonial rule, and so on. They just failed to mention that the first edition of the book appeared in 1922, and that the 523 pages selected for translation constituted less than one-third of its original size. Just as frivolous an interpretation was accorded to *A Modern Law of Nations* by Philip Jessup, imaginatively labeled a "cosmopolitan troubadour of imperialism." Professor David Levin—who reviewed the book in the same issue of *SGP*—capitalized on the fact of Jessup's employment in the US State Department (while teaching international law at Columbia University) to claim that the author had been rationalizing the "criminal designs of American bandits comparable to Hitler's 'New Order.'"[20]

SOVIET SCHOLARSHIP ON GENOCIDE

Joseph Stalin did not live to see the Korean War armistice agreement. The last years of his life were marked by an upswing of ideology in both the domestic and foreign policy of the Soviet Union. The Soviet position vis-à-vis international law was no exception. The Mutual Security Act of 1951 sanctifying subversive operations against the Communist bloc brought renewed vigor into the debates over the draft Code of Offenses against the Peace and Security of Mankind.[21] The Civil Rights Congress's (CRC) 1951 petition *We Charge Genocide* made Soviets fully realize the advantage of the Genocide Convention in hitting back at Americans where it hurt most, that is, race relations (for more on *We Charge Genocide* see Chapter 7).[22] On the legal front, the USSR seemed to be carrying the day. The ICJ ruling of May 1951 reaffirmed the right to have reservations to international treaties, thus making prosecution for genocide even more unlikely. The Eisenhower administration had indicated that, as of April 1953, ratification of the Genocide Convention by the United States was no longer on the agenda. On the level of perceptions, the American unwillingness to go along made the Soviet Union look morally superior. Meanwhile, the UN forced labor investigation—which made Moscow visibly nervous—wounded up with a much milder verdict than expected.[23] Once again, the Soviets felt that they were off the hook. Inside the country, the campaign against "rootless cosmopolitanism" aimed at eradicating any Western influences. Vicious propaganda bordering on paranoia made the Jews, suspected of cross-border allegiances, its prime target. Thus, the Jews arrested as part of the Doctors' Plot were charged with links to the American Jewish Joint Distribution Committee, which allegedly operated under the Mutual Security Act.[24] Bridging the domestic and international contexts, Soviet legal experts found themselves fighting the "aggressive cosmopolitanism of international law in the service of American imperialism." If quotations from Lenin and Stalin had always been a must, by the early 1950s the Soviet leader was proclaimed the sole guiding force: "Each pronouncement of comrade Stalin pertaining to international relations, as contained in his latest work on economic issues ["Economic Problems of Socialism in the USSR" (1951)], is of foremost methodological and cognitive importance to the Soviet science of international law. Every single guideline of comrade Stalin on the issues of foreign policy and international law should be a subject of monographic studies by scholars of international law of the Socialist camp."[25] But in March 1953 Stalin was no more.

After the prolonged period of silence, a string of publications on genocide appeared in the Soviet Union in 1954. The thrust of argumentation had changed significantly from the late 1940s.[26] The resurgence of interest in the crime of genocide can be attributed to the following three factors. First, the explicit pronouncements by senior US politicians had confirmed that the Congress was not going to ratify the Genocide Convention in the foreseeable future. For as long as the United States remained uncommitted, it would be difficult, if at all possible, for the US delegation in the United Nations to formally indict the Soviet Union for genocide. Second, the death of Stalin signaled the dismantlement of the Gulag system and the gradual release of the inmate population. Even though the repressive regime and the system of forced labor camps that it had operated were still in place, the worst of the violence was over. Thus, by January 1959 the number of political prisoners dwindled to 11,000 and the general camp population stabilized at around 900,000. The notion of political and ideological deviancy came to replace the heinous categories of "enemy of the people" and "counterrevolutionary crimes" in the Penal Code. The new Kremlin leadership could sigh in relief that this most brutal aspect of Soviet rule could no longer be used against it in the international arena. Finally, the process of decolonization, which began in earnest in the early 1950s, made the Soviet Union recalibrate its message to fit the moment. Scores of new states from Africa and Asia joined the United Nations, shifting the balance of power in the major world organization in favor of the Soviet Union. In short, by the mid-1950s the Soviets had less to fear and more to gain from evoking the resounding word *genocide*.

The most matter-of-fact account appeared in the 1954 volume of *SGP*. The author of the article, S. Volodin, recapitulated the 1948 drafting process, emphasizing the positive role played by the Soviet delegation and the negative by the American. Only the last part of Volodin's article, which brought the status of the

Genocide Convention up-to-date, contained any new information. The Soviet Union, Ukraine, and Belorussia signed the convention but with reservations to Article IX and XII. The Soviet delegation objected to the default jurisdiction of the ICJ, while the Ukrainian delegation demurred about the nonextension of the Genocide Convention to colonial and dependent territories. Poland, Czechoslovakia, Romania, Hungary, and Bulgaria registered the exact same reservations when depositing the instrument of ratification. The ruling of the ICJ confirming the right to extend reservations frustrated the plans of the "imperialist bloc" to cut the Soviet Union out, stated Volodin. The last three paragraphs of the article sketched the new streak in the Soviet discourse on genocide. As the Genocide Convention was becoming a reality, Volodin wrote, the Anglo-American camp began dissociating itself from this important international treaty. Neither Great Britain nor the Union of South Africa adhered to the convention (not coincidentally, the two countries were singled out in the final report of the UN Ad Hoc Committee on Forced Labor). The United States did sign the document, but failed to ratify it; recent statements of American politicians destroyed the hope that it would happen any time soon. The Soviet commentator quoted from a *New York Times* article of November 8, 1953, which conveyed the apprehension of some American senators that the Genocide Convention could potentially target the United States, specifically in the case of discrimination against "Negroes." Staying outside the convention, concluded the *SGP* article, did not lessen the accountability of the United States and several other countries for the acts of racism and genocide.[27]

The later theme was picked up by Aron Trainin, a leading Soviet authority on international criminal law. Gone were the references to class struggle and world revolution, less frequent became allusions to fascism and Nazism; twenty years after Trainin had come for the first time to discuss this subject, he abandoned the last vestiges of scholarly analysis endowed by his Nuremberg clout.[28] Impudently, he was pushing through the (new) official Soviet line. The chapter on genocide in his 1956 book, *Zashchita mira i ugolovnyi zakon* (*Safeguarding Peace and Criminal Law*), had no misgivings on what it was all about. Since the defeat of Hitler's Germany, genocide had taken place not only in colonies but also in some imperialist states, stated Trainin from the outset. Genocide carried out against the Negro population in the United States had been both preconceived and systematic, he argued. Genocide was born out of racism, and lynching was one of the examples within its physical form. From the perspective of the persecuted racial and ethnic groups, establishing harsh labor and living conditions with no adequate medical aid also constituted an element of the crime. And that is exactly what was going on in the United States, contended the grand old man of *ius sovieticum internationale*. As incriminating evidence Trainin offered the 1951 CRC petition and most recently the death penalty meted out to the Martinsville Seven.[29] Framing racial discrimination in the American South as "genocide" proved challenging, though. All the different forms of repression did not aim at immediate physical destruction of the Negro population, admitted Trainin. Imposing unbearable living conditions and preventing the development of indigenous culture, however, did. To describe this phenomenon Trainin coined a special term—*delayed-action lynching* (*sudy lincha zamedlennogo deistviia*). Despite his best efforts, Trainin was losing the battle against logic. He acknowledged that some American states (i.e., New York, Washington, New Mexico) had by then outlawed racial discrimination in general or in businesses with a certain number of workers. By addressing unfair practices at select enterprises, these state laws effectively tolerated racial inequality as such, insinuated Trainin.[30]

Capitalizing on the provision of the Genocide Convention concerning living conditions, Trainin pinpointed the unbearable situation of the indigenous populations in the Union of South Africa and Bolivia. Marked by grueling work in mines, poor nourishment, and ravaging tuberculosis, forced labor was a widespread phenomenon in the latter country, he said. The International Association of Democratic Lawyers (IADL, with which he was affiliated, coincidentally) in 1952 concluded that the American troops engaged in genocide in Korea and northwestern parts of China.[31] Trainin quoted from the commission's report that underlined a general pattern of killing and the blanket use of chemical and biological weapons aiming to destroy the Korean people in whole or in part. These and similar examples he negatively contrasted with the group rights guaranteed by the Soviet, but also Romanian, Bulgarian, and other constitutions.[32]

When dwelling on the drafting of the Genocide Convention back in 1948, Trainin awkwardly contradicted his earlier view that the concept of genocide should be rather delimited. Now he was in favor of a broader definition for the purpose of exacting just punishment. The prosecution of genocide, however, he was only willing to entrust to an international tribunal à la Nuremberg "organized by sovereign states." Trainin once again attacked the movement for codification of international law, his target from the mid-1930s onward. He mentioned Vespasian Pella and Henri Donnedieu de Vabres, but not Raphael Lemkin, as the partisans of the Genocide Convention. In 1935 Donnedieu de Vabres apparently gave a talk at the Academy for German Law and three years later published a book, *La crise modern du droit penal: la politique criminelle des États autoritaires*, which Trainin said included slanderous fabrications (*klevetnicheskie vymysly*) about the Soviet Union. The three legal experts' commentary accompanying the 1947 Secretariat draft Genocide Convention did as well contain certain "fascist tunes," according to him.[33]

Like other legal theorists in the Soviet Union, Trainin had adjusted his argument concerning the crime of genocide in accordance with the shifting political agenda. The meaning of *genocide* was as fluid as the Communist Party line. Thus, in 1935 Trainin excessively referred to revolutionary movement and class struggle, in 1948 he frequently mentioned "fascism," and by 1956 he decisively shifted his focus to the issue of decolonization. Indeed, he was merely illustrating the official definition of genocide as it appeared in the 1952 edition of the *Great Soviet Encyclopedia*. Volume X of the encyclopedia asserted that genocide was an offshoot of decaying imperialism, manifest in the extermination of peoples by means of creating conditions leading to the premature death of individual members.[34]

Yet Trainin's era in the Soviet legal studies was over: he had died one year after completing his book. As far as the interpretation of genocide is concerned, Mikhail Andriukhin had emerged in the mid-1950s as Trainin's successor. With three major publications under his belt, Andriukhin had become the foremost Soviet commentator on the Genocide Convention during the following decade. His was the first and only doctoral dissertation written on this subject in the Soviet Union. Supposedly scholarship, Andriukhin's writings were nothing but hollow ideology. The dissertation abstract appeared in print in May 1954 under the title *Genotsid—prestuplenie protiv chelovechestva* (*Genocide: The Crime against Humanity*).[35] As a reason for selecting this particular subject for his dissertation, the author stated its political significance while "imperialist states, first and foremost the USA, are continuing to carry out this policy until today." The abstract opened with a quotation from Lenin praising the peaceful policy of the Soviet state. The earlier discourse of two camps, socialist and capitalist, negotiating the Genocide Convention, Andriukhin replaced with a singular theme of the Soviet Union fighting against fascism, imperialism, and ethnic hatred by means of its 1948 proposal. His analysis was Marxist through and through. Drawing heavily on Lenin and other Communist classics, the prospective candidate of science argued that genocide was engendered by an imperialist economy aiming to enslave millions of people. In his definition, fascism was a terroristic dictatorship of the most reactionary, chauvinist, imperialist elements of capitalism. Nazis unleashed an imperialist war in order to prop up financial oligarchy. Without ever mentioning Jews, Andriukhin contended that the policy of genocide manifested most vividly in the regime of Nazi occupation. Death camps such as Auschwitz, he falsely claimed, had been set up two years prior to the German attack against the Soviet Union. Consequently, "monopolist predators" used genocide to exterminate the nations that put up resistance to the imperialist aggression. Racial ideology, as a cornerstone of genocide, was adopted by the imperialist bourgeoisie for the purpose of distracting the populace from class struggle.[36] Essentially, Andriukhin interpreted as *genocide* any attack on any group potentially sympathetic to the Soviet Union.

In a few broad strokes Andriukhin linked imperialism and fascism to the United States and its postwar policy. Whatever the latest words of abuse in the Soviet Union, the author crudely weaved them into his discourse on genocide. Neo-Malthusians, eugenics, and genetics-Weismannists—all got a beating from an upcoming legal expert. Since genocide was the most extreme form of racial discrimination, obviously the United States was not the only criminal state.

Therefore, Andriukhin added to the list of offenders Britain, France, and the Union of South Africa. The British allegedly resorted to genocide when enslaving the populations in places such as Kenya and Malaya; the suppression of the Boxer Rebellion in China fell into the same category. The harshest words, however, the Soviet legal scholar reserved for the United States. Thus he argued that the US administration carried out "bestial reprisals" against the black population, Native Americans, and "colored" people as a means of extracting maximum profit and simultaneously silencing political opponents. Whatever the advances in civil rights legislation, he dismissed them as a scrap of paper. Andriukhin singled out the US Congress and the US Supreme Court as the major American institutions that had sanctioned the policy of genocide. By so doing, he claimed, the US ruling elite grossly violated the UN Charter and the Universal Declaration of Human Rights (UDHR; curiously, he failed to mention the Genocide Convention). Building upon the experience of the Nazis, the American imperialists perpetrated genocide in Korea against both the civilian population and the prisoners of war. As an additional proof, Andriukhin referred to the missing signature of the United States under the 1925 Geneva Protocol banning the use of chemical and bacteriological weapons.[37]

At the end of his dissertation abstract Andriukhin returned to the 1948 debates in the United Nations. In his interpretation, rejecting the many Soviet proposals was a pity and adopting those advanced by "imperialist states" just a shame. "Reactionary forces" viewed the Genocide Convention as a stumbling bloc to their misanthropic plans. This is why the United States had not ratified the convention, reasoned the doctoral candidate. The analysis of the postwar policies of the American bloc demonstrated that, as far as the Genocide Convention was concerned, the main goal of the imperialists had always been setting subversive activities against people's democracies under the protection of international law.[38] This overall conclusion was shared by the dissertation committee, which bestowed upon Andriukhin the degree of candidate of science.

The revised dissertation appeared in print seven years later, in 1961. The book bore the same title, except that genocide was now qualified as the most heinous (*tiagchaishee*) crime against humanity. The book offered little new as compared to the 1954 dissertation. However small the differences, they are indicative of the changing political, and by extension propaganda, discourse. The punishment of perpetrators of genocide was now regarded as part of a struggle *for* peace, not only *against* the "imperialist aggression." Under the heading of peace offensive, the Soviet Union posed as the country advancing international security and friendship among nations. The collapse of the colonial system was another important development. According to the author, it simultaneously extended the scope of application of international law and reduced the probability of imperialist states carrying out genocide. Colonialism, or rather attracting the loyalty of the newly independent states, was essentially the leitmotif of the book.

Otherwise, Andriukhin used the causal framework advanced earlier in his dissertation: Incitement of genocide had occurred most commonly in colonial and dependent territories, thus making racist theory an ideological foundation of genocide.[39] Whether this logical nexus could actually be sustained is a different question altogether.

Indeed, the author of the treatise demonstrated very little analytical prowess, occasionally mixing cause and effect. Imperialist powers widely implemented the policy of genocide in colonies, stated Andriukhin. As the liberation movement posed a challenge to imperialist domination, the colonial rulers resorted to unprecedented repression, leading to physical destruction of hundreds of thousands of people and ultimately genocide. As specific genocidal techniques he mentioned dispossession of land and creation of reservations, and as particular examples the man-made famine in the Indian state of Bengal in 1943 and the suppression of the Mau Mau Uprising between 1952 and 1956. In chapter after chapter, Andriukhin discussed the policy of "genocide" and racial discrimination by the British in India, Swaziland, Kenya, Tanganyika (Tanzania), and Rhodesia (Zimbabwe); by the French in Algeria; by the Portuguese in Angola, Mozambique, and Guinea; and the Belgians in Congo and Rwanda-Urundi. Another tendency in Andriukhin's study was to ascertain guilt by association. For instance, when talking about atrocities committed by the French troops in Algeria, he identified NATO and specifically West Germany as the source of arms deliveries. He used the new buzzword in the Soviet lingua, *revanchism,* to draw a link to the Nazi war of aggression.[40] By inference, West Germany was a party to genocide and, consequently, the heir to Nazi Germany. It could hardly be a coincidence that the book went to print in July 1961 as the Berlin Crisis escalated.

Predictably, the spear of Andriukhin's attack targeted the United States. According to the author, "imperialist circles" in that country widely practiced racial discrimination and genocide against ethnic and racial minorities, especially black Americans. The suppression of the Negro population further intensified in the postwar period, he claimed. He estimated about 200,000 excess deaths among blacks due to the unbearable living conditions deliberately created by US authorities to cause their physical demise. Reportedly, certain congressmen incited genocide (i.e., killings) and urged resettlement of blacks from the United States to Africa. Although the Ku Klux Klan did not commit mass murder of blacks—Andriukhin developed his thread—lynching carried out by that particular fascist organization was a glaring example of the program of extermination of so-called lower races. Just as horrendous was the policy carried out by American imperialists against the indigenous populations. Without specifically mentioning genocide, Andriukhin went on to say that millions in the United States were suffering under racial discrimination: Mexicans, Filipinos, Chinese, Japanese, Malaysians, Hawaiians, Jews, Poles, Yugoslavs, Czechs, Slovaks, Ukrainians, and even Russians.[41]

The second half of the book outlined the history of the Genocide Convention. Andriukhin situated his analysis squarely within current affairs. As before, he defined genocide as part and parcel of an aggressive policy of monopolist capitalism. Western powers, first and foremost the United States, undermined the Soviet efforts to justly punish German and Japanese war criminals on charges of genocide, seeking to deploy them in preparation for a Third World War instead. The UN resolution 96(I) of December 11, 1946 had some merit, but also substantial faults, argued the Soviet expert on genocide. With the same degree of conviction, he praised the comprehensive Soviet proposal of spring 1948 as a "profoundly scientific and politically acute" analysis of genocide. Andriukhin concurred with Trainin that the stipulation concerning confiscation of property in the Secretariat draft would have provided ammunition to "bourgeois states." Had it been proclaimed a punishable act, "genocide charges could be advanced against authorities of people's democracies, who have confiscated—in the interests of the broader masses of population—the wealth robbed by a handful of monopolists and war criminals." The reluctance to implement domestic legislation in order to prosecute genocide Andriukhin explained by the unwillingness of the "imperialist quarters" to have their hands tied.[42]

More revealingly than any Soviet author before or after him, Andriukhin explicated the Soviet position on political groups. Among major faults of the draft Genocide Convention was the suggestion to extend protection to political groups. According to him, such broadening of the convention's scope bolstered "antidemocratic elements in the people's democracies." Newly established socialist countries successfully uncovered numerous plots hatched by imperialist agents and sponsored by the United States. Had the reference to political groups stayed, any efforts by Communist authorities to eliminate the "fascist" underground could become a matter of international law. Remarkably, Andriukhin brought Lemkin back into the picture, depicting him as a tool of American imperialism. Lemkin said nothing about political groups in his 1944 book, but changed his position along the lines of US foreign policy during his tenure as an (unofficial) legal adviser to the American delegation at Nuremberg in 1946. Around the same time, the United States launched subversive operations in Communist bloc countries. Probing any means of intervention, the US administration evoked the fight against genocide. Under the pretext of protecting political groups, the United States rallied support for all those who had been charged with high treason, criminal activities against the state. While decrying "political genocide," in fact the United States and Britain were trying to both distract attention from their illicit practices and preserve their intelligence network. Hence, not bothered about logical consistency, Lemkin suggested at Nuremberg extending protection beyond ethnic and national groups. Even more grotesque, according to Andriukhin, was the imperialists' attempt to hang "genocide" on countries of Eastern and Southeastern Europe during the 1946 Paris Peace Conference.

This time around, Lemkin attempted to insert the reference to genocide in the peace treaties with the former Axis (e.g., Bulgaria, Hungary, Romania), thus preparing the ground for interfering in their internal affairs. Simultaneously, Western powers objected to provisions targeting fascist groups and organizations in those countries.[43]

Despite these and similar "machinations," the final wording of the Genocide Convention excluded the reference to political groups. Curiously enough, the American delegation eventually came to support that motion. To explain this metamorphosis, Andriukhin invited his readers to consider the deteriorating international situation of the late 1940s. The Americans continued pushing for the inclusion of political groups until mid-1948. During that period the nascent "people's democracies" were still relatively weak, locked in the fight against "hostile elements" (read: political opposition to the brazen imposition of Communist rule). An allegation of political genocide was a means by which the United States sought to violate the sovereignty of Communist bloc countries. By 1948, however, East European states had entrenched themselves, destroying the "counterrevolutionary forces" in the process. American imperialism had no choice but to change its tactics. Meanwhile, gearing up for a new world war delineated by the Truman Doctrine and the Marshall Plan, the American administration sought to destroy any domestic opposition to its expansionist goals. In pursuit of that goal, US authorities launched in 1947 a vehement campaign against all the "democratic organizations" within the country. The proactive use of the Smith Act from 1948 onward was a part of that strategy. Thus, as the protection of political groups in Eastern Europe became less topical while the threat of prosecution for the maltreatment of similar groups in the United States grew, the American government made a complete volte-face. If anyone wanted to raise the issue of political groups, scoffed Andriukhin, they should look at the United States first. As for the US dithering, it further attested to the imperialists' hypocrisy in attuning international law to their current interests. Not "scientific arguments but reactionary political disposition" determined the US position on genocide, concluded the Soviet author. One of the last paragraphs of Andriukhin's treatise read like a slogan from a propaganda textbook: "Grave violations of the Genocide Convention by the imperialist states once again exposed before the peoples of the world the misanthropic essence of imperialism, demonstrating that imperialists resort to signing such conventions only under the pressure from the international democratic movement. However, nothing will prevent the collapse of imperialism."[44]

The candor of Andriukhin's exposé on political groups is truly unprecedented. One can only wonder what made the Soviets, thirteen years after the Genocide Convention had been signed and seven years after the Soviet Union had ratified it, show their hand. If anything, Andriukhin exposed Soviet vulnerability in relation to the territorial expansion in Eastern Europe. His discourse further proves that it was not the Great Terror of the 1930s in the Soviet Union but the territorial acquisition of the 1940s in Eastern Europe that Stalin loathed discussing within the framework of protection of political groups and, by extension, genocide. It also demonstrates the renewed vigor with which the Soviet propaganda machine incorporated the notion of "genocide" in the aftermath of Stalin's death. Historian Vladimir Tismaneanu has concurred in the opinion that the main weakness of the Communist system in Eastern Europe was its "chronic deficit of legitimacy." Mass violence that accompanied the imposition of foreign rule, specifically the show trials of 1949–1953, served in this context as "infernal pedagogy."[45]

Remarkably, the omission of political groups from the Genocide Convention came to be commonly understood in the West in much the same way, namely as relieving Communist states of responsibility for "exterminating political resisters to their expansionism."[46] In real terms, a certain conservative lobby group referred to liquidation of political dissenters in the Soviet Union.[47] Hence the definition of "genocide" as it appeared in 1959 in *The New Century Dictionary of the English Language* (p. 645): "Mass murder of a race, people, or minority group for political reasons or the like." Several other dictionaries in the 1950s incorporated political groups in their definition of genocide.[48]

Andriukhin's third and last publication on genocide, a forty-seven-page study called *Genotsid v politike imperialisticheskikh gosudarstv* (*Genocide in the Policy of Imperialist States*), hardly fit the category of scholarship at all. Published in 1967 in a State and Law Series, his extended essay had dutifully signposted areas of concern within Soviet foreign policy. Marxist pathos became more evident, and impartial analysis, well, it just was not there. Genocide was the "most cynical expression of criminal policy by the exploiter classes," he wrote in the opening chapter called "What Is Genocide?" Since the bulk of decolonization had already been carried out by the late 1960s, he had to acknowledge that the peoples of Asia and Africa no longer experienced the brunt of genocide at the hands of monopolist capitalism. Where the flares of genocide still raged was in Vietnam, and one country that perpetrated it was the United States. The history of the United States, according to the Soviet author, was punctuated by genocide. "Negrophobia" in the United States intersected with no less violent propaganda of racial hatred toward Native Americans. Living conditions on reservations were designed to cause extinction. Mass extermination of the native population went hand in hand with racist slander directed at the peoples of Asia and Polynesia, Slavs, Jews, Italians, and others. Atrocities committed by US troops in the Philippines in the aftermath of the Spanish-American War of 1892 were yet another example of genocide cited by Andriukhin. Semantically linking genocide and racial discrimination—as he did in his previous book—Andriukhin returned to the issue of race relations in the United States. In this context he mentioned the *We Charge Genocide* petition of 1951; mass arrests carried out by the police in Albany, Georgia, in 1962; and the race riots in Los Angeles in 1965.[49]

What Andriukhin really wanted to discuss, however, was the ongoing Vietnam War. In the second half of his essay he continued advancing a thesis that placed genocide at the crux of the imperialist war of aggression. The United States allegedly used genocide in order to enslave the Vietnamese people and to simultaneously crush the liberation movement, thus cowing other peoples into submission. In support of his position Andriukhin referred to "many progressive scientists in bourgeois countries" such as Victor Perlo. Brutalities committed by US troops supposedly exceeded those of the Nazis. Not coincidentally, the present West German government had been waging a war against the peoples of Asia and Africa under the banner of revanchism, argued Andriukhin. Bonn supplied the US military with bombs and toxic agents, while West German pilots deliberately destroyed the Vietnamese civilian population by partaking in aerial bombing. American and West German imperialists both provided military and technical assistance to Portuguese, South Rhodesian, and South African colonial regimes carrying out the policy of genocide. The British government as well was complicit in genocide, using man-made famine (e.g., in West Bengal in 1943) as a technique. To situate his argument in a legal framework, Andriukhin stated that acts of genocide went against the grain of the UN Charter and the UDHR, but also of the 1960 UN Declaration on the Granting of Independence to Colonial Countries and Peoples and the 1965 Convention on the Elimination of All Forms of Racial Discrimination. He rounded up his message with a solemn declaration that "Socialist commonwealth countries are carrying out the relentless struggle against the criminal encroachment of imperialists on the life and security of entire peoples—genocide. . . . In their declaration concerning the US aggression in Vietnam, the Warsaw Pact member states unequivocally state that they extend and will continue extending multifaceted assistance to the Democratic Republic of Vietnam . . . required for the victorious deterrence of American aggression."[50]

The last book on the subject to be published in the Soviet Union came out in 1985. Unprecedentedly, the book with the poignant title *Genocide* simultaneously appeared in Russian, English, and Spanish. (The Spanish translation reflected the shifting geography of the Cold War, in which Latin America started playing an increasingly important role.) One did not even have to read *Genocide* to know it was all propaganda. The Soviets themselves said so, conveniently. An overview of current research by Soviet historians that appeared in the July 1985 issue of *Voprosy istorii* contained, unexpectedly, insider information. Professor Sergei Tikhvinsky wrote that the History Section of the Soviet Academy of Science now featured counterpropaganda units, which had developed a long-term plan of "measures of propaganda and counterpropaganda character." The studies in progress utilized "anti-Marxist conceptions of the global historical process." *Genocide* was mentioned among the books that had been translated into foreign languages.[51]

The book comprised nine thematic chapters and a selection of documents. Written by professional historians, journalists, and lawyers, the chapters sketched the following cases: Nazi Germany, the United States, Israel, South Africa, Northern Ireland, El Salvador, Guatemala, Cambodia, and the composite "Judgment of the World Community." The documentary part included the text of the Genocide Convention and the findings pertaining to the use of chemical weapons in Vietnam, the crimes of Pol Pot, and Israel's invasion of Lebanon. Political violence in Ulster, El Salvador, and Guatemala, and the policy of apartheid in South Africa had a section of three to eight pages each. Predictably, these materials originated from trusted sources such as the Socialist Republic of Vietnam, the People's Revolutionary Tribunal in Phnom Penh, and the International Commission of Inquiry into Israeli Crimes against the Lebanese and Palestinian Peoples. The preface to the book cast the net as wide as possible, essentially stating that Western civilization was born into genocide. The history of the colonization of both Americas was marred with genocide, the advance of Christianity into Eastern Europe resulted in a nearly complete destruction of Slavonic and Baltic tribes, and so did the colonial policy in Africa and Asia in the second half of the nineteenth century. This historical trajectory rendered genocide a "hideous deviation born of decrepit and outdated social relations." More recently, the preface identified two major offenders: the United States and Israel. The former was said to have launched a deliberate campaign of extermination of the Vietnamese in an attempt to gain a foothold in Indochina, while the latter resorted to genocide against Palestinians and Arabs to realize the chauvinistic idea of a mono-ethnic Zionist state.[52]

The discourse that followed effectively summarized the headlines in the Soviet press over the intervening twenty or so years. The chapter on the United States argued that the country was founded and developed out of genocide against the Native Americans—the governmental policy still in place. Those in doubt should be looking for parallels no farther than Vietnam. The US armed forces widely used chemical weapons and other means of terror to cause a man-made famine. As evidence of genocide, historian Robert Ivanov referred to the findings of the people's tribunal set up by Bertrand Russell (on this occasion described as a "prominent British philosopher"). The "wealth of experience" accrued in Vietnam the United States used in supporting and encouraging genocide by the "terrorist regimes" of Israel, El Salvador, Guatemala, and South Africa. Publicist Konstantin Teliatnikov promptly extended this discussion to Israel. The Zionist genocide in Lebanon could only be compared to the crimes of the Nazis during the Second World War and the Americans in Vietnam, he averred from the get-go. In its infamy, Sabra and Shatila belonged in the same category as Khatyn, Lidice, Guernica, Oradour, and My Lai. One of the gravest crimes imputed to the Israeli military was the murder of hundreds of Palestinian children by means ranging from execution-style killings to toy bombs. Making a bridge to the subsequent chapters, Teliatnikov stated that the bulk of weaponry imported by countries such as El Salvador and South Africa came from Israel.

"There is nothing surprising about it," he insinuated, "because the Salvadorian junta practices the same type of genocide with regard to its people as the Zionists do with regard to the Palestinians." Israel armed South African racists in their aggression against Angola much like the United States supplied weapons to Zionists to help them wage genocide against the Arabs, not forgetting that America in the 1930s assisted Nazi Germany in building up its military capabilities. This abstraction made the author reach a grandiloquent conclusion: "This bears fresh testimony to the fact that genocide often goes beyond national frameworks and in global terms develops into an instrument of international reaction and monopoly capitalism . . . blinded by anti-communist hatred and prepared at any moment to plunge the world into the holocaust of a thermonuclear war."[53]

The chapter on South Africa followed the same pattern, emphasizing the role of Israel and the United States in prompting the "regime of death." Economist Inna Cherkasova defined apartheid as a series of "measures aiming at the methodical extermination of the non-white population" and asked rhetorically if it was not "genocide in a more refined form." The author contrasted the US veto in the Security Council blocking comprehensive sanctions against Pretoria to the charges of genocide allegedly perpetrated against American blacks, as voiced by certain speakers at the Second World Conference against Racism in Geneva in August 1983. For the lack of a better argument, the conflict in Northern Ireland was also framed as an open-ended question: "And isn't it genocide that the British authorities are practicing in Ulster?" The situation in El Salvador—which the Soviet news channels covered most extensively during the first half of the 1980s—was rendered as the governmental forces carrying out reprisals against the rural population under the pretext of combating guerrillas, who in their turn emerged due to the severe socioeconomic crisis. Those punitive expeditions, according to historian Ilia Bulychov, were still an integral part of the policy of genocide, carried out in compliance with the pacification plans of the Reagan administration. The chapter ended with a quotation from the late Soviet leader Yuri Andropov. In his statement of September 28, 1983 Andropov spoke of false moralizing by the United States, which showed its true colors in Vietnam, was militarily assisting Israel in Lebanon, and was presently backing the genocidal regime in El Salvador. When it came to Guatemala, the United States was specifically accused of complicity in genocide and incitement to commit genocide under Article III of the convention. Unlike in El Salvador, the army and the police in Guatemala waged a campaign of terror predominantly against the indigenous population. The United States provided military air and logistics to the dictatorship engaged in the war of extermination against its own people, wrote diplomat Vsevolod Sofinsky. The allegations of genocide were earlier sounded by the Guatemalan Bishops' Conference and the Working Group on Indigenous Populations of the CHR, on which Sofinsky served as a member.[54]

In what might be the most revealing chapter in the volume, legal scholar Victor Menzhinsky reflected on the politics of the Genocide Convention. The historical overview, stretching as far as the 1951 ICJ ruling on reservations to international treaties, effectively followed Trainin's original outline. Significantly, Menzhinsky picked up where Andriukhin left off, explicating the connection between the genocide treaty and subsequent UN legislation on racial discrimination. International criminal law recognized racism as the basis of genocide and thus the gravest offence against the peace and security of mankind, argued the Soviet legal expert. The International Convention on the Elimination of All Forms of Racial Discrimination of December 21, 1965 was followed, if not superseded, by the International Convention on the Suppression and Punishment of the Crime of Apartheid of November 30, 1973—both adopted by the UN General Assembly on the Soviet initiative. Elaborating on the provisions of the former convention, the latter listed specific acts constituting the crime of apartheid, including the following: "infliction upon the members of a racial group or groups of serious bodily or mental harm" and "deliberate imposition on a racial group or groups of living conditions calculated to cause its or their physical destruction in whole or in part." The similarity was unmistakable: Menzhinsky explicitly stated that the anti-apartheid treaty had compensated for the shortcomings of the Genocide Convention.[55]

Thus, from 1948 to 1985, Soviet commentators made a full circle explaining *against whom* Moscow conceived of the Genocide Convention. As time went on, *genocide* had slipped off the priority list for the Soviet Union. Consider that the text of the lecture that Trainin delivered in 1948 at Moscow was printed in 130,000 copies, Andriukhin's 1961 book had a print run of 7,000, and the rare 1985 Spanish-language *¡Genocide!* aimed at exactly 5,895 readers. The more propaganda, the more specific audiences it targeted. As the international disposition changed, so did the message incorporating genocide. Tellingly, in a book format, the full text of the Genocide Convention, including the reservations to Article IX and XII, was published in the Soviet Union for the first time only in 1961 (by Andriukhin).

2 · TRIAL BY WORD

The Gulag Condemned

THE GULAG LIABILITY

The vast forced labor camp system commonly known as the Gulag and the mass deportations that had been feeding it since the late 1920s proved a liability for the Soviet Union when it tried to expand its political influence internationally. According to US intelligence information, as of December 1948 the Gulag contained some thirteen million prisoners, of whom nine million were Russians, two Germans, and the remainder dozens of other nationalities.[1] (This figure likely encompasses the total number of prisoners who passed through the camp system to date.)[2] The earlier analyses suggested that the Soviets used mass deportations mainly to ensure a constant supply of free labor and as a means of control.[3]

The discourse on "Soviet genocide" during the late 1940s and 1950s begs the question of how much information about Stalin's terror was actually available in the West. A survey of literature that had appeared prior to the publication of Alexander Solzhenitsyn's *One Day in the Life of Ivan Denisovich* in 1963 suggests a negative answer. Some studies were better than others; the overall quality suffered under the burden of ideology and/or international politics. As far as genocide is concerned, the first scholarly accounts did not appear until the early 1980s. Some authors did use the word *genocide* during the intervening period, though mainly as a figure of speech or as a synonym for mass violence (in Russian, the most commonly used expression is the neutral *mass repressions*).

No matter how much the Soviets wanted to keep the Gulag a strictly domestic issue, it had broader international ramifications, obviously. Random accounts of appalling conditions in Soviet forced labor camps that started appearing in the West by the mid-1920s had assumed both political and economic significance.[4] When the first stowaways reached England and Scandinavia in 1930, the stories of their ordeal in Stalinist camps created a stir. The subject of forced labor remained for a couple of years a subject of heated discussions in legislatures, the press, and public debate. In the United States, the first such reports coincided with the arrival of Soviet lumber, manganese, and matches. The Tariff Act of 1930, restating the provision from 1922, banned the entry into the United States of any goods mined, produced, or manufactured by convict or forced labor. Consequently, the US Treasury Department imposed an embargo on Soviet pulpwood and matches. In the end, commercial interests prevailed: the State Department lifted the embargo placed by the Treasury after just one week, in August 1930. A few months later the English-language newspaper *Moscow News* pressured a group of American professionals working in Russia to publish a statement asserting that there had never been such a thing as forced labor in the Soviet Union.[5]

Earlier travelogues-cum-memoirs contained passing references to the Gulag in lieu of a far-reaching statement of fact. As a sign of things to change, in February 1946 Congresswoman Clare Boothe Luce charged the Communist regime with keeping "18 million out of 180 million in concentration and forced labor camps." No other publication had a bigger impact than Victor Kravchenko's *I Chose Freedom*, which hit American bookstores in April 1946. Hailed by the *New York Times* (*NYT*) as "one of the most important books of our time," Kravchenko's personal account came as a bombshell.[6] It was not just the content but the personality of the author that drew attention. A Communist Party member since 1928, former director of an industrial plant, and briefly a political commissar in the Red Army, Kravchenko was the most prominent Soviet citizen to defect. Having jumped off the Soviet purchasing commission in Washington, DC in March 1944, Kravchenko went into hiding. His status of a high-ranking Soviet bureaucrat was a blessing in disguise. Although one may suspect whitewash, his intimate knowledge of the internal workings of the Stalinist regime was unsurpassed. Kravchenko witnessed the horror of the famine of 1932–1933 as a member of a Communist brigade dispatched to the Ukrainian countryside for the purpose of speeding up collectivization. Twice, in 1936 and 1937, he became subject to political purges. Having escaped with a mere "reprimand" the first time around, he was mentally and physically tortured at the apex of the Great Terror. His familiarity with the Gulag remained superficial though, mainly in his capacity as a technocrat advancing industrialization behind the Urals.[7]

In the wake of his defection, on April 4, 1944 Kravchenko published a statement in the *New York Times*. No doubt bitter at Stalin's regime, he proved prophetic when asserting: "The Russian people are subjected, as before, to unspeakable oppressions and cruelties, while the NKVD [Soviet secret police], acting through its thousands of spies, continues to wield its unbridled domination over the peoples of Russia. In the territories cleared of the Nazi invaders, the Soviet Government is re-establishing its political regime of lawlessness and violence, while prisons and concentration camps continue to function, as before."[8]

What Kravchenko had to say about Stalinist terror, its scope and trajectory, has withstood the test of time. Indeed, many of his conclusions since then became standard in historiography. Kravchenko held responsible Stalin, the Soviet Politburo, and the Communist Party. Simultaneously, he cautioned against laying the blame exceptionally at Stalin's door, and thus taking one's eyes off the murderous Soviet system at large. Having mentioned literally hundreds of names among both victims and perpetrators, Kravchenko projected an indiscriminate, nonethnic character of Soviet terror (an ethnic Ukrainian, he kept referring to himself as "Russian"). The title of his respective chapters, "Horror in the Village" and "Harvest in Hell," was hardly an exaggeration. A witness to the crime, his condemnation of the Soviet regime reverberated mightily. "The first dividends of collectivization were death," and "death by starvation is a monotonous subject," enunciated Kravchenko. He emphasized the slavishness and callousness of Soviet officials tasked with extracting the last ear of wheat from the dying peasants: millions had perished "by a political decision made in a far-off capital around conference and banquet tables." While exporting butter and sometimes letting tons of grain rot in undisclosed locations, the Soviet state reduced its subjects to living skeletons, made them into cannibals. The famine was man-made under the ideological slogan of war against the peasants. Kravchenko correctly pointed out that, although the Great Terror began as a purge of the Communist Party, it eventually engulfed all strata of the population. Each and every one lived under the threat of imminent "unmasking," with each new arrest justifying the previous one and the executioners often sharing the fate of their victims. Effectively, it was the last stage in eliminating the vestiges of free thought. Kravchenko emphasized the complicity fueling the political violence, described the ritualistic element of denunciations and self-incriminating confessions, and provided examples of "verbal lynching" in the futile attempt to save one's own skin. Following a near-lethal experience in his native Ukraine, Kravchenko was dispatched to streamline industrial production in Siberia. There and then he came to realize the sheer size of the Gulag. Predating the Soviet attempts to exploit race relations in the United States for propaganda purposes, Kravchenko underlined the main difference in the treatment of slave laborers in both countries. The slaves in pre–Civil War America represented an economic value and therefore received at least the kind of care and protection given to draft animals, he insisted. In the Soviet Union with its endless supply of slave labor, however, the state apparently regarded it "more economical to let them die in droves than to feed and clothe them." As for the causes of mass violence, like many of his countrymen, Kravchenko was unable to get deep into the "strange Soviet morality play."[9] What makes *I Chose Freedom* even more credible is the lack of anti-Jewish bias, which often marred similar accounts.

Unexpectedly, the issue of Soviet forced labor camps had reappeared two days before the Genocide Convention was eventually adopted on December 9, 1948. It came up during the lively discussion of the formal complaint launched against the Soviet government by Chile. The Chilean representative accused the Soviet Union of refusing exit visas to Soviet wives of foreign citizens, and thus of violating basic human rights, traditional diplomatic practices, and other principles enunciated in the UN Charter. In his ranting response, Soviet delegate Alexei Pavlov attempted to shift the focus to colonialism. Luis D. Cruz Ocampo, former ambassador of Chile to Moscow whose son was married to a Russian woman, did not let Pavlov off the hook. He suggested that working conditions in the Soviet Union were not unlike slavery. While the ancient Romans and Babylonians had only exploited conquered peoples, the Soviet government reduced to helotry its own people. The blatant denial issued by Pavlov is worth reproducing in full:

> The representative of the USSR once again denounced the slander regarding the system of forced labor which was alleged to be practiced in his country. He was well aware of the source of those calumnies, and was surprised that representatives could credit the statements of a certain author who was a traitor to his country. The figures which the latter had quoted were absurd; if they had been accurate there would not be one free man in the Soviet Union. There were forced labor camps, but only condemned criminals were sent there, since the Government of the USSR considered it advisable for condemned persons to work, both for their own sake and for the sake of society. The number of condemned persons, however, was very limited. Mr. Molotov had stated in 1931 that there were about 60,000 in Karelia. Moreover, he had pointed out that they performed eight hours of work each day, under normal conditions; that they received a salary of from twenty to thirty rubles a month; that they were adequately fed and had books and newspapers at their disposal, so that unemployed workers in capitalist countries might well envy the lot of those condemned criminals.[10]

It was clear to everyone that Pavlov was telling brazen lies. According to classified Soviet sources, as of September 1947 the Gulag contained 2.1 million prisoners divided between 205 major camps and prisons, 31.7 percent of whom were sentenced on political charges. As regards the formal grounds for refusal of exit visas, the marriages between foreigners and Soviet citizens were banned by the Communist Party decision of February 15, 1947.[11]

Although the Chilean demarche did create a precedent, it laid bare the difficulties of filing an international legal challenge, especially against the Soviet Union. A majority of the General Assembly's Sixth Committee (Legal) endorsed the resolution condemning the Soviet Union. At the same time the delegates found Chile's case weak from a legal point of view. The draft resolution was too sweeping with regard to its allegation of both violation of international law and the UN Charter. Consequently, the United Kingdom introduced an amendment stating that the Soviet conduct violated "international usage and courtesy" rather than "international law." The Australian delegation then proposed seeking an advisory opinion of the ICJ as to the extent of privileges and immunities conferred by international law upon members of the family of the head of a foreign diplomatic mission. The Australian draft resolution was eventually defeated, informed by the sentiment that such a strategy might prove counterproductive; since Chile's case was weak legally, the ICJ would probably render an opinion that the Soviet action did not violate international law. Either way, it was expected that the Soviet bloc would counterattack by charging mistreatment of women in Chile, the United States, and the United Kingdom and claiming that Chile, as an economic colony of the United States, acted on behest of the latter state in this matter.[12] The US delegation received explicit instructions to abstain from a vote on any resolution stating that the USSR violated international law or the provisions of the charter. Using the opportunity to label the Soviet refusal of exit visas as inconsistent with standards of human decency, however, was encouraged.[13] If such a seemingly innocuous case proved so difficult to push through, one would think twice before taking a country like the Soviet Union to court on charges of genocide.

Decades-long experience made the Soviets excel at carrying out police mass operations. Ethnic deportations in North Caucasus and Crimea from November 1943 onward only became common knowledge in the West after *Izvestia* had published the decree abolishing the respective autonomous republics several years later, and the new edition of the Soviet Atlas no longer showed them. This is what an undated British document currently deposited in the American Jewish Historical Society (AJHS) in New York had stated. The analysis, which might have appeared shortly after the reprint of the decrees in June 1946, provided a remarkably accurate picture. Since the end of the Second World War the Soviet government had systematically removed from their homes and dispersed throughout remote parts of the country several small nationalities that had historically resisted the process of Russification and later Sovietization. The author of the report found it mindboggling how over one and a half million souls—the Ingush, the Crimean Tartars, the Balkars, the Kizliars (*sic*), the Kalmyks, the Karachai, and the Chechens—could be deported over enormous distances and in absolute secrecy. The document elaborated on the example of the Chechens. Even though the ex post facto decree admitted that the bulk of the Muslim Chechen population stayed neutral rather than collaborate with the Nazis, it condemned not individuals but a whole nation. This was probably the clearest expression of the "genocide habit of mind," according to the report. Thousands of NKVD troops entered the Chechen-Ingush Republic in early 1944 (the report spoke mistakenly of 1943), and on February 22 of that year they began rounding up the entire population. In the following few weeks, having shot those who had resisted, the security troops herded the victims into trucks and dispatched them to Central Asia and Siberia. Many deportees died of starvation and exposure during the long winter journey. The rest were locked in improvised camps where they were forced to fell trees and build roads. Under dreadful physical conditions, deprived of their ancestral homes, property, and culture, the Chechens, like other small nations of North Caucasus and Crimea, were rapidly dying out. "Even now the story is not clearly known," stressed the report, "owing to the dark veil of secrecy which the Soviet Government wraps around these grim events."[14] Perhaps the only significant detail that the report had failed to mention was that the Soviet mass deportations targeted specifically borderland minorities.

Thanks to contemporary research we now have a fairly accurate picture of the Soviet camp system and the mass deportations that sustained it. The mortality rates among the deportees were staggering. Approximately 7,900 Crimean Tatars, or 4 percent of the total population, died in the course of the deportation. Authorities made no special provisions for the arrival of hundreds of thousands of people, most of whom were forced to live in factory barracks, dugouts, or mud huts.[15] Having endured a punishing three-week train journey, the deported Chechens and Ingush had arrived at their destination in Kazakhstan physically weakened. Local party leaders were alarmed by the multiplying cases of dystrophy and typhus among the "special settlers." Kazakh government officials had warned that without additional food supplies the very survival of "utterly exhausted people" was in question. A significant number of deportees from the Caucasus, who had been mainly engaged in animal husbandry, could not sustain grueling labor in industry and/or on collective farms. Used to a milder climate, they had a hard time adjusting to extreme temperature fluctuations across Kazakhstan. According to survivors, hunger conditions persisted until the late 1940s, also among the indigenous population.[16] Nicolas Werth has provided further harrowing details about the plight of the deportees. Many of the Kalmyk settlers had no underwear, no shoes, and very little clothing. Crammed by tens of families in one apartment, the destitute people had to take turns sleeping inside, or were forced to camp outside with their children all night long. The mortality rate remained persistently high, taking into account that between 40 and 50 percent of the deportees were under sixteen. For the period 1943 to 1949 Soviet police authorities estimated excess deaths for Chechens, Ingush, Balkars, and Karachai at 23 percent; for Kalmyks at 21 percent; for Crimean Tatars at 10 percent; and for ethnic Germans at 9 percent.[17]

In 1950–1951 the British Foreign Office mulled over the issue of "Soviet genocide" and specifically its propaganda value. A white paper prepared by the Information Research Department (IRD), "The Dispersal and Destruction of Small Nations by the Soviet Government," painted the picture of a comprehensive purge of the borderland areas since the beginning of the Second World War. The report emphasized two prime concerns for the regime in targeting specific ethnic groups: opposition to the Communist rule and/or the policy of Russification and contacts with the outside world. Spelling out the provisions of Article II of the Genocide Convention, the report concluded, "It appears to His Majesty's Government that to deport a nation from its home country, deprive it of its material and cultural property, split up its families and scatter the remnants over a vast area of inhospitable territory under appalling living conditions is to commit genocide."[18] The question was how to frame this finding. The opinions within the Foreign Office varied greatly.

The IRD's Robert Conquest set the tone for the (internal) discussion. Conquest thought of the word *genocide* as the "most effective disruptor of the legend of the fine Soviet national policy." He reluctantly agreed with those of his colleagues in the Foreign Office who regarded "genocide" unsuitable for propaganda purposes. Indeed, it better served the legal argument that connected the Soviet practice of "destruction of nations" with the specific provisions of the Genocide Convention. In his opinion, the most important thing was to keep reminding of the tragic fate of the Chechens and the Crimean Tatars. Conquest suggested using *Chechens* as a buzzword while keeping a few real Chechens at the ready to tell their stories. Perhaps an Arab country or Turkey could pick up the Chechens' cause, Conquest speculated. Even better if Yugoslavia could lead the charge, possibly by "put[ting] up a Bosnian Muslim to do the operation." Foreign Office officials were preoccupied with the name recognition: what the man in the street could better relate to—a particular Soviet nationality he had probably never heard of or a legal concept that had been increasingly linked in the popular imagination to "race murder" and "destruction of nations." Capitalizing on many a newspaper headline, the campaign centering on genocide might be relatively easy to get off the ground. Ideally, it might snowball as the forced labor investigation did. Conquest's peers pointed out in the case of forced labor that the ordinary person could imagine it happening to him, at any time. That realization might make small nations pause before falling for Communism. As for genocide and the Chechens, it might still generate little public interest.[19]

Conquest, however, kept hammering home his point. He now argued that the significance of the "genocide theme" was *not* that it exposed the Soviet Union as a criminal regime but that it was the most potent antidote to Communist anticolonial propaganda. His emphasis on the Chechens and Crimean Tatars Conquest explained as follows. The Soviet policy toward the Chechens was more radical than that against the Baltic nations, for example. Besides, as "Asiatics and colored people," their case would resonate more with the colonial audiences. Whenever the Communists started exhorting Africans and Asians on the ills of colonialism, someone in the audience would shout: "What about the Chechens?" A series of leaflets distributed around the world and possibly a speech by Britain's prime minister would thus demonstrate the hypocrisy of "communist attacks on our colonial system."[20] In November 1951 Conquest and the IRD prepared yet another memorandum on "Soviet genocide." Distributed to Britain's diplomatic missions, the memorandum stressed that it was using the word *genocide* as "merely a convenient label" and warned against getting involved in an argument about whether any given action against a smaller nation constituted real genocide. The cover letter further specified: "We hope in the course of the next few months to develop Soviet genocide as an anti-Communist propaganda theme, since our evidence suggests that it may prove to be one on which the Soviet Union are almost as vulnerable as they were on forced labour."[21] During the subsequent decades, Conquest—who was a member of the Communist Party briefly in the 1930s and worked for British military intelligence in the 1940s—joined the ranks of academic hardliners. Conquest's influential books from the 1960s, *The Soviet Deportation of Nationalities* and *The Great Terror: Stalin's Purge of the Thirties,* were widely praised by his peers but not necessarily regarded as works of scholarship. The review of Conquest's 1970 book, *The Nation Killers: The Soviet Deportation of Nationalities,* in the *Chicago Tribune* carried the title "Stalin's Quasi-Genocide." Conquest's thesis that linked Soviet internal repression to external aggression had eventually propelled him into a political arena.[22]

Before Conquest came out with his books, one of the most authoritative accounts of the 1943–1944 mass deportations remained Abdurakhman Avtorkhanov's *Narodoubiistvo: Ubiistvo chechenskogo naroda* (*Genocide: The Murder of the Chechen People*), published in 1952 in Germany. Arrested during the Great Terror, Avtorkhanov had for five years languished in jail on fabricated charges. In 1942 he was released, but reneged on the NKVD assignment to infiltrate the Chechen anti-Soviet movement and crossed over to the Germans instead. Writing for a Nazi propaganda outfit, Avtorkhanov was tapped by the Americans after the war to work for the US Army Russian Institute and in 1950 went on to cofound the Institute for the Study of the USSR in Munich. The Russian compound word *narodoubiistvo* conveys more or less the same meaning as Lemkin's *genocide.* The tenet of Avtorkhanov's book, however, was that Stalin had accomplished what Russian czars had vowed to do a hundred years earlier, namely squash the Chechen-Ingush resistance. The two Caucasian peoples fought the hardest against the Russian oppression and so they became the first victims in that battle of liberation, according to Avtorkhanov. As yet another reason for the wholesale deportation he suggested Stalin's desire to safeguard the home front in the event of a future war with the West, specifically against Turkey. A brief overview of the Russian punitive expeditions in North Caucasus during the nineteenth century was followed by the detailed description of Soviet efforts to pacify Chechnya during the interwar period. Every new attempt to enforce the Soviet rule in the region provoked determined opposition by the Chechens, engendering a cycle of violence. Soviet authorities consistently used violent means such as suppression of Islam and forced collectivization to subdue the restive population. In the process, the NKVD resorted to provocation by first referring to the nonexistent "counterrevolutionary nationalist center in Chechnya" and later to the extensive Chechen collaboration with the Nazis. After all, the latest mass revolt began in Chechnya at the time of the Soviet-Finnish War, in January 1940, long before the German attack on the Soviet Union—argued Avtorkhanov.[23]

Avtorkhanov was among some fifty émigrés who had been affiliated with the Institute for the Study of the USSR. As officially stated, the institute welcomed into its ranks anyone who could prove that he was not a Communist Party member or a sympathizer. In 1958 the institute printed by far the most extensive volume on the subject, *Genocide in the USSR: Studies in Group Destruction.* The book came out of a symposium and contained six chapters discussing the patterns of destruction of national, religious, political, and social groups. The longest sections addressed the plight of the Jews, Russians, Azerbaijanis, and North Caucasian peoples respectively. The book's three major arguments can be summarized as follows: (a) Communism is an ideology bent on destroying national identity; (b) continuous repression against certain minority groups in Russia had intensified under Stalin; and (c) Soviet slave labor camps, the way the system was set up, needed fodder. Since the ultimate Soviet goal was creating a new "socialist" nation, genocide was not exclusively associated with Stalin but the Communist system at large. Consequently, genocide affected every nation and/or geographic region of the Soviet Union. The intensity of genocide correlated with the extent of opposition to the Soviet rule by any given national group. This discourse translated into the presumption that, insofar as Communism was immutable to change, the scourge of Soviet genocide would persist indefinitely. Rhetorical flare tended to undermine the factual data presented in individual chapters. The manifest anticommunism made some authors exclude the period of Nazi occupation from their analyses. One of them, for example, compared population statistics for Belorussia between 1940 and 1956, blaming the losses on a "persistent campaign of genocide against the Belorussian people" by the Soviet regime. Another claimed that Hitler murdered half of Soviet Jewry "with the connivance of Soviet authorities." The editors of the volume, Nikolai Deker and Andrei Lebed, did not just fail to smooth away the numerous contradictions and plain illogic displayed by individual contributors but actually muddled it up even further. Thus, none of the following questions received adequate treatment in the book: Did genocide mark the concluding stage in the long history of oppression, or was it a defining feature of the entire period of suffering? Did the fact of "rehabilitation" of the exiled peoples by the Khrushchev government amount to the confession of genocide? Would not the lesser intensity of violence since the death of Stalin work against the assumption that Communism was inherently genocidal?[24] The exact opposite of the Soviet analysis of imperialism, the incoherent argumentation advanced in this and similar émigré publications helps to explain the proliferation of genocide charges in the period up to the dissolution of the USSR: it sustained the Cold War dichotomy.

Like many others, Lemkin fell back on the existing literature on the Gulag in his analysis of "Soviet genocide." David J. Dallin and Boris I. Nicolaevsky's *Forced Labor in Soviet Russia* was probably the best known single study at the time. Cast into the debates in the United Nations, the book caused a political storm.

Vyshinsky characterized the authors as "total idiots and patented gangsters of scribbles" and the content of the book as a "bunch of lies and slander supplied by the Fifth-columnists and Hitler's agents."[25] The authors threatened a $1 million libel suit against Vyshinsky, only to find him protected by diplomatic immunity.[26] Effectively, it was a collection of essays comprising factual accounts and eyewitness reports. Published by Yale University Press in 1947, the book gave high estimates for the Soviet slave workforce—ten to twelve million in 1940. However, it failed to provide a viable analysis of the phenomenon of Soviet forced labor, seeking precedents in prerevolutionary Russia instead. Former Mensheviks, Dallin and Nicolaevsky attacked the Bolshevik regime using the very same Marxist language.[27] The authors described the Gulag as both a revival of the traditional Russian penal system and an organic element of the Soviet social order. The analogy with slavery, though not incorrect, oversimplified the giant project going back to the 1920s. "Forced labor in Soviet Russia, like any kind of slave labor, is cheap, and therein lies its first and foremost virtue," Dallin stated.[28] Lemkin did not go into details either. Altogether, he preferred quoting from Dallin's thirty-five-page pamphlet, *The Economics of Slave Labor,* that appeared two years later. Typically, Lemkin saw what he wanted to see in the statistics presented by Dallin. The composite picture that Lemkin had derived incorporated German and Japanese prisoners of war as well as the victims of the 1941 and 1943–1944 deportations. What mattered most was the overall conclusion that the combined number of Soviet prisoners was larger than that of German slave laborers.[29]

Otherwise, Dallin provided a rather stimulating, functionalist analysis in spite of the fact that his main sources of information were displaced persons (DPs) whom he had interviewed in 1948 in Europe. Following the defeat of Hitler's Germany, the Soviet Union remained the foremost country exploiting slave labor, stated Dallin. Roosevelt and Churchill at Yalta, not without hesitation, yielded to the Soviet demand concerning the use of German POW labor. The roots of the Soviet industrial enterprise and the mass deportations that had propped it up were both economic and strategic, according to Dallin. For him, the Gulag represented an immense labor exchange balancing supply and demand. The system of forced labor compensated for the lack of foreign investments and technical equipment, as well as offset the dilemma of high wages versus taxes. The degree and methods of compulsion varied depending on the personality of a camp commander, invested with substantial autonomy. Dallin argued that the Gulag differed from both the Nazi concentration camps and the Soviet camps of the 1920s, and that "planned extermination is not a function of the corrective labor system." Disproportionately high mortality in the Soviet forced labor camps Dallin attributed to the general lack of resources, cynical disregard for human life, and a periodic shift of purpose from economic gain to punishment, which sent hundreds of thousands of victims to destinations that were unequipped to receive them.[30]

At the end of his pamphlet Dallin mentioned the two ongoing investigations of slave labor by the United Nations and American labor respectively. Albert K. Herling, assistant chairman of the Commission of Inquiry into Forced Labor under the aegis of the Workers Defense League, had compiled the 1949 proceedings as a stand-alone volume. In the preface to the book, Herling thanked, among other people, Dallin, Nicolaevsky, and Constantin R. Jurgėla of the Lithuanian American Council (LAC). In the words of the editor, *The Soviet Slave Empire* was aimed at fellow travelers who had looked at the USSR as a hub of modernity and progress. An exposition of Communist horrors would not only help win over those misguided individuals but also fill with substance anticommunist propaganda. The book did not explore the issue of genocide as such. In fact, it was mentioned only once, in a quotation from Kaarel L. Pusta, former foreign minister of Estonia and one of the witnesses who had appeared before the commission. The crux of the argument was stated in the final two chapters, posed as questions: "America Next?" and "Are the Chains Eternal?" Herling painted a dystopian picture of the United States ruled by the Communist Party. In his view, the Soviet colonialism was worse than anything the white man had done to the native populations of Africa, Asia, and both Americas. The only qualification was that the Soviet forced labor system showed "absolutely no discrimination because of color or nationality, or previous condition of servitude." In that sense, the Stalinist regime was indeed "democratic." "The hydra-headed monster of the Communist movement must be exposed," declared Herling.[31]

"CAPTIVE NATIONS" ON THE OFFENSIVE

In the fall of 1950 the national delegations at the UN General Assembly each received a pamphlet titled *Human Rights and Genocide in the Baltic States*. Written by Aleksander Kaelas, the pamphlet was printed at the behest of the Estonian National Council and the Estonian Information Center, both in Stockholm. Despite its title, a mere five out of fifty-seven pages of the pamphlet dealt specifically with the issue of genocide. In the foreword, the two esteemed Estonian diplomats Hans Rebane and August Rei presented the annexation of the Baltic States in 1940 as the initial salvo in the long chain of Soviet aggression culminating in the invasion of Korea. While Western democracies were fighting to liberate Korea from Communist occupation, millions of "old and civilized European peoples," too, sought help to regain their freedom and their human rights. What Kaelas essentially did in the pamphlet was pitch selected articles from the UDHR against Soviet laws and decrees on the basis of which Estonia had been incorporated into the USSR. The reference to genocide was rather strategic, as explicated in the foreword: UDHR was a declarative document whereas the Genocide Convention was an internationally binding treatise. By the same token, the provision against slavery in Article 4 of the UDHR received mention in connection with the nascent UN investigation of forced labor. Like many other similar publications, the pamphlet sponsored by the Estonian émigré organizations failed to address several logical inconsistencies within the discussion of genocide. The numerous instances of mass terror described in the pamphlet were not accidental occurrences, the author argued, but part of a consistent pattern going back to Lenin. Whether it was slavery or torture, remuneration or standard of living—contended Kaelas—it fell under both the UDHR and the Genocide Convention and applied to the whole of the Soviet Union. At the same time, he argued that genocide was not an integral part of the Soviet political system, yet aimed to destroy specifically the Baltic nations. Mass deportations "can not be said to be anything but plain *genocide*." As a proof, Kaelas referred to the testimonies of recent refugees, who unanimously stated that the number of Estonians in Estonia was decreasing while the number of Russians was increasing. Right after that, he explained the act of destruction through imperialist and pan-Slavic policies (i.e., forced assimilation on account of Russian migrants) that had been implemented since the czarist times.[32]

Lemkin was among the first recipients of the book *Genocide: Lithuania's Threefold Tragedy*. "Hoping that you will find in it valuable factual material on the Genocide, as it is being perpetrated by Soviet Russia," wrote the LAC's Pius Grigaitis in his cover letter.[33] The book was published in 1949 in West Germany by Bronius Kviklys, who wrote under the pseudonym "K. Pelékis." During the Second World War Kviklys served in the press department of the Lithuanian Security Police and later ended up in a DP camp in the Western zone of occupation. The account was based on "facts known to its authors [Kviklys and the book editor, Jonas Rumšaitis] from dire personal experience in the enslaved homeland," and it fit within the emerging discourse of "three occupations." The chapters on the first Soviet occupation, 1940–1941, featured the graphic description of various methods of torture administered by the NKVD, accompanied by unidentified photographs of mutilated corpses. According to Kviklys, Soviet authorities had plans to deport up to 700,000 Lithuanians. Moving on into the period of Nazi occupation, 1941–1944, he unequivocally stated that the Lithuanians had nothing to do with the mass murder of the Jews: the Lithuanian underground press condemned the killings while individual Lithuanians, braving the threat of the death penalty, helped Jewish children to safety.[34]

The part of the book describing the present situation in Lithuania bore the subtitle "The Great Sin of Genocide." Why was it that Lithuania remained off limits to foreign visitors after the "return of red pestilence," was the question Kviklys posed. Because the ongoing genocide did not tolerate witnesses, was his answer. Accompanied by an "orgy of Asiatic propaganda," about 1,500 Jews who had been saved by the Lithuanians emerged from their hideouts to exact revenge. "Imported Russian peasants" took over the possessions of the deported Lithuanians and sometimes even their names. In the author's opinion, the Soviet slave labor camps differed from the Nazi concentration camps only on account of the direct exploitation of prisoners prior to their death from exhaustion or execution by bullet. The statistics on population losses in Lithuania (complemented with a drawing of the Grim Reaper) revealed that—subdivided into numerous categories—95 percent of the victims described as killed or murdered were actually Jewish. The pattern of Soviet extermination, as laid out by Kviklys, included military draft, technical training, labor duty, and repatriation. Using this rather dubious methodology, he arrived at the conclusion that since 1940 Lithuania had lost close to 40 percent of its population, more than any other European nation. "Today there are very few people who still accuse the Germans, Italians, or their satellites of being guilty of the last war," wrote Kviklys. At the same time, "the Russian genocidal practices continue with no end in sight."[35]

Two years later, the Supreme Lithuanian Committee of Liberation published a document compendium, *Appeal to the United Nations on Genocide*. Established in Nazi-occupied Lithuania, the committee in the fall of 1944 moved its operations to Germany proper. Perusing the eighty pages of documents, one is left with the impression that the committee—which claimed to be the legal representative of the Lithuanian people—could not quite decide what it was charging, genocide or gross human rights violations. This confusion was exemplified in the following excerpt from a memorandum from October 3, 1949 addressed to the United Nations: "the contempt of human rights has led to acts of barbarity—the genocide crime perpetrated in Lithuania is to be regarded as an act of barbarity and a menace to peace." The preface stated that the committee since 1946 had presented memoranda on genocide to every plenary session of the General Assembly. In fact, the earliest such document found in the collection is from October 15, 1947, with all the previous references made to the UN Charter and the UDHR. Otherwise, the select documents rehearsed the familiar themes, namely that a systematic genocide in the Baltic States began in June 1940, and that Soviet authorities were replacing the native populations with "racially alien elements, chiefly of oriental stock." Allegedly, forced marriages with "semi-savages" constituted yet another policy contributing to the "biological annihilation of the Baltic nations." Baltic émigré politicians welcomed the State Department document release on German-Soviet relations in 1939–1941, specifically the Molotov-Ribbentrop Pact.[36] Their own presentation of the historical record, however, was rather spurious at times. The memorandum from May 9, 1949, for example, insisted that "the Baltic Peoples valiantly resisted the Nazi occupant and suffered disproportionately great losses in manpower and resources in behalf of the cause of the Western Democracies."[37]

Whereas the Supreme Lithuanian Committee on Liberation was still trying to address the Soviet annexation of the Baltic States and the accompanying mass terror via existing international channels, Albert Kalme's book was an emotional outcry against injustice. *Total Terror: An Exposé of Genocide in the Baltics* appeared the same year as *Appeal to the United Nations on Genocide.* The author presented himself as a member of the Latvian underground since 1940. Reportedly, he was later captured by the Germans but in 1944 managed to escape to Sweden. Kalme rejected the legal definition of genocide out of hand: "Genocide, to me, is a pompous word. It is a word for polite conversations in civilized homes and for the conference tables of the United Nations. I hate it! . . . I call genocide 'cold, bloody mass murder' and charge Russians with practicing such inhuman homicide systematically for years. I back up my accusation with facts. Let them dare to deny them!" Kalme failed to deliver on his promise, however, while citing the anecdotes of forced marriages and purposefully encouraging drinking (just as the Japanese had promoted opium smoking among the conquered Chinese, he explained). At the same time, he acknowledged that the Soviet policy of forced collectivization did succeed in undermining the armed resistance by cutting food supply routes. To sustain his claim that the Latvians, Lithuanians, and Estonians were on the brink of extinction, he came up with the broader argument concerning the progressive Soviet expansion worldwide. The fate of the Baltic States was a warning to the rest of the world unless the Bolsheviks had been pushed back, Kalme concluded.[38] Mikola Abramcyk advanced a similar argument in the case of Belorussia. "The further annihilation of the Byelorussian people is still continuing," stated Abramcyk point blank in his pamphlet, *I Accuse the Kremlin of Genocide of My Nation: Based on the Secret Documents of the Military Persecutors and N.K.V.D. of the U.S.S.R,* which was published in Toronto by the Belorussian Alliance of Canada in 1950.[39] These and similar publications attested to the acts of genocide reportedly committed in the Soviet Union and its satellites on a daily basis. On the basis of the "strict evidence of facts and figures," genocide was proclaimed a major tool of Soviet political strategy. This conclusion prompted a rhetorical question from Wacław Szyszkowski: "If the Genocide Convention is not merely and solely a scrap of paper, a valueless document of human naivety, may we ask what practical benefit can it bring to us."[40]

Replete with accusations of genocide, none of the abovementioned publications suggested how to formulate and file the charges against the Soviet Union. The ideological polarization that marked the first postwar decade stalled rather than encouraged collecting prima facie evidence of Soviet mass crimes. In that respect, genocide allegations proved counterproductive. The following example, dealing with the wholesome deportation of the Kalmyks, helps to explain why. Out of the eight Soviet nationalities deported to a single person in 1943–1944, Kalmyks were the only one with political representation in the United States. Several thousand Kalmyks moved across the Atlantic at the end of the Russian Civil War. The émigrés of the first wave joined forces with the fresh arrivals from the DP camps in Europe to form a formidable, if numerically small, Kalmyk diaspora in the early 1950s.[41] In June 1954 Lemkin had a conversation with David Martin of the American Council on NATO. Earlier that year, the Kalmyk Committee to Combat Bolshevism had submitted to the United Nations a memorandum on genocide. Taking this issue one step further, Martin considered sending a member of the Kalmyk minority to the Buddhist conclave in Burma. Since, to his knowledge, the Kalmyks were the only Buddhist people who had been the victims of a "clear-cut and total act of genocide," one of the survivors could share the story of the destruction of his people with the Buddhists who came from all over the world. Martin inquired if Lemkin would be willing to have lunch with him and the Kalmyk leader in Greater New York.[42]

Seizing upon the émigré Kalmyk initiative, the American Committee for Liberation from Bolshevism (bankrolled by the CIA) intended in the fall of 1954 to present the incriminating evidence of "Soviet genocide." According to a plan, the formal document would be worked out by the Assembly of Captive European Nations, which convened in New York City during the Ninth Session of the UN General Assembly. Djab Naminov of the Kalmyk Committee to Combat Bolshevism, however, argued that such evidence was hard to come by and therefore suggested an alternative course of action. Naturally, it would be good to obtain additional eyewitness accounts, agreed Naminov. He could not help thinking, though, that the legalistic insistence on material evidence might "hopelessly delay the indictment of the Soviet regime before the bar of the United Nations and world opinion." The longer the delay, the weaker the case became politically and the fewer chances remained to alleviate the fate of the survivors. From the standpoint of evidence, Naminov drew a distinction between the charge of murder in criminal law and the charge of genocide, "which we now prefer against the Soviet regime." According to him, a *corpus delicti* and rules of evidence required to convict someone of murder in a democratic court of law did not apply to genocide as practiced by totalitarian governments. First, the chances of finding any *corpus delicti* in the latter case were very slim. Second, when an entire people disappeared from the face of the map, the governing authority could safely be held accountable. Naminov advanced the idea of an indictment based on fundamentals. A collective disappearance was tantamount to genocide. If the Soviet government were to deny these charges, it would have to inform the international community of the present whereabouts and welfare of the Kalmyks, Chechens, and other deported peoples. Sending a UN fact-finding commission would also be an option. By remaining silent, the Soviet Union would automatically plead guilty.[43] Effectively, this kind of argument sidestepped the legal challenge of carrying the burden of proof. As one Ukrainian American supporter of the Genocide Convention once put it, "clothing the facts with the suit of law."[44]

Then, again, the question arose (as directly posed to Lemkin in the case of the Kalmyks): what individuals should be charged with genocide—the Presidium of the Supreme Soviet, perhaps?[45] Going beyond rhetoric, Lemkin and his political allies had difficulties answering straightforward questions pertaining to "Soviet genocide." Could Lemkin please provide factual material demonstrating that genocide was indeed committed through the Soviet deportation of Baltic citizens, Toni Sender of the American Federation of Labor requested in January 1950?[46] To Cardinal Francis Spellman Lemkin wrote that he found "appalling evidence of genocide carried out systematically on the Lithuanian nation"—in the records of the Lithuanian American Information Center in New York and the Latvian Legation in Washington, DC.[47] Two years later, the cardinal was to receive another piece of evidence—a report of an unidentified Catholic prelate from Czechoslovakia in a misplaced newspaper article.[48] Among other sources of information Lemkin referred to the Vatican Radio broadcast from July 1950 and the Nazi-sponsored investigation of the Katyn massacre in 1943.[49]

After all, proof of "Soviet genocide" might not even be necessary, since it was just a means to an end for Lemkin, and increasingly the American propaganda machine. As he elaborated in the just-mentioned letter to the archbishop of New York, the destruction of the clergy in Lithuania could serve as a good illustration of "Soviet genocide" when the treaty came up for ratification in the parliaments of Latin America. This argument might work well with the Catholic nations, and besides it might help to counteract the Communist propaganda, which was picking up in Latin America. According to Lemkin, the claim that Russia was killing small nations would keep those nations on guard against Communist penetration.[50] In this and similar cases, the ultimate purpose of the Genocide Convention became increasingly hazy. Was it the preservation of religious groups as such that mattered, or was it rather their "special mission . . . in opposing Communism, materialism and political cynicism," and saving "our civilization from the onslaught of new barbarity"?[51]

Since 1953, the famine had provided the ethnic Ukrainian organizations in the United States and Canada with a most potent reference to "Soviet genocide." The UN Genocide Convention, which was called into life for the purpose of preventing and punishing the crime of genocide, had metamorphosed into a means of condemnation. A resolution adopted by the Ukrainian Evangelical Alliance of North America on the twenty-fifth anniversary of the famine, for example, put it as follows: "Whereas Communist Moscow perpetrated genocide in Ukraine and for this crime should be condemned by the free world. Whereas Communist Moscow, and especially its present dictators, used similar though less extensive methods of genocide after having occupied the territories of other nations. [We] call on all countries in the free world to sign the Convention on Genocide."[52]

Ukraine featured prominently in the report, "The Crimes of Khrushchev," released by the House Un-American Activities Committee (HUAC) on the eve of the Soviet premier's historic visit to the United States in September 1959. The report contained the testimony of witnesses heard in closed-door sessions. The witnesses were all East European émigrés such as Lev Dobriansky, president of the Ukrainian Congress Committee of America. The argument had been formulated earlier by George Sokolsky, a conservative commentator and son of an émigré rabbi. For the first time in the Soviet Union, genocide occurred in Ukraine, as a consequence of the collectivization program. Nikita Khrushchev was in charge and, consequently, responsible for genocide, argued Sokolsky.[53] Eugene Lyons, a Communist fellow traveler who made a 180-degree turn, pointed out that Khrushchev in his celebrated speech passed in silence over the horrors of forced collectivization and "genocide visited upon captive peoples." Nikolai Prychodko was more direct in describing the Soviet premier as "one of the esteemed executioners of Stalin's genocide of the Ukrainian population." A Ukrainian nationalist leader and former guerrilla fighter, Mykola Lebed, added that Khrushchev's crimes also included the "genocide of the Catholic Church" in the wake of the Second World War. Another witness presented it as part of the "political and cultural genocide that Khrushchev is presently perpetrating." As HUAC gradually stirred the discussion into the postwar period, Dobriansky identified yet another act of genocide—the recruitment of Ukrainian youth to toil on previously uncultivated lands in Kazakhstan (the notorious Virgin Lands campaign). Vitaut Tumash made a similar case for ethnic Belorussians dispatched to Central Asia.[54] The urge to situate the plethora of minor and major crimes under the single heading manifested itself in the title of a full-page advertisement in the *New York Times* eight years later. Paid for by the Ukrainian Congress Committee of America, the ad in the newspaper's November 16, 1967 issue read: "50 Years of Oppression, Fraud and Genocide—50th Anniversary of Russian Bolshevik Revolution!"[55]

During the following decades the tragedy of the Ukrainian countryside had somewhat faded from public memory. The fiftieth anniversary of the famine, however, thrust it back into the headlines. The National Committee to Commemorate Genocide Victims in Ukraine 1932–33—a coalition of some seventy Ukrainian organizations in North America—organized a series of events in the fall of 1983. As a culmination, an estimated 8,000 people marched on October 2 from the Washington Monument to the Soviet Embassy on Wisconsin Avenue. Although the main thesis stayed the same, namely that the famine was genocide, the tenet of the commemoration had slightly changed in the 1980s to emphasize the lack of debate on the deliberate withdrawal of foodstuffs by the Stalinist regime.[56] The following year the focus shifted even further, as some 7,000 Ukrainian Americans gathered outside the Soviet Embassy to protest "cultural genocide." The march of September 16, 1984 was sponsored by the National Committee to Protest Russification of Ukraine.[57]

THE CONCEPT OF *SOVIET GENOCIDE* BECOMES HARDER TO SUSTAIN

The formal rehabilitation of "unlawfully repressed peoples"—to use the Soviet terminology—began with ethnic Germans in December 1955. During the following year legal restrictions were lifted on the rest of the deported minorities.

In December 1957 the US officials reported on the latest in a series of steps taken since the death of Stalin to abolish some of the worst features of Soviet penal practice. According to the State Department: "These actions in part would seem to be a logical consequence of the post-Stalin regime's greater emphasis on persuasion rather than coercion and its avowed intention to correct some of Stalin's excesses. At the same time, the impending drop in manpower availability and the recognition of the low productivity of forced labor also doubtless induced the regime to alter the penal system." The comprehensive report "The Current Status of Human Rights in the Soviet Bloc" stated (referring to an article from the March 1957 issue of *SGP*) that Soviet authorities only now came to acknowledge that the Gulag had reneged on its purported goal of reeducation in favor of exploitation of prisoners' labor.[58] The US government learned about Nikita Khrushchev's so-called "Secret Speech" in March 1956. By early June the CIA had obtained the text of the entire speech, which it passed on to the *New York Times* for publication. The essence of Khrushchev's revelations about "Stalin's excesses," as interpreted by the Department of State, was that everyone in the Soviet Union knew what was going on but kept silent in order to survive.[59] At the same time, the American press had continuously stressed the element of cultural genocide in Soviet deportations of whole nations, since dispersing minority populations over vast areas suggested the intent to destroy those peoples as cultural and linguistic entities.[60]

In June 1957 the International Labor Organization (ILO) adopted the Convention Concerning the Abolition of Forced Labor, a supplement to the 1930 document addressing the same problem. Lemkin extended his halfhearted congratulations on the occasion, only to complain that the convention duplicated a substantial part of the genocide treaty. He was specifically referring to the provision dealing with the deliberate infliction of conditions of life calculated to cause physical destruction of a group. Since forced labor was usually performed in conditions pernicious to health, argued Lemkin, the Genocide Convention effectively had it covered. Among other faults of the Forced Labor Convention, he found that the definition of *forced labor* was missing while the term *discrimination* was too vague. In his opinion, the Genocide Convention was a more extensive document containing enforcement mechanisms. After a brief tutorial on the principles of lawmaking, Lemkin suggested inserting a direct reference to the Genocide Convention in the supplement treaty shortly to be taken up by the ILO at Geneva.[61] His advice went unheeded. Furthermore, neither the Soviet Union nor the United States bothered to ratify the 1957 convention for as long as the Cold War was in effect. Tellingly, the Soviet Union did not become a party to the 1949 International Convention for the Suppression of the White Slave Traffic either, unlike the czarist empire back in 1910.[62]

If Communism and Nazism were two sides of the same coin, then the future of small nations in Europe, Asia, and Africa looked grim indeed. According to

Lemkin, all present and prospective victims of Soviet genocide must understand that the totalitarian regimes of the brown or red tinge were committing mass murder to impose conformity. To avoid obliteration, the targeted peoples must unite under the guidance of the free world.[63] As time passed, however, selling this message became more difficult. Following the death of Stalin in 1953, Khrushchev's "Secret Speech" in 1956, and the subsequent dismantling of the Gulag, the comparison between the Nazi and Soviet terror invited a qualification. In May 1957 Lemkin addressed the Foreign Ministry of the Netherlands in the attempt to induce an extra ratification. The smaller nations of Western Europe might need the protection of the Genocide Convention from the Soviet threat as much as they needed protection earlier from the Nazis, wrote Lemkin. As he put it: "This danger appears to be slower, but in the long run it is visible."[64] Despite his efforts, the Netherlands did not ratify the Genocide Convention until nine years later, and hardly because of the fear of Soviet invasion. More likely, the Dutch government wanted to steer clear of its heavy-handed policy in Indonesia in 1947–1948, formally condemned by both the Soviet Union and the United States.

By the 1960s calls for US ratification and/or indictment of the Soviet Union for genocide became much less frequent and the tenor milder—the trend across East European émigré communities. Upon receiving a pertinent letter from the Baltimore Lithuanian Women's Citizens Club in the summer of 1962, the State Department spoke of "extinction" only with regard to Lithuania's independence, emphasizing the fact of American nonrecognition of Soviet annexation. As far as the Soviet treatment of the Lithuanian people was concerned, State Department officials used the euphemism "deplorable acts of . . . diminution or dispersal."[65] The émigré organizations were altogether in decline, especially following the termination of government funding in 1971. As of that year the annual commemoration of Soviet mass deportations was still known as the Baltic Genocide Day. Unexpectedly, it was the Soviet *Pravda* that carried a reference to genocide in one of its December 1972 issues. As part of the celebration of the Soviet Union's fiftieth anniversary, the Central Committee of the Communist Party in Moscow sponsored a trip for a group of foreign journalists. Sure enough, only the newspapers of the "brotherly communist parties" had received an invitation. As they fanned out across the country, a journalist of the Italian *l'Unità* traveled to Latvia. In his travelogue, the journalist set out to disprove the Western assertion that "something akin to genocide was happening in Latvia with regard to the national culture." He beat back this allegation by referring to the number of books and films released in Soviet Latvia annually.[66] One can only speculate whether this reference had anything to do with an episode that took place in the public gallery of the General Assembly a few years earlier. On November 18, 1968 a debate was interrupted when a group of young people unveiled signs reading "Stop Soviet Genocide," "Free Latvia," and "Stop Communism."[67] In the 1980s the Baltic case rarely featured in the context of genocide. Since the screening of the TV documentary series *The Holocaust* in 1978, the commemoration of the mass deportations of June 1941 proceeded under the heading "another holocaust." In the eyes of certain Baltic émigré politicians, genocide was still ongoing, though, by means of slave labor camps and psychiatric wards.[68]

Jewish support for the Genocide Convention became less pronounced, too, following the exit of Stalin and the marked decline in state-sponsored antisemitism in Eastern Europe. The Adolf Eichmann trial, which opened in Jerusalem on April 11, 1961, however, galvanized Jewish organizations. The American Jewish Congress (AJC) used the occasion to urge ratification of the Genocide Convention. Addressing Secretary of State Dean Rusk later that month, the AJC called upon the US government to join in the international pledge to prevent mass murder of the kind perpetrated by the Nazis. The sole reference to Moscow at that time was that the Soviet ratification of the treaty had embarrassed the United States, undercutting its moral leadership in the field of human rights.[69] The following year, as Jewish communities throughout the United States gathered to commemorate the Warsaw Ghetto Uprising, Nazi mass crimes and the resurgence of the American radical right remained their sole point of reference. The letter sent in April 1962 to President John F. Kennedy by the United Warsaw Ghetto Memorial Committee contained, unwittingly, central elements of Soviet propaganda. The committee members viewed with apprehension the emergence of the American Nazi Party, while hatred toward Jews and blacks spread by such fringe groups as the John Birch Society, the Minute Men, and Billy J. Hargis's Christian Crusade reminded them of the early days of Nazi Germany. The rise of Nazism in the United States constituted a great threat not only to the Jews, but to all minorities, and eventually to all Americans. An integral part of American democracy, freedom of speech, must nevertheless be checked, or else "Nazism . . . [will] come to our country in full force." The memorial committee, in the name of six million murdered Jews, passed the resolution demanding US ratification of the Genocide Convention, with particular emphasis on Article III dealing with "direct public incitement to commit genocide."[70] The truth is, however, that during the 1950s and 1960s the Genocide Convention never became a prime concern of the American Jewish community. The National Community Relations Advisory Council (NCRAC) had to admit that, as of 1951, the genocide treaty "has not become a burning issue in the general public." Although NCRAC's 1967 Program Plan adopted US ratification as a public relations priority, the Six-Day War that same year attracted considerably more attention.[71]

3 · SOVIET SATELLITES SHIFT ALLEGIANCES

Hungary, Yugoslavia

THE SOVIET UNION BARELY ESCAPES THE WRATH OF THE GENOCIDE CONVENTION OVER HUNGARY

As far as action on genocide was concerned, within the Communist bloc Hungary proved most likely to cause a backlash against the Soviets. Genocide charges against the Soviet Union were spearheaded by Monsignor Béla Varga. A Catholic prelate, Varga was a member of Hungary's Independent Smallholders Party and parliament speaker in 1946–1947. Varga found himself among the seventy-four Hungarian politicians spirited away to the West by the CIA while the Communists were consolidating their power in the country. Under his leadership, the Hungarian National Council (HNC)—encouraged and funded through the US State Department—became one of the most cohesive East European émigré organizations in the United States. Among its primary goals was highlighting the shortcomings in the Soviet system, including mass deportations and political repression.[1]

Beginning in 1950, Communist authorities deported some 70,000 Hungarians deemed "socially dangerous." Some of them wound up in squalid agricultural labor camps in the Hungarian countryside, others in forced labor camps in the Soviet Union. By means of deportations the new rulers intended to simultaneously ease the housing pressure and to root out potential political dissent.[2] In December 1951 Varga accused the government and the Communist Party in Budapest of conspiring with Moscow to commit genocide against the Hungarian people. He claimed that all but one clause (killing members of the group) of Article II of the Genocide Convention applied. The evidence that he cited, as it often happened in such cases, was scant. To prove serious mental harm done to the nation, Varga spoke of two thousand persons who had lost their equilibrium as a result of the "torturous conditions" and had committed suicide. The forced transfer of children was illustrated by an anecdote of two children of two and four years of age wandering the streets of Budapest. Even less credible was his claim that some parents in Hungary had tattooed the bodies of their infants with their names in anticipation of separation. Varga called for an international embargo on goods acquired through genocide, while blaming the Soviets for having tried to thwart the Genocide Convention first and then to dilute its meaning through the draft Code of Offenses and Human Rights Covenant. Finally, he invited the General Assembly to put the issue of Soviet genocide on its agenda.[3] Unlike other émigré organizations, however, Varga and the HNC did not address the United Nations and/or the US State Department directly. Instead, as Lemkin had done earlier, he approached the government of Panama. "Hungarian nation mortally in danger through deportation," he cabled President Alcibíades Arosemena; "appeal Your Excellency invoke Genocide Convention Paris to save Hungary."[4] Lemkin swiftly capitalized on Varga's appeal, adding that Hungary and other East European nations must be kept alive as a cordon sanitaire against further Soviet aggression.[5]

In early 1952 the US delegation to the United Nations received further appeals to condemn expulsions from the borderlands and to indict both the Soviet and Hungarian Communist governments for genocide. Some letter writers boosted their plea by invoking their moral obligation and their Christian duty. The State Department's reply was identical to that routinely sent to other ethnic organizations. The US delegation shared the concern about Communist human rights violations and promised to do all possible to expose slave labor, the mistreatment of prisoners of war, and the breach of treaty agreements in the Soviet bloc.[6] This polite rejection did not dishearten Varga and the HNC, though. Béla Fábián, in a letter to the *New York Times*, cited numerous anecdotes that were supposed to illustrate the "continuous practice of genocide behind the Iron Curtain." Evictions carried out in the Hungarian countryside meant certain death for the afflicted; Romania's Jews had been forced to work in the uranium mines in Saxony; Lithuania had been repopulated with "Tartars and other Asiatic tribes"—these and similar charges fed into a general conclusion that the Soviet camp system was identical to the Nazi one.[7] Dulles barely got time to settle into his new position, as Varga was already touting the secretary of state to have the Soviet Union declared guilty of the crime of genocide. Varga argued that the Soviets were trying to put the Genocide Convention on ice by diluting its definition in two other UN projects—the draft Code of Offences and the Covenant on Human Rights. Simultaneously, the formula of crimes against humanity, which had been advocated by Moscow since Vyshinsky's infamous "warmongering" speech in 1947, enabled the USSR to indict the United States for lynching. To give more weight to his words, he attached a copy of the book *Genocide by Deportation: An Appeal to the United Nations to Enforce the Law*.[8]

Coincidentally, the book was published by the HNC and included a foreword by Varga. *Genocide by Deportation* was comprised of three parts: analysis of the

Genocide Convention; outline of the Soviet terror in Hungary; and a selection of documents, taking up 90 pages out of the book's 131. "Chronically progressive genocide goes on in lands behind the Iron Curtain," stated the book from the get-go. To reach that conclusion, the HNC utilized a peculiar interpretation of genocide. Capitalizing on destruction of groups *as such* and infliction of *mental harm*—the clauses identified as the most problematic by the American diplomats—Hungarian émigrés made the case that the imposition of Communism and the supplementary concept of *Soviet man* was tantamount to genocide. They made it sound as if the discussion of "national consciousness" was incorporated in the text of the Genocide Convention. On that premise, they presented as evidence of genocide documents as different as the so-called Serov instructions, the Cardinal József Mindszenty trial transcripts, and a quotation from a high-ranking member of the Presidential Council.[9] These records meant to prove that genocide started in Hungary the moment the Red Army arrived and suggested the existence of a "master plan for the extermination" of East European nations. When it comes to the documents reproduced in the final part of the book, none of them actually spoke of mass arrests and deportations in Hungary in the context of genocide. Western politicians and journalists variously accused the Soviet Union of oppression, uncivilized conduct, inhuman treatment, human rights violations, aggression, terrorism, crimes against humanity, but not specifically genocide.[10]

Little did the Hungarian émigrés know that, as early as February 1949, the US government decided against formally evoking violations of human rights or indirect Soviet aggression against Hungary, not to mention genocide. To do so would be both futile and politically disadvantageous—concluded a secret report of the State Department. Based on past experience in the Iranian, Greek, Korean, Czechoslovakian, and Berlin cases, the United States should not bring this matter before the United Nations or encourage a similar action by any other member state. An effective UN action required a convincing proof of abuses and the "psychologically right time when the world public opinion is intensely interested in the matter," or else it might end in an air of embarrassment and frustration without any tangible result. Effectively, the State Department declared Hungary, Czechoslovakia, and other Soviet-dominated countries a lost cause. "Although the Mindszenty 'trial' will for some time revive the interest in the outrages of the Communist regimes in Eastern Europe," related the report, "it is submitted that the present time is hardly the psychological moment for reopening the problem after such a lapse of time." The Hungarian government was sufficiently strong to withstand any UN condemnation. The inability of the United Nations to take effective action beyond condemnation, however, would only weaken the morale of anticommunist forces. The only viable option would be ascertaining the violation of the 1947 Peace Treaty, the claim Hungary would no doubt reject. A UN procedure would probably end up in a recommendation that Hungary was not legally bound to accept. Beside, the Soviet Union might counterclaim a violation of the Peace Treaty with Italy regarding Trieste. Worse still, insofar as this undertaking was construed as a legal obligation to stand against discrimination, the Soviet bloc might as well bring before the United Nations any discriminatory practice in the United States or elsewhere in the Western orbit. An Indian complaint against the Union of South Africa, presently pending before the General Assembly, established a precedent pointing in that direction.[11]

Varga expanded on the issues outlined in the 1951 book three years later in a letter to the president of the Synagogue Council of America, Norman Salit. A Catholic priest, Varga said he prayed for the memory of those who perished through genocide perpetrated by both the Nazis and the Communists. According to him, the Code of Offenses was a devious substitute for the Genocide Convention that aimed to relieve the Communists of accountability for the crimes they were committing against the Jews, Catholics, Protestants, Muslims, and Buddhists. At the same time, it would establish criminal responsibility for the "Free World helping the peoples behind the Iron Curtain."[12]

In August 1954 the Select Committee on Communist Aggression (formerly the House Baltic Committee) under the chairmanship of Congressman Charles J. Kersten (R-WI) heard testimonies on the Soviet takeover of Hungary. The hearings were subsequently broadcast by the Voice of America and Radio Free Europe. Among the principal witnesses was the ubiquitous Varga. As before, he argued that the "system of wholesale deportations has reached the proportions of genocide." Although Varga admitted that, since a year earlier, it had no longer been the case, he could not help adding: "But even this seemingly conciliatory measure has become a part of a diabolical scheme to break the backbone of the nation." Alongside individual testimonies, the Select Committee admitted sixteen exhibits, including the "Indictment against Responsible Members of the Russian and the Hungarian Government."[13]

Originally, the document was presented by the Federation of Free Hungarian Jurists in America before the United Nations. Of all the many such texts drafted by East European émigrés, this one was perhaps the most professionally executed. The federation was established for the purpose of observing the newly implemented laws and decrees violating the rights and interests of the Hungarian people. The most significant criminal acts under their watch were said to have infringed the letter of the Genocide Convention. The essence of the offense, "hurting the vital conditions of life of the whole Hungarian people," suggested the broadest possible interpretation of genocide by the émigré lawyers. Operating on this premise, the president of the federation, Vince Nagy, charged Soviet and Hungarian government officials, as well as Soviet military and police leaders, with genocide. Specifically mentioned were the head of the KGB, Ivan Serov, Marshall Klement Voroshilov, and Lieutenant General Vladimir Sviridov. The problem of retroactivity was solved by the émigré lawyers as follows: they incorporated in their indictment acts committed prior to December 9, 1948 insofar as they continued past that date, thus constituting a "consecutive series of crimes." Hence the list of crimes included the detention of Hungarian prisoners of war, the "abduction" of Hungarian citizens since 1945, mass deportations from Carpathian Ruthenia, the liquidation of the Catholic Church, the "kidnapping" of Hungarian national leaders, and others. In a typical Lemkinesque fashion, the document interpreted the arrest of eminent Hungarian politicians and churchmen as "inflicting serious mental harm" to the entire nation. Also borrowed from Lemkin was the argument that, since the Communists were incapable of assimilating some ten million Hungarians who "adhered to Western civilization," the former intended to destroy them gradually, group by group, through genocide." The cause and effect relationship came under strain whenever the "Indictment" used sentences like "This brutal act of genocide leaves no doubt about the premeditated intent of the competent Russian leaders to liquidate the Hungarian population." While acknowledging that deportations had been eventually discontinued and transit camps closed, the federation insisted, à la Varga, that this was a "diabolical method" executed by the Hungarian and Soviet governments to destroy the repatriates by other means. These and similar assertions, Nagy added, had been earlier submitted by the HNC as a part of two memoranda to the UN Economic and Social Council (ECOSOC) Ad Hoc Committee on Forced Labor.[14]

It was rather predictable that some nationalist leaders and Western politicians labeled the suppression of anti-Soviet uprising in Hungary, which went into history as the 1956 Revolution, as genocide. Varga, for example, argued that the Soviet troops indiscriminately targeted innocent men, women, and children. According to him, the scope of the destruction of civilian population qualified as genocide. He further reminded that both Hungary and the Soviet Union had ratified the Genocide Convention, and thus could be internationally prosecuted.[15] The United States, which many believed would relentlessly pursue the issue of genocide, found itself in a fix when hostilities broke out in Hungary. On the one hand, Washington explicitly stated that the United States would not intervene militarily under any circumstances. On the other hand, the Voice of America and Radio Free Europe broadcasts to Hungary, twenty-three hours a day, made it sound as if the West would do exactly that. Encouraging the Hungarians to demand freedom without inciting the overthrow of a Communist system proved a major contradiction in US policy. The Suez Crisis was a blessing in disguise for the US policymakers, who now shifted their attention from Europe to the Middle East. Since the United States was unable to influence the situation on the ground without risking a war with the Soviet Union, moral condemnation remained the only (face-saving) option.[16]

As far as the formal charges of genocide are concerned, the Hungarian Revolution of 1956 was indeed the closest call for the Soviet Union. On November 4, the General Assembly convened an emergency session on Hungary, on the heels of a similar session on the Suez Crisis. During this session, Cuba, Italy, Ireland, Pakistan, and Peru introduced a joint resolution charging the Soviet Union with a violation of the UN Charter, the Peace Treaty with Hungary, and the Genocide Convention. Dr. Emilio Núñez Portuondo, head of the Cuban delegation and author of the draft resolution, claimed that some 65,000 Hungarians had been killed and many more deported to Russia. He stressed that this was not the first time that the Soviet Union had committed genocide. According to the Cuban delegate, Khrushchev himself accused Stalin at the session of the Politburo on January 24, 1956 of genocide perpetrated by the latter against the Crimean Tatars, the Kalmyks, and the North Caucasian ethnicities.[17]

The very next day, November 5, the Soviet Foreign Ministry tasked the Institute of Law in Moscow to collect information on human rights both at home and abroad in anticipation of an attack on the USSR in the General Assembly.[18] Imre Horváth, head of the Hungarian delegation to the United Nations and newly appointed foreign minister, described claims of ongoing mass deportations as "slander." *Pravda* did the same, wondering if the authors of the Cuban resolution were sane in leveling the accusation of genocide against the Soviet Union, which had sacrificed millions of lives while saving the peoples of Europe, including the Hungarians, from sure destruction at the hands of the Nazis. Predictably, the Soviets portrayed the discussion of the Hungarian question as a distraction from a truly urgent international problem, that is, the Suez Crisis. Simultaneously, they adopted a tu quoque tactic, capitalizing on the initial response to the Cuban draft resolution by Acting US Secretary of State Herbert Hoover Jr. As regards genocide, maintained *Pravda*, the chief defendant should be in fact the United States. The United States had refused to ratify the Genocide Convention, and for a good reason: the Native American population had been long exterminated, while racial discrimination against blacks and propaganda to destroy entire nations were rampant.[19]

The Soviet position on Hungary was articulated on November 19 at the General Assembly's plenary session by Dmitry Shepilov. The Soviet foreign minister, who made good as former propaganda chef of *Pravda*, told the audience that the Cuban draft resolution had the "fetid odor of provocation" about it. Even in the worst times of the Cold War one could hardly find a similar example of "slanderous allegations" violating rules of evidence. As an example, Shepilov referred to the "mythical" broadcast of the Budapest radio regarding mass deportations to Russia. He unsavorily described "this disgraceful insinuation" as the "reeking canard" that the Cuban delegation dragged out on the UN floor "from the dump of refuted fabrications." The American press had already backed down from the "malicious lie" about the alleged destruction of a children's hospital in Budapest. Now, using "some of Joseph Goebbels's most refined tricks," it was spreading the "myth" of deportations. Shepilov then gave the Soviet version of what happened in Hungary: the misguided Nagy's government, the attempted fascist counterrevolution, the white terror, and the invitation to the Soviet troops to restore peace and order. Allegations of Soviet genocide aimed to give legal clout to the rabble-rousing document submitted by Cuba. The Genocide Convention condemned acts carried out for the purpose of destroying national, ethnic, racial, or religious groups—stated the speaker—but that had nothing to do with the situation in Hungary. If the Cuban delegation were genuinely concerned about combating genocide, it should have looked elsewhere. Shepilov then ventured into a lengthy account of atrocities recently committed by the British in Kenya and the French in Algeria.[20] Shepilov's rebuttal harked back to the UN debates on the definition of genocide and specifically political groups. What the Soviet foreign minister was essentially saying was that Moscow was suppressing the political dissent in Hungary, an act not covered by the Genocide Convention (at the insistence of the Soviets).

The Soviets proved wrong in their intimation that the United States stood by the Cuban allegations of genocide. Portuondo made no secret that the reason behind including in the original resolution the charge of a violation of the 1947 Peace Treaty between Hungary and the associated powers was to get the Americans onboard. The United States, however, had no appetite for invoking the genocide treaty, which it had expressly refused to ratify. The United States circulated a substitute resolution that eschewed any reference to genocide or the demand that the Soviet troops should withdraw from Hungary.[21] Faced with US obduracy, Cuba had dropped the charge of genocide against the Soviet Union. The watered-down resolution merely recalled the "principles" of the Genocide Convention, specifically Article II(c) and (e), when urging a halt to Soviet deportations of Hungarians. Lemkin, who had argued that the reference to the Genocide Convention opportunely "dramatized" the situation in Soviet-dominated Eastern Europe, promptly issued a statement. Treading softly on the USSR, he claimed, "opened the door for enemies of the convention to kill it."[22] The latest version of the Cuban resolution was adopted on November 21 by a vote of 55 to 10, with 14 abstentions. For the first time ever, a UN resolution included a *hint* that a member state might have committed genocide. This was probably the strongest wording acceptable to countries that had not ratified the genocide treaty, wrote Michael James in the *New York Times*. Otherwise, as the argument went, the resolution might achieve little but irritate the Hungarian regime and stiffen its opposition to the admission of observers. Even that expectation was far-fetched; it was generally believed that the "Hungarian question would be allowed to die down."[23] The text of the resolution reflected the United States' ultimate decision to avoid a direct confrontation with the Soviet Union over Hungary.

It did not help that some of the facts and figures cited by Portuondo, Varga, and others proved false. An estimated number of Hungarians who died during the fighting in November 1956, for example, stood at 2,700.[24] Khrushchev delivered his famous speech at the Communist Party Congress on February 25, 1956, without mentioning the word *genocide* even once. Furthermore, it was not Khrushchev but János Kádár who stood behind the judicial murder of Imre Nagy in June 1958, contrary to what had been widely believed at the time. The overlap between the Warsaw Pact invasion of Hungary and the Anglo-French of Egypt did not serve well the discussion about genocide either. During the plenary debates, the Iraqi delegate spoke of genocide in the Gaza Strip, extended to Egypt and Algeria by his Sudanese counterpart.[25] The Soviet Union, too, was eager to refocus the discussion on the Middle East. When explaining why his country voted against UN Resolution 1127(XI), Shepilov insisted that the Cuban delegation had failed to substantiate its charges. The debates on so-called deportations and genocide were nothing but a smokescreen for the imperialist aggression as presently waged against Egypt by Britain, France, and Israel, he argued.[26]

Otherwise, Cuba obviously struck a raw nerve with the Soviets. A few weeks after the vote on the Cuban resolution, *Pravda* had inquired "Who Violates Human Rights?" The question mark was unnecessary, since the answer was obvious: the United States and . . . Cuba. The article claimed hypocrisy on the part of President Dwight D. Eisenhower when he used the eighth anniversary of the UDHR to speak on the suppression of democracy in Hungary. *Pravda* countercharged voting rights violations in Louisiana; instances of racism in Montgomery, Alabama; and discrimination against workers of Latin American descent. As for the island state, the Soviet newspaper reported on a recent demonstration against the Batista regime in front of the UN headquarters in Manhattan. The demonstrators declared a "protest against the genocide perpetrated by dictator Batista against the civilian population of Cuba." The United States did not heed these calls since it propped up the regime in Havana militarily. Bizarrely, chided *Pravda*, the American bosses were now pushing their Cuban vassal to spearhead the attack against Hungary in the General Assembly. "Indeed, dirty hands are doing dirty bidding!"[27]

YUGOSLAVIA RETRACTS GENOCIDE ALLEGATIONS

In the immediate postwar years Socialist Yugoslavia famously asserted its independence from the Soviet Union, acerbated by a personal spat between Marshal Josip Broz Tito and Generalissimo Stalin. Consequently, Yugoslavia was thrown out of the Communist Information Bureau (Cominform), with Stalin for a while plotting to remove Tito from power by force. A very public divorce in the summer of 1948 translated into a propaganda war between the two countries. The Soviet claims of fascist tendencies Tito's regime countered by charging Stalin with genocide.[28] Conspicuously, the references to "Soviet genocide" in Yugoslavia all but vanished following the death of Stalin and the rapprochement between the two countries. Cyrus L. Sulzberger of the *New York Times*, who was documenting the course of de-Stalinization in the Soviet Union in the wake of Khrushchev's "Secret Speech," noted a "curious jerk" in April 1956. The process of erasure resumed in May and early June, in preparation for Josip Broz Tito's state visit. Mutatis mutandis, Marshall Tito was now hailed in the Soviet Union as a man who stood up to Stalin and his false principles. Less publicly, observed Sulzberger, China's Mao Zedong received similar credit.[29]

Most vividly, the sudden change of conversation came to the fore in the mid-1960s in the case of Mihajlo Mihajlov. Back in the day Mihajlov enjoyed in the West a celebrity status on par with that of Alexander Solzhenitsyn. In the summer of 1964, thirty-year-old Mihajlov traveled to Moscow as an exchange student. Immersed in literary studies, Mihajlov was a Slavophile, not least because his parents originally came from Russia. Enjoying the relative freedom of what turned out to be the waning months and days of the Thaw, Mihajlov published a two-part travelogue upon his return to Yugoslavia. "Moscow Summer" appeared in the January and February 1965 issue of the Belgrade literary review *Delo*. The first part in the series, in stimulating prose, related the travails of Soviet authors coming to terms with Stalinism. It was the second installment that got Mihajlov into trouble. Titled "Camp Themes," the article compared the literature on Soviet deportations with the annals of the crimes of the Spanish inquisition. There he wrote—sometimes accurately reflecting on recent Soviet history, sometimes not—that the first *death* camps were formed not by the Germans, but by the Soviets, in 1921 at Solovetsky Islands. As far as genocide is concerned, Hitler was not the first to implement it either, argued Mihajlov. Prior to the Second World War, Stalin deported several small nations from the regions bordering Turkey and Iran. At their final destination in the inhospitable climate of Siberia, they died like flies. Hence so many Kalmyks, Tatars, and others went over to the German side, concluded the newly appointed lecturer of Slavic literature. He had no way of knowing that by the time his piece appeared in print, Khrushchev would be removed from power and the program of de-Stalinization that the former Soviet premier had half-heartedly introduced would be shelved. A Soviet diplomat in Belgrade expressed his displeasure with Mihajlov's series. Not even American journalists had written that critically, he maintained. At the same time, the diplomat expressed his doubt as to filing a formal protest, since the views expressed in *Delo* were those of the author and not of the magazine.[30]

Yet Tito decided to act assertively in this case, out of precaution. The magazine's February issue was withdrawn from circulation after the Western media had picked up on Mihajlov's findings concerning death camps and genocide. (Later that year *Moscow Summer* was published in the United States in a book format.) Tito confronted the State Prosecutor's Office, which instantly shut down *Delo* under a press law against insults to foreign nations. Within a few days the author himself was arrested for questioning. Indicted on two counts, Mihajlov was consequently fired from his position at the University of Zadar. Article

175 of the Yugoslav Penal Code prohibited bringing foreign powers into derision, which carried a maximum penalty of three years. The prosecution argued that Mihajlov's discussion of Russian forced labor was an offense to the Soviet Union. According to Article 125, Mihajlov was also guilty of having mailed a copy of his manuscript to an Italian publisher after it had been banned. Mihajlov's letters to the president of the Yugoslav Supreme Court and to President Tito remained unheeded.[31] Tito maintained that Mihajlov was a "reactionary who . . . slandered the great October Revolution." Mihajlov's trial began on April 30, 1965. According to the judgment, he "belittled and scorned" the Soviet Union and "published false facts" harmful to it. The critics accused Tito of hypocrisy, since in his earlier speeches and at the 1952 Yugoslav Communist Party Congress he himself had charged the Soviet Union with genocide. In its defense, the regime hinted at political expediency: in recalling the hideous past *now*, Mihajlov must have had political, anti-Soviet motives. Although his original nine-month sentence had been shortly overturned by the Supreme Court of Croatia, Mihajlov remained in and out of jail until 1977.[32]

Yugoslavia is also a case in point when it comes to the phenomenon of the accuser becoming the accused. The arch-Stalinist regime of Enver Hoxha in Albania, which once relied on Yugoslavia for support, had now submitted its former protector to a relentless ideological barrage. At some point Hoxha reopened the highly sensitive issue of Kosovo by alleging that Tito's clique was carrying out genocide against ethnic Albanians in that province.[33]

4 · THE STRUGGLE FOR INFLUENCE IN POSTCOLONIAL AFRICA AND THE MIDDLE EAST

Algeria, Congo, Nigeria, Iraq

THE SOVIETS CASH IN ON DECOLONIZATION

In the wake of the Second World War, more than ever, colonial domination awoke guilty conscience and stigma. The Soviet Union stood for a radical interpretation of the doctrine of self-determination and posed as an advocate for dependent nations totaling some 250 million people. In the long run, the relationship that Moscow had established with the developing world was defined by expediency. With no experience of administering oversee possessions, the USSR nevertheless attempted to get a foothold in North Africa and the Middle East through the UN system. Rebuked by the United States and Britain, Stalin effectively decided not to participate in any assistance program. The active Soviet engagement with former colonies began in earnest only with the ascent of Khrushchev. Along with Communist ideology and military hardware, the Soviets backed their prospective clients with a barrage of rhetoric.

As soon as the issue of non-self-governing territories (a euphemism for colonies) appeared on the General Assembly's agenda in the fall of 1946, the Soviet delegation in the United Nations received a directive from Moscow to argue for the broadest possible definition of this new old concept. The Soviet representative attempted to push through a motion according to which the UN member states should periodically submit to the secretary-general reports on individual freedoms, the status of women, and specific measures to stop racial discrimination in the dependent territories under their supervision.[1] As with virtually any other matter on the UN agenda, the Soviets exercised a significant degree of cynicism when it came to dependent territories. The Soviets feigned disappointment when the United States, aware of the British sensitivity, suggested omitting any discussion of the colonial question from the Dumbarton Oaks agenda. Eventually, however, they agreed to the deletion, which effectively banned any discussion of Soviet territorial expansion in Eastern Europe.[2] The Soviet delegation withdrew its support from the Trusteeship Council, contending that the five permanent members of the Security Council should be recognized as the "states directly concerned," thus raising the possibility of a veto. The USSR did not indicate specific territories with which it regarded itself as directly concerned. In a private conversation, the Soviet representative told his American counterpart that Moscow would not press claims to the African mandates and the Pacific mandates south of the equator, yet protect its position with respect to Japan and the former Italian colonies. Consequently, the Soviet Union refused to participate in the election of members to the Trusteeship Council and abstained from its work.[3] After a while, however, it seized the opportunity to help break the colonial systems of European powers and therefore joined the council in the summer of 1948.[4]

The Soviet interest in Libya, Somalia, and Eritrea—left up for grabs after the defeat of fascist Italy—was ultimately geostrategic and tactical rather than ideological or economic. As an emerging superpower, the USSR regarded even secondary international issues as a matter of prestige and simultaneously as leverage against the former Allies. It essentially belonged to the same set of questions as Greece and the Turkish Straits. In their push to dislodge the British, the Soviets greatly overestimated the discord between its Western Allies. The United States thwarted the Soviet ambition to secure control over Tripolitania, the western province of Libya. With regard to Eritrea, the Soviet Union had to eventually acquiesce to transferring this issue to the General Assembly. The Soviet decision to capitalize on the rising anticolonial sentiment did not transpire until May 1949. Encouraged by a show of popular support in Tripoli, the Soviet delegation proposed a resolution granting independence to *all* colonies at the earliest possible date.[5]

While negotiating access to non-self-governing territories, the Soviets briskly used anticolonial rhetoric. The British counterattacked by negatively contrasting the living conditions of the workers and peasants in the Soviet Union to those in the Commonwealth. As far as "imperialist domination" was concerned, the USSR was said to have increasingly practiced just that in Eastern Europe. The discussion inevitably slid into mutual recriminations of political subterfuge and fact-free comparisons of living standards. Undeterred, the Soviets kept pressing on. In order to provide for the adequate protection of minorities, insisted a Soviet delegate, colonial powers should explain their discriminatory policies, however loath they might be to do so.[6]

Decolonization proved a tricky issue also for the United States, which found itself maneuvering on a precarious middle ground between European colonial powers and their critics. The highly emotional and symbolic nature of the "colonial question," however, rendered ineffective the US middle-of-the-road position. The West and the Soviet Union both claimed to be champions of such principles as equality, national self-determination, freedom from oppression, prosperity for all, human rights, and tolerance of other races and cultures. While feeling the heat of a revolt against colonial domination, the United States encountered difficulties with its principal NATO allies whose position it understood yet did not accept. At the same time, potential political crises in the European metropolises and turmoil in their colonial possessions could jeopardize common security interests. Specific economic and strategic interests, for example uranium deposits in the Belgian Congo or air bases in North Africa, had as strong an imprint on policymaking. The fact that the United States served as an administering power of certain dependent territories such as Puerto Rico, Guam, and Samoa did not help to win the argument either. The Communist bloc had turned this cleavage to its advantage, evoking human rights to discredit the West.[7]

Regardless, for as long as Stalin was alive, the Kremlin adhered to the ideological prescript of the early Cold War. Perceiving the world as a bipolar system, Stalin contended that "those who are not with us, are against us." Since only the Communists fit the category of a progressive force, the native leaders of the emerging Third World countries were automatically relegated to the enemy camp. Preoccupied with the absorption of Eastern Europe, the Soviet Union had thus missed an opportunity to gain influence within the national liberation movements during the immediate postwar years.[8] Soviet material aid to noncommunist countries did not begin until after the death of Stalin. Afghanistan was the first major recipient in 1954; the aid program accelerated in the wake of Khrushchev's Asian tour the following year.[9] Khrushchev capitalized on Lenin's argument that the peoples of the colonial world were natural allies of the proletariat, and by extension of the Soviet Union. Consequently, decolonization would further weaken the imperialist West and specifically the United States. In the spring of 1960 Khrushchev, with his patent enthusiasm, unveiled his African policy.[10]

The policy reappraisal vis-à-vis the Third World showed immediate results, as scores of African and Asian countries declared their friendship with the Soviet Union and sided with it on a number of international issues. The Soviet emphasis on heavy industry coincided with their aspirations toward economic independence and power. Unwittingly, however, the Soviets perpetuated stereotypes of Western colonialism in the eyes of their professed clients.[11] As it soon turned out, the declared allegiance was rarely ideological, and Khrushchev's grandiose scheme of attacking the colonial empires through their "backyards" strained Soviet resources. The backlash from the Cuban Missile Crisis and the subsequent ascent of Leonid Brezhnev to power brought yet another change to Soviet policy. While staying true to the concept of global competition with the West, Moscow scaled down its ambitions significantly. From then on abstract "struggle against capitalism" became subject to a cost-benefit analysis. It meant that military, technical, and/or economic assistance to any given client state had to be of practical advantage to the Soviet Union.[12] Accordingly, the situation on the ground was interpreted from the point of view of short-term utility—whatever advanced Soviet power and influence. Taking as a basis Soviet policies in the Middle East, Galia Golan has identified the following guiding principles in Moscow's relationship with the developing world. During the Khrushchev period Soviet economic interests had been subordinated to political and strategic interests. In the 1960s the military interest took unprecedented priority. The expansion of the Soviet fleet and its deployment in distant seas accelerated the quest for bases and facilities. In the early 1970s Moscow elevated the economic factor in its foreign policy considerations. To improve its own situation, the USSR now sought a return on its investments. By that time arms and oil exports constituted some 20 and 50 percent of Soviet hard-currency earnings respectively. By the late 1970s and early 1980s, however, the political interest once again trumped Soviet military-strategic concerns: the American expansion was consistently undercutting the tentative Soviet gains.[13] This analysis undermines the thesis of Odd Arne Westad, according to which the Soviet intervention in the Third World was mainly driven by ideology yet consistent with the historical practices of the Russian Empire.[14] Throughout this entire period, whenever the Soviets spelled out the word *genocide*, it served their geopolitical goals. Their audience had been growing exponentially meanwhile: by the early 1960s the UN membership had increased to 111, among them 32 African states, which constituted the largest regional group in the General Assembly.

RHETORICAL TUG-OF-WAR IN AFRICA

While the genocide discourse by the mid-1950s became less prominent in the Soviet-American propaganda wars, the issue was picked up by the growing Asian-African bloc in the United Nations. In late August 1956 the seventeen member states of the Asian-African Group met in the UN headquarters to discuss the deteriorating situation in Algeria and Morocco. The meeting concluded that the French military conduct far exceeded "measures of repression alone but could, if allowed to continue, be tantamount to mass extermination."[15] Algeria was one of the first colonial possessions to descend into violence. On May 8, 1945 French troops opened fire on an independence rally in the town of Setif, killing hundreds of civilians. By the time the French withdrew from North Africa in 1962, about half a million Algerians had been killed. In parallel, as Odd Arne Westad has remarked, the war in Algeria had become the prime symbol of Third World unity.[16]

The year 1956 marked the period of the most brutal repression of the Algerian insurgency, which began in earnest in November 1954. Torture and retaliatory executions became commonplace while military tribunals replaced civilian courts.[17] Later that fall the bloc members filed on behalf of Algeria a genocide charge against France. Extensive military operations caused significant loss of life and thus violated the letter of the Genocide Convention, to which France was a party. The Algerian rebel leaders called upon the United Nations to halt "France's war of genocide."[18] Lemkin hailed the motion on Algeria (which he coincidentally helped to formulate), though for different reasons. According to Lemkin, the French concocted plans to nullify the Genocide Convention. They worked through both the International Law Commission and the General Assembly to introduce a formula that on the one hand linked genocide to discrimination and on the other absolved individuals acting without state authorization.[19] The original report of the Arab Information Center in New York contained the passages easily attributable to Lemkin. The evidence presented in the report pinpointed mass reprisals carried out by the French troops and/or colonists in Algeria. "It is also clear," continued the report, "that French authorities are committing national genocide by persecuting, exiling, torturing and imprisoning arbitrarily and in conditions pernicious to their health, the Algerian leaders." The rest of the paragraph spoke of the "forces of cohesion," the destruction of culture, and the deliberate creation of life-threatening conditions, accompanied by the familiar allegory of targeting the brains of the nation in order to paralyze its body (not unlike the discourse that Lemkin had developed in the case of Ukraine, for example).[20] France was unable to match the efforts of the insurgents and their Arab backers in mobilizing international public opinion. The best the French could do in their counterpropaganda campaign was to use Soviet-style rhetoric. Thus, they presented the massacre at the village of Melouza perpetrated in May 1957 by the National Liberation Front as an act of genocide, comparing it to Oradour and Lidice and the rebels to the Nazi SS.[21]

The ill-fated Anglo-French intervention in Egypt generated similar accusations. The killing of forty-eight Arabs in the village of Kafr Qasim by Israeli border police on October 29, 1956 was later in December denounced before the United Nations as "genocide" by the Iraqi foreign minister Muhhamad Fadhel al-Jamali.[22] As mentioned in the previous chapter, the Soviet foreign minister on November 19, 1956 spoke extensively about French atrocities in Algeria at the General Assembly plenary session—as a means of detracting attention from the Warsaw Pact invasion of Hungary. Having nearly burned their fingers on the issue of Hungary in the United Nations, though, Soviet diplomats treaded carefully when the discussion shifted to Algeria. Thus the Italians cowed the Soviets into tabling Ceylon's proposal from April 1957 to put the worsening situation in Algeria on the agenda of the UN Commission on Human Rights—by threatening to bring up Hungary.[23] Other than that, the Algerian War of Independence was one of those quintessential events that prompted Soviet efforts to capitalize on decolonization. It also marked the shift from defensive tactics to offensive with regard to genocide. By the late 1950s the Soviets had developed a discourse on Algeria, applied later to similar conflicts worldwide. In that discourse, France had been waging a colonial war with the purpose of exterminating the Algerian people, exemplifying genocide. In their repressive policies, the French received the support of the United States, which sought to simultaneously carve a strategic bridgehead and capture mineral resources in Africa.[24]

In September 1960 Soviet premier Khrushchev lent his name to the decolonization struggle and, by extension, the genocide narrative. In a declaration, which he submitted to the Fifteenth Session of the General Assembly in his capacity as formal head of the Soviet delegation, Khrushchev condemned racial discrimination as "justification of criminal genocide." The news spread and, about three months later, the president of the provisional Algerian government-in-exile, Ferhat Abbas, requested Khrushchev's personal assistance in stopping "overt genocide" of the Algerian people. Abbas was specifically referring to the siege laid by the French troops to the Casbah neighborhood in Algiers (the stronghold of the National Liberation Front). TASS immediately issued a communiqué, quoting Abbas on genocide and demanding a stop to mass reprisals. As France was trying to exit the conflict—unpopular at home and abroad—the terrorist Secret Armed Organization (OAS) had stepped in. OAS dramatically increased bombing attacks in Algeria to thwart the ceasefire negotiations that began in March 1962. The Algerian press instantly labeled it "genocide of the Muslims."[25] The genocide discourse, as applied to France in the United Nations, had broader ramifications for Africa and the world. Thus the head of the Malian delegation in the General Assembly evoked genocide to demand that France relinquish its former colonies at once.[26]

Proxy wars engendered proxy wars of words, of which *genocide* was the most potent. As the Algerian War was winding down, numerous other decolonization wars broke out. Angola was one among many military conflicts of the 1960s described as "genocide." Indian prime minister Jawaharlal Nehru in his May 1961 speech to the delegates of the All Indian Congress Committee claimed that the Portuguese were committing genocide in Angola.[27] A similar claim was made a few days later by the Afro-Asian People's Solidarity Organization in Cairo.[28] The violence continued well into the next decade as the Portuguese stubbornly refused to give up their colonies. So did the accusations of genocide, now expanded to apply also to Mozambique and Guinea-Bissau.[29] The response of Portugal's prime minister to the charges of genocide was no less awkward. His government was engaged in the "legitimate defense" of territories that had been Portuguese for 500 years, he said at a press conference in London, while alluding to the fact that the guerrillas were armed with Soviet and Chinese weapons. Simultaneously, he emphasized that Lisbon "tolerated no genocide against Africans" and would punish any perpetrator.[30]

The most dramatic news yet of 1961 arrived during the opening phase of the war in Angola—the assassination of Patrice Lumumba. As the first democratically elected prime minister of Congo, Lumumba had squandered all goodwill and accumulated a powerful array of adversaries. In an effort to rein in the breakaway state of Katanga (established with the connivance of Belgium), in mid-August 1960 Lumumba formally requested Soviet military assistance. Even though the Soviet Union possessed few means to influence the events on the ground, it was eager to assert its anticolonial credentials in Africa. Potential Soviet meddling, in its turn, alerted the CIA. Since Congo was the largest and richest among the newly independent African states, the prospective Soviet decision to send arms and military advisers to Lumumba might have had a major impact on the rest of the continent. It was indeed the first time that the USSR had intervened in a conflict in Africa, and thus a matter of prestige for Khrushchev, who was just about to address the UN General Assembly. Eventually, the Soviet government had ruled out providing military assistance, making Khrushchev pour out his frustration at UN secretary-general Dag Hammarskjöld. The United Nations, and personally Hammarskjöld, was averse to both the secessionists in the mineral-rich eastern Congo and the erratic method of governance by Lumumba. The latter, among other things, authorized a military expedition to Kasai Province, resulting in a massacre of Baluba tribesmen and a massive refugee flight.[31] When addressing the Security Council, Hammarskjöld subsequently accused Lumumba of "genocide in trying to wipe out the Baluba tribe."[32] The violent death of Lumumba prompted a series of condemnatory statements, including one issued by the Polish delegation to the United Nations. The document, among other things, warned of impeding genocide in Kivu Province by Colonel Joseph Mobutu and his Belgian backers.[33] The charge of genocide was renewed after the joint Belgian-US-Congolese force ended the hostage crisis in Stanleyville in November 1964, effectively squashing the Lumumba-inspired rebellion.[34]

Given Moscow's uncompromising position vis-à-vis political groups in the United Nations in 1947 and 1948, occasional references to "political genocide" in the Soviet press during the 1960s came across as phony to say the least. This was the case, for instance, when *Izvestia* wrote in November 1968 of "genocide on political grounds" presently committed in Indonesia. What Soviet authorities had in mind was actually the mistreatment of political prisoners.[35] Remarkably, the mass slaughter of members of the Indonesian Communist Party in 1965 barely registered with the Soviets. The massacres only came into the picture as a scanty background to the present plight of the Communist prisoners in Indonesia.[36]

Counterintuitively, the Soviet Union did not press the charge of genocide against apartheid South Africa until after the decolonization movement began in earnest, and even then mainly by proxy. It was then Chairman of the Presidium of the Supreme Soviet Leonid Brezhnev who restated this allegation. The reference to genocide adored the joint communiqué signed during the summer 1961 visit to Moscow of the president of Ghana, Kwame Nkrumah. A visiting delegation from Mali two years later prompted a similar statement by the Soviet Afro-Asian

Solidarity Committee.[37] The news of an antiracist demonstration in New York City in February 1969 was transmitted in a mere two sentences. The first of them told of the "Stop genocide in RSA" placards carried by the protesters.[38]

Neither did Ian Smith's Rhodesia feature high on the Soviet Union's agenda. In 1965 Rhodesia unilaterally proclaimed independence under white minority rule. The apartheid state par excellence, Rhodesia successfully thwarted international sanctions and even managed to attract further European settlers. The tide turned in 1974 following the coup in Lisbon and the end of Portuguese rule in neighboring Mozambique.[39] For the first time, Rhodesia posted a negative net migration rate. To arrest this development, Smith's government introduced family planning, aiming specifically at black Africans. *Pravda* qualified the efforts to change the racial makeup of the population in Rhodesia as "genocide."[40] The following year the charge of genocide traveled further west, to Namibia, which had been administered by South Africa in defiance of UN rulings. The allegation of genocide came from the pro-independence South West Africa People's Organization, which intensified guerrilla warfare following the Portuguese collapse.[41] The word *genocide* in relation to South Africa resurfaced around 1979. Typical of the Soviets, whenever they wanted to act from behind, the honor of rendering judgment was delegated to the third party, in this case Cuba. At a forum in Havana, President Fidel Castro compared "genocide perpetrated by imperialism in South Africa" to the crimes of the Nazis.[42]

EVERYBODY'S BUSINESS: THE BIAFRA CRISIS

For a short while, Biafra became simultaneously a symbol of immense suffering, humanitarian goodwill, and political manipulation. The Nigerian civil war had triggered perhaps the biggest genocide tug-of-war. The secession of eastern provinces in May 1967 and the mass violence that precipitated it was a classical case of Cold War proxy wars of words. Independent since 1960, Nigeria had been torn by tribal politics. Each of the country's three regions produced its own political party dominated by the major ethnic group, all fighting for supremacy over the federal government. Vying for power, politicians on all sides whipped up ethnic fear, suspicion, and jealousy. Doctored census data and forged election results were among the contributing factors leading to the 1966 army coup. Celebrated in the South, the coup caused wariness in the North, which until then held the upper hand. The abolition of the federal system by the military government, which saw it as the root cause of Nigeria's problems, sparked a countercoup in the North accompanied by massacres of Igbos. Subsequently, over a million refugees sought safety in the East. Lieutenant Colonel Odumegwu Ojukwu sought independence for the oil-rich region where he then served as military governor. To rally popular support, Ojukwu skillfully played on fears of genocide. The pro-independence message stressed details of the atrocities, inflated the numbers of dead, and warned of worse things to come. Rejecting concessions offered by the federal government and dismissing the sentiment of the region's minorities, Ojakwu and his inner circle of Igbo advisers eventually proclaimed the independence of the new state of Biafra. The Nigerian civil war, which broke out in July 1967, lasted for two and a half years and cost roughly one million lives. In Martin Meredith's opinion, Ojukwu was a master of manipulation who portrayed Biafra as a nation threatened by genocide in his marathon speeches and interviews. The sheer determination of the Igbo to keep on fighting lent credence to these allegations.[43] Enter Cold War politics.

Until the 1966 coup the Soviet Union had been effectively shut off from Nigeria by its unabashedly anticommunist government. The Biafra War presented the USSR with a unique opportunity, which no Western or African observer saw coming. The reversal of Soviet fortunes in Nigeria, as Maxim Matusevich has noted, marked the critical shift in Moscow's policy toward the developing world. The overthrow of the key (nominally) Communist regimes on the continent in the late 1960s made the Kremlin substitute ideology for political expediency in its dealing with the African leaders. Initially, the Soviets found it difficult navigating at the news of the two consecutive coups d'état. Interpreting it as sympathetic neutrality, the federalist leadership sought Soviet guarantees in the face of the anticipated Eastern secession. Once the Republic of Biafra became a reality, the North requested immediate arms deliveries from the United States and Britain, but was rebuffed. (Britain agreed to sell antiaircraft guns but nothing else.) The Soviet Union, however, promptly answered the call through its Czechoslovakian proxy. The fact of Soviet military assistance to Lagos came as a shock to the Easterners, who saw themselves as the oppressed minority fighting off the "feudal overlords" of the North, and therefore cultivated friendly relations with the Communist state. Meanwhile the federalists, emboldened by the Soviet support, grew increasingly bellicose, vowing "total destruction" and the demise of the "vandal Ojukwu."[44]

Great Britain and the Soviet Union supplied arms to the central government while Portugal and France backed the separatists. Eager to secure oil concessions, the French secretly shipped arms to the rebels from neighboring Gabon. The French Foreign Ministry seized upon the issue of genocide in order to drum up public support for Biafra's cause. The ministry's influential African unit passed on the genocide narrative to *Le Monde*, to be picked up by the rest of the French media.[45] The British wanted to get out of their former colony for good, whereas the Soviets hoped to parlay military aid into political influence. The result was the same, though, stated the guest editorial in the *Chicago Tribune*: both powers were "subsidizing the federal government's genocidal campaign against Biafra."[46] Moscow saw the situation through different lenses, obviously. The civil war in Nigeria was but one example of the struggle waged by the newly independent states against former colonial powers, wrote *Izvestia*. Acting on selfish interests, Biafra separatists forsook the unity of their country. That artificial entity was an outcome of machinations by international monopolies. Seeking to prolong the tragedy, the foreign powers pressured the federal government to give more concessions to the insurgents. *Genocide* and *famine* were among the terms utilized by imperialist propaganda in order to misinform the world opinion, to conceal the essence of the ongoing struggle in Nigeria.[47]

Famine was certainly not a propaganda ploy, making up a great proportion of the victims. The federal government's blockade of Biafra was only offset through a massive Western relief operation. Some of the relief funds Ojukwu channeled toward military purchases, thus keeping Biafra afloat. The allegation of genocide, however, did indeed prove far-fetched. To investigate Biafra's genocide claims, the federal government invited a neutral observer team. The team representing the Organization for African Union, the United Nations, Canada, Poland, Sweden, and Britain reported on its findings in early October 1968 in Lagos. The unanimous report presented no evidence of any intent by Nigerian troops to wipe out the Igbo people in the civil war with Biafra. Regardless, Ojukwu continued charging Britain, the Soviet Union, and even Egypt with collaboration in genocide.[48]

Richard Nixon decried "genocide" in Biafra as a campaign issue against Lyndon Johnson in 1968.[49] Once Nixon won the presidential election, however, the US assessment of the situation in Nigeria became more nuanced. Potential relief for over one million people in danger of starvation could not be separated from the political tangle, National Security Adviser Henry Kissinger informed the president in January 1969. Kissinger described the Igbos as the "wandering Jews of West Africa—gifted, aggressive, Westernized; at best envied and resented, but mostly despised by the mass of their neighbors in the Federation." He saw no qualms on the part of the federal government at winning the war by means of starvation, yet claimed the rebels ripped "political profit in going hungry." Kissinger dismissed the rebels' charge of genocide as exaggerated and unproved, putting his faith in General Yakubu Gawon, who he believed would not risk Nigerian unity by engaging in mass murder. The Soviets did not have a vital interest in Nigeria, but neither did the Americans, Kissinger concluded when suggesting the United States tread carefully on Biafra.[50] This earlier analysis effectively persisted for the duration of the Biafra War. The National Security Council, the State Department, and the CIA all concurred in the opinion that the positions of the warring sides appeared irreconcilable, that both subordinated humanitarian objectives to political ones, and that Igbo fears of genocide were understandable though blown out of proportion. For as long as the Soviet influence in Nigeria seemed to be only fleeting, the analysts regarded a direct US intervention in the conflict undesirable. Crucially, they could not ascertain the intent to commit genocide.[51]

The fear of imminent demise intensified as Biafra formally surrendered on January 15, 1970. An organization representing 1,500 Eastern Nigerians living in the United States charged the government in Lagos with waging "systematic genocide on the people of defeated Biafra."[52] Conservative American commentators such as Robert Morris deplored "genocide being perpetrated in Biafra" while opposing US ratification of the Genocide Convention.[53] The Soviets felt vindicated. The leader of the Nigerian federalists delivered an emotional "thank you" to the Soviet Union, which he said had contributed most of all toward the victory, in contrast to the calculating West.[54] Now that the regime had been defeated, Western benefactors of Biafra were feverishly looking for a new means of interference in Nigeria's internal affairs. This is why imperialist propaganda was making noises about saving the population of Biafra from genocide and famine. *Izvestia* quoted a Nigerian representative at the United Nations who had "refuted and unmasked the vile lies of the enemies of the Nigerian people." The same kind of talk came from the Nigerian ambassador in Moscow at the press conference on January 20. A few days latter *Literaturnaia Gazeta* announced that Ojukwu and his inner circle had maintained a close liaison with the CIA. Having fled by then, Ojukwu continued slandering the Nigerian federal government. The "genocide lie," eagerly promoted by his American sponsors, had been exposed by numerous foreign journalists.[55] As Meredith has observed, the aftermath of the war was marked by the lack of repression so that the memories of Biafra soon faded.[56] The Soviet influence in Nigeria faded as quickly. According to Matusevich, Nigeria emerged from the civil war vociferously independent. No longer pro-American and never pro-Communist, Nigeria allied its foreign policy with that of the USSR only when opportune. To cite just one example, the federal government refrained from condemning the Warsaw Pact invasion of Czechoslovakia in 1968, but started doing so once the war was over.[57]

IRAQI KURDS BETRAYED

The Soviet Union had never been more opportunistic than in its policy vis-à-vis Iraqi Kurds. Realpolitik at its worst, at different times Moscow supported the Kurdish armed rebellion, helped the regime in Baghdad to suppress it, or silently observed it being crushed. In 1963, Kurdistan was for the Soviet Union what Hungary was for the West in 1956. For the first and only time, the Soviets tried to file charges of genocide in the United Nations, unsuccessfully. The case of Iraq demonstrates that the politically motivated charges of genocide were sometimes also applied by superpowers to the countries within their orbit.

Following the dissolution of the Ottoman Empire, the Kurds found themselves split between four Muslim states: Turkey, Syria, Iran, and Iraq. Yet only Iraq, where the Kurds constitute over 20 percent of the country's population, officially recognized them as a minority. The Kurds received specific constitutional rights in 1925 courtesy of the League of Nations, as a condition for the inclusion of the oil-rich Mosul area in the Iraqi state. This particular clause had generated Kurdish demands for autonomy. The Soviet Union had consistently backed those demands as legitimate.[58] Mulla Muṣṭafā Barzānī, who had emerged as a leader of the Kurdish insurgency, had spent twelve years in exile in the USSR. On the eve of the Second World War an estimated 100,000 ethnic Kurds resided within the Soviet borders, mainly in Armenia (in November 1944 Soviet authorities deported close to 9,000 Kurds, along with other Turkic peoples, from the areas bordering Turkey). At Soviet bidding, Barzānī in 1946 established himself as the leader of the newly established United Kurdistan Democratic Party (UKDP). He was able to return to Iraq following the overthrow of the monarchy in 1958. Allied with different groups at different times, Barzānī and UKDP joined in the revolt for greater autonomy of the Kurdish region. Immediately after the Ba'ath coup in February 1963 both sides had negotiated a ceasefire. Mutual suspicion remained, however, since the new regime never defined the "rights of the Kurds on the basis of decentralization," which it had promised to guarantee. In June 1963 the fighting between Barzānī and Baghdad commenced. The Iraqi army launched a brutal attack, assisted by Kurdish tribes hostile to Barzānī (there were some 22 major and 54 minor Kurdish tribes in Iraq). The latter counterattacked, burning anti-Barzānī Kurdish villages in the process. The Iraqi air force, using Soviet-made aircraft, dropped napalm and fired rockets at rebel villages in the effort to spread terror.[59] The Soviets instantly intervened, though their geopolitical interests extended beyond the immediate support for Barzānī and UKDP.

Iraq's strategic position in the Middle East, the anti-Western ideology of the ruling Ba'ath Party, potential support for the Soviet causes across the developing world, and the revenues from prospective arms deals—these were the main factors that made Moscow seek an alliance with Baghdad. It was not as simple, though, due to attending complications. As in many other countries, ethnicity and ideology to an extent overlapped in Iraq. The Ba'athists never claimed Marxist allegiances, championing pan-Arabic nationalism instead. Most of the members of the Communist Party of Iraq were ethnic Kurds (even though Communists constituted a minority of the Kurds). In effect, the Soviets used the Kurdish issue as leverage against Baghdad. In other words, the Kurds were pawns in the political game, as they had been since the First World War. The Soviet Union advocated autonomy for the Kurds as part of its general policy of support for national liberation movements. When backing the continual Kurdish unrest in the north of the country, the Soviets made sure it never escalated to the degree of hampering Soviet-Iraqi relations. For that matter, they remained on the sidelines during the Kurdish rebellion of 1961.[60] The way they presented it publicly was pure rhetoric.

On June 16, 1963 TASS published a statement condemning the military campaign against the Kurds by the "Ba'athist pseudo-socialist leaders of Iraq." Acting in concert with the "imperialist circles," the new regime set out to drown in blood all patriotic and democratic forces in the country, including Iraqi communists and Kurdish autonomists. The methods used by Baghdad rulers in suppression of political opposition were no different from those of the Nazis. In Kurdistan, stated the Soviet news agency, the Iraqi government was carrying out the policy of mass destruction, that is, genocide. A few days later *Pravda* enunciated Moscow's concerns. Kurdistan lay in immediate proximity to the Soviet borders and could be used by imperialist states as a bridgehead for aggression against the Communist bloc. As for Ba'ath, the Soviet media portrayed it as a petty bourgeois party with fascist leanings on the CIA payroll. Conspiring with the reactionary circles in neighboring Iran, authorities in Baghdad were committing genocide against the Kurdish minority.[61]

Instead of taking action on Iraq directly to the United Nations, the Soviets acted once again by proxy. Their choice fell on Mongolia, which was highly unusual given that the country was not even a party to the Genocide Convention (yet participated in the consultation meetings of the Communist bloc countries in the United Nations). Mongolia's foreign minister on June 1 sent a letter to the secretary-general requesting the General Assembly to consider the "policy of genocide carried out by the Government of the Republic of Iraq against the Kurdish people." A supplementary note explained why the government of the People's Republic of Mongolia regarded the large-scale military operations in northern Iraq as genocide of a clearly defined ethnic group.[62] Moscow upped the ante when, on June 4, Soviet delegate Sergei Borisov called upon ECOSOC to urgently request the Iraqi government to "stop the inhuman treatment of the Kurdish people." Yet, following Jordan's lead, ECOSOC overwhelmingly rejected Borisov's demand to immediately discuss a Soviet resolution charging Iraq with genocide.[63] The Soviet proposal found little support on the grounds that specific instances of genocide fell outside the competence of ECOSOC.[64] The negative vote, commented TASS, revealed the true face of the Western delegations as advocates of lawlessness and violence.[65] The Soviet Union was not yet ready to give up on this issue and once again accused Iraq of waging genocide against the Kurdish rebels. Next it warned the governments of Iran, Syria, and Turkey against interference, comparing their actions with the tripartite aggression against Egypt seven years earlier.[66] Baghdad radio entered the fray, challenging Moscow's right to speak on genocide. Every move by the Red Army and the Communist Party had been accompanied by atrocities, an Iraqi spokesman declared. "The Soviet Union has exterminated whoever would not accept the Communist way of life. The world remembers the fate of Poland, Hungary, East Germany." The *New York Times* expanded on this argument in a July 11 editorial: "The Soviet Union's brutal treatment of troublesome national and religious minorities of its own such as the Crimean Turks, peoples of the North Caucasus, the Kalmyks, the Volga Germans and others hardly qualifies Moscow to charge the Iraqi Government with genocide because of its campaign against the Kurds." The *NYT* editors hit the spot by maintaining that the USSR had long championed the Kurds as a means of furthering its political objectives in the Middle East. Moscow's diplomatic moves were obviously motivated not by humanitarian considerations but by power politics.[67]

Meanwhile the Soviet propaganda machine mobilized—actually faked—popular opinion in support of the official line, the practice it had perfected in the 1980s in the case of Israel. *Pravda* had reportedly received hundreds of letters from common Soviet citizens demanding to stop the extermination of the Kurdish people. Among other readers "guided by the spirit of internationalism" was a certain Ashirberdy Muhammedov from Krasnovodsk: "I, dock worker, in the name of the Turkmen and the entire Soviet people am calling upon all the honest people around the world to protect the human rights of the Kurdish people. Soviet people are deeply offended by the Iraqi fascists' policy of genocide." Moscow State University was a site of a protest rally in early July 1963. One of the participants in the rally took part in a Kurdish students' congress held at Munich the following month. The congress commended the governments of Mongolia and the Soviet Union for their attempts to raise the issue of the Ba'athist onslaught in Kurdistan in the General Assembly and ECOSOC, respectively.[68] Nobody at the congress had the courage to mention, though, that those efforts had been ingloriously aborted. Bowing to Asian, African, and particularly Arab pressure, the Communist bloc in the last week of July decided not to pursue the Kurd issue any further. Mongolia quietly withdrew its request for a General Assembly debate on "Iraq's genocide." This was taken as a tipoff, speculated Louis Fleming in the *Los Angeles Times*, that the Soviet Union would drop its threats to press for Security Council action against Iraq. Soviet diplomacy made a costly error, apparently counting on divisions in the Arab world. On the contrary, solid opposition from the Asian and African states prompted unusual unity among the Arabs themselves.[69] That was indeed a blow, contravening even an earlier analysis by the US State Department, according to which the Arab-Asian bloc in the United Nations on occasion supported Soviet positions in exchange for Soviet "friendliness" toward Arabs and Asians.[70] The Soviets learned the hard way that the Third World's loyalties were in flux. As for the Western countries, the anxiety that Kurdistan might fall under Soviet domination outstripped their sympathy for Kurdish aspirations.[71]

The Soviet hypocrisy was plain for everyone to see when, in 1974, Moscow militarily assisted the Iraqi government in suppressing the Kurds. During the intervening period, the Soviet relationship with the Ba'ath regime in both Syria and Iraq had turned from hate to love. Having ceased power in early February 1963, the Arab Socialist Ba'ath Party took pains to emphasize that its battle against the Iraqi Communist Party did not diminish its willingness to maintain friendly relations with the Soviet Union. The initial Soviet attitude toward Ba'ath was hostile, however. In the aftermath of the terror, the Communists fled to the region controlled by the Kurdish rebels, where they were granted political asylum. A prominent Kurdish Communist, Aziz Mohammed, who was shortly elected first secretary of the party, had survived the terror by staying in the Soviet bloc and displayed particular loyalty to Moscow. As Haim Shemesh has noted, Khrushchev had displayed idiosyncratic sensitivity to the persecution of Communists abroad. Soviet solidarity also had to do with the ideological rivalry between the USSR and China, wherein the Iraqi Communists took the former's side. At the same time, Iraq as a whole still held little promise for the Soviet Union. Egypt was by far the most important Soviet client in the Middle East, and the relations between Cairo and Baghdad had already soured. In Moscow's assessment, the Ba'ath regime would not last long.[72] The events on the ground proved just that: a military coup of November 1963 forced the Ba'athists out.

The bloodshed stopped in the aftermath of the coup, even though persecution of the Communists and the Kurds continued for some time. Limited economic reforms introduced by the new government were hailed in Moscow as "progressive" and aid started to flow again. There is some evidence of Soviet support for the Kurds after Ba'ath had ultimately seized power in 1968. Almost instantly, the fighting resumed. The president of Iraq warned the Kurds that he would not tolerate secession, while Barzānī accused the Ba'ath authorities of waging a "war of genocide" and appealed to the United Nations to send a fact-finding commission to Kurdistan. The Soviets kept mum on the issue of genocide this time around and were altogether glad to see the end of the revolt in 1970. Such wavering has an easy explanation: the USSR was interested in the naval facilities in the Persian Gulf and determined to prevent Iraq's defection to the West. The 1972 Treaty of Friendship and Cooperation prodded Iraq to nationalize Western oil companies and the Soviet Union to pick up the bill for the lost markets. Within the following few years Iraq had doubled the size of its army, as the Soviet Union doubled arms deliveries; since 1958 the USSR had been a major arms supplier to Iraq. Meanwhile the accord that ended the latest Kurdish insurgence (the so-called March Manifesto) was gradually eroding. Full-scale hostilities that broke out in 1974 were complicated by the involvement of Iran. To preserve the close relationship with Baghdad and to keep the "imperialist powers and their agents" at bay, the Soviets sacrificed their purported Kurdish allies. The Soviet media criticized the "reactionary elements" within the Kurdish movement, claiming that enough progress had been achieved. The latter decried betrayal and accused the Iraqi government of obtaining "poison gas from the Soviet Union in preparation for an attempt to exterminate the Kurds" (as related in 1973 by *Arab Report and Record* in London). Beyond words, Moscow provided warplanes and pilots to fly sorties against the Kurds. Yet it sought to avoid the prospect of an Iran–Iraq war, which was indeed averted as a result of the bilateral agreement in 1975; without Iranian help the Kurds could not go on fighting. Another round of military hardware arrived in Iraq from the Soviet Union, only to be discontinued in 1978 in the aftermath of a crackdown on the Communists initiated by Saddam Hussein, the new de facto head of state.[73] Barzānī, when appealing to Iran for protection, claimed the Ba'ath regime and its Soviet patron were bound on genocide. Subsequently, the shah of Iran condemned the Iraqi bombing of the Kurdish population as genocide against an ethnic group related to Iranians. The US State Department attempted, but failed, to ascertain these claims. When addressing the shah of Iran in July 1973, Barzānī alerted the latter to the imminent resumption of the Iraqi assault on the Kurds, including by poisonous gas.[74]

As far as the Kurds were concerned, the Soviets fired the last shot of duplicity at the very end of the Iran-Iraq War. The Islamic Revolution held a promise for a Soviet-Iranian rapprochement. With Soviet-Iraqi relations at its lowest ebb, Moscow came out against Hussein's invasion of Iran in September 1980 by declaring neutrality in the conflict; the least the Soviet Union wanted was instability on its southern border, as exemplified by the decision to enter Afghanistan the previous year. As the war progressed, however, Moscow became increasingly discouraged by the anticommunist policies of Ayatollah Ruhollah Khomeini and the support accorded by Iran to the Afghanistan mujahideen. As early as mid-1982 the Soviet Union resumed direct arms deliveries to Baghdad and ever since has displayed an unmistakable pro-Iraqi tilt. The renewed bond with the Ba'ath regime came into view in the spring of 1984 during the discussions in the UN Security Council. Iran complained of Iraq's recourse to poison gas on the battlefield. The Soviet press reported that the Security Council had condemned the use of chemical weapons, but did not single out Iraq as the perpetrator of this particular crime. When mediating a solution to the military conflict, the Soviets emphasized that Iraq was the party seeking a negotiated settlement. Meanwhile, the supplies of Soviet weapons helped to turn the tide of the war in favor of Iraq. By 1987 Moscow had moved even further away from Tehran and closer to Baghdad, holding Iran responsible for the war and, by extension, for enabling Washington to strengthen its foothold in the Gulf region. The reciprocal shelling of cities in the winter of 1988 further escalated the conflict, leading to a sharp deterioration in relations between the Islamic Republic and the USSR.[75]

As it did back in 1974, Iran continued supporting Kurdish rebels as proxies in its war against Iraq. To quell the insurgence, some 150,000 Iraqi troops were withdrawn from the Iranian front. In order to undercut the enemy state and to crush the rebellion once and for all, Saddam Hussein in 1987 launched a comprehensive program of depopulating Kurdish villages. The so-called Anfal campaign, which picked between February and September 1988, eventually killed up to 100,000 Kurds. The most notorious crime took place in the town of Halabja close to the Iranian border on March 16, 1988. Teaming up with the Iranian Revolutionary Guards, Kurdish insurgents had turned Halabja into a stronghold. As the Iraqi forces intensified ethnic cleansing of the surrounding villages, the population of Halabja doubled on account of fleeing civilians. Some 5,000 of them died a horrible death as a result of a chemical attack by the Iraqi air force that day.

The deadliest such attack, it was one of at least forty targeting the Kurds. Saddam's regime used poison gas against the Kurds with increased frequency in June and July. The final attack occurred on August 25, 1988, five days after Iraq and Iran had signed an armistice. This fact reinforced the claim of genocide by the afflicted side and some Western politicians, who saw it as a proof that the Iraqi junta was seeking to do away with the Kurds as a distinct group.[76]

As for the Soviet officials, the "G" word never touched their lips. Since Gorbachev's coming to power, public manifestations of Soviet support for the Kurdish rebellion in Iraq remained few and far between. As it had done throughout the 1980s, the Soviet media typically referred to the support for a "real autonomy" in Kurdistan, as expressed by the Iraqi Communist Party. Perhaps the only exception to the rule was Aziz Mohammed's article in *World Marxist Review* in September 1987, in which he condemned the use of chemical weapons against the Kurds.[77] Appearing in late March 1988, the Soviet Foreign Ministry spokesman said that the reported use of chemical weapons was a violation of the 1925 Geneva Protocol and should therefore be condemned by the international community. He added, though, that this conclusion applied to both belligerents.[78] Iraq's Saddam was off the hook. The local proverb "the Kurds have no friends" proved true once again.

5 • SOUTHEAST ASIA AND THE RISE OF COMMUNIST CHINA

Tibet, Bangladesh, Cambodia

MAO'S CHINA INVITES, OR DISINVITES, ACCUSATIONS OF GENOCIDE

Lemkin was known for having his hand in anything and everything related to genocide. That is what a friend of his, Clara Hoover, assumed when reading two pieces on "genocide in Tibet" in the *New York Times* in early June 1959.[1] Whether Lemkin was personally involved or not (he passed away two and a half months later), on July 24 the International Commission of Jurists pleaded for a UN investigation of Chinese conduct in Tibet, including the "supreme crime of attempted genocide."[2] The organization was founded in 1952 in West Berlin as a counterweight to the Soviet-controlled International Association of Democratic Lawyers. Funded by the CIA, it was part of the propaganda operations against the Soviet peace offensive and similar Communist initiatives.[3] Unsurprisingly, then, the commission's 1960 report concluded that the Chinese had committed genocide in an attempt to destroy the Tibetans as a religious group. Based heavily on refugee testimonies, the report spoke of the intent to wipe out Buddhism in Tibet. At the same time, the commission did not find sufficient proof that the acts of destruction targeted the Tibetans as a racial, ethnic, or national group.[4]

The Soviet reaction to the Chinese aggression in Tibet was instructive in its cynicism. By the mid-1950s Soviet authors still argued that the "national question" had been successfully solved in the People's Republic of China.[5] The Soviet-Chinese relations had been steadily deteriorating after the death of Stalin, though they had not yet reached the point of rupture when the Lhasa Uprising broke out in March 1959. The death toll from the uprising was estimated at anywhere between 2,000 and 10,000, accompanied by the exodus of some

100,000 Tibetans, mainly to neighboring India and Nepal.[6] The Soviets measured their response to Tibet and other thorny issues against potential gains for the United States. This sort of strategic calculation, as Austin Jersild has pointed out, increasingly frustrated the Chinese leadership, who believed that the Soviet Union had sold them down the river in pursuit of a global agenda. The Soviet diplomats did a bad job reporting from below, while the Chinese deliberately limited the channels of communication to Moscow.[7] The Soviet ambivalence was reflected in the fact that the only comprehensive article on the subject to appear in the Soviet press was penned by American journalist Anna L. Strong, who had been sympathetic to both regimes. "Does the 'Tibetan Question' Exist as Such?" queried Strong in *Literaturnaia Gazeta* (*LG*). The way the situation in Tibet was presented by some actors in the United Nations had nothing to do with reality, she bluntly stated. The biggest lie of them all was "genocide fabrication" (*basnia o genotside*). Genocide in Tibet had indeed existed—for the past seven centuries. The Tibetan people were slowly dying out as children succumbed in infancy and a substantial part of the male population became Buddhist monks who reneged on their progeny. The suppression of the uprising put an end to that "long-lasting genocide." "No-one will any longer prevent the people of Tibet from making a happy, prosperous life on the Roof of the World," Strong finished her optimistic piece.[8]

According to a conversation between the Soviet ambassador in China and Deng Xiaoping on May 27, 1959, both Communist nations regarded Tibet as Chinese territory and would work against putting this issue before the United Nations. Ambassador Pavel Yudin stated that Tibetan peasants had gained most from the "Tibetan events."[9] The tone of the discussion was much less cordial when Nikita Khrushchev met Chairman Mao Zedong later that October. Khrushchev blamed the escape of the Dalai Lama to India on the Chinese, saying he would have rather seen the Tibetan spiritual leader dead.[10] Meanwhile, during the debates concerning Communist China's membership in the United Nations, the Dalai Lama had appealed to the secretary-general to save the people of Tibet from extermination. He suggested that some member state might bring up this issue within the purview of the UDHR and the Genocide Convention.[11] The representatives of El Salvador and Venezuela indeed briefly referred to genocide during a debate on the Tibetan question in the fall of 1959. The final resolution proposed by Malaya and Ireland, however, only called "for respect for the fundamental human rights of the Tibetan people," without mentioning genocide.[12]

Within the following few years, however, the Sino-Soviet alliance had collapsed. Mutual criticism led to severance of diplomatic relations in 1962 and a military buildup along the common border. The tensions boiled over in the spring of 1969 as both sides exchanged fire resulting in casualties. Mao's strategy was war and famine, declared *LG* on June 4, 1969. Among the many mass crimes committed by Beijing the newspaper mentioned, mutatis mutandis, the "policy of genocide in Tibet."[13] Although not front-page news, Tibet had thus become one of the few cases that both the Soviet Union and the United States classified as "genocide"—for as long as China remained at loggerheads with the USSR and until the West embraced the Middle Kingdom as a strategic partner.[14]

As the United States came to replace the Soviet Union as China's partner in the 1970s, Moscow used the word *genocide* with increasing frequency. Typically, the adversaries embraced each other's enemies as friends. It was not surprising perhaps that on the eve of the Indo-Pakistani War of 1971 Prime Minister Indira Gandhi had accused Islamabad of genocide. The Indian representative at the extraordinary session of the UN General Assembly in December of that year used the same term with regard to the situation in East Pakistan. Earlier, the Indian foreign minister described American military aid to Pakistan as "collaboration in genocide." What is more instructive is how the Soviet Union framed the conflict that eventually led to the creation of independent Bangladesh. In an interview with TASS in early January 1972, the freshly appointed foreign minister of Bangladesh condemned China for its tacit support of mass murder perpetrated by Pakistan. Instead of encouraging revolutionary movements around the world—as Communist China was expected to after it had reclaimed its seat in the United Nations—Beijing joined forces with the United States in furthering the policy of genocide, he said. The task of presenting the Soviet position was delegated to the Czechoslovakian *Rudé Právo*, duly outlined in *Pravda*. Finding itself in isolation, wrote the organ of the Czechoslovakian Communist Party, China began flirting with imperialism. Guided by the foolish doctrine of two superpowers, China was actually promoting anti-Sovietism and chauvinism. Taking the side of Pakistan and American imperialism against India and the people of Bangladesh was yet another example of that ruinous trend. In effect, China had emerged as an even bigger culprit than the United States in what was described as genocide in East Pakistan/Bangladesh.[15] Radio Moscow made a direct link between President Nixon's visit to China in late February 1972 and the increased bombing of North Vietnam. These crimes, a domestic broadcast said, were committed with the connivance of Beijing; China and the United States were assisting in genocide presently being carried out by the Pakistani military in East Bengal.[16]

Remarkably, the word *genocide* touched the lips of Soviet officials only after India had intervened in the conflict, and not when the news of mass atrocities first broke. Equally disturbing was that the American diplomats on the ground evoked genocide as soon as the slaughter of Bengalis began, only to be hushed up by the White House. The stifling atmosphere of the Cold War was to blame. Gary J. Bass has laid bare how President Richard Nixon and National Security Adviser Henry Kissinger willingly ignored the plight of the victims in their pursuit of rapprochement with China. The United States was the single most important backer of Pakistan, which served as a liaison between Washington and Beijing. Nixon and Kissinger approved a covert supply of sophisticated weapons to America's ally in the full knowledge of an ongoing assault on the Hindu minority in the western part of the country. In a telegram from Dacca on March 28, 1971, US consul general Archer Blood notified the US State Department of what he called "selective genocide." Neither this single piece of information nor further intervention by Blood and the US ambassador in Delhi, Kenneth Keating, swayed the White House to withdraw support from the military junta in Islamabad. Besides its immediate usefulness in building bridges to Mao's China, Pakistan was important to the United States as an anti-Soviet ally and a counterweight to India. Hence, the term *genocide* could not apply to Pakistan by default. When emphasizing the urgency of the situation, Blood correctly pointed out that the continued carnage in Bangladesh played into the hands of the Soviets. For their part, the Soviet leadership dissuaded India from going to war over Bangladesh, trying to refocus Delhi's attention on China. Thus, the evocations of genocide by the Indian ambassador in Moscow in August 1971 fell on deaf ears.[17]

By parting ways with the Soviet Union, China invited a sudden interest in its minority policy. Incriminating evidence was in abundance at any time, but Soviet propagandists got a signal to start digging only then. The Cultural Revolution wreaked havoc in the autonomous regions of Xinjiang, Tibet, and Inner Mongolia, stated *Izvestia* in February 1972. The persecution of ethnic minorities had been carried out under the guise of Mao's theory of permanent revolution. Anyone resisting assimilation risked being branded as a "class enemy." In real terms it meant expulsion, forced labor in so-called reeducation camps, or even death. The newspaper got hold of a letter by Buddhists from Inner Mongolia and Tibet that "contained facts of undisguised genocide carried out by the Beijing authorities against ethnic minorities." What the Soviets aimed at with this exposé transpired in the article's last paragraphs. Repressions in China were no different from those by Pakistani authorities in West Bengal. The Chinese propaganda shifted the blame onto millions of refugees who had crossed into India, drawing a parallel to the exodus following the suppression of the 1959 uprising in Tibet. It was out of desperation that members of various minority groups had been fleeing from China, was the conventional wisdom shared by *Izvestia*. Next, however, it quoted a Communist official in Inner Mongolia who swore to turn the autonomous region into a "stronghold against Soviet revisionism." Such provocations exposed Great Han chauvinism taken up by the Maoists in their hegemonic aspirations, the organ of the Soviet government eloquently summed up.[18]

Having condemned China's "treacherousness," Soviet ideologists set out to reinterpret Chinese history accordingly. Maoists thought of themselves as the successors of Genghis Khan and Batu Khan, dreaming of recreating the Middle Kingdom. For starters, they claimed a chunk of territory belonging to the Soviet Union; with the same degree of success they could have laid claim to the other side of the moon, scorned *LG*. According to the newspaper, in the nineteenth century authorities in Manchuria carried out a "brutal policy of genocide." Seeking Russian protection, thousands of ethnic Uighurs, Kazakhs, and Kirgiz fled to the Fergana Valley and what is nowadays Kazakhstan. By the same token, the establishment of the Second East Turkestan Republic (1944–1949), with the help of the Soviet Union, supposedly halted genocide perpetrated by the Kuomintang in Xinjiang. When it comes to persecution of ethnic minorities such as Uighurs, Mongols, and Tibetans, however, Mao Zedong and his clique by far exceeded Chiang Kai-Shek and the Kuomintang in their cruelty. They reneged on the 1945 promise to introduce a federal system for the benefit of non-Han peoples in the wake of the successful Communist revolution in China. Maoists had been trying ever since to portray their expansionism and near-genocidal policy of forced assimilation as the "inevitable course of history."[19] Later on the Soviet press focused on the plight of ethnic Mongols in China. Communists were the first victims of mass "repressions bordering on genocide" in Inner Mongolia during the Cultural Revolution, followed by other minorities in subsequent years. The lesson learned—*LG* abruptly shifted the focus—was that the same destiny could affect any other Asian country within the China's sphere of influence, for example Cambodia.[20]

By the mid-1970s the Sino-Soviet relations hit rock bottom, making Moscow propagandists seek their all-time favorite rhetorical device—comparison to Hitler's fascism. "Dangerous Similarity: A Letter from China" was the title of the article that appeared in August 1974 in *LG*. Xinhua News Agency and China's Foreign Ministry had learned a great deal from the likes of Joseph Goebbels and Alfred Rosenberg. In order to win over peasants and workers, Mao followed in the footsteps of Hitler, who had distributed property confiscated from the Jews among artisans and petty traders. As early as 1938 Mao outlined his idea of nationalist Marxism. Like the Nazis, Maoists had been preaching anti-Sovietism, expansionism, and racism. In the latter's case racism was less blatant, merged with Great Han chauvinism. Inside China, that policy primarily targeted ethnic minorities who resided in the territories that had been annexed earlier by Chinese feudal lords. Even though Mao and his cohort did not adopt the Nazi policy of genocide directly—argued the Soviet newspaper—they pursued the very same objective of forced assimilation.[21] This conclusion alone demonstrates just how little thought the Soviets gave when brandishing the word *genocide*.

Following the Soviet invasion of Afghanistan, Western observers started taking Moscow's rhetoric more seriously, perhaps too seriously. The anger at China's territorial claims and its closer than ever ties to the United States made the Soviets play the ethnic card. Capitalizing on the grievances of the Uighur minority, who suffered disproportionately during the Cultural Revolution, Soviet propaganda encouraged ethnic unrest in Chinese borderlands. As of early 1980, the question was when, rather than if, the Kremlin would heed a call from Soviet

Central Asian republics to rescue their oppressed kinsmen from "cultural genocide" by the Chinese.[22]

INTERNATIONAL REALIGNMENT AND POL POT'S CAMBODIA

When it comes to putting a name on mass atrocities, Cambodia perfectly demonstrates the primacy of geopolitics. To be fair, Communist countries alleged genocide even in Lon Nol's Cambodia. In April 1970 Lon Nol's government attempted to dislodge North Vietnamese from their sanctuaries in neutral Cambodia. While the military offensive choked, army and police units massacred thousands of Vietnamese civilians in and around Phnom Penh. Subsequently, Cambodian authorities allowed about half a million surviving Vietnamese to leave for South Vietnam. The killings were widely reported in the international press.[23] Among the reporting newspapers were *Pravda* and *Izvestia*. Both referred to the Swiss *La Tribune de Lausanne,* which designated targeted violence as "genocide." The organ of the Soviet Communist Party further described it as "political genocide," orchestrated by the CIA with the purpose of drawing Cambodia into the grand US design for Indochina.[24] The centrality of geopolitics transpired also in the arguments of the Cuban delegate during the discussion in the UN Third Committee in December 1972. "The new type of Nazism" was now perpetrating genocide, war crimes, and crimes against humanity in Vietnam, Laos, and Cambodia, he said. He went on to argue that, of all the US military officers carrying out such acts in Indochina, only Lieutenant William Calley Jr. had been convicted, and even then symbolically.[25] (Three years earlier to the day, the Cuban Committee of Solidarity with South Vietnam situated the My Lai massacre within the scope of genocide.[26])

Willing to record a relatively minor episode in the tide of violence sweeping Cambodia, the Soviets essentially passed in silence the bloodbath unleashed by the Red Khmer in so-called Democratic Kampuchea (DK). Whatever official information—a brief mention at best—had circulated, it inevitably related to the USSR's main ally in the region, Vietnam. Then and again, the changing political constellations defined how and when the word *genocide* was used. As Saigon fell and the Americans withdrew from Indochina, the Soviets saw the opportunity to extend their influence in that region. Capitalizing on the Sino-Soviet differences, the United States began cultivating Beijing as a counterbalance to Moscow. The historical visit of President Nixon to China in February 1972 heralded the beginning of the rapprochement between the two countries. The second half of the 1970s saw the China-Vietnam divide becoming the epicenter of Soviet-American proxy wars, both real and virtual. Consider, for example, that at the UN Conference on the Human Environment in June 1972 China accused the United States of genocide and ecological warfare. In its reply to the talk of "monstrous atrocities" in Vietnam, Cambodia, and Laos, the United States expressed regret rather than anger, according to the *Boston Globe*.[27]

The Pol Pot regime, which seized power in Cambodia in April 1975, enjoyed the full support of Mao's China. Despite the persecution of the Chinese minority and the lack of manifest gratitude by its client, China conceived of Democratic Kampuchea as a bulwark against Vietnam. Wary of supporting a Chinese client, Moscow let North Vietnam call the shots on Cambodia. Once the victory was theirs, the Khmer Rouge lashed out against the Soviets, expelling the diplomatic personnel in Phnom Penh in a most humiliating manner. Faced with a fait accompli, the Soviet Union had no choice but to jump on the bandwagon. The earlier attempts to mend fences had failed, however: the new regime maintained no diplomatic relations with the Soviet Union, occasionally engaging in hostile acts against the Communist superpower. The Khmer Rouge regarded the USSR as an enemy state and the subsequent Soviet-Vietnamese alliance as a conspiracy against Democratic Kampuchea (DK).[28]

The horrors that took place inside Cambodia during the following three and a half years, specifically their interpretation, had been colored by the standoff between Vietnam and the Soviet Union on the one side and China and the United States on the other. For the first time, the Soviet press characterized Pol Pot's policy as "genocide" in the summer and fall of 1978. *Pravda*, *Izvestia*, and *LG* all referred to the mouthpiece of the Vietnamese Communist Party *Nhân Dân*, which spoke of China as the "true inspirer of genocide in Kampuchea." The death of up to two million people in what had been deemed the "barrack socialism state"—not incorrectly, pinpointed *Izvestia*—should be attributed to the Maoist ideology blindly implemented in Cambodia. *LG* reprinted a Vietnamese cartoon featuring Mao Zedong leisurely smoking a pipe on a couch while observing the ongoing atrocities in the background. The caption read: "Beijing authorities betrayed the cause of people's national-liberation movement."[29] Apropos the article in *Nhân Dân*, apparently it was reacting to an earlier commentary in China's *Xinmin ribao*. That commentary, unprecedentedly, accused Hanoi of launching a war of aggression against Cambodia and acknowledged Chinese backing of the Phnom Penh government.[30] The emerging narrative and its timing is hardly coincidental. By the spring of 1978 the fault lines had been drawn: Vietnam's leader ship had settled on a military intervention in Cambodia while China reached an understanding with the United States on containment of Vietnam.

Much like the Soviets, US authorities by and large kept mum on the issue of genocide in Cambodia, gingerly raising the human rights concerns. As William Safire observed in April 1978, the only ambassador to the United Nations ever to evoke genocide was Israel's Chaim Herzog.[31] Interesting enough, among the first public figures who spoke of "Cambodian genocide," as early as December 1975, was Alexander Solzhenitsyn. True, Solzhenitsyn did not elaborate, using it rather as a reference point; the celebrated Russian writer was critical of the

Ford administration for making, in his view, too many concessions to the Communist bloc—the true perpetrator of genocide.[32] Perhaps less unexpected was the stubbornness with which the far left in the United States denied the fact of large-scale atrocities in Pol Pot's Cambodia. There were a few Americans who rejected the charge of genocide outright. To accept that "slander," one *Boston Globe* reader argued, would be equivalent to accepting the invasion of Cambodia by Soviet-backed Vietnamese troops. The number of executed was vastly exaggerated, whereas some deaths were unavoidable as the Khmer people shook off the bonds of colonial and imperialist oppression. "Revolution isn't pretty!" summed up the callous observer from Somerville. Daniel Burstein of the Communist Party (Marxist-Leninist) claimed to be the first American to visit Kampuchea since the Khmer Rouge takeover. The week-long tour of Kampuchea in 1978 made him speak of a propaganda war waged against the country by both the United States and the Soviet Union. According to him, forced labor was just a rumor, and so were the stories of summary executions spread by the refugees. The most slanderous of all charges leveled against Kampuchea was that of "mass genocide," claimed Burstein. He readdressed this question to Deputy Premier Minister Ieng Sary. Brother no. 3 stated in an interview that there had never been anything like that in DK—how ludicrous! If one could talk of genocide at all, it was committed by the United States, responsible for the deaths of some 800,000 people during the war. Burstein endorsed this view and added that the "genocide myth" had been perpetrated by refugees in Thailand, some of who were allegedly paid to "tell good horror stories." Otherwise, "no revolution is immune to . . . some excesses" was the familiar refrain repeated by the Maoist devotee. It was actually the execution of some of "Lon Nol's traitors" that made Jimmy Carter designate Kampuchea as the "worst violator of human rights in the world."[33]

Quite so it was not, of course. In his statement on human rights violations in Cambodia on April 21, 1978, Carter spoke of "genocidal policies" implemented by the Khmer Rouge government during the past three years. By that he meant mass killings, forced deportation of city dwellers, persecution of political opposition, suppression of religion, and withdrawal of food.[34] The overthrow of the regime in early 1979, however, induced a correction to the president's strong words. The dilemma of the US foreign policy on Cambodia was most vividly summarized by Art Buchwald, an American humorist and syndicated columnist. Buchwald rendered his conversation with an unidentified State Department official at the beginning of 1979. The latter shared with Buchwald the difficulties of picking the lesser of two evils. Pol Pot, no doubt, held the "modern genocide record in all of Southeast Asia"—he explained—yet the new National Salvation government in Phnom Penh had the backing of both Vietnam and the Soviet Union while the crumbling Khmer Rouge regime enjoyed the support of China. Essentially, it had to do with the power struggle between Moscow and Bejing, surmised Buchwald. That was exactly right, confirmed the veteran Pol

Pot watcher. The United States had to tilt toward Pol Pot only because the Soviet Union was tilting toward Hanoi, or else the newly won friend China would lose face. Buchwald's lighthearted conclusion on how to get out of the quagmire proved prophetic: "Oh boy, I said. Look, I have a suggestion. Why don't we let the Vietnamese-backed Cambodians and the China-backed Cambodians fight it out among themselves? If Pol Pot loses, we can always let him open a restaurant in the United States." And fight it out they were allowed to do, as illustrated in a *Chicago Tribune* cartoon, except that instead of a sickle and a hammer they used actual weapons, including the word *genocide*.[35]

The fight soon shifted from the battlegrounds of Cambodia to the conference rooms of the United Nations. Days before the Khmer Rouge had been sent packing, the regime complained to UN secretary-general Kurt Waldheim about Vietnam's invasion. In response, Vietnam charged the Pol Pot regime with genocide and acts of aggression in the border areas. The statement issued by the Kampuchean United Front for National Salvation upon entering Phnom Penh on January 7, 1979 contained similar formulations.[36] Debates in the Security Council began over the question of who would represent Cambodia in the United Nations. The opinion was split between the countries that supported and opposed the Vietnamese invasion. The supporters consistently referred to brutalities committed by the Khmer Rouge regime as partial justification for its ouster. The Vietnamese delegate contended that three million people had been killed in a "ferocious act of genocide." The Soviet press did not find it opportune to invoke Carter's statement on Cambodia until after the Vietnamese had swept Pol Pot from power. To substantiate the allegations of genocide, the Soviet representative was now quoting the US president in the Security Council.[37] Suddenly, the Soviets found themselves citing such unlikely sources as the *Christian Science Monitor*. The newspaper reportedly depicted the "policy of genocide against its own people" in Cambodia as an extension of the Chinese Cultural Revolution and compared it to the Nazi mass murder.[38] The debate became even more acrimonious following China's invasion of Vietnam in mid-February 1979. While Vietnam condemned China's "open and deliberate aggression," a representative of the ousted Khmer Rouge regime accused Vietnam of a "deliberate policy of genocide" against Cambodia.[39] This barb put Vietnam on the defensive and, in the long run, contributed to the emergence of a double-genocide thesis.

The Vietnamese invasion of Cambodia disrupted the rice harvest. Food shortages had been exacerbated through a deliberate disruption of foreign aid by the new government, which was fighting Khmer Rouge guerrillas in areas bordering Thailand. Beginning in April 1979, Western officials and journalists began speaking of widespread famine. "Starvation at the worst Biafra level" was said to have threatened the very survival of the Cambodian people. With the international coverage of the food crisis increasing dramatically, a DK representative in the UN General Assembly claimed genocide. Countering Communist bloc accusations of genocide, on several occasions he stated that the Hanoi authorities were planning to transform Cambodia into a vast crematorium, acting out Hitler.[40] China weighed in by charging Vietnam with "aggression and genocide" vis-à-vis refugees. At that, the Chinese deputy foreign minister accused a superpower—meaning the Soviet Union—of aiding and abetting Vietnam.[41] A Polish representative kicked the ball back, comparing the Khmer Rouge to Nazis. His Belorussian counterpart went one step further, calling for the DK leadership to be tried under provisions of the Genocide Convention.[42] Indeed, Australia at one point indicated willingness to initiate proceedings against the Khmer Rouge, but later reconsidered so that it might not be misinterpreted as recognition of the government in Phnom Penh installed by the Vietnamese.[43]

With international prosecution not in the cards, the authorities in Phnom Penh went ahead and staged a trial of Pol Pot and Ieng Sary on charges of genocide. Building upon the precedent established by Bertrand Russell, the People's Revolutionary Tribunal on August 15, 1979 convened in the capital city. Nearly one hundred foreign lawyers and journalists, mainly from Communist countries, were flown in for the show trial. Among the observers were the Soviet Afro-Asian Solidarity Committee and the IADL. During their stay in Phnom Penh, the foreign guests got the opportunity to visit the Tuol Sleng Museum of Genocidal Crimes recently established by the Vietnamese. The trial began with a statement by an American lawyer representing Pol Pot and Ieng Sary. Contravening the principle of presumption of innocence, he unequivocally declared the defendants guilty of genocide. Having heard the total of twenty-one witnesses and eight commission reports, after four days of deliberations the tribunal sentenced both men to death in absentia. Simultaneously, emphasized *Pravda*, the verdict had also been passed on Maoism as the ideology of genocide.[44]

Semiofficial English-language publications hastily printed in Vietnam and the Soviet Union portrayed China as a driving force behind the "genocidal crimes of the Pol Pot–Ieng Sary clique." The title of one such book, *Kampuchea: The Crimes and the Collapse of Maoism*, was pretty much self-explanatory.[45] By inference, if Chinese advisers stirred up "genocide and repressions . . . following Maoist recipes" in DK, the continuous support for Pol Pot insurgents in post–Khmer Rouge Cambodia might produce the same outcome. At this point the Soviet Union took to reminding—as it had been consistently doing with regard to the United States—that China had not yet ratified a single humanitarian treaty, including the Genocide Convention. The Chinese responsibility for the crime of crimes had become a dogma, as reiterated by the World Peace Council (WPC) at its session in Berlin in early February 1979. The ideological self-righteousness was still on display when the Communist authors enumerated the deadly elements of Khmer Rouge terror: withdrawal of medicine, forced labor brigades, concentration camps, manmade famine—all in the name of "socialist revolution, the complete eradication of classes and social relics."[46] Had they dug deeper in history, they would have been forced to admit that Pol Pot's main inspiration, Mao Zedong, was a true student of Joseph Stalin, and that the roots of violence stretched from Phnom Penh to Moscow via Beijing. This inconvenient truth, though, bothered no one, since designating China as an architect of genocide was just a means to check China's expansion in Southeast Asia, that is, geopolitics.

Perhaps the only Soviet scholar who attempted a dispassionate analysis of Pol Pot's terror, if only in passim, was political scientist Fedor Burlatsky. Burlatsky in May 1979 was asking if mass atrocities committed in Democratic Kampuchea qualified as genocide. Genocide signified the destruction of certain ethnic or racial groups, whereas in Cambodia people belonging to their own ethnic group had been destroyed. If so, asked Burlatsky, what principle guided the selection of victims, social status perhaps? Actually it was the destruction of so-called suspicious elements and the feeble—the ideological genocide concealed behind Socialist and Communist slogans, he concluded.[47] Meanwhile, the world war of words had continued unhindered. The bulk of the evidence supplied by Western officials, nutritionists, and nongovernmental actors in the summer and fall of 1979 suggested that the extent of famine in Cambodia had been exaggerated. Representatives of the toppled DK regime, however, kept lambasting the Vietnamese for alleged acts of genocide all the same. One press release from the DK mission to the United Nations claimed that the Hanoi agents had long since infiltrated the Khmer Rouge apparatus, implying that the Vietnamese were responsible for the abuses during the 1975–1978 period as well. The Chinese representative on the UN Commission on Human Rights later also qualified as genocide Vietnam's mining rice fields and using chemical weapons. The moral equation between the crimes committed by Khmer Rouge and the Vietnamese policy in Cambodia—the tale of two genocides—received a further boost following the Soviet invasion of Afghanistan in December 1979.[48] The Soviet Union, for its part, continually dwelled on the hypocritical application of the term *genocide* to post–Khmer Rouge Cambodia by the Americans and their Chinese allies. How come, pointedly asked *Pravda*, that the president of the United States, who had condemned Pol Pot and his associates in the past, was now styling them a resistance movement? Obviously, the fate of the long-suffering Cambodian people was nobody's business.[49] This conclusion—minus the prerequisite ideology—was echoed by a few American observers. As Louis Wiznitzer of the *Christian Science Monitor* put it: "The Chinese still play the Pol Pot card; and the United States plays the Chinese card. The Soviet Union plays the Vietnamese card; and Hanoi plays the Heng Samrin card. Both sides are ready to fight to the last Cambodian."[50]

The Soviets dropped the ball on Cambodia as abruptly as they picked it up. Except for a brief mention of recently discovered mass graves in October 1982, the Soviet press during the 1980s rarely referred to the Khmer Rouge genocide in Cambodia.[51] After all, it was all about Cold War politics rather than the victims or the crime.

6 · (SOVIET) PIGGY IN THE MIDDLE

American Liberal Left versus Radical Right on US Ratification of the Genocide Convention

LESS UNIFORM OPPOSITION TO US RATIFICATION IN THE 1960S AND 1970S

In the aftermath of the Cuban Missile Crisis, the Soviet Union and the United States decided to step back from the brink of nuclear war. Known as détente, the easing of strained relations between two superpowers appeared to extend beyond international politics. The emergence of a more favorable atmosphere in Washington prompted over fifty labor, religious, and civic groups to form in 1964 the Ad Hoc Committee on the Human Rights and Genocide Treaties (CHRGT), under the aegis of the Jewish Labor Committee (JLC). The coalition launched a nationwide campaign to oblige the US government to commit itself more vigorously to international humanitarian law. In February 1965 the CHRGT convened a national conference in Washington, DC (attended by 175 delegates from fifty-four organizations); it received further publicity during International Human Rights Year in 1968.[1] Yet the prospects for US ratification of the Genocide Convention still remained dim. To persuade the politicians and the general public, the proratification lobby had to cut through the thick of prejudice and ignorance (e.g., the idea that the United Nations was a Communist spy nest controlled by Soviet Russia).[2]

"Anticommunism was the refuge of white supremacists in Mississippi," has remarked historian Herbert Shapiro.[3] Southern segregationists had a long tradition of attacking the US government for having allegedly made too many concessions to the Communists. Governor of Georgia Herman Talmadge—described by one reviewer as the "self-appointed prophet of Jim Crow forces"—was thus inquiring in his 1955 book:

> How many times have you read in your newspapers and magazines or heard over the airwaves this question: "What will Russia say if our government does this?" How many times have you read or heard this: "What will the Reds say if we don't do this?" or "What will the Communist newspaper *Pravda* print about the United States because we do this or that?" In some instances we have shaped our national policy by trying to please the Communists. . . . Too many things are being done in our country and by our country because we keep looking back over our shoulders at the Communists. Who cares what the Reds say? Who cares what *Pravda* prints?[4]

Senators from the Southern states had earlier emphasized that they regarded the Genocide Convention as nothing more than a "backdoor method of enacting federal anti-lynching legislation."[5]

Thus, more than anything else, it was the dynamics of race relations in Dixie that stood in the way of US ratification. In an unusually frank interoffice memorandum, the Department of State in June 1962 explained why. The Genocide Convention had by then been ratified by sixty-five countries, including the Soviet Union, which "cut the guts of the thing out" by means of reservations, though. The core of the problem was Southern opposition to "signing anything that deals with race relations." The problem therefore was purely political, and as such relatively low on the administration's priority list. The Senate and the State Department were waiting for each other to act first, which amounted to the US government dragging its feet on the Genocide Convention.[6] Aghast at the authorities' indecision, Senator Estes Kefauver wittingly compared the State Department and the Senate to Alphonse and Gaston from an old comic strip.[7]

The failure to ratify several international conventions, alongside the human rights questions, created major difficulties for the United States in the United Nations. Growing US reluctance to join voting majorities mustered behind these projects, according to the State Department, "has placed the US more frequently in the minority opposition that it was wont to be in the early years of the UN."[8] The Soviet Union was quick to strike at America's Achilles heel, as William Korey has put it. One of the earlier documented encounters that put the United States on the spot occurred in January 1964 in the CHR's Sub-Commission on Prevention of Discrimination and Protection of Minorities. The Soviet member of the body confronted the US expert Morris B. Abram, who advocated forceful measures of implementation. He reminded the subcommission that the United States was not even a contracting party to the Genocide Convention. The hint of duplicity made the embarrassed American express his regret about the fact of US nonratification. Two years later the very same Abram received a scolding from the Soviet delegate for having supported creating the office of independent UN commissioner for human rights. It was "indecent and hypocritical," charged the latter, since the United States had "resolutely refused to accept legal obligations." The article in *Pravda* on April 24, 1966 intimated that continuous racial discrimination in America was the reason why the United States had not ratified the genocide treaty.[9]

Typically, the genocide refrain played alongside the Soviet mantra of the United States reneging on international humanitarian treaties. Soviet propagandists tried to vary the message over time. In support of their argument, for example, they would quote an American politician like William Proxmire (D-WI), who made US ratification his life's work. Another time they would stress that international humanitarian law, like everything else, was a subject of class struggle and thus had two mutually exclusive interpretations—socialist and capitalist. The Soviet signature under the Genocide Convention and a series of international covenants that came into force in 1976 provided the answer as to whose interpretation was the correct one.[10] Ordinary Soviet people, supposedly, shared these views. For instance, in the spring of 1980 *Pravda* printed a selection of citizens' letters under the title "When We Are Spoken To in the Language of Threat." "Why does the United States shield genocide, apartheid, racism," rhetorically asked a reader from Orenburg Oblast. "Why do they violate the rights of entire nations?" Residents of Tambov and Kaliningrad concurred that the "American imperialists were spitting venom every time a hated dictator" such as Pol Pot, Anastasio Somoza, or Augusto Pinochet fell.[11] Eventually, the entire discourse amounted to nothing more than the affirmation of their own right versus their adversary's wrong. Defensive self-righteousness never let go in the Soviet Union's case.

February 23, 1970 marked a symbolic watershed in the history of US nonratification. On that day the American Bar Association (ABA) at its biannual meeting in Atlanta once again rejected the Genocide Convention, if only by a slim majority (130 to 126). The ABA verdict rallied conservatives of all stripes in the United States.[12] A voluntary association of lawyers and law students such as the ABA did indeed wield significant power. Anticipating a favorable vote by the ABA, the State Department proposed holding Senate hearings on the Genocide Convention *after* the meeting in Atlanta. However, the chairman of the Foreign Relations Committee, James W. Fulbright, had been reluctant to engage the Senate, since obtaining the necessary two-thirds majority in the upper house was considered unlikely.[13] Secretary of State William P. Rogers, following the lead of the US representative to the UN's Commission on Human Rights, Rita E. Hauser, had specifically advised President Nixon to send a message to the Senate ahead of the ABA House of Delegates meeting. The ABA support was essential insofar as Nixon was intent on seeking Senate consent to ratification, Rogers exhorted his boss on February 5.[14] Nixon heeded the advice and, two weeks later, had sent the appropriate message to the Senate.

At Atlanta, the ABA veteran Alfred J. Schweppe spoke on behalf of the opposition. He reminisced about the 1949 ABA meeting in St. Louis. Nothing had happened on the subject of genocide in the House of Delegates, "except some loss of memory," insisted a former dean of the University of Washington Law School. Schweppe proudly declared that he had voted for every Republican presidential candidate beginning in 1916. He had voted for Nixon twice and liked the man very much. The more was Schweppe's consternation when he learned that President Nixon had sent the treaty to the Senate for approval. In his judgment, the Americans "were always making major concessions, the Communists none." Due to the "pathetic performance" of the US delegation in the United Nations, out came a defective convention that the Soviets could readily approve. If it were now ratified by the United States—Schweppe presaged—it would be a "useless but troublesome piece of paper." The Communist bloc proved immune against accusations of genocide, while charging the United States with the crime was fair game. He would only accept a totally rewritten genocide treaty "with teeth in it."[15]

To articulate his concern, Schweppe in mid-March addressed Nixon directly: "Having voted for you twice, apart from genocide, I am very pleased with your conduct of the difficult office of President." The letter lamented that the Genocide Convention did not cover the "Hitler-Stalin-African-Asian type of genocide." At the behest of the president, State Department legal adviser John R. Stevenson alleviated Schweppe's fears by saying that US ratification would be a symbolic act at most. There was nothing unusual about the Communist countries' reservations regarding the jurisdiction of the ICJ; besides, those reservations did not substantially weaken the convention or affect the US attitude toward the treaty. As for the sinister Soviet plot to deny protection to political groups, Stevenson made an unexpected admission: It actually might protect the United States from propaganda charges that the United States was committing genocide against political groups at home or abroad.[16]

In March 1970, upon the request of Senator Fulbright, Secretary of State Rogers prepared a summary of pro and counter arguments vis-à-vis the Genocide Convention. He started off with the most topical, namely the speculation that American servicemen who had fought in Vietnam could be subject to extradition under the terms of Article VII of the convention. This was not going to happen, assured Rogers, since the United States did not have an extradition treaty with the Democratic Republic of Vietnam. It was altogether inconceivable that any act committed by US soldiers in Vietnam could fit the definition of genocide; all they did was help the South Vietnamese defend themselves. Contrary to yet another argument, Rogers told the chairman of the Senate Committee on Foreign Relations, the provisions of the Genocide Convention did not infringe freedom of speech guaranteed by the First Amendment of the US Constitution. As to the specific provision regarding causing serious mental harm, which could open the door to numerous charges of genocide by minority groups, Rogers evoked rigid enough standards protecting against frivolous allegations of genocide.[17]

The arguments in favor of US ratification, as put forward by Nixon's secretary of state, proved too vague to be convincing. That is what the hearings before a subcommittee of the US Senate Committee on Foreign Relations in late April and May 1970 had effectively demonstrated. It did not help that the line of argumentation advanced and the groups that testified in 1970 were similar to those at the 1950 Senate hearings. The eleven proponents and five opponents of the convention were equally apprehensive that, as long as the United States did not ratify the treaty, the sentiment would persist that genocide had been committed in that country, too.[18] Perhaps the biggest difference from the earlier deliberations was that the notion of genocide—as presented by Senator Proxmire—now also included anti-Jewish pogroms in czarist Russia and the mass murder of Armenians in Ottoman Turkey. Lev E. Dobriansky, president of the Ukrainian Congress Committee of America, represented East European émigré organizations at the hearings. Dobriansky appeared frozen in time, unaware of the political changes that had taken root since the 1950s, when framing genocide as the preserve of totalitarian regimes such as China and the Soviet Union. With détente in effect, American politicians participating in the hearings were no longer united in their opinion of whether charges such as the transfer of Greek children by Communists actually constituted genocide. The senators came to gradually realize that the political phraseology of genocide rarely, if ever, translated into legal cases. This equally applied to the Soviet Union and the United States. If the charge of genocide against Americans in Vietnam was preposterous, then so was one against Vietnamese in Cambodia. The statement by Lawrence C. Smith of the US Constitution Council to the effect that black Americans were the "largest victims of genocide in the world" obviously fell into the same category of unsubstantiated claims.[19]

As Schweppe's statement at Atlanta had demonstrated, the old guard in the American legal establishment still held sway. Whether "lingering Brickerists," in the words of Korey, constituted a cohesive group or not, John W. Bricker and his legacy were all too real. Writing to President Nixon in 1970, Bricker said that both Eisenhower and Johnson had promised him never to submit a treaty that would violate the terms of his amendment. Every passing day made the amendment even more important, insisted Bricker. In support of his claim, he referred to an article in the July issue of the *American Bar Association Journal*.[20]

Sure enough, in their article Orie L. Phillips and Eberhard P. Deutsch quoted from Dulles's testimony before the Senate Judicial Committee in April 1953. They argued that the "jurisprudential sorcery" of the Genocide Convention might subject American citizens to trials in disregard of US constitutional safeguards. Even in the absence of an extradition treaty with North Vietnam, the authorities in Hanoi—using the Nuremberg Tribunal as a precedent—were eager to try members of the US military for genocide. The authors abhorred the prospect of other countries (i.e., the Soviet Union) determining if genocide had ever taken place within US borders. Indeed, a sympathetic lawyer (i.e., William L. Patterson) had recently revealed plans to go before the United Nations and charge the United States with genocide against the Black Panthers. The notoriously vague provision of mental harm could well have applied to racial segregation prior to 1954; the Supreme Court's statement in *Brown v. Board of Education* regarding separation of black children could tendentiously be interpreted to mean exactly that. The United States lost big, argued Phillips and Deutsch, by having traded political groups for ethnic in the final wording of the Genocide Convention. Hence Communists had been able with impunity to inflict intolerable conditions of life on a political group and to target its members for destruction. Genocide was thus ongoing in Czechoslovakia, Hungary, and several countries in Africa and Asia. The doomsday scenarios painted by Phillips and Deutsch in the *ABA Journal* contrasted with their matter-of-fact conclusion: "In the final analysis, the prohibition of genocide by treaty must become an exercise in futility. Adolf Hitler would hardly have restrained the frightful acts of genocide that gave rise to the convention, even if it had been in existence and Germany had been a party to it during the Nazi reign of terror. The Soviet Union and her Communist-bloc allies were not deterred from the 1968 invasion of Czechoslovakia by the nonaggression provisions of the Charter of the United Nations."[21]

Coming back to Bricker, he had been as much opposed to the Genocide Convention as he was to the Covenant on Human Rights. This is an indication as to the extent to which these two documents/conceptions were intertwined within the Cold War discourse. According to Bricker, if ratified, the covenant would have had more adverse consequences for the United States than the convention. Writing to Nixon's counselor Bryce N. Harlow in June 1970, Bricker instantly interjected a conspiracy theory of his own: he could not help thinking that someone was lobbying for ratification in the interest of a small minority and not that of the American people. He also knew the name of the culprit—Mrs. Hauser, who was promoting the Covenant of Human Rights "on behalf of the New York crowd that opposed my amendment."[22] Bricker's intervention further demonstrates the extent to which the opposition to the United Nations—as an organization purportedly seeking to establish a "world government" by means of a genocide treaty and similar instruments—translated into American domestic politics. Thus, along with the Genocide Convention, the Daughters of the American Revolution condemned liberal immigration policies, disarmament, and excessive federal spending. Simultaneously, the women's service organization urged screening textbooks for "patriotic" contents and sounded the alarm over rising crime rates.[23] Ironically, the arguments advanced by the conservative opponents of US ratification of the Genocide Convention since the 1950s echoed the Soviet position of thirty years ago. The Soviets, too, argued against the principle of universal jurisdiction as a purported violation of state sovereignty.[24]

THE AMERICAN FAR RIGHT SAVAGES THE GENOCIDE CONVENTION

The most fascinating thing about the 1970s political mobilization against the Genocide Convention in the United States is that the difference between the arguments advanced by the conservatives and those on the far right fringe was only of degree, not kind. Equally significant is the number of contradictions in those arguments. Majorly, the convention was regarded at the same time as being too weak and too strong. Not a single case had been brought before the ICJ since 1951—argued the San Diego chapter of the Federation of Republican Women's Clubs—whereas the crime of genocide "obviously" had been perpetrated in Tibet, Belgian Congo, Biafra, and at Hue in Vietnam. Simultaneously there were "dark hints" of US servicemen at My Lai potentially being prosecuted under the Genocide Convention. "Our nation is presently in dire distress over both domestic and foreign problems and does not need the fears, suspicious [sic], anxieties and divisiveness which this Convention would endlessly compound," concluded the Republican women's organization.[25]

The Anti-Defamation League (ADL) kept track of organized opposition to US ratification by groups and individuals to the right of the American political spectrum. The ADL distinguished three segments of the right wing: (1) ultra-conservatives; (2) the political far right; and (3) the neo-fascist fringe that disseminated racial and religious bigotry. Even though the rightist organizations, publications, or broadcasts represented only a small minority of the American electorate, they were capable of creating the appearance of a public opinion groundswell. The scope and thrust of their operations was indeed substantial, especially when considered in the aggregate. In practical terms, the zealots proved able, generating a substantial flow of mail and telegrams to members of Congress.[26] In that respect, the proratification lobby was reportedly losing to ultra-right and conservative groups by a factor of 100.[27]

In retrospect, the American far right's "life-or-death campaign . . . to kill the genocide hoax" was quite unprecedented. It was anti-everything—liberal, Jewish, black, Catholic, but foremost anticommunist. "Immediate action necessary to prevent ratification, misled Americans victimized by propaganda from 'free press,' emergency truth campaign under way"—screamed *Liberty Letter* in June 1970. "A tight knit band of White Christian patriots" fought against and stopped two "evil pieces of leftist legislation"—the Genocide Convention and the Family Assistance Plan (Guaranteed Annual Wage)—proudly declared *The Thunderbolt* later that fall.[28]

The far right, to be sure, excelled in its favorite pastime—conspiracy theory making. Images, one darker than another, filled the pages of the radical press. Under the distinctive title "World Government Trap," *The Herald of Freedom* filed a potent hyperbole of the United Nations saying to the United States, like the spider to the fly: "Won't you step into my genocide parlor?" The UN monstrosity of the Genocide Convention was the ambiguous and sanctimonious document meant to destroy freedom of speech for every American. The UN Charter was the work of Soviet agent Alger Hiss and the genocide treaty nothing but an old Communist trick, pounded the editorial. After all, most of fifty-one groups comprising the CHRGT, which had been playing a major role in the drive for Senate ratification, were left-wing.[29] Meanwhile, president of the ABA Bernard G. Segal, a supporter of the treaty, happened to be Jewish. "Right-wing patriots were shocked" to learn of Nixon's overtures. The president had either been misled or he had "colluded with diabolical elements." Under the terms of the Genocide Convention publications such as *The Thunderbolt* would no doubt be banned and all groups fighting race-mixing driven underground—raved the white supremacist tabloid with the same name. American citizens would be dragged to trial by an alien international court à la the "monstrous" Nuremberg Tribunal, which did injustice to the Nazi leaders but failed to prosecute real criminals like Churchill and Stalin. *The Independent American* had this image of kangaroo trials held in Moscow, Tibet, or Ghana—necessarily presided over by Communist judges, insisted *The Thunderbolt.* Anyone, even President Nixon, could be arrested and tried in a "foreign 'war crimes' trial or worse," warned Liberty Lobby. That UN tribunal—feigned a racist outfit that went by the name Cinema Educational Guild—"could sentence you to be hanged, or shot, or imprisoned for life in a Siberian Slave Labor Camp." Unsurprisingly, then, added *Life Lines,* the Communist Party of the United States was all fired up about genocide. The enemy camp comprising Zionists, blacks, and Communists such as William L. Patterson and Ralph D. Abernathy (who took over after Martin Luther King) set out on a dirty mission to "finish off the racists in America." Racial slurs just kept coming from the hatemongers like *The Thunderbolt, White Power,* and *The Cross and the Flag*: "Remember, the only race being threatened with genocide is the White race. The leftists are working day and night for mongrelization of our people with the Blacks. This is real genocide, but of course the U. N. would never take any action to save the White race. The legislation is designed to tape our mouths closed because anything we might say in defense of racial purity causes negroes and Jews 'mental harm.'"[30]

The former FBI agent and conservative activist Dan Smoot used specific examples to illustrate the American racial dystopia. Conviction and sentencing of any black, or worse Black Panther, may be considered an international crime under the provisions of Article II of the Genocide Convention, insinuated the self-titled *Dan Smoot Report.* All public officials and private persons who had anything to do with the arrest, trial, and incarceration of a criminal—from witnesses and law enforcement officials to judges and governors—could hypothetically be accused of genocide. "Criticizing communist and other agitators (domestic and foreigner) who are creating criminal anarchy and trying to incite racial war in the United States could be construed as genocide," insofar as the alleged victims are identified as members of a protected group by the convention. Smoot rallied on behalf of officials acting under sterilization laws in some twenty states and dismissed the "alleged massacre of Vietnamese civilians at My Lai." As Schweppe and the ABA had done for a good thirty years, Smoot argued that the Genocide Convention exempted Communist governments. The Communists have all ratified the treaty, yet they "have more genocidal blood on their hands than Nazis ever had," practicing mass murder on political grounds. Robert Morris and John B. Gest in the *Wanderer* made a similar argument against an "old constitutional monstrosity, the so-called Genocide Treaty."[31] A "UN monstrosity," "deadly document," "deceitful treaty," "Communist-backed hoax," "Jewish scheme," "nightmare of deceptive and dangerous wording," "diabolical plot," "egregious concoction," "tyrannical treaty"—these were the typical epithets the American right attached to the Genocide Convention. It was nothing but a means to suppress all criticism of the leftist establishment, summed up *Liberty Letter*. To illustrate this point, the mouthpiece of the Liberty Lobby featured a somewhat stereotypical Cold War cartoon featuring the Russian bear and Uncle Sam. The beast was taking the shaky gentleman off the "free speech" pedestal by placing the "genocide treaty" towel over his mouth.[32] *The Red Line*, a bimonthly publication of the archconservative Cardinal Mindszenty Foundation in St. Louis, Missouri on September 17, 1970 sported the headline "Reds Ordered to Push 'Genocide' Propaganda." The Communist Party USA ordered its membership to mount a full-scale campaign for Senate ratification so that American prisoners in North Vietnam could be legitimately prosecuted as war criminals, claimed the article.

Yet the prize for the most apocalyptic piece of writing belongs to the antisemitic *Common Sense* of the late Michael Conde McGinley. The article from December 1, 1970 announced the coming of the antichrist, no more and no less. "Anyone shouting 'Communism is Jewish' under the Genocide treaty will be LEGALLY apprehended and taken away to a distant place, never to be heard from again," prophesized the anonymous author. After John Kennedy and Martin Luther King, more assassinations of the "left wing darlings" might follow: Ted Kennedy, George McGovern, William Fulbright, Ralph Abernathy, and a few others. In response, "they (the chosen few)" would start purging the leaders of the right. The sentencing of Robert DePugh of the Minutemen and Robert Shelton of the Ku Klux Klan was just the beginning, the article "How It Might Happen" continued. As the next step, horror of horrors, leftists would try to take away from the Americans their firearms. The doomsday, as predicted by *Common Sense*, would arrive in the form of martial law, while "Abbie Hoffman, Jerry Rubin, and the rest of the Jewish Rat pack are out roaming the streets of America encouraging the youth to break every law." "With the Black Plague moving in on us in the form of the Black Panthers," claimed the tabloid, "it was easy to see that the Christian Purge is on."[33]

The alleged assault on constitutional rights was sometimes directly linked to Soviet treacherousness. Why did Americans waste their time making treaties with the Russians, while the latter never intended to abide by them—angrily inquired a high-ranking official of the Church of Jesus Christ of Latter-Day Saints—"can't our men in Washington see what's going on?" So bound up in treaties and so weak militarily was the United States, he prophesized, that one day the Communists would walk in and take over the country. Dismiss all avowed Communists in high policymaking positions and do not enter into the genocide treaty, was his advice to President Nixon.[34] A newspaper reader in California took it one step further, suggesting that the United States should get out of the United Nations altogether. The latter's sole purpose was the furtherance of international Communism, according to the resident of Monterey Park, whereas the best genocide treaty was in fact the US Constitution.[35]

INTERNATIONAL OBSERVANCE OF HUMAN RIGHTS PUTS THE GENOCIDE CONVENTION BACK IN FOCUS

The US Senate failed, on February 5 and 6, 1974, to break a filibuster against the Genocide Convention. The efforts of the proratification lobby simply did not measure up to those of the political right. The latter's campaign had reached such a fevered pitch that mail and phone calls were running 200–1 against.[36] However significant was the contribution of the CHRGT and its affiliates, their humanistic message was just not enough to break the ice of the Cold War. Consider the president of B'nai B'rith Women, who spoke of the survival of the human race on behalf of 140,000 members of the organization. The ratification of the Genocide Convention, she said, not only would epitomize the morality and ethical values on which America had been built, but also signal the start of the US "involvements in peace and people."[37] The White House did occasionally invoke humanitarian values, too, though mainly to draw a contrast with the Soviet Union. As President Nixon interjected in his February 1970 message to the Senate, "some of our detractors have sought to exploit our failure to ratify this Convention to question our sincerity."[38] This was indeed the biggest factor that made the administration eventually move on this issue.

In the summer of 1975 in Helsinki thirty-five states signed the Final Act of the Conference on Security and Cooperation in Europe (CSCE). The Helsinki Declaration, which incorporated clauses on the inviolability of national frontiers and respect for territorial integrity, was meant to improve relations between the Communist bloc and the West. Having legitimized its territorial acquisitions in Eastern Europe in the wake of the Second World War, the Soviet Union emerged a winner. As a trade-off, Moscow acquiesced to Article VII of the Helsinki Accords, which proclaimed respect for human rights and fundamental freedoms. This proved to be a costly mistake for the Soviets, who underestimated the international fallout of the dissident movement.[39]

To implement the provisions of the Final Act, the signatories in October 1977 gathered at a follow-up conference in Belgrade. In the run-up to the meeting, the Soviet Union found itself on the defensive, as it had in the past in the United Nations. In the CIA's assessment, the Soviets were anxious to prevent further Western exploitation of their weakness in the field of human rights. Moscow was seeking to head off those efforts by counterattacking the Western record on implementation, focusing specifically on racial discrimination. The sense of Soviet vulnerability spurred a propaganda blast against Jimmy Carter's "demagogy" on human rights. The personal involvement of the US president in public appeals on behalf of Soviet dissidents infuriated the Soviets. To face up to the Soviet countercharges, National Security Adviser Zbigniew Brzezinski ordered a review of national security aspects of US policy on human rights.[40] One of his recommendations was making ratification of the Genocide Convention a "high spot on our list of legislative priorities." In the opposite case, criticism would keep coming not only from the Soviets but also from the American human rights groups.[41]

That was the context that made the CHRGT insist on speedy ratification of the Genocide Convention. This act should, then, strengthen Carter's hand in his efforts to raise major human rights issues at the forthcoming talks in Yugoslavia. "Unless we put our own house in order," wrote CHRGT's executive secretary, Betty Kaye Taylor, "our credibility is surely open to serious question."[42] Coincidentally, a former Supreme Court assistant justice, Arthur J. Goldberg, who served as president of the American Jewish Committee and chairman of the CHRGT, was appointed US ambassador to the 1977 conference. As expected, the Soviets at Belgrade attacked the US human rights record. Goldberg had no chance but to craft a convoluted response to the effect that "our effort to redress wrongs lays the foundation for our concern about wrongdoing elsewhere."[43] The KGB correctly predicted that Carter's human rights campaign would for long remain a staple of US foreign policy. To arrest this development, it proposed identifying the population groups in the United States and other capitalist countries who claimed violations of their fundamental rights. For this purpose, it recommended creating in a third country a private international relief fund where the "victims of imperialism and colonialism" could take their grievances. Simultaneously, the Western media outlets under Soviet clout would continue lambasting the ills of the capitalist world, including racial discrimination. As regards the accusations of human rights violations within the Soviet Union, the KGB set out to discredit Amnesty International as an offshoot of the CIA.[44]

The reminder that the United States had failed to ratify the Genocide Convention, along with another fifteen human rights treaties, encapsulated the talking points of Soviet propaganda circa 1977. Racism battered all visible minorities in the United States, effectively cancelling out the main tenet of the Declaration of Independence. In violation of the principle of nonapplicability of statutory limitations, US authorities continued sheltering Nazi war criminals and refused their extradition. Globally, the United States had been propping up the regimes inimical to human rights such as South Africa, Israel, Chile, South Korea, Haiti, Paraguay, Nicaragua, Guatemala, and others. While flagrantly intervening in other states' internal affairs under the "false slogan of protection of human rights," Washington actually violated the Helsinki Final Act by having refused ratification.[45] For affirmation, Soviets turned to the CPUSA and its recent report "unmasking Washington's hypocrisy." Signed by Henry Winston and Gus Hall, the document claimed that the human rights drive was yet another "anti-Soviet trick" among those the American imperialism had been using against socialism during the past sixty years. Along with the standard accusations, CPUSA top brass lashed out against the East European émigré groups. Sponsored by the CIA, those groups strove to violate the Soviet Union's territorial integrity, while Radio Free Europe/Radio Liberty was making a handful of renegades into heroes.[46] Bringing the émigrés into the picture was indeed remarkable, since the Soviets never mentioned the 1950s mass campaign to indict the USSR for genocide or the émigré organizations (and Raphael Lemkin) that stood behind it.

In 1979 the CSCE held hearings and issued several reports on the infringement of the Helsinki Final Act by the Soviet Union. A semiannual report by President Carter from December of that year further documented the violations of the freedom of movement, thought, and religion. The United States found particularly troubling the suppression of various Helsinki monitoring committees in the USSR. Without commenting on the American charges of noncompliance, the Soviets shifted the discussion to a very different plane. On November 13, 1979, *Pravda* reminded readers that, of the forty existing international agreements on human rights, the United States had ratified only ten. Even more pointed was a Radio Moscow broadcast on December 9, the thirty-first anniversary of the Genocide Convention and the Universal Declaration of Human Rights. The radio program "International Observers Roundtable" highlighted the failure of the United States to ratify the genocide treaty. Noting the large number of contracting parties, one commentator observed: "it can hardly be that the whole world is out of step, while the United States is in step." Another analyst charged that the "Senate's position speaks quite eloquently of the present American 'enthusiasm' for human rights."[47]

The disposition at the second CSCE follow-up meeting at Madrid between November 1980 and September 1983 was no different from that at Belgrade in 1977–1978. According to a memorandum sent out to the KGB stations, the West would be trying to turn the Madrid meeting into a propaganda blitz against the Soviet Union. The issue of human rights, alerted the KGB headquarters, would be used to discredit the Communist bloc in much the same way as at Belgrade.[48] Moscow's response remained the same: the Soviets just kept pestering the United States for not having ratified the Genocide Convention. Every time the Senate Foreign Relations Committee urged ratification, TASS published scathing commentary. Thus, in May 1985 the Soviet News Agency referred to the genocide treaty's diehard opponent, Jesse Helms (R-NC). Helms had repeatedly warned of a potential international prosecution of American citizens had the United States become a party to the convention. This fear was totally justified, interjected TASS, since genocide had since long been a constituent part of US policy, of which the dismal treatment of Native Americans was just one example.[49] The latest reminder was issued by TASS on December 10, 1987, marked by the United Nations as Human Rights Day.[50]

Quite instructive was Soviet reaction to the so-called Whitaker Report. Benjamin Whitaker, a retired British politician and historian, was commissioned by ECOSOC to review the Genocide Convention with the purpose of making it more operational. Building upon a similar report from 1978, in July 1985 Whitaker presented the results of his labor, the Revised and Updated Report on the Question of the Prevention and Punishment of the Crime of Genocide. The Soviets took the report apart. Not only did Whitaker inadequately cover the history of genocide, but he also passed over the current outrages in silence. Among the past cases of genocide, Whitaker was said to have paid lip service to the colonial period and the Nazi policy toward the Slavs. As for the present, Israel's treatment of the Palestinians was nowhere mentioned in Whitaker's report. Furthermore, according to *Izvestia*, the Special Rapporteur attempted to illegitimately broaden the definition of genocide by applying it to any situation resulting from a violent change of power, including interparty struggle. As expressed by Vsevolod Sofinsky during the subsequent debate on the findings in the CHR subcommission, equally unacceptable was the suggestion to include among the protected groups economic, social, and sexual groups. (Notably, Whitaker's call for consideration of ecocide, ethnocide, and cultural genocide met no resistance from the Soviet delegate.) Sofinsky argued that the Whitaker Report had political undercurrents aiming to subvert state sovereignty. While the United States had not ratified the Genocide Convention, an attempt had been made to emasculate this document of international law, indeed to make it a tool of Western aggression.[51]

Echoing Lemkin and his earlier idea of NATO as an antidote to genocide, Konstantin Rusakov made a point about the Warsaw Pact as a bulwark against racial discrimination and genocide, among other ills. A high-ranking CPSU official in charge of contacts with foreign Communist Parties, Rusakov was speaking in May 1985 on the occasion of the treaty's thirtieth anniversary.[52] A symbolic list of the most egregious instances of genocide, drawn by the Soviets, could be derived from an interview with Anatoly Karpov. Chess world champion between

1975 and 1985, Karpov served as chairman of the Soviet Peace Foundation. Since its inception twenty-six years earlier—he told a *Pravda* journalist in October 1987—the foundation had been providing relief to the victims of aggression, genocide, and natural disasters. Among the victims' countries of origin Karpov specifically mentioned Vietnam, Cambodia, Lebanon/Palestine, South Africa, and Chile.[53]

7 · MOSCOW TAPS THE NEW LEFT

The Vietnam Antiwar Movement, Black Panthers, the American Indian Movement

THE SOVIET NARRATIVE OF THE VIETNAM WAR

Mass protests against the Vietnam War, which exacted an enormous human cost, led to the emergence of the so-called New Left in the West during the 1960s. In the United States, the radical left alliance comprised, among others, the Vietnam antiwar advocates, Black Panthers, and Native American activists. The Soviets traditionally viewed the grassroots movement with suspicion insofar as it did not take orders from Moscow. From the perspective of propaganda, however, public discontent in the noncommunist world was worth tapping. With a great many ideological strains and tactics on display, charges of genocide against the US government proved one of the common threads that bound the New Left together.

The charges of genocide in Vietnam had dotted the Soviet newspapers since 1963. Put in the mouth of a certain Saigon attorney, genocide might be an American policy to prevent the inevitable unification of the country. A *Pravda* journalist conspicuously used the word *liudoguby*, which is the literal translation of *genocidaires*.[1] As of 1965, it was still Communist fellow travelers such as *L'Humanité* journalist Madeleine Riffaud, president of the WPC John D. Bernal, or *Le Figaro littéraire* contributor Fernand Gigon whom the Soviets quoted on genocide in Vietnam.[2] The Western press took notice.[3] By the following year Soviet political commentators had found their own voice. In September 1966 *Pravda* printed the longest such article ever, "Genocide." Under the pretext of fighting Communism, the United States had been effectively exterminating all the Vietnamese. This kind of crime had been recognized as genocide already by the Nuremberg War Tribunal, asserted Yuri Zhukov. The author was obviously contradicting the previous Soviet discourse on the Korean War by stating that the use of chemical and biological weapons on a massive scale took place for the first time in Vietnam. There was no mistake, of course, in his description of the deadly efficiency of napalm bombs dropped on Vietnam in the millions by the US Air Force. Even the engineers of Nazi gas chambers faded in comparison with "American genocide experts," he added. Zhukov's sympathy lay with a court-martialed draft dodger who stated his objection to the "policy of genocide in Vietnam."[4] In the spring of 1967 *Pravda* reported on a group of draft dodgers protesting against the war in Vietnam in front of the American pavilion at the Montreal Expo. Among other slogans carried by the protesters was "Shame to the Policy of Genocide." A more creative way of showing the opposition to the Vietnam War was on exhibit in London later that summer. The demonstrators who gathered in front of the US embassy in Grosvenor Square sported boards styled after London street plaques: "Genocide Sq., City of Westminster."[5]

The reference to Nazi gas chambers was not coincidental, and it was carried all the way into the General Assembly's Special Political Committee. In the fall of 1966 Hungary sponsored a resolution stigmatizing the United States for chemical warfare in Vietnam. Western countries eventually managed to water down the harshly worded resolution through an amendment. The amendment replaced sections deploring the use of chemical and bacteriological weapons with an innocuous call for all nations to observe the 1925 Geneva Protocol against the use of poison gas. Some observers believed that the Soviets—acting in this particular case through one of their satellites—had renewed the verbal offensive in order to cover their own embarrassment in the ideological fight with China. The worse the state of Moscow's relations with Beijing, the more virulent became the Soviet criticism of the West. The Soviet Union walked an extra mile to avert Chinese charges that it was in league with the American "imperialist-warmongers." Moscow effectively took its struggle against Mao Zedong into Vietnam. A broadcast in the Vietnamese language on March 16, 1967 told the people in North and South Vietnam that Maoists were wiping out non-Chinese minorities in an act akin to genocide.[6]

Meanwhile the Soviets kept looking for quotations on "genocide in Vietnam," from UN secretary-general U Thant to famed columnist Walter Lippmann.[7] Like Korea in the 1950s, Vietnam in the 1960s functioned as a reference point for other alleged instances of genocide. While the use of napalm by Israel in the Six-Day War served as a direct mean of comparison, a random remark by H. Rap Brown, who linked the war in Vietnam to racial discrimination and police brutality in the United States, hardly did so.[8] With the antiwar movement in the United States gathering momentum, the Soviet press had much to report. In mid-December 1969 a few thousand protesters massed in front of the Waldorf Astoria hotel in New York City to demand "Stop the War! End the Genocide of the Vietnamese People!" Yet another slogan decried "Terror against Black Panthers." Joseph

North of the *Daily World,* as rendered by *Pravda,* argued that participating in the Vietnam War was not an act of duty but that of genocide. Had Mark Twain ventured to Wall Street today (i.e., summer 1970), speculated North, he too would be denounced as unpatriotic.[9] Soviet scholar Alina Koroleva linked the issue of genocide, the American war in Vietnam, and racial discrimination in the United States in a rather unorthodox fashion. In need of cannon fodder, the US Army enlisted a disproportionate number of blacks to fight in Vietnam. This, according to Koroleva, was one of the more subtle forms of genocide.[10]

The brutal tactics used by the US military in Vietnam, no doubt, provided ammunition to the ever-growing allegations of genocide: forced population transfers, burning down villages, carpet bombing, destruction of dams and crops.[11] Set up by the philosopher and pacifist Bertrand Russell in November 1966, a people's tribunal "tried" the US government for war crimes in Vietnam, accusing the United States of genocide. One of the five major issues examined by the tribunal was formulated as follows: "Have there been unjustifiable reprisals against the civilian population, namely the execution of hostages? Has there been creation of hard-labor camps, deportation of the population or other acts tending towards the extermination of the population which can legally be called acts of genocide?" Even though the philosopher Jean-Paul Sartre, in his capacity as executive president, conceded that the members of the tribunal were not fully aware of criminal intent, he nevertheless insisted that the logic of American imperialism presupposed genocide. Specifically, he argued that genocide underlined the antiguerrilla strategy of neocolonialism, the Pax Americana. The tribunal accepted Sartre's analysis to unanimously declare, on December 1, 1967, the United States guilty of genocide. The publication, and the quasi-legal exercise that preceded it, was predominantly moralistic in tone.[12] As is the case with international citizens' tribunals in general, Russell's attempt to rally public opinion fell short due to overly aggressive procedures tainted by partisanship.[13]

As a matter of fact, Russell's was not the first such tribunal in existence. Neither was it the first to charge genocide in Vietnam. In 1966 and 1967 a body with a rather long name, Committee for the Denunciation of War Crimes Committed by the US Imperialists and Their Henchmen in South Vietnam, published in Vienna a series of black books, or rather pamphlets of twenty-odd pages. The personalities behind the committee and its publications were Isabelle Blume and Heinz Badner of the WPC. The third pamphlet, with the leaden title *US Imperialists' "Burn All, Destroy All, Kill All" Policy in South Vietnam,* came out in early 1967. The pamphlet attributed over one million dead and wounded Vietnamese to the deliberate policy of genocide and was distributed at a press conference in Hanoi.[14]

It was perhaps unsurprising that US officials refused to comment on the entire affair. Remarkably, the Soviet media did not utter a single word about the Russell tribunal either. Neither did North Vietnam pay much attention to the tribunal's proceedings. On August 29, 1968 the Communist Party of Vietnam Central Committee considered a report on recent achievements on the diplomatic front. The lengthy report had just one paragraph dedicated to the tribunal. It merely stated that two (public) sessions of Russell's "International Court of Justice" had taken place in Sweden and Denmark respectively. The conclusion drawn by dozens of investigating delegations had exposed that the United States had committed the crime of aggression against Vietnam and were presently carrying out genocide against the Vietnamese people.[15] A North Vietnamese official had expressed in private that the Soviets opposed the tribunal, aware that it lacked legal authority. Among the forty-odd witnesses who appeared before the tribunal, not a single one came from the Soviet Union.[16]

The Soviets had a reason to distrust the Western liberal left. Thus, Sartre defined the 1968 military invasion of Czechoslovakia by the Communist bloc as a war crime under international law, though adding that it could not be compared to American actions in Vietnam—"ignoble genocide."[17] As for Russell, he had the stigma of a "philosopher obscurantist" among the Soviet legal experts. His advocacy for a world government as a means of preventing a nuclear war allegedly played into the hands of the American monopolists.[18] Furthermore, Russell was one the five Western intellectuals who oversaw the Congress for Cultural Freedom. Underwritten by the CIA, the congress came into existence as a counterweight to the Soviet-backed WPC and held its inaugural meeting in Berlin in June 1950.[19] The Soviets apparently preferred to the Russell tribunal quasi-legal entities that sprang directly from the American antiwar movement. One such entity, the International Commission of Inquiry into U.S. Crimes in Indochina, came into existence in late 1969 in response to the notorious My Lai massacre. In 1970–1972 the commission held public hearings in Stockholm, Oslo, and Copenhagen, respectively. Some of the witnesses traveled to Norway via Moscow.[20] In fact, the citizens' commission was established upon a public call from the Bertrand Russell Foundation, which *Pravda* failed to mention when reporting on its proceedings. Falling back on the Nuremberg precedent, the Oslo session charged US Army personnel with war crimes and crimes against humanity, and qualified the war in Vietnam as "genocide."[21] The print version of the proceedings, in Swedish, actually had *Genocide* for a title. As a follow-up, WPC's magazine *New Perspectives* printed in the summer of 1972 an article with the title "Ecocide, Biocide, and Genocide in Vietnam."[22]

Literaturnaia Gazeta in August 1968 printed a piece by the German writer Peter U. Weiss. Weiss sat on the Russell tribunal and contributed a book of his own on the "US genocide in Vietnam." In his analysis, the indiscriminate bombing of civilians and infrastructure aimed at annihilating the Vietnamese people as such.[23] Soviet academics weighed in on the subject of the Vietnam War, too. On March 21, 1968 the Ethnographic Institute of the Soviet Academy of Science held a one-day seminar. The event marked the International Day for the

Elimination of Racial Discrimination. One of the eight papers delivered at the seminar examined the "US policy of genocide in Vietnam."[24]

Capitalizing on the Russell tribunal's findings, the IADL and the World Federation of Trade Unions both accused the United States of genocide in Vietnam. As the debates on US ratification of the Genocide Convention came to a head in 1970, the critics made it known that it was just a matter of time before Moscow began agitation to indict the United States on those charges. The genocide treaty was, and had always been, "subject to abuse by those who wish ill to the United States," concluded the conservative *Human Events*.[25] On March 31, 1971 prospective US ratification suffered yet another, psychological setback. On that day second lieutenant William L. Calley was sentenced to life imprisonment for ordering his men to murder unarmed Vietnamese civilians at My Lai three years earlier. Even though twenty-five of his co-defendants walked out free, and Calley himself later received a limited presidential pardon, disputes over his conviction had placed additional obstacles in the pathway to Senate approval. The same applied to the Geneva Protocol barring the use of poison gas and germ warfare. The State Department disputed that the protocol covered herbicides and tear gas, which the United States extensively used in Vietnam.[26]

The American far right decried the Calley verdict as "part of a subversive plan to downgrade the military" and a sure sign that, under the terms of the Genocide Convention, Nixon could be tried for mass crimes in Vietnam.[27] The Soviet propaganda gave no reason to doubt this conclusion. In the period after 1975, Moscow had consistently made a connection between the fact of US nonratification and the refusal to prosecute individuals accused of mass crimes during the war in Vietnam. Some of them maintained their positions in the Pentagon, US governmental agencies, and even international organizations. No surprise, then, speculated *Pravda* in August 1977, that those malefactors did not want to bind their hands and feet.[28]

The opponents of the Genocide Convention such as Senator Strom Thurmond (R-SC) turned the issue on its head. Vietnam had reportedly used poison gas against anticommunist tribal groups, yet on June 9, 1981 the country became party to the Genocide Convention. Thus, Thurmond's statement before the Foreign Relations Committee later that year read: "The Genocide Treaty, where it should restrain atrocity is not observed, and where it would be observed [i.e., United States], it is unnecessary." Among other examples illustrating potential abuse of the convention, specifically the clause on incitement to commit genocide, he dwelled on the hostage crisis in Iran. Should the genocide treaty become supreme law, speculated Thurmond, Iran could have taken the United States to the ICJ for enabling any number of American citizens with the freedom to urge retaliatory military action.[29]

As the war in Vietnam spilled over to neighboring countries, the Soviet bloc and the United States kept trading accusations of mass crimes, including genocide. Thus, the Lao Patriotic Front charged the US military with genocide by means of waging chemical warfare in North Laos. The Soviets reiterated the charge, on occasion defining genocide as the "barbarian extermination of people serving the imperialist interests of the USA in Southeast Asia." To help defeat the Communist insurgents and the invading military forces of North Vietnam, the CIA recruited the Hmong tribesmen. Once the Communists emerged victorious in the civil war, they targeted the Hmong people for retribution. Systematic reprisals in their turn prompted allegations of genocide.[30]

SOVIET PROPAGANDA AND RACE RELATIONS IN THE UNITED STATES

The Soviet Union had systematically failed to reach out to nonwhite population groups in the United States. Soviet policy vis-à-vis American blacks—if there ever was one—can be defined as reactive. By denouncing racial discrimination in the United States, the Communist regime sought to shift attention from endemic human rights violations at home. Soviet satellites promptly adopted a tu quoque technique in their counterpropaganda. For example, a Bulgarian delegate in the General Assembly reportedly warned his Ceylonese counterpart against going to Little Rock because of his skin color. The Hungarian Communist leader János Kádár in 1957 went on the record to argue that those who tolerated racial persecution (i.e., the United States) had no right to preach human liberty and human rights.[31]

More consequential battles ensured around specific UN treaties in the making. Recurrent instances of antisemitism in several parts of the world, including the Soviet Union, prompted an initiative to draft an international convention banning all forms of racial discrimination. As usual, the preparatory work began in ECOSOC's Human Rights Commission, in 1961. Following a bitter exchange between Israel and the Arab states, the United States and the Soviet Union threw themselves into the fight. Capitalizing on a recent race riot on the University of Mississippi campus in Oxford, the Soviet delegate counterattacked charges of persecution of Jews in the USSR. In her lengthy rebuttal to Marietta P. Tree of the United States, Tatiana Nikolaeva attacked the "punitive provisions" against blacks in a number of states and cited incidents involving African diplomats in Washington, DC and New York City. She recalled the 1951 *We Charge Genocide* petition and proclaimed antisemitism a "unique American phenomenon proving that Hitler is not dead." This harangue, in its turn, was denounced by the American delegate as "vicious half-truths." Tree voiced her objections also when the Soviets, a few years later in the same commission, proposed listing *antisemitism* alongside such odious terms as *Nazism* and *genocide*. Antisemitism could not be covered up forever by recalling the crimes of Hitler, Tree argued.[32]

The Soviet reaction to the bombing of a Baptist church in Birmingham, Alabama serves as yet another proof that Moscow did not have a clear policy on race relations in the United States. As part of an intimidation campaign against school desegregation in the American South, the Ku Klux Klan on September 15, 1963 detonated a bomb killing four black girls. It took over a month before *Pravda* reacted with an article by Henry Winston. A Marxist civil rights activist and high-ranking official in the CPUSA, Winston juxtaposed in his piece the "barbarity" of the United States and the "humanity" of the Soviet Union. He placed the killing in Birmingham among other "genocidal acts against the black people," a manifestation of supremacist white culture and its Christian ethics. The exact opposite was a Young Pioneer meeting, which Winston said he had recently attended in Moscow. The more sincerity he claimed there was in the Pioneers' affirmation of solidarity with the American blacks, the less genuine it sounded. Just as disingenuous appeared the appeal signed by well-known Soviet children's authors published in the same issue of the newspaper.[33] As if to prove Winston right, the World Festival of Youth and Students issued a declaration. One sentence in the declaration read: "we express our solidarity with the glorious patriots of South Africa, Negros of America, all those who stand up for their human rights in the persistent struggle against the criminal policy of genocide."[34]

However, even the Soviets were forced to acknowledge, if indirectly, the advances in American race relations. "We no longer read in the newspapers about lynching of Negros," admitted *Izvestia* in September 1963. Yet the sentence continued: "but that does not mean that the most radical forms of genocide against the Negro people ceased to exist or have been banned in the United States."[35] This is a fascinating postulate that can be extended to the entire genocide discourse during the Cold War. If one of the two ideological warring sides had determined that any given case constituted genocide, exemplified by a particular technique of destruction, no matter what policy changes the other side might have introduced, the label stayed. The basic principles of propaganda dictated so. To back down meant losing face. At that, the article in *Izvestia* was called "Modern Cannibals."

From the early 1960s onward the Soviets found "genocide" in each and every manifestation of racial intolerance in the United States. The reference points changed as the Cold War conflicts traversed from Africa to Southeast Asia and from the Middle East to Latin America. In August 1965 it was the Watts Riots in Los Angeles and continual air bombings in Vietnam. The Soviet press provided no details of the race riot, which it framed as an organic transition from conventional discrimination to armed suppression of the African American population by US authorities. The process of decolonization ignited the liberation movement among the American blacks, according to *Pravda*. The April 1968 riot in Chicago, which flared up following the assassination of Martin Luther

King and left at least eleven dead, was designated by the same newspaper as the "beginning of the second mass genocide in America." It laid the blame on Chicago mayor Richard J. Daley, who did indeed give police the shoot-to-kill authority. Along the way, *Literaturnaia Gazeta*, paraphrasing John Hersey in his book *Algiers Motel Incident*, qualified the July 1967 race riot in Detroit as "genocide."[36] An African American newspaper, *Minority Report*, essentially concurred with this opinion. "Every major black ghetto in the country was put into what amounts to the verge of genocide," stated the Dayton, Ohio–based newspaper in October 1969. To illustrate the extent of police violence, it made a subtle reference to the Soviet invasion of Czechoslovakia the pervious summer. The smoldering neighborhoods of Chicago made "Prague look like Switzerland," wrote *Minority Report*.[37]

The surge of political activism in the United States in the wake of the Vietnam War breathed new life into the CRC's 1951 petition *We Charge Genocide*. The petition campaign had rebound, yet only as a shade of its former self. Malcolm X of the Nation of Islam was reportedly the first to revive the issue of genocide when in 1964 he unsuccessfully pleaded with several African nations to sponsor an appeal to the United Nations. His initiative came in the wake of a race riot in Harlem in July of that year, during which a picketer was spotted carrying a sign reading "U.N. Must Intervene to Stop U.S. Genocide."[38] By that time allegations of genocide had acquired more and more abstract form. Contraception pills, drugs, and involuntary sterilization bills introduced in some states came to be construed as a covert means to destroy the black communities.[39] Numerically, it should be noted, black Americans had become a larger force to reckon with. By 1960 there were an estimated 19 million blacks in the United States—a significant minority that made up about 92 percent of the nonwhites in that country.

The radical black organizations had appropriated *We Charge Genocide* in the attempt to replicate the relative success of the CRC petition campaign. For support, they turned to William Patterson, the driving force behind the original effort to indict the United States for genocide. In fact, it is not even clear whether it was the Black Panther Party or the "man of legend"—as Gerald Horne has designated Patterson—who traded the idea to resuscitate the genocide crusade. Due to his firebrand personality, Patterson quickly emerged from the shadows following the demise of the CRC in January 1956. The following month Khrushchev had delivered his famous "Secret Speech," which American authorities made sure to disseminate as widely as possible. Damning revelations about the Stalinist terror caused disarray within the CPUSA ranks. Membership plummeted. Patterson was not among the thousands of deserters. Patterson renewed his pledge of allegiance, convincing himself that Moscow was instrumental in driving Jim Crow into oblivion.[40] His ideological steadfastness and political agility were appreciated; two years later Patterson was appointed general manager of the *Worker*.[41]

Established in October 1966, the Black Panther Party (BPP) had acquired notoriety among the far-left groups for its advocacy of violence. As one of its members declared in 1969, "black people have abandoned the non-functional and ineffective tactics of the 'Civil Rights' era and have now resolved to attain their long overdue liberation by any means necessary."[42] Patterson, who chaired the CPUSA Black Liberation Commission, did not rush to condemn the Panthers' militancy on account of their commitment to the cause of black emancipation. His affiliation with the BPP was at the same time rational and emotional: Patterson was reliving his revolutionary past. He viewed the Panthers, as he did earlier the Communists, as "modern Abolitionists." Whereas Patterson and Chairman of the CPUSA Gus Hall had denied any involvement in the Harlem Riot, the word *genocide* spelled out during the disturbances brought back memories. Young militants, who held a certain reverence for Patterson, kept coming to him for advice. Patterson had established a particularly close relationship with the Student Nonviolent Coordinating Committee (SNCC). By early 1967 the SNCC was facing bankruptcy and, following in the footsteps of the CRC, expressed the desire to reprint an updated edition of *We Charge Genocide*. The SNCC had circulated a memorandum in which it alerted African and Asian member-states of the United Nations to "brutal suppression of black people in the United States as a matter of international concern." Simultaneously, SNCC heeded Patterson's counsel and applied for observer status at the United Nations. Although these desperate moves did not save the SNCC from its ultimate demise, the rallying cry of genocide was picked up and carried further. SNCC's fiery leader, Stokely Carmichael, who in mid-1967 hopped over to the BPP, invoked Patterson's "we charge genocide" at a major protest against the Vietnam War and altogether saw a great potential in the theme.[43]

Eventually, it was the BPP that contributed most toward the reenactment of Patterson's genocide campaign of twenty years earlier. Patterson's contention that CPUSA should stand in the forefront of the defense of the Black Panthers became reality when he joined, in 1969, the legal defense team for the BPP cofounder Huey P. Newton. Shortly, he joined forces with Bobby Rush of the BPP's Illinois chapter and few other activists in the defense of Rap Brown. Curiously, the cable that Patterson sent to the Black Panthers congratulating them on the first national conference on antifascism, held in Oakland in July 1969, arrived from Moscow, of all places. The BPP paid back in kind, glorifying Patterson as a "crack warrior, strategist, and organizer of Black liberation and working class movements." Whatever ambivalence persisted, CPUSA and BPP had developed a mutually beneficial relationship (there were cases of double membership), in no small measure thanks to Patterson. *We Charge Genocide* was on the reading list of the BPP; in March 1970 *Black Panther*, the party's news organ, quoted Patterson in urging comrades to "take black genocide before [the] U.N."[44]

And so they formally did, at the Emergency Conference to Defend the Rights of the Black Panther Party, held at Chicago's Malcolm X College that same month. It was an open secret that CPUSA stood behind the conference.[45] According to *Daily World*, over five hundred conference participants represented 128 groups and organizations. The session chaired by Patterson (with the participation of Ralph D. Abernathy, Ossie Davis, and Dick Gregory) unanimously endorsed reviving the genocide initiative.[46] The conference consequently resolved sending to the United Nations a petition claiming violations of the Genocide Convention by the United States. The text of the petition appeared as a part of the BBP's ten-point program, made public by Rush in December 1969, and was later that fall endorsed by the newly established National Coalition Against War, Racism, and Repression. Reportedly signed by over one million people, the petition eventually made it to the United Nations. The delegation that delivered the document included artistic personalities Davis and Gregory. As to the substance, the petition made a case for systematic oppression of American blacks, manifesting itself in short lifespan, high infant mortality, deficient health care, poor education, and substandard housing. As before, "inflicting serious bodily or mental harm" and "creating conditions of life calculated to bring about physical destruction of a group" were among the specific provisions of the Genocide Convention that have been deemed applicable.[47] To boost the petition campaign, the Communist International Publishers in New York reprinted *We Charge Genocide*. The Soviet media rounded up the issue of police harassment of the Black Panthers by stressing the growing reprisals against those opposing the US policy of genocide, for example Angela Davis. The arrest of Davis, an academic and CPUSA member with links to the Black Panthers, on charges of conspiracy in murder caused a universal outcry. Her subsequent acquittal by jury trial cemented Davis's celebrity status in the Soviet Union and throughout the Communist world, especially in Cuba and East Germany.[48] The United States Information Agency mounted a worldwide campaign to portray the trial as an example of democracy at work. Among other things, the policy paper emphasized that "loose charges by Angela Davis Committees of genocide against black militants are not justified by the facts."[49] The person who helped organize the legal defense for Davis was Patterson.[50]

Despite the best efforts of the "anticapitalist" camp, the manifestly violent tactics made it hard to sell Black Panthers as victims of genocide. There is no indication that, say, the telegram of protest sent by the Communist Party of Canada to US president Nixon and the CHR in January 1970 had any effect at all. The telegram condemned the "criminal policy of genocide" of the US government vis-à-vis the black population.[51] The opponents of the Genocide Convention drew a direct line between the 1951 CRC petition—a "ticking time bomb"—and the Black Panthers' propaganda. Although the radical group had openly admitted to a calculated campaign to kill police, wrote *Human Events,* it actually accused police of waging a genocidal war against them.[52] Sometimes the argument against "sloganeering black militants" in the United States was contrasted with the allegations of genocide in Africa. Roy Wilkins of the *New York Post,* for example, in January 1971 angrily dismissed the charge of the Black Panthers by referring to a petition recently filed with the United Nations by two black Sudanese. With the death toll approaching 500,000, the petitioners accused the Arab-led Khartoum government of carrying out a policy of genocide in South Sudan. The fact that the government of Sudan used Soviet-built aircraft against the rebels served as aggravating circumstances.[53]

It will not be an exaggeration to say that in 1970 the Genocide Convention became a battlefield between the American Communists and the far right. The September 1970 issue of *Political Affairs,* a monthly of the CPUSA, carried a three-page editorial, "Against Genocide." It pointed out that the CPUSA had been charging the United States with genocide for twenty years, that is, since the publication of the CRC petition in 1951. The editorial called upon "every Communist and progressive, every reader of *Political Affairs*" to support the proratification campaign. A nationwide drive culminated in a series of demonstrations held in mid-November in New York City. The march down Fifth Avenue to the UN headquarters on November 21 was spearheaded by Patterson. This time it was the John Birch Society that did the monitoring. One of the organization's faithful from Illinois sarcastically noted that such advocacy caused great mental harm to a minority group—the John Birch Society—and should therefore be prosecuted as genocide.[54]

The November 1970 public appearance in connection with the Genocide Convention was also Patterson's last. The petition campaign was faltering, unable to reach the levels of publicity generated by the CRC back in the early 1950s. The State Department, which painstakingly monitored the international fallout of *We Charge Genocide* back then, spent no time reporting on the new edition of the book. Crucially, Patterson, who hit the rewind button, had lost faith in his utmost ally. After all was said and done, Patterson had remained an unreconstructed Communist who drew inspiration from the annals of Marxism-Leninism. He had hoped, but failed, to bring the Black Panthers into the ideological fold. Confronted by judicial terrorism—he charged in July 1970—the BPP still failed to appreciate the political power of mass action. He envisaged a broader black liberation front under the leadership of the Communists to stand against "racism and genocidal policies and practices of American imperialism." He further insisted, "One who wishes to be a revolutionary should mark well the centenary of the birth of Vladimir Ilyich Lenin which so recently took place in Moscow to say nothing about studying the theoretical conferences on 'Leninism and Contemporaneity' which took place in Prague late in 1969." Newton, Patterson's legal client, begged to differ. In his rebuttal in September 1970 he chastised Patterson for having failed to understand the intellectual debt of the BPP to Malcolm X. More than just a self-defense group, he argued, the BPP was at the vanguard of the struggle against imperialism in the United States. As for a comparison with the CPUSA, Newton challenged Patterson that the BPP did more in three years in mobilizing the black masses than the former had done in twenty. He altogether dismissed the CPUSA as having embraced the "bourgeois democratic electoral politics line."[55] Patterson, who had dutifully condemned "leftist deviation"—the catchall charge that Stalin, Molotov, and Vyshinsky used to do away with scores of Old Bolsheviks in the mid-1930s—spoke out against Maoism as espoused by Newton and Carmichael. With Patterson charging "counterrevolution" and Newton "revisionism," the split between two individuals, and essentially between the CPUSA and the BPP, was complete by 1972. The concomitant rapprochement between the United States and China made the divide unsurmountable. In effect, Patterson stuck (for life) to Moscow while the BPP sought inspiration in Beijing.[56]

On November 5, 1979 the National Black Human Rights Coalition, an umbrella organization that came into existence a year earlier, organized a march of some five thousand to the United Nations. The participants carried the slogans "Black People Charge Genocide" and "Human Rights Is the Right to Self-Determination."[57] Some of the protesters broke through the police cordons and presented to the UN officials a document analogous to the CRC's 1951 petition. *Pravda* made it sound as if the organization, whose name was not mentioned, represented the entire black population of the United States.[58]

The decline of the Black Panther Party in the 1970s and its eventual demise by 1982 was reflected in the dramatically reduced coverage in the Soviet press. The issue of genocide with regard to black Americans actually came up only once during the 1980s. On May 13, 1985, following an armed standoff, the Philadelphia police dropped a bomb on the house at 6221 Osage Avenue. The explosive killed eleven people, including five children, belonging to a radical black group, MOVE, who had holed themselves up in the house. A further sixty-five houses burned down as a result of the explosion. TASS insisted that the objective of the police operation was not dislodging the members of the organization but "physical destruction of the 'undesired.'"[59] *We Charge Genocide* was briefly in the news in March 1980. TASS singled out the CRC 1951 petition campaign as the most important achievement of William Patterson, who passed away earlier that month at the age of 89.[60]

THE PLIGHT OF AMERICAN INDIANS AIRED IN MOSCOW

By the late 1970s Soviet propaganda had increasingly identified Native Americans as the main target of genocide in the United States. The most fascinating aspect of the 1970 Senate hearings on the Genocide Convention had been reduced to a sentence and therefore completely overlooked. Deutsch, who testified against the convention for the ABA, and Fulbright, who variously promoted it, reached a consensus on one particular issue. As reported by the State Department, they agreed that US treatment of American Indians "had probably been genocide."[61] One gets the same sense from perusing the proratification arguments by the lobby groups. The American Jewish Committee, for instance, prepared a series of responses to the criticisms most commonly advanced against the Genocide Convention. One of these criticisms was that, if the United States acceded to the convention, the treatment of the blacks and "Indians" would fall under the terms of the treaty. In respect to the latter case, argued the document, the treaty's application was prospective, so that responsibility lay only with respect to future conduct.[62] From the perspective of the afflicted group, this sentence could be easily interpreted as an unwitting admission that the Native American population had been subject to genocide in the past. The opponents of the Genocide Convention, to be sure, wasted no time in making it part of their argument. Not to be outdone by the Black Panthers, wrote Michael S. Kogan in *Ideas*, the Indians of Wounded Knee had also considered leveling charges of genocide against American leaders.[63]

The first documented instance of Soviets referring to the extermination of Native Americans as "genocide" is from November 1948. To back up the Soviet argument that linked fascism, racism, and genocide, *Izvestia* printed a lengthy exposé of racial theory in the United States. The newspaper went particularly hard after the late Ellsworth Huntington and his *Mainsprings of Civilization*. The Soviet critics were not alone in questioning the scientific value of the book, including Huntington's theory of the demise of the Native Americans. They were first, though, in calling it a form of genocide.[64] Half a year later, *Sovetskaia Litva*, of all newspapers, compared Indian reservations to Nazi death camps.[65] Those probably would have remained passing references had not it been for the following precedent that made the Soviets realize the propaganda value inherent in the plight of the indigenous population. In the fall of 1950 a delegation of Iroquois approached Vyshinsky in New York. The head of the Soviet delegation at the Fifth General Assembly was handed a copy of the complaint that stated discrimination against Native Americans by the US government. Professor Vsevolod Durdenevsky promptly developed a legal discourse, according to which the Indian treaties—approved by both the Senate and the US president—had been within the domain of international law. The Native Americans, therefore, had the right to invoke the violations of the UN Charter.[66] *Novoe vremia* put it in less academic language by arguing that the US authorities set out to "destroy the surviving indigenous population of America." Truman was, then, a mere hypocrite and dissembler when he claimed that genocide "has not occurred in the United States."[67]

Nevertheless, it still remained a fleeting reference, with the issue lying dormant until the 1970s. The Russian-language edition of *We Charge Genocide* listed

Native Americans as victims of genocide, and so did Mikhail Andriukhin in his books. In June 1961 *Izvestia* carried a short story on the American Indian Conference in Chicago. According to the article, "Empty Words of Freedom, Reality of Genocide," over one thousand chieftains came together to condemn the continuous governmental policy aiming to eradicate the vestiges of aboriginal culture.[68] Never mind the exaggerated number of participants; the policy document drafted by the conference, Declaration of Indian Purpose, did not speak of genocide but of "duress, undue influence, unwarranted pressures, and policies." In May 1968 the Soviet press reported on the Poor People's Campaign in Washington, DC led by Reverend Ralph Abernathy. Abernathy was quoted as saying that, by condemning the Native Americans to death by starvation (e.g., through restrictions on fishing), the US Supreme Court had effectively authorized genocide.[69] *Izvestia*, ex post facto, narrated the symbolic occupation of Alcatraz Island by Native American activists. Dislodging the occupants in June 1971 was presented as part and parcel of the policy of racism and genocide by US authorities.[70]

Speaking out on behalf of ethnic minorities in the United States had a double function for the Soviets. The dominant motive, as the core argument of this book goes, was reinforcing the general front against the West. The defensive posture, characteristic of the first Socialist society, did not completely disappear as the Soviet global imprint grew, however. Moscow rulers cherished positive reviews, whatever the source. Traditionally, the biggest friends of the Soviet Union were found among American blacks. Now that the American Indian movement started taking shape, the Soviets could count on a larger pool of supporters. And so Claude Lightfoot, black activist and CPUSA member, chastised the "imperialist bourgeoisie and misguided left" for their criticism of the Soviet nationalities policy. Obviously, those who had tolerated genocide of Native Americans and slavery would now slander the proletarian internationalism of the USSR. Lightfoot swore in the name of American Communists to propagate Soviet achievements, especially its contribution to decolonization, and to protect it against defamation.[71] Taken up by the likes of Abernathy and Lightfoot, the cause of Native Americans since the mid-1960s had become a part of a broader New Left alliance. Influenced by the African American civil rights, Black Panthers, and Vietnam antiwar movements, Native American activists had borrowed some of their strategies, tactics, and rhetorical tools.[72] It was unsurprising, therefore, that the word *genocide* was soon injected into the conversation.

The State Department's white paper "Status of Indians in the United States" from January 1947 did not mention the crime of genocide or the treaty in the works that was supposed to address it. Once the Genocide Convention had been drafted, however, some perceptive commentators picked up on the past instances of mass violence that had so far eluded discussion. A few weeks before the genocide treaty went to a vote in the General Assembly, the UK delegation reported back to London on November 25, 1948 that the Americans "were afraid of accusations which may be made against them as a government in respect of the treatment of the negro and Red Indian populations of the United States."[73] Half a year later English-born author and historian William H. W. Sabine as well mentioned "extermination of the Redskins by the white Americans."[74]

The State Department's premonition proved correct and, as time passed, the Soviets sought further minority groups in the United States subject to genocide. In 1977 the list of alleged victims expanded on account of Puerto Ricans. According to an unofficial race chart, averred *Izvestia*, Puerto Ricans in the United States ranked second from the bottom, just above "Indians" yet below "Negroes." Claiming that the substandard living conditions in the Bronx borough of New York constituted genocide, though, was too much even for the experienced propagandists. So they settled on the term *social genocide*.[75] By 1984 genocide had allegedly also consumed Mexicans and a few other unspecified ethnic minorities in the United States. *Pravda* excelled in casuistry when noting that these minority groups were "cast by racism into the category of deprived of rights [*bespravnye*]."[76] Along the way, the Soviets incorporated the indigenous populations of Canada and Australia on the ever growing genocide roster. The reference for the former was Claude Fournier's 1974 western film *Alien Thunder*, and for the latter a statement issued by the World Council of Churches at its conference in Melbourne in May 1980. The issue of genocide came up also in connection with a conference on aboriginal constitutional matters held in March 1983 in Ottawa. As mediated by *Pravda*, the Canadian government was guilty of bending the land property rights of the native peoples in favor of American oil companies.[77]

The State Department once again proved prophetic in its earlier observation that the faraway trust territories of the United States might eventually become a target of Soviet propaganda. Sure enough, not all Pacific islands mentioned in an October 1983 issue of *Izvestia* belonged to that category or were administered by the United States for that matter: Samoa, Tonga, Fiji, Hawaii, Marquesas. The thrust of the Soviet argument was the same, though—certain indigenous peoples residing on those islands had since the nineteenth century become victims of virtual genocide. As elements of genocide *Izvestia* listed alcoholism, noxious diseases, and widespread desperation.[78]

By 1977 Native Americans replaced black Americans in the top spot of the genocide index as designed by Soviet propagandists. The recalibration of the message was due to both international human rights politics and a violent turn in the American Indian civil rights movement. A conflict on the Pine Ridge Indian Reservation resulted in the lethal shooting of two FBI agents on June 26, 1975. The suspect, Native American activist Leonard Peltier, two years earlier took part in an armed standoff with federal forces at Wounded Knee. On April 18, 1977 a jury trial in Fargo, North Dakota delivered its verdict, sentencing Peltier to two life sentences on charges of first-degree murder. Three days later, *Izvestia* denounced the verdict as fabrication and described the sentencing of Peltier as a continuation of the policy of genocide against the Native Americans.[79] What Angela Davis was for the Soviets briefly in the early 1970s, Peltier remained throughout the 1980s. Voiced internationally, doubts over legal proceedings sustained the image of Peltier as a quintessential victim of genocide, as construed in the Soviet media. In the wake of the trial, the first UN Conference on Indians in the Americas, held in September 1977 in Geneva, condemned the "policy of discrimination and genocide carried out against the Indians by the USA and other imperialist states on the American continent."[80] The message was shaped by the International Indian Treaty Council, an offshoot of the American Indian Movement (AIM)—a radical advocacy group with a nongovernmental consultative status in the United Nations. The conference opened with a presentation by Russell Means, former leader of the AIM. Means called President Carter a "racist" who talked about "human rights the world over when my people are suffering planned genocide." By so doing he obviously played into the hands of the Soviets, who were eager to counter Western criticism of reported Soviet human rights abuses. Indeed, the director of the Treaty Council had earlier taken AIM's contention and supporting evidence to the Soviet Mission to the United Nations for delivery at the forthcoming CSCE conference in Belgrade.[81] Means, too, acknowledged the Soviet enthusiasm for the conference. As he further explained: "[T]hey wanted anyone who dissented against the United States in their camp." Following the Geneva conference, Means went on a sponsored tour of Bulgaria, Hungary, and East Germany.[82] As for specific charges, the Soviet press typically mentioned widespread poverty, high child mortality, disproportionate unemployment rates, deficient antenatal care, and prosecution of activists. A wretched existence on reservations, compared to concentration camps, supposedly constituted economic, social, and cultural genocide.[83]

In 1978 the AIM organized the Longest Walk across America to protest against abrogation of Indian treaties. Starting, symbolically, on Alcatraz Island in February, participants reached Washington, DC in July. There, one activist used the word *genocide* to illustrate the attempts of transnational corporations to seize Indian lands rich in mineral resources. An AIM co-founder, Clyde H. Bellecourt, made a much more serious claim related to forced sterilization when characterizing US policy vis-à-vis Native Americans as "genocide." Yet the tenet of an interview with Bellecourt, as conducted by a Soviet journalist, was that the United States had no right to pinpoint human rights violations abroad (read: in the Communist bloc) before putting its own house in order.[84] Smaller in scale, the Long Walk for Survival traversed the same route in June–November 1980. As before, the fight against genocide was among its slogans. Around the same time the United Nations received a formal complaint, in which the tribal leaders charged the US government with genocide of the Native Americans.[85]

In the first half of the 1980s the AIM had received substantial coverage in the Soviet press. Ironically, by then the organization had long been defunct, crushed by the persistent legal assault of the US government on the one hand and vicious infighting and paranoia in the wake of the Wounded Knee occupation on the other. Needless to say, no mention had been made that the AIM was never the whole of the American Indian movement.[86] The controversial AIM figures such as Means and Dennis Banks were using various international forums to expose the "policy of genocide vis-à-vis the Native population of America." Simultaneously, they sought international recognition for the Indian treaties binding the US government. *Pravda* reported, with a two-year delay, on the people's tribunal organized by Banks in Davis, California. With the participation of dozens of organizations and tribes from both Americas, the September 1982 tribunal found the state of South Dakota—the site of the massacre at Wounded Knee in 1890 and the shootout at the same location in 1973—guilty of murder and genocide.

Imprisoned for his alleged role in the Wounded Knee incident, Peltier had established a permanent presence in the Soviet media. He was typically portrayed as an antigenocide rebel and a symbol of the duplicity of the United States, which was "censuring other countries on human rights." The constant references to genocide and racial discrimination in the United States earned a reproof from the State Department, which accused Soviet authorities of misrepresenting Peltier's case. Nonchalantly, the Soviet media created an allegory of the American "civilization" scalping Peltier, now portrayed as a chieftain and one of the few Native Americans still alive. Peltier was described as "prisoner of conscience," the term commonly used by the West with regard to jailed human rights activists in the Communist bloc.[87] A delegation of Peltier's defense council and Native American activists had on several occasions traveled to Moscow to plead for international attention. When Mikhail Gorbachev, sometime in late 1985, got a question about Andrei Sakharov, he countered it with the name of Peltier. In May 1988 the Soviet Peace Committee gave a hero's welcome to Tony Gonzales of the International Indian Treaty Council and Nilak Butler of the Leonard Peltier Defense Committee. In an interview broadcast by *Vremia* (the main Soviet TV news program), they accused the United States of genocide and demanded a meeting with Ronald Reagan on Indian issues. The interview was part of a commentary criticizing the US president for meeting with dissidents and Jewish refuseniks.[88]

The focus on Native Americans had rendered a broader perspective on genocide reflecting the present status of Soviet-American relations. The accelerating nuclear arms race made a Soviet commentator speak of mass psychosis in the United States comparable with the situation in Germany on the eve of the Nazi takeover. *Izvestia* and *LG* political analyst Vitaly Kobysh emphasized the cult of power, which he said was born during the conquest of the American West. The method of genocide originally tested by white settlers on American Indians had recently been applied in Korea, Indochina, Nicaragua, and El Salvador.[89] The revelations about the forced sterilization of an estimated one-fourth of all Native American women in the first half of the 1970s reinvigorated the Soviet criticism of the United States' failure to adhere to the Genocide Convention.[90] For the last time, it appears, the Soviet press commented on the situation of Native Americans within the context of genocide in November 1988. The article that appeared in *Pravda* was prompted by the brief arrest (for contempt of court) of an AIM leader, Vernon Bellecourt, two months earlier.[91]

8 · SOVIET-TURKISH RELATIONS AND SOCIALIST ARMENIA

THE ARMENIAN ETHNIC TRAUMA AS A FOREIGN POLITICAL ISSUE

Specific to the Soviet Union was an academic study of genocide pioneered by ethnic Armenian scholars. Obviously, it had to do with the collective trauma of mass murder committed in the late 19th and early 20th centuries by Ottoman Turks. When it comes to commemoration, the Armenian Communist leadership ended up performing a balancing act between their ethnic identity and party discipline. The issue of genocide came up on the wave of ethnic nationalism during Khrushchev's Thaw and reflected the status of Soviet-Turkish relations. The latter, in its turn, were largely dependent on the state of Turkish-American relations, cutting through Cold War politics.

The Orthodox Armenians traditionally perceived of Russia as a protector against Muslim Turkey. The Armenian Soviet Socialist Republic emerged out of the tumult of the First World War and the Bolshevik Revolution. To placate Turkey, Lenin's government in 1918 ceded the provinces of Kars and Ardahan in Eastern Anatolia and in 1923 formally transferred the Mountainous Karabakh (Nagorno-Karabakh) region, predominantly settled by Armenians, under Azerbaijani jurisdiction. This territorial adjustment made Stalin, then commissar for nationalities, declare the Armenian Question solved once and for all. To Stalin's dismay, in October 1939 Turkey signed a mutual assistance pact with Britain and France. Nevertheless, in March 1941 Ankara committed to a neutrality agreement with the USSR. Eventually, on February 23, 1945, Ankara declared war on Germany. Negotiating from a position of strength, in June of that year the Soviet Union demanded from Turkey the return, on ethnic grounds, of the provinces of Kars and Ardahan. More consequentially, Moscow sought the revision of the 1936 Montreux Convention that gave Turkey full control of the Black Sea Straits, thus provoking an international crisis, which in its turn led up to the Truman Doctrine. Turkey's alignment with the West was formalized through NATO membership in 1952. In the wake of Stalin's death Khrushchev sought rapprochement with Turkey, once again renouncing Soviet territorial claims. In spite of the Kremlin's overtures, the bilateral relations only began to improve by 1963, in the advent of the Cyprus crisis and the rise of the Turkish left, to name just a few factors.[1]

Not coincidentally, the first academic works, in both Armenian and Russian, examining the destruction of the Armenian communities in Ottoman Turkey started appearing also in 1963. Thus, the historical-philological journal of the Armenian Academy of Science printed an article with the title, "The Genocide of Armenians in the Ottoman Empire and the Accountability of Imperial Germany." The fiftieth anniversary of the massacres, perhaps for the first time in the Soviet Union, was marked with a series of academic lectures and publications. One of the papers delivered at the joint session of the Armenian Academy of Science and the University of Yerevan in April 1965 held British imperialism accountable for the ethnic violence perpetrated by the Young Turks. Another examined falsifications in Turkish historiography. Yet the final presentations advanced the politically correct thesis, according to which the regeneration of the Armenian people was only possible within the framework of the Soviet Union. Naturally, the authors writing on this subject were obliged to fit their narrative into the procrustean bed of Marxist ideology. Whereas the selected documents published in the Proceedings of the Armenian Academy of Science was a difficult format to mold ideologically, a major monograph by John Kirakosyan that came out the same year in Yerevan proved not. The 512-page-long book, *The First World War and Western Armenians, 1914–1916*, originally appeared in Armenian and was later translated into Russian. Kirakosyan, a professional historian and Communist Party propagandist, emphasized the connivance of British imperialism in the slaughter masterminded by Turkish "reactionaries." Simultaneously, he lashed out against Armenian nationalists represented by the Dashnaktsutyun Party (the Armenian Revolutionary Federation). However, even this fairly balanced analysis did not measure up to the official Soviet version of history. That is what Grigory Akopyan implied in his book review in *Voprosy istorii*. Akopyan argued that the author did not sufficiently explain the failure of Armenian nationalists to reach out to "Turkey's progressive forces." Only the unified toilers' front against the common enemy could have alleviated the situation of ethnic minorities, including the Armenians, in Ottoman Turkey, insisted the reviewer.[2]

Kirakosyan was one of the three Armenian academics who proposed—perhaps for the first time ever—the idea of building a genocide memorial. The suggestion came in the form of an open letter sent in July 1963 to the Central Committee of the Communist Party of Armenia. Notably, the letter suggested financing the construction through private donations. The ever-growing number of initiatives coming from various quarters left the Armenian Communist leadership no choice but to react. On November 13, 1964 the head of the Armenian

Party branch, Yakov Zarobyan, proposed to the Central Committee in Moscow a series of events marking the mass destruction of Armenians in 1915. Zarobyan made his case by enveloping it in ideologically correct language. According to his reading of history, genocide of the Armenians was a corollary of the Pan-Turkish agenda to sever the Caucasus from Russia. Soviet Russia, on the other hand, not only brought the Armenian nation back from the dead but also propelled it into the Communist era. The influential, numerically strong Armenian Diaspora had traditionally commemorated genocide on April 24. Acting on selfish and provocative grounds, the reactionary Dashnaktsutyun was now claiming that a mere absence of formal commemoration of genocide in the Soviet Union amounted to denial, Zarobyan pressed his point. His proposal was thus supposed to neutralize the nationalist forces and to simultaneously highlight the genius of the Soviet Communist Party. Specifically, he suggested (a) preparing propaganda materials that would interpret the 1915 genocide from the Marxist-Leninist position and unmask the "Imperialists and their Dashnak proxies"; (b) organizing in Yerevan a closed event with the general theme "The October Revolution and the Renaissance of the Armenian People"; (c) erecting an obelisk in memory of the Armenians fallen in the First World War; and (d) arranging cultural programs in the Armenian émigré centers abroad to trumpet the achievements of Soviet Armenia. None of these proposals should jeopardize the current normalization of Soviet-Turkish relations, added the secretary of the Communist Party of Armenia, censoring himself.[3]

Then and later, the top Armenian officials spoke more like representatives of the people than Communist functionaries. Their higher-ups in Moscow saw it as a problem. Soviet foreign minister Andrei Gromyko did not want to revive the territorial dispute with Turkey, member of the CPSU Politburo Mikhail Suslov sought to preserve ideological purity, and one of the few surviving Old Bolsheviks, Anastas Mikoyan, just exercised caution.[4] Consequently, as the sad anniversary drew nearer, the Armenian Communist Party had to consistently renege on both the ethnic and legal aspect of mass atrocities. As of early March 1965, the heroism of the Armenian nation and its resurrection under Communism became the centerpiece of the planned commemoration. Another slogan designated the USSR as the homeland of the Armenians worldwide. In the end, all that remained on the agenda for April 24 was a closed session at the Yerevan State Academic Theater.[5] The article by Mkrtich Nersisyan and Nikolai Ushakov that appeared in *Pravda* on April 24 made all the right noises. The masterminds of mass crimes earned the wrath of the broader toiling masses of Turkey, contended historian Nersisyan and scholar of international law Ushakov. This is why, following the collapse of German imperialism, the Turkish people threw the Young Turks into the dustbin of history. Due to its anti-imperialist policy, the new Turkey was able to quickly establish friendly relations with the nascent Soviet state. Otherwise, the article bore the exact same title as the book by Mikhail Andriukhin, "Genocide:

The Most Heinous Crime against Humanity," and exercised the familiar themes. Endemic to capitalist exploitation, genocide made appearances in Nazi Germany and presently plagued the United States, South Africa, South Vietnam, and Portuguese colonies. The article's conclusion, however, reflected the growing Soviet confidence in the ultimate victory of Socialism. The defeat of Nazism saw the expansion of Communism into Eastern Europe; the developing countries of Asia, Africa, and South America were all seeking Soviet support. "Imperialism will not be able to implement its darkest designs even by means of genocide," declared Nersisyan and Ushakov, "the future belongs to socialism, to communism."[6] Three years later the Soviet media went even further, promoting the thesis that the Armenians, as the first people ever to experience genocide, were able to attain statehood only within the Soviet Union.[7]

The academic-cum-ideological discourse on the destruction of Armenians in Ottoman Turkey had broader, political implications. An article similar to *Pravda*'s—though apparently with a tougher line on contemporary Turkey—also appeared in *Sovetskaia Armeniia*. In a show of solidarity, Armenian students in Moscow planned a demonstration in front of the Turkish embassy, but were forced by the police to disperse. Remarkably, it was not the Soviet press but the *New York Times* that reported on the attempted demonstration.[8] What happened in Yerevan that same day—merely twelve years after Stalin's death—was truly unprecedented in the context of the Soviet state. Authorities had gravely misjudged popular sentiment, as close to one hundred thousand people gathered at the central Lenin Square. The gathering was spontaneous and featured a handful of slogans, none of them using the word *genocide*. One of the placards demanded "Return Our Lands" (i.e., Eastern Anatolia and Mountainous Karabakh), another pleaded for a "Just Solution to the Armenian Question," while still another simply reminded "1915."[9] The KGB reported a group of five thousand breaking into the theater building during the commemorative meeting.[10] Panicked calls to bring in the army were overrun by both First Secretary Zarobyan and the supreme military commander in Armenia.[11] Remarkably, no criminal charges were laid, and no top officials of the MVD or KGB lost their job. The purge within the Armenian Communist Party and state apparatus, however, was extensive, culminating in the dismissal of Zarobyan in February 1966.[12]

In a powerful demonstration of the people's will, the protesters demanded an official recognition of genocide by the Soviet government and the construction of an appropriate memorial to its victims. To avert further ethnic tensions, the work on the memorial commenced in 1966, and on November 29, 1967 (i.e., the forty-seventh anniversary of Soviet Armenia) it stood ready, on a hill overlooking the capital city and conveniently separated from the latter by a river. In the architectural tradition of Soviet war memorials, which started appearing throughout the Soviet Union in the mid-1960s, the Yerevan monument bore no particular national symbols. By interpreting the Armenian suffering in the same language and visual forms as the Soviet sacrifices in the Second World War, the Communist leadership aptly incorporated the Turkish atrocities into the amorphous category of fascism. At that, the Tsitsernakaberd memorial complex did not have any inscriptions—a compromise to Soviet foreign policy, which proscribed unnecessarily antagonizing Turkey.[13] Indeed, after two decades of confrontation, in the 1960s the Soviet Union set out to normalize its relations with Turkey. Gromyko traveled to Ankara in 1965, followed by the visit of Prime Minister Süleyman Demirel to Moscow two years later. Upon concluding his trip, Demirel proclaimed a new era in Soviet-Turkish relations. In a newspaper interview on October 14, 1967 he stated, "Today there is no enmity between Turkey and the Soviet Union." This trend persisted all the way through the late 1980s.[14]

As just mentioned, the demonstrators in Yerevan articulated the territorial claims against both Turkey and Azerbaijan. The nexus between the issue of land and that of genocide, Mountainous Karabakh and Eastern Anatolia, is more significant than it may first appear. Even earlier, Armenian intellectuals had on several occasions appealed to the Communist authorities to restore Karabakh and Nakhichevan (an Azerbaijani enclave within Armenia) to Armenia. One such appeal served as a basis for a similar request by the Armenian leadership to the CPSU Central Committee in September 1966. Signed by First Secretary of the Armenian Communist Party Anton Kochinyan and Prime Minister Badal Muradyan, the letter identified the territorial loss rather than genocide as "Armenia's greatest national tragedy." The Turkish policy of denial, therefore, aimed to exculpate both those concomitant acts. The Armenian leaders rubbed their superiors the right way by saying that the "toiling masses" shared in the wisdom of Soviet foreign policy. However, insofar as an argument against raising the territorial issue with Turkey had been met with a certain understanding, authorities in Yerevan had problems explaining to the people why both autonomous regions had not been duly rejoined with Armenia.[15] According to political scientist Richard H. Dekmejian, the upsurge of nationalism in Armenia correlated with the improvement in Soviet-Turkish relations. The Armenian Communist leadership thus took a calculated risk by opening the discussion on genocide in the attempt to dampen nationalist sentiments. This decision, however, had the opposite effect and, in the long run, weakened the central authority.[16] In retrospect, the genocide discourse manifestly failed to reconcile the demands from above with those from below, and not only in Socialist Armenia.

Part and parcel of the Soviet propaganda, the discourse on Armenia, by Armenians, was tightly controlled. The unauthorized mass demonstrations that took authorities by surprise three years previously had been channeled, from April 1968 onward, into organized, though not officially sanctioned, mourning processions to the Tsitsernakaberd. Beginning in the mid-1970s, senior government and Communist Party officials took a more visible role in the march of remembrance by laying wreaths at the memorial early in the morning. Ordinary participants followed, carrying wreaths with black ribbons and the standard inscription: "To the Victims of Genocide/name of the agency." At the same time, April 24 was not a public holiday, and employees were penalized for leaving work to attend the commemorative ceremony. As a way out, people made the trek after working hours or simply slipped away.[17]

Exactly ten years had elapsed since the 1915 atrocities for the first time became a subject of conversation in the Soviet Union. Brezhnev had summoned his top ideologist, Mikhail Suslov, to discuss an action plan in the run-up to the sixtieth anniversary.[18] The intervening period, needless to say, was marked by complete silence. Yet, the word was out, and the word was *genocide*. Armenian dissidents used it, for example, in a 1974 issue of the underground journal *Faros* to describe purported plans by Soviet authorities to bring more ethnic Russians into Armenia.[19] As became clear during the discussions within the Communist Party ten years earlier, the so-called Armenian Question had broader international ramifications. The Armenian émigré organizations did indeed attempt to insert references to the mass murder of 1915 in a major UN study of the Genocide Convention commissioned in the late 1960s by ECOSOC. The preliminary report by Special Rapporteur Nicodéme Ruhashyankiko of Rwanda included, as part of a historical survey, a short paragraph that spoke of the "massacres of Armenians, which have been described as 'the first case of genocide in the twentieth century.'" As the CHR's Sub-Commission on Prevention of Discrimination and Protection of Minorities came to discuss Paragraph 30 on March 6, 1974, among other observers in the meeting room, unexpectedly, was a delegation from Soviet Armenia. In a subsequent report to the KGB, Kirakosyan—who in 1975 was appointed foreign minister of the Armenian SSR—related that the Soviet and British delegations had abstained from the vote and that the reference was eventually excluded from the final text. According to Kirakosyan, the Armenian Diaspora, which stood behind Paragraph 30, had then launched a massive campaign to get the reference reintroduced.[20] These efforts proved in vain and Ruhashyankiko's study, when it finally appeared in July 1978, failed to mention Armenia and Armenians. The Soviet reluctance to back the inclusion of Paragraph 30 was seen as contradictory, especially since the Special Rapporteur did cite in support of the claim that the Armenians were the first victims of genocide in the twentieth century, among others, the document collection edited by Nersisyan and published in 1966 in Yerevan.[21]

Appearing in *Pravda* on April 24, 1975, a lengthy article, "Imperialism as Perpetrator of Genocide," attempted to reclaim the conversation. The date of publication was predictable, while the personality of the author was not. Academic Victor Ambartsumyan had built his international reputation as a founder of theoretical astrophysics. The longest serving president of the Armenian Academy of Science had superb expertise in stellar astronomy and the cosmogony of galaxies, but not necessarily in international law and European history. It did not matter after all, since the ideological matrix had existed for a long time. Most likely, it was Ambartsumyan's affiliation with the Armenian Society for Cultural Relations with Foreign Countries that landed him the job of writing the newspaper piece. The entire article could be summarized in one equally rambling sentence: The Armenian nation was only able to survive as part of the Soviet Union, which defeated Nazi Germany and thus stopped genocide, that definite manifestation of imperialism.[22] The magnanimity of the Russian people served also as the underlining theme of the Armenian film *Nahapet,* based on a 1965 novel. The film's main character, a lone survivor, was shown rebuilding his life in Soviet Armenia.[23] Released in 1977, the film made it to the Cannes Film Festival the following year. By 1979 the formula had appeared: "the first genocide in human history had been perpetrated in 1915–16 in Western Armenia."[24] Soviet propagandists failed to explain why this and similar pronouncements did not translate into an official Soviet position on the Armenian genocide, articulated both domestically and internationally.

At the conclusion of yet another ten-year cycle, on April 24, 1985 Ambartsumyan received the task and/or was able to print the conventional article on Armenia and genocide. Along with the familiar themes of Western imperialism and Nazi racism, Russian high-mindedness and Armenian attainments within the family of Soviet peoples, Ambartsumyan tackled two new topics. Playing by the book, he described how the Armenians had implemented the decisions of the June 1983 Plenum of the CPSU Central Committee. More instructive, however, was his ideological wrapping of genocide denial. On the eve of the fortieth anniversary of V-Day, some bourgeois historians were trying to distort the causes and lessons of the Second World War to whitewash the Nazi crimes, he claimed. Within this context, "certain elements [*takie golosa*] in the West" took to denying the fact of genocide perpetrated against the Armenian minority in Turkey, disallowing massacres as a facet of population transfers.[25]

The article in *Pravda* was sanctioned by the CPSU Politburo as a concession to the Armenian Communist leadership. The Politburo earlier that year considered the proposal to declare April 24 the Day of Commemoration of the Victims of Genocide. The proposal was turned down, and the meeting's transcript explained why. Among other items on its agenda, the February 21 meeting discussed "measures in connection with the 70th anniversary of genocide against the Armenians." The debate projected the Soviet leadership's desire to reconcile domestic and foreign policy, less so to accommodate the needs of the Armenian population, when dealing with the issue of genocide. First Secretary of the Armenian Communist Party Karen Demirchyan apparently spoke on behalf of his people while using the politically correct language. The Armenian Diaspora, under the guidance of the CIA, had claimed Soviet indifference toward the 1915 genocide in the attempt to harness anti-Soviet sentiments among the Armenian population. The US House of Representatives, at the same time, had adopted a resolution declaring April 24 the Day of Remembrance of Man's Inhumanity to Man. Turkey pressured the congressmen to withdraw the resolution and simultaneously sponsored terrorism inside Armenia as well as against Soviet diplomats abroad. To stop the tide of anti-Sovietism, Demirchyan suggested introducing an official day of commemoration, accompanied by a public address broadcast on radio and TV.[26]

In his proposition the top Armenian Communist received unlikely support from the KGB. KGB deputy head Philipp Bobkov anticipated up to 300,000 people taking part in the 1985 commemoration. Meanwhile he said he was alarmed by increased nationalist activity inside Armenia, the agitation by Turkey—which argued that genocide had been provoked by Armenians themselves—and the rising number of terrorist acts, especially by the Armenian Secret Army for the Liberation of Armenia. In his opinion, Demirchyan's proposal would have helped in seizing the initiative and exercising better control over the population. The members of the Politburo, however, were unconvinced. Would not it have had the opposite effect of aggravating ethnic tensions, wondered Soviet premier Nikolai Tikhonov. Gromyko warned against playing up to the Armenian Diaspora. Had Turkey installed on its territory nuclear missiles aimed at the USSR, that would be a serious threat indeed, he contended. Otherwise, the country's history was replete with sad anniversaries, beginning with the invasion of Batu Khan in the 13th century, to warrant a decree at Republican level. *Pravda* editor in chief Mikhail Zimianin said his newspaper had in the past printed editorials on the issue under discussion, dedicating a mere paragraph to genocide. He believed that the United States was trying to play off the Soviet Union against Turkey on account of genocide. An official endorsement of the Day of Commemoration in Armenia would thus be regarded as an act hostile to Turkey. Tikhonov reminded that Istanbul could at will close the Dardanelles and the Bosphorus. Now that the Soviet-Turkish relations were improving, the Americans would have been clear winners had this relationship deteriorated once again. Tikhonov said he found only five sentences concerning genocide in the *Pravda* article from April 24, 1975, and that was more than enough. After all, the Soviet people had gone though much greater tragedies such as in Belorussia during the Nazi occupation. Gorbachev, who chaired the meeting, sided with the majority. He proposed a resolution allowing the Armenian Communist Party to conduct the commemoration of genocide, but to no greater extent than in the past. The Politburo concurred that, in accordance with the class position, the focus of the commemoration should be on the present achievements of the Armenian people rather than on the past trauma.[27]

Top Armenian officials continued emphasizing the foreign policy aspect in their quest for a countrywide recognition of the genocide, but to no avail. This was a leitmotif, for example, of a 1986 white paper by Shavarsh Simonyan,

Minister of Education of the Armenian SSR. Claiming the profound sympathy of the Armenian Diaspora toward the Soviet Union, Simonyan argued that the United States was trying to break this bond by distorting the Soviet position on the Armenian genocide. Driven by military and political considerations—not incorrectly, contended the minister—the American administration and NATO were supporting Turkey on this issue while trying to make the international community believe otherwise. In order to retain the support of the émigré Armenians, Simonyan proposed publishing a relevant piece of research. Such an academic publication would pinpoint the genuine efforts of Soviet Russia and specifically of Lenin to undo the consequences of the Armenian genocide, and simultaneously reveal the pernicious role of British and German imperialism as well as the hypocrisy of the present US/Western diplomacy.[28]

Yet the Soviet Politburo did not bite into this argument. As discussed earlier, since the mid-1960s the Soviets had pursued a policy dictating that a pound in the purse was worth two in the book. In this particular context, maintaining the high moral ground on the issue of the Armenian genocide did not match up to the immediate concerns over Turkish military capabilities. Coincidence or not, Soviet-Turkish relations had received a boost shortly preceding the anniversary of the genocide. By courting Ankara, Moscow was effectively seeking to discredit Washington. Following the deep freeze of the 1950s (e.g., in 1959 the Americans placed in Turkey ballistic missiles with nuclear warheads), the relations between the two countries improved significantly by the mid-1960s. The United States had refused NATO assistance in the event of Turkish intervention in Cyprus, while the Soviet Union promised to remain neutral in the crisis. The creation of the Mediterranean naval squadron in 1964, as part of the new Soviet military doctrine, required talking to the Turks. In the summer of 1965 the USSR extended a line of credit to Ankara, so that by the end of the decade Turkey had become one of the largest Third World recipients of Soviet economic aid. Turkey permitted the transfer of Soviet arms to Syria and Iraq over its territory in 1970, and overflights of equipment to the Arabs in the 1973 Yom Kippur War. Moscow reciprocated by refraining from criticizing the Turkish invasion of Cyprus in the summer of 1974. The United States, however, early the next year cut military aid to Turkey in response to the invasion. The Soviets won big when Turkey, in retaliation, closed the American bases. Yet the victory proved ephemeral since the Turks did not mean to lose their leverage against the USSR and, three years later, reopened the bases. This news was all the more humiliating as it came on the heels of the Turkish-Soviet agreement on the Principles of Good Neighborly and Friendly Cooperation. Subsequently the Americans stepped up their efforts to cement Turkey's allegiance to the West by negotiating a new economic package and making it into a base for the new Rapid Deployment Force. In spite of that, in 1984 Turkey signed the largest ever economic agreement with the Soviet Union involving supplies of crude oil and gas.[29] The 570,000-strong Turkish army, 500 nuclear warheads stored in the country, and the US promise of coproduction of 140 nuclear-capable F-16s—these figures alone were enough to keep the Soviets on their toes.[30] Outnumbering Soviet divisions in the region, including those in Afghanistan, by two to one, Turkey was on Moscow's mind whenever the words *genocide* and *Armenia* were spelled out.

As a matter of fact, the US position on the Armenian genocide was not significantly different from that of the Soviet, colored by similar considerations. Consecutive US administrations showed little appetite for historical controversies involving their Cold War allies. For example, on June 18, 1970 the counselor of the Turkish embassy made his way to the Department of State to warn that any mention of massacres of Armenians by Turks during and after the First World War in connection with the Genocide Convention would produce an "unfortunate effect" in contemporary Turkey. The counselor was specifically referring to US senator Proxmire, who had earlier that month drawn this parallel as an argument in favor of US ratification of the treaty. Department of State officials replied that the administration had no intention of ever referring to the "Armenian situation" in the context of the Genocide Convention.[31] This position had solidified during the first half of the 1980s, as Turkey had acquired new strategic importance to the United States. As just mentioned, the United States maintained a military air base and communication facilities in Turkey, which also functioned as the CIA's key listening post in the Middle East. Turkey maintained the largest military force of any NATO ally and received the third largest share of US military assistance behind Israel and Egypt. Hence a Department of State background briefing from 1982 regarded the historical record of 1915 "ambiguous" and censured references to genocide.[32]

THE ECHO OF GENOCIDE IN KARABAKH

The violent death of up to one million Armenians in 1915–1918 potently reverberated in the waning days of the Soviet Union. The policy of liberalization introduced by Gorbachev removed the lid from the simmering ethnic conflicts, specifically in the Caucasus. As mentioned earlier, the Mountainous Karabakh region in 1923 was formally transferred under Azerbaijani jurisdiction as a means of mollifying neighboring Turkey. Simmering tension in Karabakh burst into the open in 1978 in the form of an open letter to Brezhnev. Armenian writer and Communist Party member Sero Khanzadyan bitterly complained about the persecution of ethnic Armenians in Karabakh and Nakhichevan. A companion document invoked Article III of the Genocide Convention to argue that by destroying the vestiges of Armenian culture in the latter region, Azerbaijani authorities had created unbearable living conditions for the remaining Armenians. The same "genocidal methods" were presently extended to Mountainous

Karabakh, insisted Khanzadyan. As an example, he referred to the purge of Armenian intellectuals who in 1975 collected signatures for the absorption of the region into Soviet Armenia.[33]

The growing discontent culminated in mass demonstrations and a formal request for the unification of Mountainous Karabakh with Armenia in February 1988. In reaction, Azerbaijani mobs in Sumgait, a city northwest of Baku, staged a pogrom against local Armenians. The pogrom lasted from February 26 to March 1 and left at least thirty-two dead. Caught unprepared, the Soviet leadership allowed only muted coverage of the Sumgait pogrom in the media, unwittingly fomenting rumors of genocide.[34] At a demonstration of protest organized in Moscow, an Armenian activist blamed the massacre on the Communist leadership of Azerbaijan. "Even the Germans were more humane in their genocide than these Muslims," he told the crowd two weeks later. This claim was backed by as many as one thousand demonstrators, who hoisted banners declaring "Karabakh Was and Will Be Armenian" and "Shame to the Proponents of Genocide."[35] Coincidentally, a popular Karabakh Movement, which had advocated for absorbing the autonomous region into Armenia, started taking shape weeks before the Sumgait pogrom. The anti-Armenian violence not only reinvigorated the separatist movement but also equipped it with the potent reference to genocide. Harutyun Marutyan has argued that the subject matter of genocide had effectively propelled the Karabakh Movement.[36]

Soviet dissident historian Roy Medvedev objected that the criminal trial of Sumgait perpetrators held later that year indicted defendants for murder rather than a "programmatic act of genocide."[37] Characteristic was an exchange in the Presidium of the Supreme Soviet between Gorbachev and an Armenian delegate, Professor Sergei Ambartsumyan (the namesake of Victor Ambartsumyan). On July 18, 1988 the Presidium held an extraordinary session on the crisis in Mountainous Karabakh. Despite his visible indecisiveness, Gorbachev proved a farsighted politician as far as the issue of genocide was concerned:

AMBARTSUMYAN: Prior to entering into a dialog with you, I regard my duty as a communist, educator, dean to tell the whole truth about the difficult situation that had ensued in our Republic.

GORBACHEV: May I ask you a direct question? Are you sure that you are speaking in the name of the people?

AMBARTSUMYAN: The speaker expressed the opinion that in Sumgait has taken place attempted genocide.

GORBACHEV: Genocide is a certain policy, premeditated, racial, but not spontaneous. In Sumgait, however, the dregs of society went on a rampage. Their identity has been established. As for genocide, it is a policy of extermination deliberately carried out with regard to a certain people or minority. Why would you ascribe a bandit escapade to the whole of Azerbaijan? What sort of genocide can we talk about here? You certainly know the word's worth. You may regret your whole life throwing around such accusations.[38]

Such a cautious approach made Andrei Sakharov—top nuclear physicist, human rights activist, and Nobel Peace Prize winner—declare that the "central authorities are extremely indecisive and partial [while] Armenian people are again facing the threat of genocide." His wife and fellow dissident Elena Bonner went even further, accusing the Soviet leaders of adopting a pro-Azerbaijan position and "letting the population of Nagorno-Karabakh succumb to genocide." On the other side of the Atlantic, Governor George Deukmejian of California—then the highest ranking elected official of Armenian descent in the United States—indirectly urged Gorbachev to take action to alleviate the risk of "another Armenian genocide."[39] Gorbachev's reluctance to get embroiled in the genocide discourse can be explained in part through the just mentioned link between international law and territorial grievances. The allegations of genocide in Mountainous Karabakh strengthened the calls for boundary revision in Armenia's favor. This, however, was taboo for the (post-Khrushchev) Communist leadership. Any change in the existing status quo threatened to unravel the multinational fabric of the Soviet Union. Therefore, whatever his personal convictions, as the head of state Gorbachev had no choice but to stand by the principle of immutability of borders and consequently play down fears of genocide.

The Sumgait massacre ignited a full-blown military conflict between Armenia and Azerbaijan. The Karabakh War no doubt sped up the decision of the Supreme Soviet of Armenian SSR in November 1988 to designate April 24 as Genocide Remembrance Day. In explicating this decision, the head of the Armenian Communist Party, Suren (Sergei) Arutyunyan, was still playing by the rules. Referring to the tense political situation in Armenia, Arutyunyan had told Gorbachev that the "proletariat" were urging the authorities to sanction the commemoration of the genocide. Such an authorization would emphasize that the "Communist state respects the gloomy past of the Armenian nation that had resurrected only thanks to the October Revolution."[40] On April 24, 1989 Arutyunyan spearheaded the first ever official commemoration ceremony. He spoke of the two "pressure points [*bolevye tochki*]" in the history of Armenia, one in 1915 and another in 1988, when he pushed for a referendum on the future of Mountainous Karabakh at the Congress of People's Deputies of the Soviet Union later that summer. The newly elected Supreme Soviet should condemn genocide, he said without being specific. The vigor and bitterness of these remarks played at different levels. This was seen, for example, when an Armenian translator addressed one of her friends, an editor of a literary journal:

"You, Russians, have sunk in the eyes of the Armenians. You have failed to save us from Azerbaijani genocide."[41] The fear of impeding genocide in Mountainous Karabakh was also voiced internationally, most prominently by Baroness Caroline Cox. In her capacity as deputy speaker of the British House of Lords, Cox in the second half of 1991 led a fact-finding mission to the region. Having traveled to Mountainous Karabakh three times within a six-month period, in January 1992 Cox released a statement. In a letter to Russian president Boris Yeltsin later that month, Cox spoke of a "real danger of a possible genocide of the Armenians in Karabakh."[42] By that time, Moscow officials could reasonably argue that it was no longer *their* concern.

9 • THE ISRAELI-PALESTINIAN CONFLICT

PROPAGANDA IN LIEU OF GUNS IN SUPPORT OF THE PALESTINIANS

A survey of the Soviet press from 1948 onward reveals that, among a great many hot spots during the Cold War, the Israeli-Palestinian conflict had generated the most "genocide" hits. Paradoxically, it reflected a bad conscience rather than firm convictions on the part of the Soviets, who never fully committed to the Palestinian cause. Before the Soviet Union, or any other state for that matter, had taken to accusing Israel of genocide, the World Jewish Congress (WJC) brought similar charges against Pakistan in the ECOSOC. The WJC maintained that Resolution 96(I) of December 11, 1946—which provided for an international treaty banning genocide—gave the United Nations authority to call Arab states to account.[1] Foreign Minister Mohammed Zafrullah Khan in February 1948 categorically rejected the claim of genocide against Jews by Muslims in Pakistan.[2] The newly established state of Israel did consider filing charges of genocide, too. On March 30, 1949 Prime Minister David Ben-Gurion informed the Knesset that the Israeli delegation at Lake Success would request a UN inquiry on whether Arab states complied with the Genocide Convention. The reason for concern was the worsening situation of Jews in the Arab world. The intimation that Israel was urging the United States to exert pressure upon Arab states in this matter proved unfounded, though.[3]

For the first time, it appears, Israelis were rendered as perpetrators during the US Senate hearings on the Genocide Convention in early 1950. Representing the Women's International League for Peace and Freedom, Ruth Gage-Colby had been dealing with child welfare. At some point in her testimony, she compared the Nazi massacre at Lidice in 1942 to the Jewish at Deir Yassin in 1948. In an attack on the Palestinian-Arab village on April 9, Zionist paramilitaries killed an estimated 107 people, including several children. Gage-Colby speculated that the Jewish suffering under Nazis made some of the victims into saints while others into beasts, which in her view constituted "genocide's blackest indictment." Harry S. Berger of the National Economic Council restated the charge of genocide at Deir Yassin.[4]

Each and every war waged by the state of Israel had evoked claims of genocide. The farther in time, the more frequent and more intense became the charges. The 1982 invasion of Lebanon had unleashed a torrent of genocide accusations by the Soviet Union. In fact, no other event during the entire period of the Cold War generated as many references to genocide. The Soviet propaganda seems to have been working backward. The Lebanon War led to comparisons to the Yom Kippur War, the war of 1973 stirred the memories of the Six-Day War, and the war of 1967 was reminiscent of the First Israeli-Arab War. Thus, the expulsion of Palestinians in 1948 was for the first time described as "genocide" in the Soviet press only in 1981. As with many other instances of mass violence, the Soviets pulled out the genocide card whenever it fit their agenda.

The Soviet words did not match their deeds. Going back into the immediate postwar period, the Soviet Union had a single objective in the Middle East: to establish a political presence in the region at the expense of the British. Foreign Minister Molotov believed that Palestine was an issue that divided London and Washington. His deputy Gromyko in May 1947 delivered a speech at the UN General Assembly, which could be safely described as pro-Zionist, though with a caveat. West European states failed to protect the Jews against the Nazis, he said, and hence could not guarantee the interests of the Jewish people after the war. The failure to inject the USSR in the international settlement of British Mandate Palestine made Moscow adopt a wait-and-see position. In view of the pro-British orientation of the Arab regimes, the Soviets had little to gain from taking their side on the issue of Palestine. Uncertain about the future orientation of the Jews, the USSR nevertheless endorsed the creation of the Jewish State in 1948, to the chagrin of the Arabs; in the Soviet calculation, a binational state would hold an advantage for the British. Consequently, the Soviets regarded the invasion of the nascent Jewish state by Egypt, Jordan, and Syria as British provocation designed to thwart partition. The policy of Arab depopulation pursued by Jewish authorities prior to and after the declaration of independence went largely unnoticed in the Soviet Union. Once again, the Soviets blamed the refugee crisis on the British, who were allegedly looking for a pretext to stay put. Indirectly, the USSR sided with Israel in rejecting a Palestinian right to financial compensation. The discernable change in Soviet policy toward Israel at the end of 1948 has been attributed to a number of factors. In Galia Golan's analysis, among the major reasons was the perceived disloyalty of the Soviet Jews and, more generally, the antinationalist campaign launched domestically the previous year. This provided the context for sham trials of prominent Jews in the Soviet Union and Eastern Europe following the Stalin-Tito split. Otherwise, there is no evidence that either the Israelis became manifestly pro-American at that time, or the Soviets began explicitly currying favor with the Arab states. Most likely, the political support for Israel no longer offered any benefits to the Soviet Union.[5] The dynamics of domestic propaganda aiming at Israel confirm this point. While Israel-biting reached new levels in the Soviet Union in 1953, the message did not seem to stick with the general public. After all, Zionist Israel was consistently presented as a pathetic marionette of the United States—the real enemy of the Soviet Union.[6]

For the duration of the Israeli-Palestinian conflict, the Soviet Union had been playing power politics. Thus, Moscow remained uncommitted to the Arab states during the Six-Day War of 1967, in no small degree due to its own strategic miscalculations. Typically, Moscow accepted no responsibility for the Arab military debacle. What Golan has described as a pursuit of dualistic policy shaved off even more Soviet prestige among the Arab states during the Yom Kippur War of 1973. The USSR had supplied arms to Egypt—its biggest client in the Middle East—yet viewed the imminent attack on Israel as jeopardizing its aspirations in the region. Moscow wanted to redeem some of the lost ground in the Arab world by providing assistance, yet sought to avoid direct confrontation with the United States and to limit damage to détente. There is no way the Soviets could achieve this contradictory objective. All they could do, then, was to push for a cease-fire. In the process, the Soviets received a share of criticism from the Chinese, who contended that Moscow had sold its friends in the name of superpower hegemony.[7]

Within a week after the conclusion of the 1967 Arab-Israeli War, TASS issued an international call to stop the "genocide against the Arabs." A *Pravda* article titled "The Crime of Genocide" specifically mentioned forced evictions and the use of napalm by the Israeli air force as deliberate acts aiming to destroy the largest possible segment of the Arab population. As an emerging rhetorical device, a Soviet commentator then evoked the gas chambers of Majdanek and Auschwitz. Despite the verbal protests of the Israeli representative in the United Nations, taunted another *Pravda* journalist, the crimes committed by the Israeli occupation forces were no different from those of the Nazis.[8] Jewish survivors in the United States took the Soviet comparison of the Israelis to Nazis as a personal offense. The Jewish Nazi War Victims Organization of America bought a full-page advertisement in the *New York Times*, in which it accused the Soviet Union of "incitement to genocide."[9]

The Soviet rhetoric had rarely been sophisticated or its arguments logical. Was not it genocide, inquired *Pravda* in December 1969, when the Israeli military had deliberately razed thousands of Arab homes just because their dwellers supposedly sympathized with the guerrillas?[10] The Soviets, obviously, knew the answer even before posing the question. Indeed, a few months later the same newspaper, referring to confiscation of land, accused Tel Aviv of genocide in the occupied Gaza Strip. Around the same time Soviet ideologists started shaping the narrative that linked fascism and Zionism. The government of Israel squandered the goodwill of the "forces of peace and democracy" toward the Jewish people by unleashing the wars in 1956 and 1967. The Zionist leadership had been cynically manipulating the Nazi mass murder of Jews in order to deflect criticism against the "reactionary" policy of the Israeli government, labeling such criticism antisemitic. By so doing Zionists ignored the class nature of fascism. Jews and other nationalities had perished in millions not because Nazi racism was profoundly antisemitic, argued *Pravda*, but because fascism had been engendered by imperialism.[11] The Soviet propaganda charged genocide against Arabs in Israel and the occupied territories, while dismissing the military threat against the state of Israel as a "smokescreen." Among the individuals accused of perpetuating the "myth of Arab threat" were French philosopher Raymond Aron and American historian Theodor Draper.[12]

Meanwhile, verbal close combat in the United Nations had intensified. The link between Nazism, antisemitism, and genocide came to dominate the General Assembly's debates on December 9 and 10, 1970. American delegate Helen G. Edmonds argued that the draft resolution condemning Nazism was proposed by the Soviet Union for propaganda purposes, against West Germany. To contrast, she mentioned discrimination against Soviet Jews seeking emigration. Soviet delegate Yuri Rybakov described the reference to refuseniks as a diversion from the US atrocities in Vietnam and its pursuit of the Black Panthers. "In the eyes of the U.S.," he claimed, "genocide reflects the spirit of the 70's."[13]

The status of Jews in the Soviet Union had acquired international ramifications when the World Conference of Jewish Communities on Soviet Jewry convened in February 1971 in Brussels. In an unprecedented expression of solidarity, 760 delegates from every continent issued a joint declaration denouncing Soviet repression of Jewish culture and voicing concern over the future of the embattled minority.[14] The Soviet press instantly reacted, calling the historic Brussels conference a "Zionist orgy" prompted by the US government. Genrikh Borovik in *LG* advanced the familiar tu quoque argument that denied the United States the right to speak on behalf of the Jews. The desecration of synagogues, xenophobic broadcasts, and acts of conventional discrimination made the United States "exactly that country where racism, antisemitism, and plain genocide is an everyday occurrence." Even worse, Borovik decried the assault by Meir Kahane's radical Jewish Defense League on the Moscow Philharmonic's musicians in New York City a year earlier.[15] The orchestra's performance in the national capital in January 1970 was disrupted as well. Militant Jewish students of the New Washington Committee for the Prevention of Genocide showered the concert hall with leaflets detailing Soviet antisemitism. Later that fall the same splinter group staged a protest during the performance of the touring Moiseyev Dance Company.[16]

As a means of combating accusations of antisemitism, the Soviet propaganda apparatus attempted to create a semblance of public opinion. In the process, the outraged conscience of the Soviet Jews protesting "Zionist slander" came across as coerced and insincere. "We are greatly upset by the mayhem perpetrated by Zionist hooligans in the USA, their criminal acts against the Soviet institutions in that country. Who is behind the degenerates acting under the fake banner of 'protection of Jews'?" Signed by several individuals from the Jewish Autonomous Region, the article in *Pravda* in June 1971 denied that persecution of Jews had ever been the case in the Soviet Union. It was actually in the United States where racism and antisemitism were on the rise, while Israel—"following in the footsteps of its transoceanic masters and Hitlerite monsters"—carried out acts of discrimination and genocide vis-à-vis Arabs.[17]

The hiatus between the 1967 and 1973 wars was marked by the ascent of the Palestinian Liberation Organization (PLO). As with the Arab-Israeli conflict in general, the Soviet embrace of the PLO was dictated by tactical considerations as part of the superpower contest. For the first four years of the PLO's existence (the organization was established in 1964), Moscow did not return calls for assistance. The Communist authorities viewed the Arab-Israeli confrontation primarily as a conflict between states and the Palestinian issue as a refugee problem. China, however, instantly extended its support to the PLO (already in 1965 the PLO had set up an office in Beijing), prompting a rethink on the Soviet part. Most essentially, the Arab states such as Egypt had taken up the Palestinian cause. As it was turning into the single most potent issue uniting the Arab world, and the most vexing for the United States to handle, the Soviet Union had no choice but to assert its leadership. Thus, in 1968 the Soviets began referring to the Palestinians as a "nation," and in 1969 declared the PLO a "national liberation movement." In 1970 the PLO had secured Soviet propaganda backup and, following the visit to Moscow of Yasser Arafat—cofounder of the Palestinian armed group Fatah and the newly elected chairman of the PLO—the promise of indirect arms supplies. In 1974 the Soviet government explicitly expressed itself in favor of a Palestinian state and announced the opening of a PLO office in Moscow (the second national liberation movement to ever receive such an honor). Most significantly, the Soviet Union recognized the PLO as the sole representative of the Palestinian people, granting diplomatic status to its Moscow office along the way. In spite of the public declaration of support, however, the Soviets had harbored serious reservations about the PLO, which might get in the way of their geopolitical interests. The two sides were in disagreement on core issues. The Soviets deemed undesirable the destruction of Israel, backpedaled on the problem of Palestinian refugees, spoke softly on Jerusalem as the capital of a future Palestinian state, avoided putting a cap on Jewish emigration to the Holy Land, and, most crucially, disavowed terrorist tactics. The Soviets generally condemned PLO terrorist operations, regarding them counterproductive and adventurist. Rather, they preferred the PLO becoming a conventional military force.[18] All these differences never became part of the ongoing propaganda war.

The Israeli-Palestinian standoff kept generating violent episodes readily described as "genocide." On September 8, 1972 the Israeli air force bombed ten PLO bases in Syria and Lebanon. The bombing raid, which killed an estimated two hundred people, was carried out in response to the massacre of Israeli Olympic athletes by Palestinian militants at Munich two days earlier. The Communist Party of Lebanon instantly branded the air raid as part of the Israeli genocide of the Palestinian people, the message transmitted by the Czech and Soviet press.[19] The bus hijacking and the subsequent massacre of Israel civilians in March 1978 prompted yet another incursion into Lebanon. This time it was the Soviet Committee of War Veterans that aired charges of genocide.[20] Soviet officials contested the US State Department's formulation "isolated instances of violence" with regard to the occupied Palestinian territories, insisting that the government of Israel had been carrying out the deliberate policy of genocide.[21] This claim was backed by Egypt, Fidel Castro of Cuba, and Muammar al-Gaddafi of Libya, but disputed by Israel.[22] In between, the veteran Soviet diplomat Yakov Malik charged in the Security Council that Israel had resorted to "racial genocide" in putting down unrest in the West Bank.[23] As the Soviet Union had been repeatedly accused of "cultural genocide" against the Jews, Soviet officials took particular pleasure in reporting on the 1980 UNESCO resolution condemning the annexation of East Jerusalem and the destruction of historical monuments by Israel. The Soviet representative spoke of "cultural genocide" carried out by Israel in the occupied Palestinian territories.[24]

It so happened that in December 1981 a Soviet journalist came to visit the Palestinian refugee camp Shatila in West Beirut. He described the Palestinians who ended up at Shatila as refugees from the 1948 "Israeli genocide."[25] The significance of this remark is, of course, that eight and a half months later a Lebanese Christian militia carried out, with the connivance of Israel, a bloody massacre at Sabra and Shatila. This single event, more than any other in recent history, emboldened the Soviet claim of genocide. Yet even before the September 18 carnage, the Soviet propaganda qualified as "genocide" the Israeli invasion of southern Lebanon that had preceded it. Arguably, this was the only appropriate term to define the attempt of Tel Aviv, variously assisted by Washington, to physically destroy the PLO. Following the invasion of Lebanon in June 1982 (prompted by a Palestinian assassination attempt on the Israeli ambassador in London the previous month), the Soviet government issued a statement condemning the Israeli military operation as an act of genocide. According to TASS, the statement had attracted considerable attention in the Middle East.[26] Be that as it may, the Soviet policy in the run-up to and during the Lebanon War differed markedly from what was publicly stated.

Lebanon, with its complex religious and political spectrum, had been off the Soviet radar. The Soviets did not support the Syrian military intervention of 1976 and its alliance with the Christian forces against the PLO. Once the Syrian-PLO fighting had ended, Moscow stood by the cease-fire in the south, discouraging further PLO operations against Israel for the fear of disproportionate retaliation. By arming and training the PLO, Moscow created the impression that it did approve of armed action, even when it did not. According to Golan, there was no Soviet commitment to the PLO in Lebanon or willingness to intervene on its behalf in the event of a war. However paradoxical it may appear, the USSR was primarily concerned with placating its client, as was often the case in its dealings with the national liberation movements generally. The prospective of an all-out Israeli-Syrian war could prompt calls for Soviet intervention and potentially unleash a superpower confrontation. Bogged down in Afghanistan and unnerved by Reagan's offensive posture, the Soviets had no stomach for further escalation. Hence, as they did during the previous Arab-Israeli wars, they pressed for an immediate cease-fire. The Syrians expressed their incomprehension of Soviet passiveness, and so did the PLO. The Soviet government pleaded diplomatic support, which the PLO leadership aptly dismissed as inconsequential. The USSR did literally nothing, as the PLO had been surrounded and bombarded in West Beirut for weeks. As the war continued, the Soviets found themselves increasingly on the defensive, minimizing the Palestinians' losses and shifting the criticism onto the Arab states. To lessen the damage, the Soviet propaganda cultivated the image of the United States pulling the strings. But the crux of the message communicated to the Palestinians from Moscow remained steady: expect nothing more but supplies.[27] There was just one weapon the Soviets could resort to, however ineffectively—accusations of genocide.

Never before had the Soviets applied the word *genocide* as frequently and consistently as in the case of the 1982 Lebanon War. One-fifth of all articles with references to genocide that appeared in *Pravda* between 1948 and 1988 dealt with the Israeli mistreatment of Palestinians. The mass violence accompanying the Israeli invasion of 1982 generated the unprecedented 188 hits out of 1,037 for the entire forty-year period (in comparison, the Vietnam War, which lasted for eighteen-odd years, had been mentioned in connection with genocide 103 times). Within the context of Soviet foreign policy, these statistics alone superimpose a conclusion opposite to the one explicitly stated.

TASS instantly declared the Israeli push into southern Lebanon on June 6, 1982 a "policy of genocide against the Arab people." In the Soviet interpretation, the "fifth war against the Arabs" aimed at physical extermination of the Palestinians.[28] Hisham Sharabi, history professor at Georgetown University, concurred that Israel's action in Lebanon was part of a broader pattern, which extended to the Palestinians in Gaza and the West Bank. When claiming genocide, he falsely stated that the Geneva Conventions of August 1949 expanded the definition to include the "destruction of homes, the confiscation of property, the expulsion of people, and the destruction of social, political, and cultural institutions."[29] On June 21, Soviet foreign minister Gromyko formally accused Israel of aggression and genocide in Lebanon. Speaking at a news conference at the Soviet mission to the United Nations in New York City, Gromyko nevertheless gave no sign that Moscow was ready to react with more than just words.[30]

The most remarkable feature of the Soviet anti-Israel propaganda campaign of the early 1980s was the use of (doctored) public opinion. Weeks after Israel had launched Operation Peace for Galilee, impromptu meetings of protests took place across the Soviet Union. Photos taken at such meetings depicted the orderly "protesters" listening to the speakers, holding professionally painted slogans declaring "Shame on Israeli Occupiers!" and "No to Genocide!" Fishermen, electricians, farmers, shoemakers, miners, chocolatiers—a cross section of Soviet society offered their insightful comments on recent developments in the Middle East. Blacksmith A. Agdgomelashvili of the Moscow Automotive Plant condemned the "bloody adventure" of Israel in Lebanon. As a war veteran, he said, he knew what it was all about—the Israelis testing the new weapons at the behest of the United States, turning Lebanon into a virtual "laboratory of genocide." A cotton grower from Uzbekistan nailed the American administration for aiding and abetting the "bloody genocide perpetrated by the Israeli invaders against tens of thousands of children, women, and elderly." A loader at a Moscow milk plant perceptively noted that the "genocide against Palestinians and Lebanese was carried out within the framework of the strategic alliance between Washington and Tel Aviv." A drill press operator from the Tadjikgidroagregat factory in Dushanbe added that the Israeli invasion of Lebanon constituted a violation of international law and the UN Charter. An electrical engineer from Riga compared Israel's policy to that of Nazi Germany, projecting the same ignominious end to the former.[31]

Along with anonymous Soviet citizens, several distinguished personalities shared their views on Israeli "genocide." The director of the Hermitage Museum in Leningrad, Boris Piotrovsky, compared the State of Israel to ancient tyrannies, which razed entire cities and killed off their populations. The famed academician regarded the Israeli action in Lebanon as a contemporary manifestation of genocide. Moldavian writer Ion Chobanu spoke of "Zionist barbarians destroying the Lebanese civilian population in genocide."[32] The most weight, however, was supposed to be carried in the message coming from Soviet Jews. Members of the Legacy of Ilyich collective farm in Valdgeym, Jewish Autonomous Region, gathered around the Second World War monument. The slogans in Russian and Yiddish read: "Zionists, Get Out of Lebanon!" "Stop Genocide!" "Soviet Jews Support the People of Palestine!" "Shame on Tel Aviv Butchers!" Vegetable grower F. Feiman denounced the "bloody regime of Begin," which conspired with American imperialism to smash the PLO and to physically destroy the Palestinians. The Israelis learned the policy of genocide from the Nazis, argued the speaker. Soviet journalists advanced this historical analogy further, demonstrating their ignorance in the process. Thus a *Pravda* correspondent argued that "perhaps only the *Diary of Anne Frank*, a Jewish girl who had experienced the horrors of Hitler's death camps, could be compared to the stories of the prisoners of Zionist concentration camps."[33] The choreographed exercise in public indignation lasted for about two months, to be continued at a higher, diplomatic level.

As they had done a decade earlier in the case of the Vietnam War, the Soviets screened the international press for the allegations of genocide, readily finding them in the daily press of Mozambique, for example.[34] After the Soviet leader Leonid Brezhnev, in an interview in *Pravda* on July 21, 1982, rendered the Israeli invasion as "genocide," agencies with international exposure such as the Soviet Peace Committee were quick to follow.[35] As to the alleged American responsibility for genocide, it was mainly on account of US-produced cluster munitions excessively used by the Israeli Defense Forces in Lebanon.[36]

In the case of Israel, the Soviets were able to effectively apply the discourse that they had developed in 1948 in connection with the Genocide Convention. *Pravda* reminded that Zionism had been declared a form of racism by the UN General Assembly.[37] Indeed, UN Resolution 3379 to that effect was passed seven years earlier by a vote 72 to 35 (with 32 abstentions). The Soviet bloc, predictably, voted "yes." Since the Soviets had always regarded the Nazi theory of racial superiority as a cornerstone of genocide, the November 10, 1975 resolution could be construed as a bridge between the crime of Zionism and that of genocide. In mid-July 1982, the IADL convened an extraordinary meeting in Paris. Qualifying the military invasion as the crime against peace and the "brazen act of genocide," the IADL resolved to establish an international commission for the investigation of Israel's crimes in Lebanon. Next month, in a parallel development, the Non-Aligned Movement requested the UN General Assembly to prolong the emergency special session on Palestine. The organization's member states, which constituted a solid majority in the United Nations, called for immediate cessation of "Israel's policy of genocide against the Lebanese and Palestinian people." When the extraordinary session resumed on August 16, the head of the Soviet delegation, Mikhail Sytenko, declared Israel and the United States both responsible for the "bloodshed and genocide."[38] Soviet lawyers rendered the same verdict.[39]

Much like the Vietnam War, the 1982 Lebanon War produced not one but several commissions of inquiry. This time around, the Soviets decided to set up a citizens' commission of their own. The Soviet Public Commission of Inquiry into the Crimes of the Israeli Aggressors in Lebanon held its first meeting on August 30 in Moscow. In its deliberations the Soviet outfit went no further than endorsing the findings of yet another commission, though. The International Commission of Inquiry into Israeli Crimes against the Lebanese and Palestinian Peoples met in Nicosia, Cyprus two weeks earlier. The commission was yet another brainchild of the WPC and featured two Russians among twenty-three of its members: constitutional lawyer Alexander Berkov and the director of the Institute of State and Law of the Soviet Academy of Science, Vladimir Kudriavtsev. According to *Pravda*, the international profile of the commission—chaired by one of Britain's leading barristers, John Platts-Mills—entitled it to issue a *political* and legal verdict. Consequently, the Nicosia gathering, "on the basis of numerous irrefutable facts," charged the government and military of Israel with genocide. The rationale was stated as follows: The Israeli leaders did not conceal that their main objective was liquidating the PLO and dispersing the Palestinian people as a historical and ethnic entity. The summer 1982 invasion had created a situation that undermined the very existence of the Palestinian inhabitants of Lebanon.[40] The IADL was meanwhile pushing for the creation of a permanent commission of inquiry, whose main task would be publishing a corpus of mass crimes committed by Israel in Lebanon. The IADL meeting at Brussels in late October 1982 took cues from Brezhnev's roadmap for a Middle East settlement.[41] Such a commission had indeed been shortly established, under the aegis of the Association of Palestinian Lawyers.

The accusations of genocide in the meantime poured in from all over: Communist Party of Syria, Cypriot Progressive (Communist) Party of Working People, Communist Party of Austria, Afro-Asian People's Solidarity Organization, All India Indo-Arab Friendship Association, World Federation of Trade Unions, not to mention the PLO.[42] Not coincidentally, all those parties and organizations were typically referred to in the Soviet Union as "brotherly." Yet some indignant voices belonged to world statesmen such as French president François Mitterrand. Historical analogies varied depending on who was speaking. For example, the Ministry of Foreign Affairs of Vietnam likened "Israel's genocide in Lebanon" to the crimes of Pol Pot in Cambodia, whereas the Czech News Agency compared the massacres in Sabra and Shatila to those in Lidice, Khatyn, and Oradour. The government of Laos, naturally, drew attention to the plight of its own people at the hands of the Americans.[43]

Inside Israel, any discussion of the applicability of the Genocide Convention was effectively blocked through its peculiar interpretation in the Nazis and Nazi Collaborators (Punishment) Law. The 1950 law contained the legal definition of "crimes against the Jewish people." The newly coined crime incorporated the provisions of Article II of the Genocide Convention but identified Jews as the singular target group.[44] Along these lines, Norman Podhoretz, conservative pundit and then adviser to the US Information Agency, issued a blunt apologia for Israel. Writing on September 24, 1982 in the *Washington Post*, Podhoretz exempted Israel of any advance knowledge of the massacre at Sabra and Shatila and insisted that any interpretation to the contrary would go "against the general power of moral judgment and moral discrimination."[45] "Moral vocabulary," in the words of Podhoretz, was prominently on display during the debates at the UN

General Assembly that same day. The Soviet bloc and the Third World countries repeatedly accused Israel of genocide in reference to the massacre in the two Beirut refugee camps on September 16–18. The PLO observer delivered perhaps the harshest speech, in which he referred to the "Judeo-Nazi junta in Tel Aviv." He said the Palestinians were victims of a "Holocaust" and "genocide," as engendered by a Zionist dream of establishing an exclusively Jewish state. The Israeli delegate denounced the debate as a "disgusting orgy of hatred" and a "hypocritical and cynical exercise" for the purpose of shifting the blame for the massacre. Tit for tat, he accused the United Nations of ignoring massacres in Cambodia, Afghanistan, Syria, and Uganda. The evening of oratory at the General Assembly ended with the condemnatory resolution supported by all but two countries, Israel and the United States.[46] Resolution ES-7/9 marked a crescendo, whereas Resolution 37/123D—the apotheosis. On December 16, 1982 the General Assembly resolved that the massacre of Palestinian refugees at Sabra and Shatila was an act of genocide. With no votes against, twenty-two states abstained from voting on this resolution.[47] The UN Commission on Human Rights—never particularly appreciated by the Soviets—followed in mid-February 1983. The CHR reiterated the genocide verdict and called upon the General Assembly to declare September 17 the Day of Commemoration of the Victims of Sabra and Shatila.[48]

The Geneva Summit of November 19–20, 1985 unleashed a new era in American-Soviet relations. The Palestinian problem, however, remained just too convenient a sticking point to bring up in the tu quoque argumentation. When an Israeli reporter challenged Kremlin spokesman Leonid Zamiatin on a human rights issue, the latter fired back: "Look what's going on with the Arabs in Israel—you're destroying them, it's genocide."[49] Even such humanitarians as Sakharov sometimes found themselves caught up in genocide rhetoric. Recently released from internal exile, Sakharov was once asked by an Egyptian journalist about the "policy of genocide carried out by Israel in the occupied Arab territories." Without engaging with the term *genocide,* Sakharov replied that he considered it to be just one element of the tragedy that had been unfolding during the past few decades, and that he hoped for a compromise acceptable to both sides.[50] Charges of genocide against Israel had been promptly serialized in "scientific" books with poignant titles such as *Zionism: The Poisonous Weapon of Imperialism* (1970), *Crime Without Punishment: What Happened in Lebanon* (1983), and *Zionism: Genocide in Action* (1986). Thus, Yuri Tyssovskii claimed that "Zionists mainly count on brute force, international banditry, and veritable genocide," while Taras Klimenko plainly stated that the forty-year history of the State of Israel was defined by genocide against the Palestinians.[51] Yet even in relation to Israel, the Perestroika years saw a relative moderation in the use of the word *genocide.* As of early 1988, *Pravda* spoke of "actions bordering on genocide" in the Israeli-occupied Palestinian territories.[52]

"CULTURAL GENOCIDE" OF JEWS IN THE USSR ALLEGED

The intensity of Soviet Israel-bashing matched the amount of international attention paid to the status of the Jews in the USSR. This is where the term *cultural and spiritual genocide* comes in. For the first time, this term was used in a petition before the CHR submitted on March 21, 1951 by a delegation of American labor leaders. "We charge that the Soviet campaign to blot out Jewish cultural life and Jewish identity are brutal and uncivilized breaches of the UN Charter, of the Covenant of Human Rights, and of the Genocide Convention," stated the delegation representing the American Federation of Labor, Congress of Industrial Organizations, Jewish Labor Committee, and Workmen's Circle.[53] The AJC used a similar formulation: "The Cultural and Spiritual Genocide systematically pursued against the Jewish people by the Soviet Union [capitalized in the original]." The German-Jewish weekly *Aufbau* in New York wrote in June 1951 about "systematic state-sponsored racial murder in the Soviet Union." In reference to the JLC, the newspaper spoke of "spiritual and cultural genocide" of the Jews, drawing a parallel to "physical genocide" committed by Soviet authorities against twenty-something million forced laborers.[54] The US State Department was not ready to qualify the persecution of Jews in the Eastern Bloc as genocide, though. Choosing his words carefully, a State Department official spoke of the "brutal and inexcusable denial of human rights in the Soviet Union, Poland, Czechoslovakia, Romania, Hungary, and Bulgaria with respect to the cultural and spiritual life of the Jewish people in these countries." Although there was no available machinery at the present time in the United Nations for the adequate consideration of the AJC petition—he wrote in response to Senator William Benton (D-CT)—every opportunity should be used to press the Communist countries on human rights.[55] Ratification of the Genocide Convention in 1954 by the Soviet Union, if anything, congealed the concept of cultural genocide against the Jews. As the NCRAC's resolution from June 1954 put it, "cultural genocide has extirpated virtually all organs and institutions of Jewish culture and religion behind the Iron Curtain."[56] Even this one sentence is enough to realize that the subject of concern was actually assimilation.

Cultural genocide, as a term, had never been coherently explained when applied to Soviet Jews. For example, in August 1961 Harry Schwartz reported in the *New York Times* on a new Soviet periodical in Yiddish, which he presented as a further retreat from Stalinist antisemitism. Indeed, since late 1948 Soviet Jews were the only minority group without a national newspaper or magazine in its own language. This could, then, be a response to the criticism that Soviet leaders had embarked upon a deliberate policy of cultural genocide vis-à-vis Jews. At the same time, according to the latest Soviet census only a quarter of Soviet Jews regarded Yiddish as their mother tongue. The International Confederation of Free Trade Unions made a similar point (negatively contrasting the number of publications in Yiddish with that printed in the native languages of the Siberian ethnicities), when urging a full-scale UN investigation of antisemitism in the Soviet Union in October of the following year. Since culture and education were indispensable to the survival of Jews, by depriving Jews of these essentials Soviet authorities were committing genocide. This is how Rabbi Maurice N. Eisendrath, head of the Union of American Hebrew Congregations, had put it, for example.[57] US Representative from California Alphonzo Bell, upon concluding his visit to the Soviet Union, supported his claim of "cultural genocide" with this general statement: "It was impossible for Jews to live happily and successfully in Russia."[58] Even more farfetched appeared a case for genocide construed on the example of a certain rabbi in Russia. Engaged in illicit currency exchange, the rabbi was sentenced to death on charges of "economic crimes." By executing the men of God, the USSR was wiping out Judaism, concluded an American newspaper in October 1963.[59] Summarizing these and similar anecdotes, a Reform Judaism organization in New York City in early 1965 released a documentary, *The Price of Silence*.[60] The term *spiritual genocide* also made an appearance in academic books, for example in Gunter Lawrence's provocatively titled *Three Million More?* Released in 1970, the book was largely based on the author's interviews with Jews during his visit to the Soviet Union four years earlier.[61] Neither did some American politicians hesitate to exploit the issue of "cultural genocide" of Jews in the Soviet Union. This particular subject brought together some 250 people to a rally on Boston Common on August 9, 1970, addressed by Robert J. Drinan, former dean of Boston College Law School, who was seeking a congressional seat.[62]

The truth is, however, that the fate of the Soviet Jews was as much a subject of political expediency as any other issue. Nixon and Kissinger put it in most cynical terms when having this exchange in the White House on March 1, 1973. Kissinger: "If they put Jews into gas chambers in the Soviet Union, it is not an American concern, maybe a humanitarian concern." Nixon: "I know. We cannot blow up the world because of it."[63] Despite the public rhetoric to the opposite, even some American Jewish organizations acknowledged, internally, that the Genocide Convention did not apply to the USSR's treatment of its Jewish minority.[64] In fact, the Senate Committee on Foreign Relations had earlier entered this particular clause as one of informal understandings explaining what the treaty *did not* cover.[65] The clause on mental harm was also deemed inapplicable. In the summer of 1973 the chief proponent of the Genocide Convention in the US Senate, Proxmire, had received a letter from N. Burnett Magruder of the Christian Heritage Center in Kentucky. The latter wondered if the suppression of dissent, and specifically forced treatment of prisoners of conscience in Soviet psychiatric institutions, would be banned under the convention. In his view, as far as mental harm was concerned, the Soviet cruelty far exceeded that of the Nazi regime. Proxmire forwarded Magruder's inquiry to the US State Department, but only was able to extract a general reply to the effect that the Genocide Convention did not cover political groups and that establishing mental harm was rather complex, depending on the facts in any given case.[66]

The notion of *cultural genocide* persisted precisely because it did not make it into the final draft of the convention. That is how William Korey retrospectively described the secret trial and subsequent execution in the spring and summer of 1952 of the fifteen prominent individuals affiliated with the Jewish Anti-Fascist Committee.[67] Inside the Soviet Union, too, refuseniks picked up on the issue of *intellectual genocide*. One of the activists, cyberneticist Victor Brailovsky, was in June 1981 sentenced on charges of antistate defamation. Brailovsky was mainly known as the editor of the underground publication *Jews in the USSR*. In one of the issues of the newsletter, Brailovsky analyzed the pattern of rejection of Jewish applicants in Soviet higher education as an example of "intellectual genocide."[68]

TIPTOEING ON THE ISSUE OF THE HOLOCAUST

With the word *genocide* excessively applied to all sorts of conflicts past and present, the Soviets proved tight-lipped when it came to the Nazi mass murder of the Jews. Whenever they called it so, it was for a reason other than historical accuracy. Preoccupied with the propaganda value of their message, Soviet ideologists sometimes managed to omit the name of the victim group altogether. That is what happened when a TASS correspondent came to speculate whether the West German TV channels would air the 20-part documentary series *The Unknown War*. The American TV series on the Second World War was produced with Soviet cooperation and was released in 1978 to critical acclaim. The subsequent narrative belonged to Peter Schütt, a high-ranking official of the German Communist Party. Schütt drew a parallel with the recent screening of the TV documentary series *The Holocaust* in West Germany. By addressing the most horrible aspect of fascist genocide, the documentary helped explain to West German youth the racist foundation of Hitlerism, he said. In that respect *The Unknown War* was even more important, according to Schütt. Showing the Soviet sacrifice in the fight against fascism had the potential to dispel anticommunism and anti-Sovietism among the younger generations.[69]

Like any other subject, historical or otherwise, the Nazi extermination of the Jews, too, became a hostage of the Cold War. For as long as the persecution of Palestinians by Israel had been classified by the Soviet Union as "genocide," Jews could not possibly have been acknowledged as the specific target of the Nazis. On the contrary, any suggestion that the Soviets did injustice to history and/or memory was bluntly dismissed as a "Zionist lie." And so in the wake of the (successful) propaganda campaign to indict Israel for genocide, in April 1983 the Soviet Public Anti-Zionist Committee came into existence. Established at the behest of the CPSU and the KGB, the committee served its purpose by denouncing the United States and Israel and quelling the clamor over Jewish emigration from the USSR. At a press conference, one of the committee's founding members, Genrikas Zimanas, received the following question. A political correspondent of the Novosti News Agency wondered why the "Zionist propaganda spread slander," as if commemoration of victims of the Nazi genocide had been prohibited in the Soviet Union. However suggestive the question was, the high-ranking Lithuanian Communist Party official had a hard time getting around it. He had heard of this "Zionist fabrication," replied Zimanas. In Lithuania, like elsewhere in the Soviet Union, the sites of fascist mass executions had been properly marked, stated the wartime Jewish Partisan commander. The Zionist ringleaders knew full well, continued Zimanas, that the acts of commemoration embraced all victims regardless of their ethnicity. The Zionists told lies in order to cover up their own crimes in Lebanon, specifically the massacres at Sabra and Shatila. At the same time, they kept suspiciously quiet about the Nazi war criminals who found refuge in West Germany and other countries. Zimanas said Israel's duplicity had to do with class politics.[70]

Another press conference of the Soviet Public Anti-Zionist Committee, in October 1984, featured two members of the International Commission of Inquiry into Israeli Crimes against the Lebanese and Palestinian Peoples. A prominent Swedish Communist, John Takman, was asked whether Israel had committed genocide in Lebanon. Speaking on behalf of the commission, Takman confirmed the charge of genocide with regard to the Palestinian people. Making a link to the Israeli blockade and bombardment of Beirut, he claimed the crimes of "Zionists" in Lebanon were no different from those of the Nazis. The final word belonged to the chairman of the Anti-Zionist Committee, David Dragunsky, one of the most decorated Soviet Jewish war veterans. The established fact of the criminal alliance between Zionism and Nazism the Zionist propaganda would no doubt try to portray as an expression of antisemitism. The Zionist subterfuge of rendering any criticism of Israel as antisemitism simply would not pass, he said.[71]

Dragunsky's statement related to a cache of documents of Nazi provenance shortly released by Soviet authorities. The archival records purported to demonstrate the contacts between the "Zionists" and the Nazis, likely referring to the secret negotiations with Heinrich Himmler to secure the release of at least some Slovak and Hungarian Jews in 1942–1944. Treating these negotiations as a criminal conspiracy, Cesar Solodar, a Soviet Jewish writer and wartime correspondent, drew a direct line to the Lebanon War. "Those who posed as the victims of Nazism," wrote the author of the book on the same subject, "now feature as the executioners and perpetrators of genocide." Hence the importance of unmasking contemporary Zionism. The Soviet people were in equal measure opposed to antisemitism and Zionism, stated Solodar. As for the unsavory attempts to present the Soviet Anti-Zionist Committee as an embodiment of some sort of anti-Jewish campaign ongoing in the Soviet Union—countered one of its active members—it belonged to the arsenal of anti-Soviet intrigues.[72]

In search of further evidence for the abovementioned claims, Karen Khachaturov, a Soviet official with a PhD in history, visited the Ghetto Fighters' House in Israel. The visitor from Moscow found quite a few shortcomings in the museum's permanent exhibition. He said the role of the Soviet Army in the liberation of prisoner camps had been understated while that of Allied forces exaggerated. He objected to the use of the terms *Nazi* and *Nazism* instead of *Hitlerite* and *Fascism*. The documentary about the Jewish uprising in the Sobibór death camp, he noted, failed to mention the contribution of the Soviet prisoners of war. All of these things, according to Khachaturov, testified to the Zionists' deliberate falsification of the causes of the Second World War and the origins of fascism, with its unambiguous anticommunist and anti-Soviet streak.[73]

A French documentary, *Shoah,* played in selected movie theaters across the Soviet Union in 1988, three years after it had been originally released. Even then, the word *Jews* had not been spelled out. The article in *LG* merely stated that the film "depicted the tragedy of genocide in Hitler's death camps." According to the Soviet journalist who had conducted an interview with the film's director, Claude Lanzmann, quite a few people in the audience left halfway through the screening—unprepared to see what they saw.[74] An official commemoration ceremony for the Jewish victims of the Nazi mass executions at Babi Yar in Kiev was for the very first time held at a cemetery in Moscow on September 23, 1988. Led by a Supreme Soviet delegate, Lev Shapiro, the ceremony was framed as discreetly as possible. Shapiro spoke of "Jews, Ukrainians, Byelorussians, Moldovans, Russians, Kazakhs, Georgians—the Soviet people of many ethnicities" who perished in the Nazi genocide. The audience was described as the "Soviet public [*obshchestvennost*]."[75] *Pravda* did not tell the entire story, though. Some speakers directed their anger not at the Germans but at the Soviet government. According to the *Chicago Tribune,* a Jewish war veteran told the 500-strong audience that "Babi Yar was a prelude to the spiritual genocide of the Jewish people in our country."[76] Coincidentally, President Reagan drew a similar parallel at the ceremony unveiling the cornerstone of the US Holocaust Memorial Museum on the National Mall. In his speech to about 1,500 people on October 5, he renewed his challenge to the Soviet Union to relax restrictions on Jewish emigration.[77] Back in the USSR, the Jews featured as a deliberate Nazi target group in another *Pravda* article, though only as a counter reference to Jean-Marie Le Pen, the notorious leader of the French far-right National Front.[78]

The Pravda news digest from mid-November 1988 featured a piece commemorating the *Kristallnacht,* the nationwide anti-Jewish pogrom in Nazi Germany fifty years earlier. As it turned out, that was just an introduction to the main theme of the article. As if they were mocking the memory of the past, reported *Pravda,* the Israeli soldiers on November 9 staged a pogrom on the occupied

Palestinian territories, dispersing the general strike marking one year since the beginning of the intifada.[79] Not until May of the following year did the Nazi genocide of the Jews appear as the subject in its own right, with no ideological strings attached. A Soviet journalist found himself wandering through the Yad Vashem Museum in Jerusalem, contemplating the scope of the tragedy befallen the Jewish people. Literally days before the Soviet Union began to unravel in August 1991, an announcement appeared about the forthcoming commemoration ceremony at Babi Yar. In a rare moment, *Pravda* was telling the truth: "At the end of September 1941 on the Babi Yar ravine the Hitlerites launched genocide of the Jews in our country."[80]

10 • AN UNCERTAIN END TO THE COLD WAR AND THE REACTIVATION OF THE GENOCIDE TREATY

THE WAR IN AFGHANISTAN PROMPTS RECIPROCAL ACCUSATIONS OF GENOCIDE

Despite the strenuous efforts on behalf of the Genocide Convention in the United States during the 1970s, its future looked rather bleak at the beginning of the new decade. The fateful decision of the Soviet Politburo to invade neighboring Afghanistan, in the last week of December 1979, did anything but strengthen the foundations of international law.

Counterintuitively, the first charges of genocide on record were issued prior to the Soviet invasion. Mohammad Daud, who in July 1973 overthrew the monarchy in a bloodless coup, took a tough line on Pakistan in the attempt to garner domestic Pashtun support. Thus, the self-appointed president promoted a proxy war in Pakistan when he came up in support of the insurgency in Baluchistan Province in the fall of 1974. Afghanistan's Foreign Ministry accused Pakistan of carrying out genocide against the Baluchi population, drawing a parallel to the mass atrocities committed in East Pakistan (Bangladesh) three years earlier.[1]

The Soviet military intervention was meant to check the growing Islamic insurgency that threatened the Socialist government in Kabul. Keen to insulate its borders, the Kremlin resolved to prop up the friendly regime in Afghanistan, which had been regarded as an important geopolitical outpost throughout history. According to the so-called Brezhnev Doctrine, the Soviet Union reserved the right to intervene in order to preserve the Communist bloc and thus to forestall Western encroachment.[2] In short, the Soviets had a classical status/security dilemma on their hands. The allegations of genocide, unsurprisingly, started pouring in within months after the Soviet troops entered Afghanistan. The tone was set by CBS newsman Dan Rather. In the spring of 1980 Rather went on a clandestine six-day tour of the country in the Soviet grip. When telling about his incursion on *60 Minutes* Rather argued that genocide might be the Soviet answer to continued armed resistance. What was remarkable about the earlier assessments of the Soviet strategy in Afghanistan was the *anticipation* that Moscow would have committed genocide. Several diplomats, academics, and political pundits contended that the Soviets were bent on genocide. It was entirely within the realm of possibility, according to Theodore Eliot, US ambassador to Afghanistan from 1973 to 1978. Eliot's predecessor in Kabul, Robert Neumann, agreed: "To exterminate the entire Afghan population is not easy, but I suppose not entirely undoable, either. Dying isn't that big a thing for them [the Soviets]."[3]

Aware that the military option was fraught with danger, the Soviet leadership from the outset found itself on the defensive. This was the reason why the Soviet press felt obliged to counter the charges of genocide as soon as they appeared, even in obscure Western publications. Rather received instant rebuttal in the Soviet media. As soon as Rather went on the air, TASS labeled his story a "deliberately falsified report." His allegations of the Soviet military using nerve gas and perpetrating genocide was part and parcel of President Carter's "provocative propaganda campaign," stated the Soviet news agency.[4] In July 1980 *Izvestia* took to task a minor Paris newspaper, which printed an article, "Anatomy of Genocide," about the Soviet conduct in Afghanistan. Despite the flashy title, "stale propaganda goods" was all it was, argued the Kabul-based correspondent. While Soviet soldiers were defending the country against "external aggression," "imperialist reactionaries and Chinese supremacists were recruiting feudal lords, smugglers, drug dealers, and criminals" to terrorize the Afghan population. Those counterrevolutionaries loathed the idea that life in Afghanistan was getting back to normal. Fortunately, the Afghan people had a steadfast friend in the Communist bloc with the Soviet Union at the helm. The article in *Izvestia* ended with a quote from CPSU General Secretary Leonid Brezhnev, who had vowed to defend the "achievements of the April [1978] Revolution."[5] Author and journalist Alexander Prokhanov in *LG* identified two main themes in the Western media in relation to the Soviet military presence in Afghanistan. Browsing through *Time Magazine*, *Newsweek*, and the *Christian Science Monitor*, Prokhanov said he came across numerous allegations of atrocities bordering on genocide and speculations about the military incapability of the Afghan army. Measuring these claims against the Soviet practices, he believed the American press had received "propaganda directives from above." The then leader of Afghanistan, Babrak Karmal, further dispelled the accusations of mass murder and genocide in an interview with the French Communist *L'Humanité*.[6]

Particularly damning proved the reports about the alleged Soviet use of chemical and toxin weapons. According to US State and Defense Department experts, the Soviet Union was actively using mycotoxins—the toxic chemical agents produced by fungi, previously tested on Hmong guerrillas in Laos. In their estimates, Soviet-supplied chemical weapons had been responsible for the death of some 10,000 people in Afghanistan, Laos, and Cambodia, thus contributing to a "campaign of genocide against defenseless people." Further details appeared in the Department of State Report to the Congress on March 22, 1982. The United States accused the Soviet Union of violating the Geneva Protocol and threatened to take the issue to the United Nations, while dismissing the concomitant decision of President Ronald Reagan to revive the US chemical weapons program as unrelated. TASS vigorously rejected these charges as "dirty lies." The Soviet Union had signed the Geneva Protocol and never resorted to chemical warfare. As to the United States—reminded a Soviet political observer—the memory was still alive of tens of thousands of tons of toxic agents dropped on Indochina by the US aggressors.[7] Controversy continued for the duration of the Soviet occupation of Afghanistan. Some American experts had questioned the evidence provided by US officials. Other than tear gas, the use of chemical weapons by the Soviet Union in Afghanistan has never been definitively proven (not least because relevant CIA records remain classified). The same concerns the stories of scattered mines built to look like children's toys. In the words of Mark Galeotti, it was a brutal, hard-fought war that saw civilians targeted, villages deliberately depopulated, and torture routinely applied as a tool of terror and interrogation, yet that particular form of inhumanity appears to have been missing.[8] Unprepared to fight a long counterinsurgency war, the Soviets centered their efforts on cutting the mujahideen supply routes. In the process the Soviet troops conducted deadly raids and sweeps through rural areas, bombed villages and granaries, destroyed crops and irrigation systems, mined fields and pastures. By the time the "limited contingent of Soviet forces" had pulled out from Afghanistan in 1989, an estimated 1.25–2 million civilians were dead.[9]

Yet the biggest concern remained the endless stream of refugees from Afghanistan. Anywhere between one-quarter and one-third of the population had moved to neighboring Pakistan and Iran by 1983. Certain Western analysts described this unprecedented displacement as "migratory genocide," supposedly encouraged by Soviet authorities for the purpose of ridding the country of opposition.[10] In late 1985 the West came one step closer to pronouncing the Soviet Union guilty of genocide from the highest international rostrum. The previous year the CHR had appointed one of its members, the Austrian law professor Felix Ermacora, as special rapporteur on Afghanistan. In the past, the Soviets praised Ermacora for his human rights investigations in South Africa and Chile; now they opposed his appointment, referring to him exclusively as a "Nazi." Refused entry to Afghanistan, Ermacora toured refugee camps in Pakistan. His first report received relatively little attention, but his second made quite a stir when it went to a vote in the General Assembly on December 13, 1985. In no uncertain terms, Ermacora outlined gross human rights violations by Soviet forces, specifically targeting villages and agriculture. The report fell short of calling it "genocide," however, contrary to the expectations of the State Department. According to a secret cable from Geneva prior to the UN vote, a "charge by Ermacora of genocide would be a major development in the [United Nations] and could have significant repercussions elsewhere." "Embarrassment to the Kremlin"—that is how the cable explained the intended effect of the report.[11]

With the relentless stream of information about Soviet atrocities in Afghanistan, it was only a matter of time before Moscow uncovered "evidence" of genocide on the other side of the front line. Suspiciously, it came up about the time Ermacora was preparing his second report. According to the Soviet version of events, the Pashtuns living on the Pakistan side of the Khyber Pass took up arms against the mujahideen, who had wielded increasingly more power in this nominally autonomous region. Appearing in late December 1985 on Kabul TV, Sheikh Jamir of the Shinwari tribe told about the reprisals by the Pakistani Army. Tens of thousands of troops were engaged in destroying villages and confiscating weapons provided by Afghanistan. Jamir accused Muhammad Zia-ul-Haq's administration, in concert with the United States, of waging genocide against the Afridi and Shinwari peoples, who resented the mujahideen bands operating from their territory. The Soviet newspaper and TV reports were augmented by a proclamation issued by the Women's International Democratic Federation. The organization restated the charge of genocide, identifying Islamabad and Washington as partners in crime. Similar charges were leveled by the ambassador of Afghanistan to the Soviet Union on January 10, 1986, and the permanent representative of Afghanistan in the United Nations on February 8.[12] Meanwhile, a dissident Pakistani tribal leader had appealed in the name of the Pashtu clans to "stop genocide." His appeal went to the CHR, the Islamic Conference Organization, and the leader of the Non-Aligned Movement, Prime Minister of India Rajiv Gandhi. From Delhi promptly arrived a reply charging the Pakistani Army with genocide and gross human rights violations. The Soviet media could not resist throwing Israel in the picture. "The photograph of a bulldozer razing a house has become a symbol of Israeli colonization of the Arab lands, yet one here was taken in Pakistan," *Izvestia* made the case some six months later. "No wonder, since genocide always has the same features."[13]

The charges of "Soviet genocide" had been routinely uttered by Western politicians during the 1980s. A West German parliamentarian mentioned torture and indiscriminate bombardment of villages as elements of the crime of genocide presently being committed in Afghanistan. Pakistan's foreign minister, in his speech before the UN General Assembly in September 1986, spoke of one million Afghans who succumbed to genocide and forced migration as part of a sinister Soviet design. Israeli ambassador to the United Nations Benjamin Netanyahu in December of the same year squared on the issue of genocide with his Soviet counterpart. When the latter charged Israel with genocide in the West Bank, Netanyahu replied that the "term *genocide* better describes the Soviet behavior in Afghanistan." Perhaps the most prominent official to express his opinion on the subject was US attorney general Edwin Meese. Meese was visiting Pakistan in March 1986, in part to show American support for Pakistan's efforts to stamp out drug production. Addressing more than three hundred refugees, Meese referred to genocide as one of many markers of the Soviet military occupation. "The world asks why are the Soviets doing this in Afghanistan?" he went on. "The answer is in a way simple—it is part of their desire to dominate the entire world." One name on the indicter list was conspicuously missing, however; usually outspoken, President Reagan apparently did not feel the need to push the Soviets more than he had done already. On December 3, 1987 Reagan took questions from the journalists representing four major American news channels, including Dan Rather of CBS. Among other things Reagan was asked if he believed that Gorbachev believed that the Soviet troops in Afghanistan, "committing genocide almost daily," had been genuinely invited there. In his answer, Reagan avoided discussing the substance of the crime, merely stating that Gorbachev had inherited the Afghanistan war.[14] The Soviet war in Afghanistan had a major impact on the debates concerning US ratification of the Genocide Convention.

GROWING POLITICAL SUPPORT IN THE UNITED STATES FOR A "SYMBOLIC" TREATY

In 1982 the US Department of Justice summed up what had been known for quite some time. By then the United States, alongside Communist China and apartheid South Africa, stood in noble opposition vis-à-vis the ninety-odd states that became parties to the Genocide Convention. All of Washington's major NATO and Southeast Asia Treaty Organization allies had acceded to the treaty. Over a period of thirty-two years, the convention had been the subject of five hearings and had been reported out of the Senate Committee on Foreign Relations four times. As the joke went, the Genocide Convention was eligible for the *Guinness Book of World Records* as the oldest treaty pending before the Senate. Every time, opponents had been able to command enough support to prevent approval by the Senate. The provisions of the treaty did not conflict with the American Constitution, concluded the Justice Department. The question of ratification for the American government was, therefore, that of foreign policy and had political overtones.[15]

The two major concerns were retroactivity and the element of intent. As had been emphasized in the aftermath of the 1968 My Lai massacre, US ratification would have had no retroactive effect. To begin with, the US Constitution would not allow the Congress to enact an ex post facto criminal law.[16] Nevertheless, the Department of Justice aired a few more hypothetical scenarios to install the safeguards, whenever necessary. State Department witnesses had testified in the past that the Genocide Convention was purely prospective, but had not explained how they reached that conclusion. Article I, for example, stated that genocide was a crime under international law, which might imply a preexisting obligation. The United States could perhaps submit an understanding that the convention was limited to future acts. Even then, a state such as Vietnam—which became a party the previous year—could potentially charge the United States with genocide in the ICJ irrespective of the convention, claiming obligations of the United States under customary international law. On the other hand, such claims might be barred by lapse of time. As incorporated within the concept of genocide, "intent" should provide some protection against frivolous, propaganda-inspired charges, argued Assistant Attorney General Theodore B. Olson. As an example, he brought up treatment of Haitians detained by the US Immigration and Naturalization Service—definitely not genocide, even though detainees might claim to have been "mentally harmed" by the experience. Haitians who had a legal status in the United States were not subjected to similar treatment, and hence there was no intention to destroy them "as such." Reiterating pro and contra arguments, Olson was rather optimistic in his conclusion. By ratifying the Genocide Convention, the United States would get access to an "excellent platform to seek to expose atrocities being committed in communist nations which otherwise are largely ignored in the world community." At the same time, since the ICJ had proved to be a useful tribunal for the United States in the past, Washington should not fear countercharges.[17]

From the perspective of the Justice Department, the treaty was symbolic. As a handwritten meeting note (likely written by Special Assistant to the Attorney General Kenneth O. Simon) from December 1983 attested, "No state has ever invoked it, and no-one has ever been charged with genocide under the treaty. As far as pros and cons are concerned, we are sometimes attacked by the Soviet Union for not ratifying it."[18] Obviously, Soviet blaming and shaming did not constitute a real threat. In other words, the growing consensus within the US government regarded ratification as a safe option. Simon had subsequently outlined his position to the attorney general. Since no nation or individual had ever been formally accused of genocide, he argued, it was unlikely that problems would arise in the future. Any objections to US ratification could be addressed in the form of reservations, that is, express understandings about the meaning and operation of the Genocide Convention. The act of ratification would be seen as an "important symbolic gesture that the U.S. is committed to human rights at a time when our principal adversary has repeatedly shown it is not." It would also be advantageous to President Reagan, both domestically and internationally, as a sign of his "unique commitment to human rights," added Simon.[19]

The push for ratification was further aided by the American Bar Association, which had had a change of heart on the convention in February 1976. With the grand old men such as Deutsch (b. 1897), Phillips (b. 1897), and Schweppe (b. 1895) on their way out, the ABA had adopted a more flexible position. ABA sided with the Senate Committee on Foreign Relations in its insistence on a supplementary package consisting of three reservations and one declaration. Unprecedentedly, in the spring of 1984 an ABA delegation traveled to the Soviet Union. In Moscow, ABA president Wallace D. Riley had a meeting with the Association of Soviet Lawyers, inviting any number of them to the ABA's annual meeting later that summer. Prior to his trip, Riley had a conversation with Ambassador Max Kampelman (of later fame as chief US negotiator with the USSR on nuclear and space arms). Kampelman had said that the failure of the United States to ratify the genocide treaty was frequently thrown in his face by the Soviets. They presented it as an indication that the United States was not serious about observing the norms of the international rule of law, and certainly less concerned about basic human rights than was the Soviet Union. Riley found it "most unfortunate that the Soviets and other Eastern Bloc nations have had this vehicle with which to embarrass the U.S." He believed that the Senate action on the Genocide Convention would add to the stature of the president in his dealings with the Soviets.[20]

Encouraged by the expert opinion of the Justice Department, Reagan on September 5, 1984 asked the Senate to give its advice and consent to the ratification of the Genocide Convention—the fourth American president to do so. Next month the Senate Foreign Relations Committee unanimously endorsed ratification. Yet the early action in 1985 was not forthcoming. Conservative senators under the leadership of Jesse Helms enumerated eight amendments as the condition for their support. Six of those amendments had been considered already in 1950 and 1971 and engendered no opposition. The seventh amendment, which affirmed the superiority of the US Constitution, was also accepted as reasonable. What caused a problem was the insistence that the ICC should not exercise authority without the formal approval of the United States.[21] Senator Orrin G. Hatch (R-UT) berated Ernest A. Gross and the State Department for "confusing the nature of treaties with the nature of executive agreements." Taking into account that President Daniel Ortega of Nicaragua had already accused the United States of supporting genocide in that country, warned Hatch, signing up to an international penal court would spell disaster.[22] The senator from Utah was referring to the statement of the ICJ vowing it had the jurisdiction to hear the case submitted by the government of Nicaragua in April 1984. The court's claim sent shockwaves through the Senate.[23]

The mention of Nicaragua in the context of the Genocide Convention carries a broader significance due to the heightened role of Latin America in the global Cold War during the 1970s and 1980s. This chapter in the history of the Cold War warrants a digression.

The frequency with which the Soviet media referred to genocide was antithetical to analysis—hollow words unsubstantiated by the facts on the ground.

The "genocide" of Soviet coinage sometimes came across as cartoonish, literally. Even before the proxy wars in Latin America had reached dramatic proportions, *Izvestia* readily reprinted the *Daily World*'s cartoon "The School of Genocide." The cartoon featured an American adviser standing on top of a CIA truck and handing over diplomas to South American clients who had graduated from the "University of Genocide."[24] Not until the overthrow of the Socialist government of Salvador Allende in Chile in September 1973 did the Soviet Union (indirectly) identify any particular South American country as the locus of genocide. The graphic TV footage from Santiago added to the drama unfolding in the CHR and other UN bodies. The widow of President Allende spoke in the CHR of extrajudicial killings and "genocide" that swept Chile. Awaiting trial on political charges, the head of the Communist Party of Chile, Louis Corvalán, expressed himself on the "treachery and genocide" of Pinochet's junta vis-à-vis the Chilean people. A book published by the Chile Solidarity Committee in Panama also claimed genocide, reportedly. Two years after the coup d'état, the Soviet representative on the UNESCO Executive Board was evoking interchangeably the notions of genocide and gross human rights violations with regard to Chile.[25]

Still random in the case of Chile, charges of genocide became more prominent as the leftist Sandinistas were closing in on the corrupt regime of Somoza in Nicaragua. Cuba led the way in September 1978, declaring solidarity with the insurgents and condemning the "genocide and repressions" unleashed by the embattled dictator. The president of Mexico made a similar statement when shortly announcing the severance of diplomatic relations with Managua. The Soviets expanded this narrative by emphasizing the pernicious role of the United States in propping up the genocidal regime. Washington sent military advisers and mercenaries, and Israeli arms, to assist the Somoza clan, which had been brutalizing the Nicaraguan people for nearly half a century. In effect, the United States had abetted the genocide raging in that Latin American country.[26] The United States went on a verbal counteroffensive in the United Nations where its ambassador denounced as "genocide" the Sandinista attack against the indigenous Miskito people in late December 1982.[27]

In July 1979 the Sandinistas seized power in Nicaragua. To prevent a repeat scenario in El Salvador, the United States began pouring money into the military-led government. Opposed to them stood the leftist guerrillas of the Farabundo Martí National Liberation Front (FMLN). Already at the beginning of the decade-long civil war the FMLN charged the El Salvadoran army with genocide. Soon enough, Washington and Moscow/Havana were accusing each other of meddling in El Salvador's internal affairs. As related by TASS, "genocide concealed by lies" involved the United States sending arms and military advisers to the junta in El Salvador, with the knowledge of ongoing atrocities.[28]

In the 1980s the specter of genocide in Latin America, according to the Soviets, also came to include Venezuela and Brazil. The evangelical New Tribes

Mission reportedly used the "Nazi methods of pacification" vis-à-vis the indigenous population of Venezuela. Alongside proselytizing, the organization had been accused of serving as a front for geological prospecting. The first allegations of genocide against the Amazon tribes in Brazil—as a means of land grabbing—appeared as early as 1968. The more recent case focused on the environmental and social damage caused by Tucuruí Dam in Pará State. The controversial dam was completed in 1984, flooding a large area that included part of an Indian reserve. The concomitant problems included population displacement, malaria, mercury contamination, and loss of livelihood. The detrimental impact on health was mainly due to the defoliants used to clear the forest in the first phase of construction. The Soviets capitalized on the findings of a Brazilian environmental NGO to claim that the Pentagon had secretly tested herbicides similar to Agent Orange (employed in Vietnam) in the Amazonian jungle. The lethal experiment purportedly killed over seven thousand tribal people and was covered up by consequently flooding the area.[29] In this particular case, the stress was on the kind of toxic substance used. The Soviet Union evoked genocide in order to demonstrate that the United States was stockpiling and testing chemical weapons, ready to use them at any time, also in Europe.[30]

A FINAL PUSH FOR US RATIFICATION OF THE GENOCIDE CONVENTION

Some activists, but also scholars, have ex post facto attributed Reagan's 1984 call for ratification to the lobbying efforts of American Jewish organizations. Although this interpretation is not without merit, ultimately Reagan's decision had to do with politics, both international and domestic. The announcement came just one day before the US president was to address a biannual convention of B'nai B'rith International, the oldest and largest Jewish service organization in America. Reagan was indeed angling for votes as he was running for reelection that year. Critics of the Genocide Convention such as conservative columnist George F. Will were wondering why the administration, having allowed the treaty to gather dust for forty-four months, dusted it off just two months before an election? The Liberty Lobby, which claimed 38,000 active members, strongly criticized the US president for "bowing to the pressures" of an election year. With this action, the group claimed, Reagan was going to disaffect more of his supporters than he had ever done during his presidency.[31] Senator Helms, who had put sand in the gears of the ratification process, put his objections in the context of electoral politics, too. Thus, he told a group of reporters after the Foreign Relations Committee meeting on September 19, 1984: "The Jewish people are very enthusiastic about having this, but Israel is likely to be the first victim of this convention." He then added: "They [Israelis] have killed a lot of Arabs. Who knows what a World Court would do?"[32] Senator Hatch, inadvertently following the script of the American far right, painted a dystopia to state his opposition to the treaty. He invited the *NYT* readers to consider the following scenario. The year is 1990 and fictitious Israeli defense minister Yaakov Levin has arrived in New York to make a speech before B'nai B'rith. There he is arrested on charges of genocide against the Palestinians in the West Bank. The warrant was issued by the US attorney general's office upon a complaint filed by the UN secretary-general. Kept incommunicado, the defense minister is accorded no governmental immunity or presumption of innocence. After a three-week media extravaganza, the UN International Genocide Penal Tribunal convicts the Israeli official on all counts. He is transferred to Syria to begin his sentence of life imprisonment. Israel angrily withdraws from the United Nations in protest and shortly invades Syria. The Soviet Union immediately threatens the United States with retaliation.[33] With this take on inferno, Hatch only fell short of a prediction of a new world war.

Undeterred, Reagan crushed his Democratic challenger at the ballot box. More than potential votes, it was perhaps the blunder he had made the following year that reinforced Reagan's commitment to the Genocide Convention. The story really began with the commemoration of the Normandy invasion in June 1984, from which West Germany was shunned. To patch up relations with Chancellor Helmut Kohl, who was instrumental in the deployment of US ballistic missiles in West Germany, Reagan committed to visiting a military cemetery as part of a plan to observe the fortieth anniversary of V-Day in Europe. A few weeks prior to the scheduled visit, journalists had learned that the chosen cemetery at Bitburg, the site of a NATO airbase, contained four dozen Waffen-SS graves. Despite the public uproar and a personal plea from the celebrated author and survivor Elie Wiesel, Reagan went ahead with the plan. The fact that the May 5, 1985 trip to Bitburg also included a visit to a former Nazi concentration camp—entered on the agenda at the last minute—could not repair the political damage. The Soviets, for sure, took full propaganda advantage of what had been described as Reagan's bow to Nazi war criminals.[34] It looked particularly bad as the US president was preparing to meet the newly elected Soviet leader Mikhail Gorbachev in an unprecedented meeting at Geneva later that fall. John F. Kerry (D-MA) and forty-five other senators urged Reagan to seek Senate ratification before the summit. That would enable him to deal credibly with Gorbachev on the issue of human rights and specifically the plight of Soviet Jews, Kerry wrote. Reagan got the message, asking Senate majority leader Bob Dole (R-KS) to act before the end of 1985.[35]

The Soviet publicity machine went into high gear days before the Geneva Summit opened on November 19, 1985. Gorbachev's chief spokesman, Leonid Zamiatin, seemed to be well prepared when answering questions at a news conference he had called. Accusations of Soviet antisemitism he countered with counterclaims of extensive anti-Jewish pogroms in the United States. Rampant racism, genocide against the Native Americans, and most recently the firebombing of "dissidents" in Philadelphia (i.e., MOVE)—these were "facts of life in the US today," allegedly. In a mid-summit swipe at the United States, the Soviet government distributed an open letter to members of Congress charging the policy of genocide against the American Indians. The letter, which specifically protested the case of Leonard Peltier, was an obvious attempt to get back at Americans over the human rights issue. Another attack on the United States came at the so-called Budapest Cultural Forum (an offshoot of the 1975 Helsinki Accords) less than a week after the generally upbeat meeting between Reagan and Gorbachev. The leader of the American delegation denied the charges that his country was a "haven of cultural and physical genocide" and said that the Soviet position violated the spirit of the summit. He reminded delegates that it was Gorbachev who had told reporters at Geneva that the two superpowers agreed to "stop making stupid remarks about each other."[36]

It took almost a year to negotiate the so-called Sovereignty Package, designed to appease the dissenters. Nevertheless, during the decisive vote on December 5, 1985 two senators expressed an objection: Helms and Chic Hecht (R-NV). They argued that, once the treaty had been activated, Israel would be the first to be charged with genocide. In that view they were supported by law professors Robert A. Friedlander and Grover Rees, who testified at the Senate hearing on March 5 later that year. Among other witnesses, the floor was given to Trisha Katson, legislative director of Liberty Lobby. In her lengthy presentation, Katson spoke on behalf of the Palestinians and aptly denied the existence of Nazi gas chambers. Upon her request, the record of the hearing included the fifteen-page-long conclusion from the book of the Holocaust denier James J. Martin.[37]

As the Soviet-American relations began to ease, the holdup in the Senate was increasingly blamed on party politics. National Republican operatives had a dilemma on their hands: a vote for the Genocide Convention might alienate the conservative base, while a vote against it might lose Jewish backers and their campaign contributions. No one understood this problem better than Dole, who was considering a 1988 presidential bid. Dole had made a commitment to the American Jewish community twice, at the groundbreaking ceremony for the Holocaust Memorial Museum and in a speech to the Council of Jewish Federations. At the same time, conservative Republicans in half a dozen states who were running for reelection in November 1986 risked losing the support of the right, which could ultimately cost the party Senate control, if Dole forced a pre-election vote on the long-delayed genocide treaty. Eventually Dole did just that, on February 18, having opted to jeopardize several Republican senators in tight races to enhance his presidential prospects.[38]

On February 19, 1986 the Senate overwhelmingly approved the Genocide Convention by an 83–11 vote. While Helms, Steven D. Symms (R-ID), and other conservative Republicans voted against the ratification, they dropped plans for a filibuster, which would have prevented a vote. The legislation was officially called the Proxmire Act after the retiring Senator Proxmire, who since 1967 had delivered a total of 3,211 proratification speeches on the Senate floor—another potential entry for the *Guinness Book of Records*.[39] The Senate resolution, which was assured through the adoption of the Lugar-Helms-Hatch Sovereignty Package, found that instances of "political genocide" had taken place in Tibet, Cambodia, and Afghanistan. However, none of the senators who had voted for the resolution believed that the Soviet Union would ever agree on a treaty amendment requiring a definition of political genocide. Later that summer Robert Byrd (D-WV) called, to no avail, upon the US secretary of state to investigate Soviet actions in Afghanistan as a possible violation of the Genocide Convention.[40] The Senate completed action on US participation in the genocide treaty on November 14. Two weeks later, at an awards dinner held by the Simon Wiesenthal Center, President Reagan explicitly promised to sign the enabling legislation.[41] On November 4, 1988, he signed the treaty into law. Jewish organizations such as B'nai B'rith did not fail to comment that Reagan appropriately acted on the eve of Kristallnacht, whose fiftieth anniversary was approaching.[42]

Remarkably, *Pravda* attributed US ratification to a large extent to the lobbying efforts of Amnesty International. The article on October 21, 1988 titled "Should We Trust the 'Amnesty'?" answered this question basically in the affirmative. The organization's latest annual report had pinpointed the positive changes occurring in the USSR in the field of human rights. At the same time, admitted the newspaper, Amnesty had regularly addressed gross human rights violations in Latin America and even called for a retrial of Peltier.[43] This exposé alone serves as a strong indication that the Soviets were ready to bury the hatchet on the issue of international law in general and the Genocide Convention in particular. After all, Amnesty International traces its origins to the British section of the International Commission of Jurists, which had fought running battles with the Soviets since the 1950s.

COMMUNISM COLLAPSES, LEAVING A POISONOUS VOID

With the continuous push for ratification in the United States, the future of the Genocide Convention was ultimately decided in Moscow. On March 11, 1985 the Soviet Politburo selected the 54-year-old Gorbachev as the new CPSU secretary-general. Facing up to reality, Gorbachev embarked on a series of comprehensive reforms to enhance the competitiveness of the Soviet Union. The difference in style between Gorbachev and the previous leaders of the country was instantly felt. Known for his comprehensive, if longwinded, speeches, Gorbachev delivered one at the XXVII Congress of the CPSU on February 25, 1986. Among other things in the speech—which took up an entire newspaper—he pledged to fruitfully cooperate with foreign governments toward international peace. In the humanitarian sphere, he specifically mentioned the fight against genocide, apartheid, fascism, and various forms of discrimination.[44]

In his address at the UN General Assembly in early December 1988, Gorbachev spoke at length about the Soviet commitment to human rights. Among other things, he stated, "We consider that the jurisdiction of the International Court in The Hague with respect to interpreting and applying agreements in the field of human rights should be obligatory for all states."[45] Analyzing the results of his trip to the United States, Gorbachev had told the Politburo members that the unilateral Soviet proposals proved that Moscow meant business. In so doing the USSR had seized the initiative from the Americans, willing to build a new, post–Cold War world.[46] As an affirmation, on February 10, 1989 the Presidium of the Supreme Soviet accepted the ICJ jurisdiction with regard to six multilateral treaties, including the Genocide Convention. (Not coincidentally, for the United States the Genocide Convention entered into force on February 23.) By withdrawing the earlier reservations, pointed out Foreign Minister Eduard Shevardnadze, the Soviet Union was guided by the desire to strengthen the international legal order and to ensure the primacy of law in politics. *Izvestia* seconded Shevardnadze with the headline, "We Prioritize [International] Law."[47]

Domestically, however, Gorbachev treaded carefully on the issue of genocide, as demonstrated by his handling of the Armenian-Azerbaijani conflict. In retrospect, Gorbachev acted wisely by rejecting the broader interpretation of genocide on the one hand and avoiding directly meddling into interethnic conflicts across the Soviet Union on the other. The violent overthrow of the Communist government in Romania served as a reminder of just how badly it could all end for the country's leadership. While cultivating nationalism as a means of keeping independence from Moscow, Nicolae Ceauşescu had greatly impoverished Romania during his nearly three-decade-long rule. With most of his Communist peers swept from power by mid-December 1989, Ceauşescu sealed his destiny by staunchly refusing reforms. The false sense of invincibility made the dictator order the dreaded security force Securitate to fire at the demonstrators in Timişoara.[48] Caught while fleeing, Ceauşescu and his wife Elena were tried before a drumhead court-martial. Indicted for the genocide of some 68,000 people, they were executed by a firing squad on December 25, 1989.[49] The following month, four of the dictator's most powerful aides appeared before a military tribunal in Bucharest. Held responsible for the deaths during the Romanian Revolution of December 1989, they were originally charged with complicity to commit genocide and later with masterminding genocide. Article 357 of the Romanian Penal Code defined genocide as killing "members of the collectivity of any group," committing "grave attempts on the physical or mental integrity of the collectivity or group," and/or exposing the "collectivity or group to living conditions or treatments that are capable of physically destroying persons." With the death penalty shortly abolished, all four defendants were found guilty and sentenced to life imprisonment in late January 1990. The minutes of the Political Executive Committee of the Romanian Communist Party from December

17 and 22 constituted the crucial (and only) evidence of genocide presented at the trial—described at the time as Romania's Nuremberg.[50] Complicity in genocide featured prominently in other high-profile trials held in Romania through 1990. Among the indicted were General Iulian Vlad, chief of the Securitate, and Ceauşescu's flamboyant son Nicu.[51] If one were to disregard the fact that the capital punishment meted out to Ceauşescu Sr. was basically judicial murder, then the case can be made for Romania's leader being the first ever acting head of state standing trial and sentenced to death on charges of genocide. By the same token, while taking note of the lack of due process, the subsequent trials in Romania made the most extensive use of the complicity in genocide clause to date.

As the Soviet Union was effectively on its deathbed, all sorts of "genocide" causes entered the conversation. The decades of propaganda were to blame in that most of the speakers had only a faint idea of what they were talking about. In the run-up to the CPSU Central Committee plenum on nationalities question, a group of intellectuals in April 1989 gathered for a roundtable discussion. Among the participants in the roundtable was Jānis Peters, chairman of the Latvian Writers Union. Peters spoke of language politics in Latvia, arguing that internal migration was no different from mass deportation. As regards numerically small nationalities [*malye narody*], claimed Peters, the result was outright genocide. He hastened to add that the guilty party was not the Russian people but the "aggressive economic [policy]." His reference to genocide prompted a question from the audience about whether Peters meant it figuratively or literally. His answer was remarkable in its obliqueness: "I believe it makes no difference insofar as a people vanish due to aggressive economy. It is of utmost importance that Perestroika enables us to attack this problem head-on."[52]

Alas, Perestroika further complicated, rather than solved, a great many problems facing the ailing Soviet Union. The disaster at the Chernobyl nuclear plant in April 1986 had been increasingly referred to as "genocide" by Belorussian and Ukrainian intellectuals such as Vasil Bykov and Boris Oleinik. The fact that Byelorussia received about 70 percent of the radiation made Zianon Pazniak, chairman of the Belorussian Popular Front, declare it in 1989 a case of "radiogenocide."[53] In February 1991 a group of Russian-language speakers from South Ossetia had addressed Gorbachev, Chairman of the Russian Supreme Soviet Boris Yeltsin, and Minister of the Interior Boris Pugo. The telegram appealed for help against the genocide ostensibly waged by Georgian militants.[54] Ultimately, on the eve of the Soviet Union's collapse, the nationalist *Molodaia gvardiia* claimed "genocide of the Russian people." In the July 1991 issue of the magazine, Vladimir Zarubin went on a rampage against democrats and Freemasons in his defense of the Communist Party and the KGB.[55]

The genocide discourse has come full circle, making Soviet intellectuals reconsider the history of their own country. Their ways of looking at Stalinism, however, often came from the annals of ideological struggle, now seemingly in decline.

Was Stalin an absolute evil who committed "genocide against his own people" or a multifaceted individual who had strengthened the Soviet state? History, therefore, was a "weapon in the struggle to achieve short- and long-term goals." The bipolar vision of history made it difficult to fathom, though, how the Soviet people would be able to "successfully forecast their future, while accounting for past mistakes, to solve the current problems of revolutionary transformation of society"—to quote Nikolai Potapov in a March 1989 issue of *Pravda*.[56] If anything, in this hazy picture of the past vs. the future, *genocide* continually carried its unintended function of a curse word. The colors changed, but "revolutionary" and "reactionary" remained as loosely defined as before. No surprise, then, that the revelations about the Gulag in the Soviet Union had sparked a backlash and a reversal to a familiar theme of fascism. Learning about one's own history, however bitter it might be, was indeed important, wrote veteran *Pravda* correspondent Victor Kozhemiako in June 1990. Moving from one extreme to another, though, was not healthy, he cautioned. Since the publications about the Nuremberg Tribunal and all the atrocities committed by the Nazis became sparse—the Soviet journalist complained—the youth of today were no longer aware of what fascism had inflicted on their country and the world. Kozhemiako took to reminding readers about the "Final Solution of the Jewish Question," mass extermination of Roma, "genocide of 'inferior races' in Ukraine, Belorussia, Russia, and even the Baltic."[57] As this list of victim groups attests, the only new aspect of the Nazi policy of mass murder that had emerged during Perestroika was persecution of the Roma. Indeed, representatives of the Soviet Roma attended the fourth congress of the International Roma Union held in 1990 in Poland, for the first time ever.

A curiosity of sorts, *genocide* was entered into the *Dictionary of Perestroika* alongside the "new" words and terms such as *unemployed, racket, socialist pluralism, jury trial, Mafiosi, Glasnost, Karabakh, pesticides, Jewish cultural center, Zionization, poverty line, hunger strike, de-Armenianization*, and others.[58] The dictionary, work on which commenced in 1989, was published three years later. One can only wonder what was novel about *genocide*—the word with which Soviet citizens had been bombarded since the 1960s.

After forty years, the Genocide Convention finally became operational. Few were celebrating, though. Eventual US ratification was just a gesture, prompted by strong political undercurrents. Even the long-term supporters of the treaty had recognized the bitter truth: Even in ideal circumstances, the Genocide Convention would not have prevented the mass murder of Jews by Hitler or Cambodians by Pol Pot, the victimization of the Hutu in Burundi or the Baha'i in Iran. This was the conclusion reached by David A. Harris, the AJC's Washington representative. The only substantial enforcement mechanism to come out of the treaty was the ability to call attention to an atrocity, echoed Nicolas C. McBride in the *Christian Science Monitor*.[59]

CONCLUSION

Some scholars have dubbed the twentieth century the "century of genocide." In that case, the Cold War decades could, then, be safely described as half a century of genocide allegations. Ever since Raphael Lemkin spelled out the word *genocide,* it has been less a legal concept than a discourse. The concept is one committed to paper by the United Nations, while the discourses are many. The bulk of what we hear and read about genocide today belongs to the latter category.

During the Cold War, the Genocide Convention in general and the word *genocide* in particular belonged to the arsenals of the ideological warring sides. If there was anything "legal" about the term at all, then it was only its indiscriminate, extrajudicial use. *Genocide,* as predicted by seasoned politicians, became a hollowed-up vessel that could be filled with any meaning. Drafted by career diplomats, the Genocide Convention has failed to navigate the choppy waters of the Cold War. Like seaweed, propaganda overpowered the original idea, spread, and multiplied. Soon the international landscape was awash in irreconcilable rhetoric.

At one point or another, a good eighty countries in both hemispheres came to be accused of genocide. Communist bloc countries and Soviet republics, nearly all of them, supposedly carried out genocide or, alternatively, bore the brunt of that heinous crime: the Soviet Union, Czechoslovakia, Hungary, Albania, Poland, Romania, East Germany, Cuba, Laos, Vietnam, Cambodia, China (under both the Qing Dynasty and Mao). Noncommunist countries where genocide reportedly took place, or which were practicing genocide, at different times included the United States, Great Britain (Northern Ireland), France (both the Third and Fifth Republics), imperial Germany (and indirectly West Germany), Belgium, Portugal, Austria, Cyprus, Japan, Indonesia, Australia, Canada, Israel, Egypt, Jordan, Syria, Afghanistan, Republic of South Africa, Honduras, El Salvador, Guatemala, Nicaragua, Dominican Republic, Bolivia, Colombia, Venezuela, Brazil, Paraguay, and Chile. Among former colonial and dependent territories that experienced genocide have been mentioned Algeria, French Somaliland (Djibouti), Ethiopia, Kenya, Sudan, Tanganyika (Tanzania), Burundi, Rwanda, Swaziland, Rhodesia (Zimbabwe), South-West Africa (Namibia), Angola, Mozambique, Portuguese Guinea (Guinea-Bissau), Congo,

Uganda, the short-lived Republic of Biafra (Nigeria), Equatorial Guinea, Chad, Madagascar, Yemen, Lebanon, Pakistan, India (Kashmir), Sri Lanka, East Pakistan (Bangladesh), Burma, British Malaya (Malaysia), Fiji, Grenada, Bermuda, and British Guyana. Counting the combined population of these countries, one may inevitably arrive at a conclusion that, within a span of some forty years, genocide had affected about four-fifths of humanity.

In the postwar decades *genocide* has become an issue of semantics rather than of international law. Thus world audiences learned about "migratory genocide" (Afghanistan), "spiritual genocide" (USSR), "elitocide" (USSR), "radiogenocide" (USSR), "intellectual genocide" (Czechoslovakia), "ecological genocide" (Vietnam), "biological genocide" (Laos), "ideological genocide" (Cambodia), "psychic genocide" (United States), "industrial genocide" (United States), "social genocide" (United States), "racial genocide" (Israel), "ethnic genocide" (Austria), "cultural genocide" (Corsica, France), and so on. And so Israel was talking about "genocide" in Cambodia, the Soviet Union lambasted Israel for "genocide" of the Palestinians, and the United States periodically evoked "genocide" in the USSR. The president of Sudan rejected allegations of genocide in his own country but accused Ethiopia of perpetrating one in Eritrea. China claimed the United States was carrying out genocide in Vietnam, while some commentators in the United States ascertained Chinese genocide in Tibet—the latest charge the Soviets supported, after having first dismissed, for political reasons. The charges of genocide came and went around the world. The more frequent the allegations, the less international attention they received. By the time the United States took to ratifying the Genocide Convention and the Soviet Union to withdrawing its longstanding reservations in the late 1980s, the concept was bankrupt.

The Cold War systematically undermined the legal foundations of the Genocide Convention, making it into a venerable tool of propaganda. It should have been, but never was, about the victims, millions of victims. The narrative, as advanced in this book, suggests an alternative definition of genocide: a rhetorical tool that reflects the Cold War dynamics in pursuing specific geopolitical interests. In that sense, it was casuistry of blood, manipulated to achieve maximum short-term results.

The Soviet Union and the United States emerged bloodied from nearly half a century of propaganda war. With hindsight, there is no way the Soviet Union could prevail in the Cold War and by extension in ideological warfare. Even though the Soviets managed to score a few important victories, their overall record was poor. The Soviet scholarship on genocide effectively died together with Aron Trainin, though even the veteran of Soviet international law had no choice but to tread the Communist Party line. For all intents and purposes, the Soviet Union did not have a policy related to the Genocide Convention. It was merely a part of the Soviet "no" agenda. From the outset, *genocide* was relegated to a stockpile of propaganda, essentially being a word of abuse.

Recriminations lacked nuance. Despite an air of moral superiority, the Soviets failed to make inroads into the American protest movement or to carry the prize of decolonization. Local context notwithstanding, the USSR sought always to map the chain of command leading all the way to Washington, less frequently to London, Paris, Brussels, Lisbon, and Pretoria. The ultimate blame for alleged genocide had always been thrown at the American door. I chose to call it proxy wars of words. On occasion Moscow lashed out as hard against its ideological allies who had fallen out with the Soviet Union. Ultimately, the Soviets wanted to nail the perpetrators of the crime more than they wanted to assist its victims. It was not so much the plight of the Kurds in Iraq that the Soviets deplored but the "betrayal of socialism" by the Ba'athist regime in Baghdad, not the death of millions of Cambodians at the hand of Pol Pot but the support that he had received from China. Ideological pragmatism and defensive self-righteousness—to deliberately use oxymorons—underlined all aspects of Soviet policymaking, including the discourse on genocide.

Even though it was empty words anyway, the Soviets sometimes felt obliged to qualify their allegations: "Baghdad authorities are *effectively* carrying out a policy of genocide in Kurdistan" (1963); "American imperialism is waging the war of extermination, *veritable* genocide against the Vietnamese people" (1965). Taken in the aggregate, it amounted to an admission that quite genocide it was not, irrelevant as it might be. The Soviet media, at least on one occasion, came very close to divulging that genocide could indeed mean just anything. That is what *Izvestia* essentially wrote when marking the twentieth anniversary of the Universal Declaration of Human Rights: "Sadly, even in our times . . . people are confronting on a daily basis such sinister notions as racism, segregation, apartheid, genocide, and neo-Nazism. Not everyone can explain the origins of these words, though everyone understands that they mean the assassination of the leaders of the Negro movement in the USA, oppression of the native population of South Africa in reservations, barbaric destruction of the peaceful population of Vietnam, colonial terror in Portuguese colonies, and the ominous talk of revanchism currently coming from FRG."[1] Call it genocide for every occasion. Consider, for example, the Soviet propaganda addressing the deficient working conditions of coal miners in West Virginia. Tens of thousands of miners went on strike, reported *Pravda* in the spring of 1969. The strikers demanded compensation for physical disabilities, specifically lung diseases, incurred as a result of work in mines. The conclusion drawn by the newspaper was rather off the wall, though: the miners were "victims of industrial genocide in the name of monopolistic profit."[2]

Beyond propaganda, the Soviets felt extremely uneasy operating within the confines of international law. One may wonder why, after all, the Soviet Union did not refer racial discrimination in the United States to the ICJ. Hypothetically, Moscow could have urged Hanoi to try American POWs in North Vietnamese custody on charges of genocide. The Soviet regime might have contributed financially to the Russell tribunal, or at least carried the news. Some of their choices simply defy rational explanation. There is nothing unusual in *Sovetskoe gosudarstvo i pravo* having declared war on the *American Journal of International Law*. At the same time, the Soviet law journal never mentioned by word the International Commission of Jurists, the Western counterweight to the Communist-influenced International Association of Democratic Lawyers. Even though these two Cold War outfits were often at each other's throats, *SGP* did not join the fray. Was it because the vicious attack on the ABA's periodical ensued in the waning years of Stalin's rule when Soviet lawyers tried to outdo each other in their show of loyalty to the increasingly paranoid regime, whereas Western lawyers had incorporated in July 1952—less than a year before the death of the "great leader"—and therefore escaped excessive scrutiny? It is anybody's guess.

The same goes for Americans. Taking into account just how many cases had been labeled "genocide" during the Cold War years, it comes almost as a surprise that others were not. The suppression of the liberalization movement in Czechoslovakia in 1968 is one such exception to the rule. Both the 1952 Slansky trial in Prague and the 1956 invasion of Hungary had generated a flurry of genocide accusations. One can only speculate whether it was a relatively small number of victims during the street battles, the caution with which the Soviets handled the aftermath of the military aggression, or the onset of détente that prevented the Western politicians and the media from identifying it among the most heinous crimes. London's *Sunday Times* went perhaps the farthest, calling the crackdown on dissidents that followed "intellectual genocide."[3] Neither the Americans nor the Soviets meant what they said. Way too often, the reciprocal accusations of genocide masked the reluctance to intervene in real time, a fig leaf of sorts. Khmer Rouge Cambodia serves as perhaps the crassest example of such "genocide ping-pong." After decades of trading jabs over genocide, political expedience made both superpowers effectively turn their gaze away from the unfolding nightmare.

The thesis advanced in this book corroborates the predominant reading of the origins of the Cold War. The perception of hostile encirclement that was born into the Soviet state never let go. Soviet cooperation with the West, even during the Second World War, was always conditional and therefore did not last. Structurally unable to operate in the multilateral political setting, Moscow effortlessly slid back into the bipolar vision of the world. The word *genocide*, and the international convention that avowed stamping it out of existence, was just an element in a zero-sum game for the Soviets. The Americans, who never reconciled with Communism—antithetical to their own form of governance—came as easily to embrace genocide rhetoric. The American left and the right incessantly lobbied in favor and against the genocide treaty, respectively, especially after McCarthyism had been beaten back. The supporters of the Genocide Convention in the United States sounded just too general and too idealistic to fight off the straightforward message hammered out by the opposition. The Jewish liberal left had tried for decades, but would not have been able to defeat the far right, had not someone called Mikhail Gorbachev been left with no choice but to take the Soviet Union out of the Cold War.

A mirror-image discourse on genocide, as it had developed in the Soviet Union and the United States, does not conceal an important difference between these two countries. The fact that the United States is a democracy endowed with a free and vibrant press presupposed a self-critical view of America. Appendixes A and B in this volume—which provide a breakdown of genocide-themed articles that appeared between 1948 and 1988 in *Pravda* and the *New York Times* respectively—drive this point home. A quick look is enough to establish that the interest in the issue of genocide was much broader and more consistent in the United States than it ever was in the Soviet Union. State ownership of the media in the USSR determined a number of relevant articles and subject matter in *Pravda*. In other words, the Communist Party decided what and when to label as "genocide," as opposed to freewheeling discussions in a pluralistic society. Thus, following limited coverage of the drafting of the Genocide Convention in 1948, *Pravda* returned to the subject of genocide only four years later—to report on the CRC's efforts to indict the United States for genocide of black Americans and the alleged use of bacteriological weapons by the US Army in Korea. It took another ten years before the organ of the Soviet Communist Party started evoking genocide in earnest, in connection with decolonization. After a few years' pause, in 1977, *Pravda* renewed its attack on Western duplicity regarding genocide—as a mean of deflecting attention from the violations of human rights in the USSR. The many proxy wars fought by the two superpowers during the 1980s prompted a steady stream of genocide allegations in the Soviet press. Characteristically, the five subjects that generated roughly two-thirds of genocide hits during the Cold War were the treatment of Palestinians by Israel; Pol Pot's Cambodia (ex post facto, mainly on account of China's "treachery"); the Vietnam War; El Salvador; and racial discrimination in the United States.

The trajectory in the United States, as per the number of relevant articles in the *New York Times*, was somewhat different. A massive interest in the Genocide Convention in 1948 continued, with a lesser intensity, all the way through Dulles's announcement in 1953 that the United States would not ratify the treaty. Steady numbers during the following decade exploded in the late 1960s, mainly on account of the Vietnam War. Like in the case of *Pravda*, though earlier than in the Soviet Union, mass atrocities by the Khmer Rouge in Cambodia made references to genocide in the *New York Times* more common. Finally, Israel's invasion of Lebanon and multiple armed conflicts in Latin America in the 1980s made the American press reflect on the crime of genocide as intensely as did the Soviet newspapers. Yet the American top-five list, generating over one-third of genocide hits, did not look anything like the Soviet. The range of subject matter was greater, more self-reflective, and less governed by ideology: Nazi mass murder of Jews; nonpolitical perspectives on genocide; race relations in the United States; delayed US ratification of the Genocide Convention; and the genocide treaty as such.

Where does it all leave us with regard to prevention and prosecution of genocide? At a great disadvantage! The Cold War inserted a self-destructive mechanism into the Genocide Convention. This particular document of international criminal law exemplifies the forty-odd years of ideological confrontation. Built on opposition rather than cooperation, the existing treaty defies its purpose. In effect, it added more fuel to the Cold War flame, without extinguishing any others. We have inherited a rhetorical ticking bomb. If the ultimate goal in drawing attention to the plight of a particular minority group or nation was to deal a blow to the opposite side, what distinguishes genocide from other core international crimes or gross violations of human rights? During the postwar decades, the answer was a war of words. While the face of adversary has changed since the end of the Cold War, the toxic legacy of the ideological divide lingers on.

Undoing this damage seems like an impossible task.[4] I am glad that the revisionist historian James J. Martin has been proven wrong in his dim conclusion from 1984 that the "chances of being burned at the stake for witchcraft are probably as high as conviction for 'genocide.'"[5] In the end, international lawyers have managed to salvage what was intended as a dead letter of the law. Despite all odds the Genocide Convention lives on, having been applied, with mixed success, to a number of conflicts, both recent and more distant—Sudan, Rwanda, Bosnia, Guatemala, Cambodia. Unless we are willing to continue with the casuistic debates of the Cold War era, we better surrender *genocide* as an analytical concept and leave it to lawyers to argue in court. A prime example of power politics, the Genocide Convention makes the "crime of crimes" an ill-conceived category for historical analysis.

AFTERWORD

Genocide Rhetoric and a New Cold War

The Russian Ministry of Justice maintains a "List of Extremist Materials." Individuals producing, stockpiling, and disseminating such materials are liable to prosecution. In the summer of 2015 the list was expanded on account of Raphael Lemkin's 1953 article "Soviet Genocide in Ukraine." Translated into twenty-eight different languages, the annotated article appeared in book format in Kiev, Ukraine in 2009.[1] Censoring Lemkin's ideas on genocide tells us less about the Soviet Union of sixty-five years ago than about the Russia of today. Obviously, I am not the only one who is having a déjà vu moment. Although the factor of ideology is no longer there, the concept of *hostile encirclement* that underlined the Soviet Union's existence once again dominates political discourse.

This book ends with the collapse of the Soviet Union, which heralded the beginning of a brave new world, this time for real. Much ink has been spilled over Francis Fukuyama's *The End of History*. Back in 1992, his thesis sounded just too good to be incorrect. Fukuyama argued that the meltdown of the Communist bloc signified the end of ideology in international politics. And since the raison d'être of ideological confrontation has dissipated, the world would automatically embrace liberal values espoused by the West—a clear winner in the Cold War. An uninterrupted period of economic prosperity that followed, ushered in by the idea of a common market and global trade, seemed to confirm this optimistic prognosis. There were many reasons to believe that Russia, which succeeded the Soviet Union, was on its way to becoming a state like any other, ready to play by the rules but also to uphold those rules. Even though warning signs were plenty—the "frozen conflicts" on Russia's borders, the brutal execution of war in Chechnya, blitzkrieg in Georgia, to name just a few—foreign commentators refused falling back to the familiar discourse of realpolitik. Recalling Gorbachev's proposition from 1985 "to stop making stupid remarks," it would seem incomprehensible that the Russians, or anyone else for that matter, would behave recklessly by going back to their old ways. Alas, "many a beautiful theory was killed by an ugly fact," as Thomas Huxley once quipped.

During the first post-Soviet decade the Russians remained on the receiving end of genocide accusations. In pursuit of historical justice, the former vassal states on occasion used the émigré playbook from the 1950s. The Baltic legislation on crimes against humanity, genocide, and war crimes entail peculiar interpretations that would make experts on international law raise their eyebrows. The law on the responsibility for the genocide perpetrated against the inhabitants of Lithuania, enacted in April 1992, for example, interprets destruction of human beings for any purposes as genocide. Thus, according to this law Soviet deportations constitute genocide. In May 1998 the then chairman of the Lithuanian parliament, Vytautas Landsbergis, signed a resolution that declared mass deportations a war crime displaying characteristics of genocide. Another Lithuanian law from June 1997 combines crimes against humanity and war crimes in a single term, "war crimes against humankind." To make the application of these and similar laws easier, the president of Lithuania declared in July 1998 that the NKVD and KGB were criminal organizations that had committed genocide and war crimes against Lithuanian citizens.[2] Estonian legislation prescribes the intentional killing of anti-Soviet partisans as a crime against humanity. This interpretation informed several judgments in criminal cases resulting in the conviction of defendants.[3] One particular individual in 2008 stood trial on charges of genocide for his role in the forced deportation of a few hundred Estonians in 1949, forty-three of whom eventually died in exile.[4] Due to the defendant's death in the midst of the trial, the prosecution never got the chance to successfully demonstrate how accessory to murder would translate into collaboration in genocide.[5] Such legal interpretations led to a situation when, for example in Lithuania, a majority of genocide indictments relate to the crimes committed during the Soviet rather than Nazi occupation. This opened the possibility of individual Jews being convicted of genocide of the Lithuanian people.[6]

If the Baltic legislation on genocide still remains a largely internal matter, the public exhortations by the Polish and Ukrainian authorities got under the Kremlin's skin. The Polish government has regarded the mass execution of over 14,000 Polish officers in Soviet captivity in April 1940 as genocide. To counteract those claims, the prosecutor general of Russia in September 1998 demanded an official inquiry into the death of tens of thousands of Russian prisoners of war in Polish concentration camps during the 1919–1921 war. They were victims of genocide, he concluded. To drive this point home, in April 2017 the Russian Military History Society installed at the Katyn memorial site stands with information about the Russian prisoners in Polish captivity, predictably provoking indignation in Poland.[7] Otherwise, the Russian Katyn investigation was closed in 2005 due to the expiration of the statute of limitations, without finding evidence of genocide. Even more resolutely, the Russian government has been opposed to the evocation of genocide in Ukraine. Beginning in

1993, consecutive presidents of Ukraine referred to the man-made 1932–1933 famine—which affected Ukraine most adversely—as genocide.[8] Viktor Yanukovych, who had cultivated friendly relations with Russia, is so far the only leader of Ukraine who refused to describe the famine as genocide.[9] The most extensive commemoration took place in 2008 on the seventy-fifth anniversary of the famine and the sixtieth anniversary of the Genocide Convention. On this occasion the Russian State Duma issued a resolution stating, among other things, that the famine does not bear attributes of genocide and should not be used for political purposes altogether—the position endorsed by Alexander Solzhenitsyn. Meanwhile Russian court historians sprang into action, producing works aiming to disprove the "myth of genocide," especially with regard to the 1932–1933 famine.[10]

What can be safely described as judicial casuistry, the Russian state under President Vladimir Putin supplemented with propaganda and most recently with covert operations. "It's geopolitics, stupid," proclaimed *Time Magazine* in March 2014.[11] Having suppressed dissent at home, Putin wasted no time on niceties and, in an act of brazen aggression, sent arms and troops into Ukraine that spring. While Russian diplomats were lying without blushing in front of the cameras and Russian military provocations were growing by the day, Western observers continued debating whether Cold War 2.0 was in effect. Call it whatever you want, from the perspective of this book the answer has arrived in late September 2014. Following the musings of genocide during the summer months, the Russian authorities opened a legal inquiry into the "genocide of the Russian-speaking population in southeastern Ukraine."[12] The fact of judicial investigation put aside, the crucial adjective *alleged* was missing, as it had been during the Cold War years. This minor detail did not deter Channel One, Russia's major state TV network, from instantly weaving the genocide narrative into its coverage of Ukraine. Simultaneously, the Russian Foreign Ministry went on the offensive, decrying American hypocrisy in the case of a white police officer fatally shooting a black teenager in Ferguson, Missouri, earlier that year. Reacting to the rioting and protests in the aftermath of the jury verdict, it suggested US authorities should focus on domestic problems instead of lecturing Moscow on human rights.[13] In January 2016 the head of the Russian Investigative Committee, Alexander Bastyrkin, challenged Russian human rights activists to take up the cause of the "destruction of over 6,000 people as a result of genocide of the Russian-speaking population of Donbass."[14] Remarkably, the very same individual, then in his capacity as Russia's deputy prosecutor general, had earlier charged Georgia with the genocide of Ossetians. As evidence of genocide, Bastyrkin volunteered the bombardment of residential areas in South Ossetia during the short-lived Russo-Georgian War in August 2008.[15]

A peruse of post-Soviet legal scholarship reveals that the relationship between foreign policy and international law has never been disavowed in contemporary

Russia. Hence the preeminence of the dualist theory, according to which international law and domestic law constitute parallel legal systems. Certain Russian scholars have argued that Russia's military intervention in Georgia and Ukraine did not violate the norms of international law. Whenever this argument proved difficult to sustain, they referred to Western duplicity in cases like Kosovo and Iraq. Consequently, they treat the International Criminal Tribunal for the Former Yugoslavia with disregard. Russian textbooks and academic publications consistently depict the United States and NATO as aggressive states that have systematically violated international law since the end of the Cold War. In an apparent contradiction, the annexation of Crimea fits the definition of *aggression* commonly used in Russia prior to 2014. More crucial, Russian scholarship on international criminal law never comprehensively explained why Moscow stayed outside of the ICC—not least due to Georgia's referral of Russia's leadership to the ICC, as Lauri Mälksoo has speculated. This does not prevent the Russian government from construing itself as the guardian of international law.[16] It is not coincidental that geopolitics, which was consistently demonized in the Soviet Union, is now regarded as a respected scientific discipline in Russia, indeed promoted as a cornerstone of international relations.[17]

Like the old debates about the origins of the Cold War, it will take some time to determine if the blame for the present escalation should be put squarely on President Vladimir Putin of Russia. Even if Putin's aggressive posture contributed most to undermining the norms of international conduct, this symbolizes a larger trend. Call it a crisis of multilateralism. In October 2016 Burundi, South Africa, and Gambia one by one announced they were withdrawing from the ICC, claiming the court's perceived bias against African nations.[18] Whether the formal act of withdrawal may prevent the ICC from looking into mass violations in those countries is beside the point: the system of transitional justice as we have seen it coming to shape in the 1990s and early 2000s appears to be crumbling before our eyes. If revoking the ratification of the Rome Statute by a few states may sound bad enough, nonratification by the United States and the Russian Federation is even more troubling. For that matter, the third major player in the Cold War and in the current international constellations, China, has not even signed the statute. Much has been written about Beijing's disregard for the ICJ ruling of July 2016 concerning jurisdiction over the disputed islands in the South China Sea. A similar piece of news from December 2015 attracted far less attention internationally. That month President Vladimir Putin signed a law enabling the Constitutional Court of the Russian Federation to overthrow judgments passed by international human rights courts.[19] On November 16, 2016 Putin very publicly removed Russia's signature from the founding treaty of the ICC. Rodrigo Duterte, the vociferous president of the Philippines, had picked up the rhetoric of neo-anti-imperialism by declaring one month earlier that the Philippines was "separating" from the United States and realigning with China and Russia. His declaration followed on the heels of a public spat with the ICC, which issued a warning against the drug crackdown Duterte has been carrying out with utmost brutality.[20] One day after Putin's announcement, Duterte threatened to withdraw his country from the "useless court."[21]

Insofar as we understand transitional justice as a legal response to the wrongdoings of previous repressive regimes to facilitate political change, we may conclude it has run its course. The embrace of transitional justice after the end of the Cold War underlined the allure of democracy. Consequently, the less significance attached to democratic values, the less need for any sort of transition, especially that incorporating the judicial mechanisms. There is also an element of bad conscience, which seems to have evaporated under the relentless streak of humanitarian disasters of recent years (prompted in part by the rejection of a democratic form of rule). The debate is ongoing about the legacy of the International Tribunals for Rwanda and the former Yugoslavia. The consensus exists on just one particular count: the tribunals served the cause of advancing international criminal law; to put it differently, international lawyers had a great opportunity to hone their professional skills. Twenty-odd years after the Dayton Agreement, the balance of power in Bosnia-Herzegovina appears hanging by a thread, while political stability in Rwanda is associated with the increasingly authoritarian President Paul Kagame, who has been running the country effectively since the 1994 genocide. To avoid the complexity and the cost of such massive undertakings, the international community has since then scaled down its ambitions. The answer is the so-called hybrid tribunals like the one in Cambodia, which produced, well, mixed results. The initial enthusiasm for truth and reconciliation commissions also took a hit. Pressed to name at least one unambiguous success story, scholars typically point to South Africa—the country mired in corruption with inequality levels higher now than they ever were under apartheid. At present, the prospect for yet another commission exists only in the case of Colombia. And some countries, notably Russia, have skipped this stage altogether.

The depreciation of international criminal justice informs even those few instances that can be construed as positive. There is a tacit understanding that by proclaiming a violent conflict anywhere in the world as genocide, the claimant state or the United Nations is expected to act. Yet, when the US State Department in March 2016 defined the comprehensive assault on Syrian and Iraqi Christians by the so-called Islamic State as genocide, there was no expectation that the United States would change its policy in the Middle East to specifically alleviate the plight of the Yazidis.[22] Remarkably, this is probably the only such case in over a decade where the affirmation of genocide rings true. Obviously, it goes beyond specific countries and/or international criminal justice. Rather, it is the unfulfilled promise of a "global village." Nothing illustrates it better than the election of Donald Trump as US president and his "America first" agenda. Off-the-cuff references to genocide are, therefore, just a reflection of the growing mistrust of globalization. The more split the world, the more genocide rhetoric there will be. The only hope is that the current crisis, and a milder version of the Cold War that it has informed, is cyclical. One thing we know for sure is that geopolitics, in its primeval form, is here to stay.

APPENDIX A

TABLE A.1. Articles in *Pravda* with Reference to Genocide, 1948–1988 (by year)

Year	Articles	Year	Articles
1948	9	1969	21
1949	0	1970	27
1950	0	1971	25
1951	1	1972	41
1952	12	1973	14
1953	2	1974	9
1954	4	1975	8
1955	1	1976	8
1956	4	1977	18
1957	0	1978	32
1958	1	1979	94
1959	2	1980	53
1960	3	1981	79
1961	5	1982	188
1962	4	1983	64
1963	16	1984	66
1964	2	1985	61
1965	12	1986	36
1966	11	1987	30
1967	22	1988	40
1968	13	**Total**	**1,037**

TABLE A.2. Articles in *Pravda* with Reference to Genocide, 1948–1988 (by subject)

Algerian War	5
Angola	4
apartheid South Africa	25
Argentina	1
Armenians in Ottoman Turkey (a 1965)	13
Biafra, false allegation of genocide in	1
Bolivia	1
Canada, discrimination against the indigenous population (1983, 1987)	2
Chad	1
children as victims	2
Chile	4
China, action in Inner Mongolia	1
China, complicit in Khmer Rouge crimes in Cambodia (a 1978)	26
colonialism	5
Colombia	2
Cuba, "economic genocide" against	1
Cuba, Batista's terror in	1
Cuban resolution on Hungary (1956)	4
Dominican Republic	1
East Pakistan (Bangladesh)	4
El Salvador	73
fascism	1
French Somaliland	1
Genocide Convention drafting process in UN (1948)	10
Guatemala	11
Guinea Bissau	4
Haiti (1982)	1
the Holocaust (1988)	3
imperialism	17
Indonesia, "political genocide" in	1
Iraq, persecution of Kurds in (1963)	7
Israel, mistreatment of Palestinians (a 1967, mainly post-1979)	256
Khmer Republic, killing of native Vietnamese in (1970)	1
Khmer Rouge Cambodia (a 10/1978)	206

Korean War	5
Laos	3
Latvia, claim of "cultural genocide" in disputed	1
Mozambique	10
Mountainous Karabakh (Sumgait massacre)	1
Namibia	7
Nazi mass crimes	27
Nicaragua	25
nuclear weapons, threat of	10
Paraguay	3
Pakistan, mistreatment of Pashtu tribes (1985–1986)	3
Rhodesia (Zimbabwe)	13
Socialism as antithesis	1
state sovereignty	1
Uganda, Museveni's claims (1986)	2
UN as a body to counter genocide	1
Uruguay	1
USA complicit in the death of native peoples of Brazil (1984)	7
USA conducts subversive operations	2
USA, discrimination against African Americans in (a 1951)	54
USA, extermination of Native Americans (a 1966, mostly 1983–1986)	26
USA, "industrial genocide" in	1
USA invades Grenada (1983)	3
USA, nonratification of the Genocide Convention by (a 1954, mostly post-1977)	19
USA shields perpetrators of genocide	3
USA, strategic bombing of Cambodia	1
USSR/Ukrainian SSR/Belorussian SSR ratify the Genocide Convention	3
USSR helps victims of genocide	1
USSR as a protector against genocide	3
USSR to work toward elimination of genocide (1986)	2
Vietnam War	103
West Germany, prosecution of war crimes in	2
Total	**1,037**

APPENDIX B

TABLE B.1. Articles in the *New York Times* with Reference to Genocide, 1948–1988 (by year)

1948	169	1969	132
1949	99	1970	155
1950	109	1971	119
1951	67	1972	112
1952	79	1973	68
1953	76	1974	83
1954	37	1975	59
1955	16	1976	64
1956	42	1977	73
1957	12	1978	90
1958	11	1979	103
1959	33	1980	91
1960	38	1981	66
1961	55	1982	120
1962	24	1983	52
1963	31	1984	72
1964	38	1985	103
1965	48	1986	91
1966	43	1987	95
1967	87	1988	117
1968	119	**Total**	**3,098**

TABLE B.2. Articles in the *New York Times* with Reference to Genocide, 1948–1988 (by subject)

ABA stand on	30
Afghanistan	17
Algerian War	11
Amritsar temple in Punjab, India, massacre at	4
Angola	6
apartheid South Africa	13
Argentina	4
Armenian genocide (a 1964)	88
Armenian terrorism	31
Assyrians, ancient, used	1
Australia	1
Austria, mistreatment of ethnic Slovenes in	2
Azerbaijan, attack on ethnic Armenians in	1
Baltic states	16
Belgrade Conference of Nonaligned Nations	2
Biafra	98
birth control as a means of	29
"Black genocide" in in the United States	197
Black Panthers	14
Bolivia	1
Brazil, mistreatment of the indigenous population in	9
Bricker Amendment	4
British Guiana	2
Burma	2
Cambodia, Lon Nol government in commits	1
Cambodia, Khmer Rouge genocide in	86
Cambodia, charges South Vietnam with genocide of Khmer	4
Canada, mistreatment of the indigenous population in	3
Canada, cultural genocide against the Francophone population in	4
Chile	1
China	7
Colombia	1
Congo	13
Covenant on Political and Civil Rights (1954)	1

Cuba	5
Cyprus	19
Czechoslovakia	3
DDT	3
Dominican Republic	3
Draft Code of Offences Against the Peace and Security of Mankind	8
East Pakistan (Bangladesh)	56
ecocide	10
"economic genocide" (1952)	1
Eichmann trial	48
El Salvador	19
Equatorial Guinea	3
Eskimo people (1963)	1
Ethiopia, commits genocide against the Eritrean people	7
Ethiopia, man-made famine in	3
etymology of the word	5
forced labor in Communist bloc countries	4
French Somaliland	1
Genocide Convention, Chinese revision of (1952–1953)	15
Genocide Convention drafting process in UN (1948)	124
Genocide Convention, general	87
Genocide Convention, lobbying on behalf of	4
Genocide Convention, ratification/adherence to by individual countries	45
Genocide Convention, signing by individual countries	16
Genocide Convention, Soviet reservations to	5
Greece, forced transfer of children from	7
Greeks, ethnic in the USSR deported	1
Guatemala	12
Haiti	2
Hawaii	2
Holocaust curriculum (a 1977)	15
Hungary (a 1951, mainly 1956)	31
homosexuals facing	5
ICC	4
India, targeting Naga fighters (1962)	1
India-Pakistan, mutual recriminations in the wake of the 1947 partition	28
Indonesia	5

"industrial genocide"	1
International Law Commission	1
Iraq, persecution of Christians in (1978)	1
Iraq, persecution of Kurds in	33
Iran-Iraq War	1
Iran, persecution of Baha'i in	9
Iran, persecution of Kurds in (a 1979)	2
Iran, shah accused of	1
Israel, Arab states attempt genocide against	36
Israel, accused of genocide (a 1953, mainly post-1982)	79
Israel, legislation on genocide in	2
Italy, squeezing out German minority	1
Japan, whaling	1
Japanese POWs in Soviet captivity	1
Jewish assimilation in America as	3
Jews, the threat of genocide in the Arab world	8
Jews, cultural genocide committed against in Romania	2
Jews, cultural genocide committed against in the USSR	36
Jonestown, Guyana, mass suicide in as genocide	1
Jordan, mistreatment of Palestinians in	2
Katyn, mass execution of Polish officers in	3
Kenya, allegations of genocide by the British	1
Khrushchev's "Secret Speech"	1
Laos	6
lead poisoning as	1
Lebanon, Christians in under threat of genocide	8
Lemkin, Raphael	18
Libya	3
Lithuania	7
malaria epidemic as	1
Mariana Islands	1
Morocco	1
Mozambique	2
Namibia	3
narcotic drugs as an instrument of	11
Native Americans (a 1953, mainly post-1968)	83
Nazi genocide of the Jews	398

Nazi war criminals in America	4
Neo-Nazis in America	3
Nicaragua	14
Niger	12
Northern Ireland	9
nuclear weapons, threat of	22
Palestine, the 1947 partition	4
Paraguay	6
Peru	1
the Philippines, mistreatment of Muslims in	8
philosophical, literary, artistic, and religious interpretations of	296
PLO commits	9
Poland	4
pollution as	1
Portugal commits genocide in colonies	2
Potato Famine in Ireland	3
prevention of genocide	1
Puerto Ricans	4
Red Brigades	1
Rhodesia	1
Romania	4
Ruanda-Urundi	28
Saudi Arabia, the 1987 clash at Mecca	1
Scotland, England committed genocide in the eighteenth century	1
South Korea charges	9
Slovenes, Yugoslavia claims Italians commit genocide against	1
South America, mistreatment of the indigenous populations in	1
"Soviet genocide"	66
Soviet legislation on genocide (1988)	1
Soviet ratification	5
Sri Lanka, persecution of ethnic Tamils	14
Sudan	6
Suriname	1
Syria, accused of genocide in Lebanon	1
Tanzania	1
Tibet	34
terrorism as	1

Uganda	13
Ukraine	8
United Kingdom, ratification delayed	2
Universal Declaration of Human Rights and	1
US ratification delayed	153
US ratification, Dulles says no to	5
US ratification, lobbying for	118
US ratification, lobbying against	14
US ratification, Senate hearings on	9
Vietnam War	63
Vietnam War, Russell tribunal	15
"We Charge Genocide" petition by the Civil Rights Congress	12
Western Europe	1
West Germany, legislation on genocide and war crimes in	7
Yemen	2
Yugoslavia, mistreatment of ethnic groups in	11
Zimbabwe	2
Total	**3,098**

ACKNOWLEDGMENTS

It took nearly seventeen years for this project to mature from the level of an idea to an actual book. During the past twelve years I had the privilege of being associated with the Center for the Study of the Holocaust and Religious Minorities in Oslo, Norway. The center, led by director Guri Hjeltnes, has been extremely supportive of my academic research. This book would never have come to be had not it been for the center's institutional support. Among the scholars who have read and commented on the original manuscript, Douglas Irvin-Erickson of George Mason University was particularly forthcoming. I appreciate the intellectually stimulating conversations that I have had with Douglas, who also volunteered to compose a foreword.

I take pleasure in thanking the following individuals by name. Mikhail Tyyagly of the Ukrainian Center for Holocaust Studies made an effort to copy for me several Soviet publications dealing with the crime of genocide. Mary Curry and Anna Melyakova of the National Security Archives at George Washington University did me a favor by scanning a particular document upon request. The book covers some forty years of world affairs, with some of the episodes more familiar to me than the others. Hence I want to acknowledge the scholars who found time to reply to my queries: Mark Galeotti, Eric Konigsberg, Lauri Mälksoo, Zaruhi Shushanyan, Simo Mikkonen, and Gary J. Bass.

The book is dedicated to Krishna Das. The earth was burning under their feet as Krishna and her family fled East Pakistan (Bangladesh) for India. Millions of Bengalis like her simply did not have time to contemplate what name politicians put on their suffering.

NOTES

INTRODUCTION

1. Cf. William A. Schabas, *Genocide in International Law: The Crimes of Crimes* (Cambridge: Cambridge University Press, 2000).
2. "Is Lawfare Worth Defining? Report of the Cleveland Experts Meeting, September 11, 2010," *Case Western Reserve Journal of International Law* 2–3, vol. 43 (2010): 11–25.
3. Christi Scott Bartman, *Lawfare: Use of the Definition of Aggressive War by the Soviet and Russian Federation Governments* (Newcastle: Cambridge Scholars Publishing, 2010), 1–2.
4. Lawrence J. LeBlanc, *The United States and the Genocide Convention* (Durham, NC: Duke University Press, 1991), 28.
5. William A. Schabas, "Genocide and Crimes Against Humanity: Clarifying the Relationship" in *The Genocide Convention: The Legacy of 60 Years*, ed. H. G. van der Wilt et al. (Leiden: Martinus Nijhoff, 2012), 14.
6. Mathew Lippman, "The Drafting and Development of the 1948 Convention on Genocide and the Politics of International Law" in ibid., 23.
7. Mark Mazower, "The Strange Triumph of Human Rights, 1933–1950," *Historical Journal* 2, vol. 47 (2004): 380–381, 396–397; idem., *No Enchanted Palace: The End of Empire and the Ideological Origins of the United Nations* (Princeton, NJ: Princeton University Press, 2009), 1–27, 200–203.
8. Gearóid Ó Tuathail, *Critical Geopolitics* (Minneapolis: University of Minnesota Press, 1996), 16–17, 21, 54, 58–68.
9. John Erickson, "'Russia Will Not Be Trifled With': Geopolitical Facts and Fantasies" in *Geopolitics, Geography and Strategy*, ed. Collin S. Gray and Geoffrey Sloan (London: Frank Cass, 1999), 242.
10. Quoted in Hans W. Weigert et al., *Principles of Political Geography* (New York: Appleton-Century-Crofts, 1957), 5.
11. Cf. William Korey, *An Epitaph for Raphael Lemkin* (New York: Jacob Blaustein Institute for the Advancement of Human Rights of the American Jewish Committee, 2001); Samantha Power, *"A Problem from Hell": America and the Age of Genocide* (New York: Basic Books, 2002), Ch. 2–4; Robert Skloot, *If the Whole Body Dies: Raphael Lemkin and the Treaty Against Genocide* (Madison, WI: University of Wisconsin Press, 2006); Dan Eshet and Adam Strom, *Totally Unofficial: Raphael Lemkin and the Genocide Convention* (Brookline, MA: Facing History and Ourselves, 2007); John Cooper, *Raphael Lemkin and the Struggle for the Genocide Convention* (Houndmills, UK: Palgrave, 2008); Dominik J. Schaller and Jürgen Zimmerer, eds., *The Origins of Genocide: Raphael Lemkin as a Historian of Mass Violence* (London: Routledge, 2009); Roman Serbyn and Olesia Satsiuk, eds., *Raphael Lemkin: Soviet Genocide in Ukraine, Article in 28 Languages* (Kiev: Maisternia Knyhy, 2009); Agnieszka Bieńczyk-Missala and Sławomir Dębski, eds., *Rafał Lemkin: A Hero of Humankind* (Warsaw: Polish Institute of International Affairs, 2010); Steven L. Jacobs, ed., *Raphael Lemkin's Thoughts on Nazi Genocide: Not Guilty* (Jacksonville, FL: Bloch, 2010); Steven L. Jacobs, ed., *Lemkin on Genocide: Written by Raphael Lemkin* (Lanham, MD: Lexington, 2012); Donna-Lee Frieze, ed., *Totally Unofficial: The Autobiography of Raphael Lemkin* (New Haven, CT: Yale University Press, 2013); *Watchers of the Skies*, documentary (2015). Lemkin's book, *Axis Rule in Occupied Europe: Laws of Occupation, Analysis of Government, Proposals for Redress* (Washington, DC: Carnegie Endowment for International Peace, 1944), was reprinted in 2005.

12. Cf. Mark Lewis, *The Birth of the New Justice: The Internationalization of Crime and Punishment, 1919–1950* (Oxford, UK: Oxford University Press, 2014); Philippe Sands, *East West Street: On the Origins of "Genocide" and "Crimes Against Humanity"* (New York: Knopf, 2016); Douglas Irvin-Erickson, *Raphaël Lemkin and the Concept of Genocide* (Philadelphia: University of Pennsylvania Press, 2016). David Crowe is currently working on an ultimate biography of Lemkin grounded in primary sources.

13. Hirad Abtahi and Philippa Webb, eds., *The Genocide Convention: The Travaux Préparatoires* (Leiden: Martinus Nijhoff, 2008).

14. A. W. Brian Simpson, "Britain and the Genocide Convention," *British Yearbook of International Law* 1, vol. 73 (2002): 5–64; Frank Chalk, "The United Kingdom Genocide Act of 1969: Origins and Significance," unpublished article (2002), http://migs.concordia.ca/documents/UKGenocideAct.pdf.

15. Anton Weiss-Wendt, *The Soviet Union and the Gutting of the UN Genocide Convention* (Madison, WI: University of Wisconsin Press, 2017); Weiss-Wendt, ed., *Documents on the Genocide Convention from the American, British, and Russian Archives*, vols. 1–2 (London: Bloomsbury, 2018).

1. SOVIET SCHOLARS OF INTERNATIONAL LAW AS FOOT SOLDIERS IN THE COLD WAR

1. DoS position paper, "Principal Stresses and Strains Facing the US in the UN (III. Propaganda in the United Nations)" [1953], NARA, DoS general records, Assistant Secretaries of State for UN Affairs, 1945–1954, 59/58D33/5.

2. Ibid.

3. Harold D. Lasswell, "The Prospects of Cooperation in a Bipolar World," *University of Chicago Law Review* 4, vol. 15 (Summer 1948): 877, 887.

4. John N. Hazard, "Law Practice in Russia: The Organized Bar in the U.S.S.R.," *American Bar Association Journal* 35 (March 1949): 268–269; Władysław W. Kulski, "Soviet Comments on International Law and International Relations," *AJIL* 3, vol. 45 (July 1951): 563; Darrell P. Hammer, "Legal Education in the USSR," *Soviet Studies* 1, vol. 9 (July 1957): 21, 24–26.

5. Serge Gorny, "American Criminal Law as It Is Taught in Russia: A Translation from a Soviet Textbook," *American Bar Association Journal* 36 (July 1950): 542–543.

6. The Russian edition of Howard Fast's book *The Passion of Sacco and Vanzetti: A New England Legend* (1953) had the word *Passion* in the title replaced with *Heroic Deed*.

7. Gorny, "American Criminal Law as It Is Taught in Russia," 543.

8. Ibid. The Taft-Hartley Act, formally known as the Labor Management Relations Act of 1947, mainly targeted trade unions. Among other restrictions, Taft-Hartley prescribed union leaders to declare that they did not support Communism or seek to overthrow the US government by force.

9. Ibid., 544–545. Unsurprisingly, the textbook did not cite any prison population statistics for the Soviet Union.

10. The so-called Twelve Theses on International Law were adopted at a July 1938 conference convened by Vyshinsky. Taking cues from Leninist-Stalinist foreign policy, Vyshinsky insisted that the Soviet Union had a free hand in using some, but not all, principles of bourgeois international law in its relations with imperialist states.

11. Oliver J. Lissitzyn, "Recent Soviet Literature on International Law," *American Slavic and East European Review* 4, vol. 11 (December 1952): 257–273. The same year Krylov became the first Soviet lawyer to be inducted into the prestigious Institute of International Law (est. 1873).

12. Grigoryan and Yuri Zhdanov to Stalin, June 26, 1951; Korovin to the Academy of Political Science at Columbia University and the American Society of International Law (June 1951), RGASPI, 82/2/1318. It is unlikely that Korovin acted upon his own initiative. At the very least, he must have been pressured to sever his contacts with colleagues in the United States.
13. Georgy Zadorozhnyi, "'Amerikanskii zhurnal mezhdunarodnogo prava'—propovednik mezhdunarodnogo razboia i bespraviia," *SGP* 12 (December 1952): 80–87; idem., "Amerikanskaia pravovaia doktrina—zleishii vrag mezhdunarodnogo prava," *SGP* 1 (January 1953): 66–74; Kulski, "The Soviet Attitude Towards International Law and International Relations," *AJIL* 3, vol. 47 (July 1953): 486–489. Zadorozhnyi was a student of Krylov, who proposed the ICJ as a subject for his doctoral dissertation.
14. Kulski, "Soviet Comments on International Law," *AJIL* 4, vol. 45 (October 1951): 762–770.
15. Kulski, "Soviet Comments on International Law and International Relations," *AJIL* 2, vol. 45 (April 1951): 310–311.
16. Oleg Bogdanov, "Amerikanskaia mezhdunarodno-pravovaia doktrina na sluzhbe imperialisticheskoi ekspansii," *SGP* 5 (May 1952): 70; E. Dmitriev, "Amerikanskie 'gosudarstvovedy'—prisluzhniki reaktsii i fashizma," *SGP* 7 (July 1952): 59; Lydia Modzhorian, "Reaktsionnye iuristy na sluzhbe amerikanskikh agressorov," *SGP* 10 (October 1952): 85–90. See also Kulski, "Soviet Comments on International Law and International Relations," *AJIL* 1, vol. 47 (January 1953): 128.
17. The Mutual Security Act of 1951 came to replace the Marshall Plan. The most controversial part of the act was the pledge to assist persons residing in or escaped from Communist bloc countries who could provide military support to NATO. The McCarran Act, or the Subversive Activities Control Act of 1950, required Communist organizations to register with the US attorney general and provided for investigation of alleged party members.
18. A district court in New York in October 1949 found the twelve members of CPUSA guilty of conspiracy to overthrow the US government.
19. Boris Shabad, "Fashizatsia gosudarstva SShA," *SGP* 1 (January 1951): 38–45; Josif Levin, "Fashizatsiia gosudarstvennogo stroia SShA," *SGP* 4 (April 1951): 69–76; Alexei Lepeshkin, "Fashizatsia mestnykh organov upravleniia SShA," *SGP* 8 (August 1953): 66–77.
20. Review of Charles Ch. Hyde's book; David Levin, "'Mezhdunarodnoe pravo' amerikanskikh imperialisticheskikh razboinikov," *SGP* 3 (March 1951): 75–81.
21. The original draft of Code of Offenses against the Peace and Security of Mankind was presented in April 1951. The draft code had come under attack in the United States as a subtle Soviet attempt to subvert US support for anticommunist forces. For details see Weiss-Wendt, *The Soviet Union*, 191–199.
22. The Communist-affiliated CRC is mainly known for its 1951–1952 campaign to formally indict the United States for genocide. The campaign had essentially failed, since no member state was willing to take up the CRC's cause in the United Nations. For details see Weiss-Wendt, *The Soviet Union*, 228–246, 258–260.
23. The UN investigation of forced labor in 1948–1954 was aimed specifically against the Soviet Union. Nevertheless, the ad hoc committee's final report from May 1953 fell short of outright condemnation of the Soviet Union and its satellites.
24. The so-called Doctors' Plot signifies the final act in the state-sponsored campaign of antisemitism in the USSR. In January 1953 authorities arrested a group of physicians—all Jewish—and charged them with conspiracy to poison top Soviet leaders, including Stalin. Only the death of Stalin two months later spared the lives of the falsely accused.
25. Quoted in F. Ivanov, "Chetvertaia sessiia Komissii mezhdunarodnogo prava OON," *SGP* 11 (November 1952): 72.

26. Cf. Aron Trainin, "'Genotsid'," *Izvestia*, May 4, 1948; idem., "Bor'ba s genotsidom kak mezhdunarodnym prestupleniem," *SGP* 5 (May 1948): 1–16; idem., *Bor'ba progressivnykh sil protiv unichtozheniia natsional'nykh grupp i ras (Konferentsia v N'iu-Iiorke po bor'be s genotsidom)* (Moscow: *Pravda*, 1948), 1–15.

27. S. Volodin, "Konventsiia o preduprezhdenii prestupleniia genotsida i nakazaniia za nego," *SGP* 7 (December 1954): 125–128.

28. Cf. Trainin, *Ugolovnaia interventsiia* (Moscow: OGIZ, 1935); idem., *Ugolovnaia otvetstvennost gitlerovtsev* (Moscow: Iiurizdat, 1944). Trainin was a member of the Soviet prosecution team at the IMT.

29. The Martinsville Seven was a group of black American youths convicted and executed for allegedly raping a white woman in 1949.

30. Trainin, *Izbrannye proizvedeniia: Zashchita mira i ugolovnyi zakon* (Moscow: Nauka, [1956] 1969), 407–412. Trainin's discussion of the status of race relations in the United States is just one example of his ideological compliance. The Soviet newspapers dismissed the Supreme Court's decision in *Brown v. Board of Education* as mere propaganda, inconsequential in a social system permeated with racism. See Richard Lentz and Karla K. Gower, *The Opinions of Mankind: Racial Issues, Press, and Propaganda in the Cold War* (Columbia, MO: University of Missouri Press, 2010), 81–82.

31. IADL was established in October 1946 with the purpose of promoting international law, "democratic principles," and lasting peace. In reality, it was one of many Communist-front organizations. On the application of the term *genocide* to the warfare in Korea see Weiss-Wendt, *The Soviet Union*, 209–224.

32. Trainin, *Izbrannye proizvedeniia*, 411, 413–414.

33. Ibid., 415–421. See also a critical review of one other theoretical treatise by Donnedieu de Vabres in *SGP* 3 (1940): 136–141. The book was essentially a series of university lectures delivered by Donnedieu de Vabres in November 1937. In the two lectures dealing with the Soviet criminal law (Ch. 7–8) Donnedieu de Vabres provided a comprehensive overview of extrajudicial proceedings from the Red Terror to the Great Terror.

34. "Genotsid," *Bolshaia sovetskaia entsiklopedia*, vol. 10 (Moscow: Sovetskaia entsiklopedia, 1952), 440–441.

35. In Soviet/Russian academic tradition, the author of a dissertation is obliged to publish an abstract (Russian: *avtoreferat*) one month prior to the defense. Following the successful defense, the person in question is designated a candidate of science—the first postgraduate degree equivalent to a PhD.

36. Mikhail Andriukhin, *Genotsid—prestuplenie protiv chelovechestva* (Moscow: Moscow Law Institute, 1954), 1–4, 10–13.

37. Ibid., 5–9.

38. Ibid., 12–16.

39. Andriukhin, *Genotsid—tiagchaishee prestuplenie protiv chelovechestva* (Moscow: Gosiurizdat, 1961), 3–6, 20, 119.

40. Ibid., 22–44, 70–71. The notion of German militarism and neofascism had emerged in May 1950 (Andrei Fateev, *Obraz vraga v sovetskoi propagande, 1945–1954 gg.* [Moscow: IRI RAN, 1999], 128).

41. Ibid., 44–57, 82.

42. Ibid., 72–88.

43. Ibid., 75, 88–91.

44. Ibid., 91–93, 120. For a recent perspective on the forced Sovietization of East Europe see Anne Applebaum, *Iron Curtain: The Crushing of Eastern Europe, 1944–1956* (New York: Doubleday, 2012).

45. Vladimir Tismaneanu, "Diabolical Pedagogy and the (Il)logic of Stalinism in Eastern Europe" in *Stalinism Revisited: The Establishment of Communist Regimes in East-Central Europe*, ed. Tismaneanu (Budapest: CEU Press, 2009): 26–27.
46. San Diego County Federation of Republican Women's Clubs, Resolution on President Nixon's Request for Ratification of the U.N. Genocide Convention, April 13, 1970, NARA, DoS general records, subject numerical files, 1970–1973. Social, 59/1613/3042.
47. "Genocide Treaty Exposed," *Liberty Letter* (June 1970), WAG, 37/3/34.
48. See, for example, G. & C. Merriam Company to Elizabeth Nowinsky, February 15, 1950, NYPL, ZL-273/1. The respective entry in *Webster's New International Dictionary* also featured "cultural groups."
49. Andriukhin, *Genotsid v politike imperialisticheskikh gosudarstv* (Moscow: Znanie, 1967), 4–20.
50. Ibid., 20–47.
51. Sergei Tikhvinsky, "Itogi i perspektivy issledovanii sovetskikh istorikov," *Voprosy istorii* 7 (July 1985): 10.
52. Alexander Galkin, ed., *Genocide* (Moscow: Progress Publishers, 1985), 6–9.
53. Ibid., 37–87.
54. Ibid., 88–146.
55. Ibid., 159–170. Cf. UN General Assembly resolution 3068 (XXVIII).

2. TRIAL BY WORD

1. "Russia's Prison Camps," *NYT*, December 28, 1948.
2. Anne Applebaum has quoted the figure 18 million—the number of people who passed through the Soviet camps and colonies between 1929 and 1953. In addition, one should count among the victims some 6 million exiles, effectively forced laborers who lived outside the barbed wire. Beyond that, calculating the sum total of the Gulag population, and not least the excess deaths, may be next to impossible (Anne Applebaum, *Gulag: A History* [New York: Doubleday, 2003], xvii, 515–521).
3. "Slavery in Russia," *Chicago Daily Tribune*, November 14, 1947; Cyrus L. Sulzberger, "Soviet Forced Labor Held Economic Asset in Study," *NYT*, June 30, 1948.
4. Some four dozen autobiographical accounts written by former Gulag prisoners and occasional foreign visitors in Russian, English, German, and French had appeared by 1947. For an annotated bibliography of earlier books on Soviet terror see David J. Dallin and Boris I. Nicolaevsky, *Forced Labor in Soviet Russia* (New Haven: Yale University Press, 1947), 309–319; Jonathan D. Smele, *The Russian Revolution and Civil War, 1917–1921: An Annotated Bibliography* (London: Continuum, 2002), 161–165; Susan L. Carruthers, *Cold War Captives: Imprisonment, Escape, and Brainwashing* (Berkeley, CA: University of California Press, 2009), 101–105.
5. Dallin and Nicolaevsky, *Forced Labor in Soviet Russia*, 218–220, 222, 229.
6. Carruthers, *Cold War Captives*, 107–108.
7. Except for a confession of nearly giving up and signing up the falsified testimony under duress, Kravchenko invariably depicted himself as having helped people in peril, whether they were starving peasants, denounced coworkers, or individual camp inmates. Hard to verify, this constitutes perhaps the most problematic part of his account.
8. "Soviet Official Here Resigns; Assails 'Double-Faced' Policies," *NYT*, April 4, 1944.
9. Victor Kravchenko, *I Chose Freedom*, 105, 107, 111, 114, 116, 118, 130–131, 134–135, 211–218, 226, 236–237, 242–243, 284, 295, 336–341, 469, 475. Whether Kravchenko's ghost editor and translator should be credited for turning the incoherent typescript of 1,500 pages into powerful prose—as pinpointed by some critics—is beyond the point.

10. (Chile: Ocampo; USSR: Pavlov), UN Official Records, third session of the General Assembly, 139th Plenary Meeting (December 7, 1948): 769, 775. Pavlov was apparently referring to Kravchenko. Ocampo expanded on his thesis in a pamphlet that appeared in print on December 1, 1949. See *El neo zarismo totalitario de la Unión Soviética* (Santiago de Chile: Imprenta Chile, 1949).

11. Gulag, transfer deed of the Gulag to the Soviet Ministry of Inners, September 2, 1947, http://www.alexanderyakovlev.org/fond/issues-doc/1009232; CPSU Central Committee, decree banning marriages between Soviet citizens and foreigners, February 15, 1947, http://www.alexanderyakovlev.org/fond/issues-doc/69332. The ban on marriage stayed until October 14, 1953. Applebaum has identified at least 476 distinct camp complexes, consisting of thousands of subcamps, which operated in the USSR through 1960. See Applebaum, *Gulag*, xvi. For the Gulag population statistics see Nicolas Werth, "A State Against Its People: Violence, Repression, and Terror in the Soviet Union" in *The Black Book of Communism: Crimes, Terror, Repression*, ed. Stéphane Courtois et al. (Cambridge, MA: Harvard University Press, 1999), 203–231.

12. DoS, report of the Sixth Committee on the item proposed by Chile, March 17, 1949, NARA, DoS, Bureau of Int. Org. Affairs and its predecessors, 59/3039E/28. See also UN docs. A/C.6/296, A/C.6/311, and A/C.6/316; doc. 375, reproduced in Allida Black, ed., *The Eleanor Roosevelt Papers: The Human Rights Years, 1945–1948. Part 2* (Charlottesville, VA: University of Virginia Press, 2010), 887–890.

13. DoS, position paper, "Protest by Chile Concerning Refusal of USSR to Allow Soviet Daughter-in-Law of Former Chilean Ambassador to Leave Soviet Union," August 26, 1948, NARA, DoS, Bureau of Int. Org. Affairs and its predecessors, 59/867223/27.

14. Unidentified British report on Soviet mass deportations [after June 1946], AJHS, P-154/7/10. The NKVD used forty-six trains to deport the 26,359 Kalmyk families, or 93,139 persons, to Siberia in the first days of January 1944. Beria to Stalin and Molotov re: the Kalmyk resettlement operation, January 3, 1944, http://www.alexanderyakovlev.org/fond/issues-doc/58887. An estimated 459,486 Chechens and Ingush were slated for deportation later that February. Beria to Stalin re: the preparations for the resettlement of Chechens and Ingush, February 17, 1944, http://www.alexanderyakovlev.org/fond/issues-doc/58891.

15. Brian Glyn Williams, "Hidden Ethnocide in the Soviet Muslim Borderlands: The Ethnic Cleansing of the Crimean Tartars," *Journal of Genocide Research* 3, vol. 4 (2002): 361.

16. Birgit Brauer, "Chechens and the Survival of Their Cultural Identity in Exile," ibid., 389–392; Michaela Pohl, "'It Cannot Be That Our Graves Will Be Here': The Survival of Chechen and Ingush Deportees in Kazakhstan, 1944–1957," ibid., 404–407.

17. Werth, "A State Against Its People," 219–225.

18. British Foreign Office, Information Research Department, white paper, "The Dispersal and Destruction of Small Nations by the Soviet Government" [December 1950], NA, F.O. 1110/421/PR66/2. The Information Research Department was established in 1948 to counter Soviet propaganda, especially in Third World countries. The department employed a number of East European émigrés.

19. British Foreign Office, memoranda on the IRD's white paper, December 12–18, 1950, NA, F.O. 1110/421/PR66/2.

20. Robert Conquest, memo, "The Genocide Theme," January 18, 1951, NA, F.O. 1110/421/PR66/2. See also Karen E. Smith, *Genocide and the Europeans* (Cambridge, UK: Cambridge University Press, 2010), 49.

21. British Foreign Office, IRD, memo, "Soviet Genocide," November 24, 1951, NA, F.O. 1110/421/PR66/8.

22. David C. Engerman, *Know Your Enemy: The Rise and Fall of America's Soviet Experts* (Oxford: Oxford University Press, 2009), 264, 269–272, 274, 308; Lennart Samuelson, "A

Pathbreaker: Robert Conquest and Soviet Studies During the Cold War," *Baltic Worlds* 1, vol. 2 (April 2009): 47–51.

23. Alexander Uralov (Abdurakhman Avtorkhanov), *Narodoubiistvo v SSSR: Ubiistvo chechenskogo naroda* (Munich: "Free Caucasus," 1952), 6–8, 35–44, 50–53, 59–69. Cf. Moshe Gammer, *The Lone Wolf and the Bear: Three Centuries of Chechen Defiance of Russian Rule* (Pittsburgh: University of Pittsburgh Press, 2006).

24. Nikolai Deker and Andrei Lebed, eds., *Genocide in the USSR: Studies in Group Destruction* (Munich: Institut zur Erforschung der UdSSR, 1958), vii–viii, 1–5, 16–27, 34–35, 44–45, 54, 77, 87, 105, 138, 219, 226–242, 251. See also the book review in *NYT*, November 26, 1958. The section on the Crimean Tatars mentioned a "Committee for the Investigation of Genocide in the USSR" (p. 25), the only such reference on record. Most likely, the author was referring to the research conducted at the Munich institute leading up to the symposium and eventually book publication.

25. Gunnar Helge Carlsen, "Altså—så var det sant!" *Bergens Tidende*, September 28, 1991.

26. Carruthers, *Cold War Captives*, 111.

27. Marc Szeftel, review of Dallin and Nicolaevsky's book, *American Historical Review* 3, vol. 54 (April 1949): 603–605.

28. Dallin and Nicolaevsky, *Forced Labor in Soviet Russia*, ix, xiii–xiv, 40, 88, 92–107, 299, 304.

29. Lemkin to Sidney Ruttenberg, no date, AJHS, P-154/1/10.

30. Dallin, *The Economics of Slave Labor* (Chicago: Henry Regnery, 1949), 3–4, 9–20, 28–29.

31. Albert K. Herling, *The Soviet Slave Empire* (New York: Wilfred Funk, 1951), v–x, 72–76, 197–207.

32. Aleksander Kaelas, *Human Rights and Genocide in the Baltic States: A Statement Submitted to the Delegations to the United Nations General Assembly, September 1950* (Stockholm: Estonian Information Center, 1950), ii, 3, 10, 49–55. An Estonian lawyer, Kaelas fled in 1944 to Sweden.

33. Grigaitis, LAC, to Lemkin, February 2, 1950, NYPL, ZL-273/1.

34. K. Pelékis, *Genocide: Lithuania's Threefold Tragedy* (Bielefeld: Venta, 1949), 7, 42–82, 152–153.

35. Ibid., 183, 192–195, 201, 206, 231–239.

36. Released by the State Department on January 21, 1948, the document collection, *Nazi-Soviet Relations from 1939 to 1941*, was hailed in the American press as perhaps the best piece of propaganda against the USSR to date. See Weiss-Wendt, *The Soviet Union*, 61–62.

37. *Appeal to the United Nations on Genocide* (Reutlingen: Supreme Lithuanian Committee of Liberation, 1951), 4–24, 35, 40–41, 46, 49.

38. Albert Kalme, *Total Terror: An Exposé of Genocide in the Baltics* (New York: Appleton-Century-Crofts, 1951), 8–11, 216–219, 225, 229–234.

39. Abramcyk initially collaborated with the Nazis but in 1943 was elected president of the Belorussian People's Republic in Exile. In parallel, he chaired the League for the Liberation of the Peoples of the USSR.

40. Wacław Szyszkowski, "Should the Genocide Convention Remain a Dead Letter?" *Intermarium: Bulletin of the Central European Federal Clubs in Paris and in Rome* 15, vol. 7 (May 1951): 12–14.

41. Curtis Richardson, "Stalinist Terror and the Kalmyks' National Revival: A Cultural and Historical Perspective," *Journal of Genocide Research* 3, vol. 4 (2002): 442, 447.

42. Martin to Lemkin, June 25, 1954, AJA, 60/2/8.

43. Francis Macy to Naminov, October 23, 1954, AJA, 60/2/9. Naminov was among the seventy Kalmyks who in December 1961 paid a visit to the US State Department. The delegation formally thanked US authorities for having accepted Kalmyk refugees. Although it was not a focus of the conversation, genocide was mentioned. See Rasa Gustaitis, "Kalmyks Trek Here, Thankful to Be in U.S.," *Washington Post and Times Herald*, December 16, 1961.

44. Dobriansky, statement before the Senate Foreign Relations Committee urging the ratification of the Genocide Convention [January 1950], AJHS, P-154/7/10.
45. Dorothy Weber to Lemkin, December 16, 1954, AJA, 60/2/17-W. Weber was writing a paper on the Soviet deportation of Kalmyks.
46. Sender, AFL, to Lemkin, January 16, 1950, AJHS, P-154/2/3.
47. Lemkin to Spellman, Archbishop of New York, September 13, 1949, AJHS, P-154/2/2.
48. Rosenberg to Lemkin, October 26, 1951, NYPL, ZL-273/1.
49. Lemkin at college roundtable on the UN Genocide Convention [no date], AJA, 60/4/2.
50. Lemkin to Spellman, September 13, 1949, AJHS, P-154/2/2.
51. Lemkin, draft letter no. 1 [no date], AJHS, P-154/2/5.
52. Ukrainian Evangelical Alliance of North America, resolutions, September 23, 1958, AJA, 60/4/3.
53. George E. Sokolsky, "These Days: Minorities Here and in Russia," *Washington Post and Times Herald*, July 9, 1958. See also Lewis, *The Birth of the New Justice*, 227.
54. *The Crimes of Khrushchev*, pt. 1, September 4, 1959 (Washington, DC: Government Printing Office, 1959), 9; ibid., pt. 2, September 9–11, 1959, 2, 5–7, 13, 41, 45, 51, 66; ibid., pt. 6, December 17, 1959, 22–24. See also "Khrushchev Crime Report Tells of Terror, Death," *Hartford Courant*, October 12, 1959. Lebed and Tumash were paid CIA agents; the former had been implicated in the mass murder of Jews and Poles during WWII.
55. "Ukrainian National Revolution vs. Russian Bolshevik Revolution!" *NYT*, November 16, 1967.
56. Caryle Murphy, "Ukrainian Americans Commemorate Famine in Homeland 50 Years Ago," *Washington Post*, October 1, 1983; "March in Washington Protests Famine in Ukraine 50 Years Ago," *Los Angeles Times*, October 3, 1983.
57. "7,000 Ukrainians Hold March in Washington," *NYT*, September 17, 1984.
58. DoS, report, "The Current Status of Human Rights in the Soviet Bloc," December 27, 1957, NARA, DoS general records, Bureau of Int. Org. Affairs and Its Predecessors, position papers, 1945–74, 59/82D211/44. The 49,000 exiled Kalmyks were released only in March 1956 and their autonomy was restored in January 1957; the 245,000 Karachai, Chechen, and Ingush were able to return in July 1956, though not to their ancestral home in the Caucasus. See Steven A. Barnes, *Death and Redemption: The Gulag and the Shaping of Soviet Society* (Princeton, NJ: Princeton University Press, 2011), 241, 245.
59. DoS, US Embassy in Moscow to Secretary of State Rusk, March 9, 1963, NARA, DoS general records, central foreign policy file, 1963, 59/939556/3252.
60. See, for example, editorial, "The Soviet Minorities," *NYT*, February 13, 1957.
61. Lemkin to ILO Office [before June 25, 1957], NYPL, ZL-273/2.
62. Cherif M. Bassiouni, "Enslavement as an International Crime," *New York University Journal of International Law & Politics* 23 (1991): 464–476, 481–482. See also CHRGT, fact sheet on the Convention Concerning the Abolition of Forced Labor [1965], WAG, 37/6/31.
63. No title, no date, AJA, 60/4/7.
64. Lemkin to Elisabeth Pelletier, May 2, 1957, AJA, 60/2/5.
65. Assistant Secretary of State for Congressional Relations Frederick G. Dutton to Congressman George H. Fallon, July 6, 1962, NARA, DoS decimal files, 1960–1963, 59/949637/570.
66. V. Skvortsov and V. Tiurkin, "Glazami druzei," *Pravda*, December 12, 1972.
67. "Criticize Soviets," *Hartford Courant*, November 19, 1968.
68. Joseph Prunskis, "We Should Also Remember the Holocaust That Befell Balts," *Chicago Tribune*, June 1, 1978; idem., "The 40th Anniversary of Soviet Captivity," *Chicago Tribune*, June 9, 1981. Prunskis was active in the LAC.

69. Julian Freeman, AJC, to Rusk, April 21, 1961; AJC resolution on Eichmann and Genocide Convention, April 16, 1961; Heinz Gelles, President of AJC, to Harlan Cleveland, Assistant Secretary of State, June 23, 1961, NARA, DoS decimal files, 1960–63, 59/949637/570.

70. Myer Klarfeld, Chairman of the United Warsaw Ghetto Memorial Committee, to Kennedy, April 29, 1962, NARA, DoS decimal files, 1960–1963, 59/949637/570.

71. NCRAC Legislative Information Committee, meeting minutes, March 9, 1951, WAG, 25/290/30; Edward S. Goldstein, draft chapter, "German Reparations/Genocide Convention" from an unfinished PhD thesis on the history of the JLC [mid-1970s], WAG, 232/1/6.

3. SOVIET SATELLITES SHIFT ALLEGIANCES

1. Katalin Kádár Lynn, "At War While at Peace: United States Cold War Policy and the National Committee for a Free Europe, Inc." in *The Inauguration of Organized Political Warfare: Cold War Organizations Sponsored by the National Committee for a Free Europe/Free Europe Committee*, ed. Katalin Kádár Lynn (Saint Helena, CA: Helena History Press, 2013), 33–35; idem., "The Hungarian National Council/Hungarian National Committee" in ibid., 238–240, 244, 258–259.

2. Ibid., 262, 304f.

3. Statement of Béla Varga, December 2, 1951, AJA, 60/4/3. See also "Hungarian Exiles Call on U.N. to Act," *NYT*, December 2, 1951.

4. US Embassy in Panama to DoS, December 5, 1951, NARA, DoS decimal files, 1950–1954, 59/862915/1341.

5. Lemkin to Samuels, *NYT*, December 7, 1951, NYPL, ZL-273/1.

6. John C. Somers to US delegation to the United Nations, January 6, 1951 [1952]; Rudolf Benedikter to US delegation to the United Nations, January[?] 1952; Porter McKeever, Director of Information for the US delegation to the United Nations, to Somers, January 28, 1952; McKeever to Benedikter, January 28, 1952, NARA, DoS decimal files, 1950–1954, 59/862915/1342.

7. Béla Fábián, "Letters to the Times: Deportations by Soviets," *NYT*, August 15, 1952. Fábián sat on the HNC's executive committee.

8. Varga to Dulles, February 27, 1953; HNC, "Soviets Undermine Genocide Convention in the U.N.," February 26, 1953, NARA, DoS decimal files, 1950–54, 59/862915/1342.

9. "Instructions on the Procedure of Carrying Out the Deportation of the Anti-Soviet Elements from Lithuania, Latvia, and Estonia," signed by the Security Police Deputy Head Ivan Serov sometime between February and June 1941, had acquired a central place in the discussion of Soviet terror in the Baltic States. Cardinal József Mindszenty was the Roman Catholic primate of Hungary who opposed the imposition of Communism. His arrest and subsequent trial in February 1949 on bogus charges of treason and espionage made Mindszenty a cause célèbre for the anticommunist movement.

10. *Genocide by Deportation: An Appeal to the United Nations to Enforce the Law* (New York: Hungarian National Council, 1951), 15–21, 27–28, 31, 63, 66, 69, 71–72, 74, 77, 92. István Kovács was mistakenly identified in the book as "chairman" rather than vice president of the Presidential Council of the People's Republic of Hungary. On the Mindszenty trial in February 1949 see Carruthers, *Cold War Captives*, 115–116, 136–139, 143–144.

11. DoS, position paper, "Hungary," February 7, 1949, NARA, DoS general files, subject files of Durwald V. Sandifer, 59/917370/8.

12. Varga to Salit, October 6, 1954, AJA, 60/2/16-U-V.

13. Investigation of Communist Take-Over and Occupation of Hungary, Fifth Interim Report of Hearings Before the Subcommittee on Hungary of the Select Committee on Communist

Aggression, House of Representatives, 83rd Congress, 2nd Session (Washington, DC: Government Printing Office, 1954), i–v, 12.

14. Vince Nagy, President of the Federation of Free Hungarian Jurists in America, "Indictment against Responsible Members of the Russian and the Hungarian Government," June 1954, NYPL, ZL-273/4. Lemkin had confirmed he "worked with the Hungarians" (Donna-Lee Frieze, ed., *Totally Unofficial: The Autobiography of Raphael Lemkin* [New Haven, CT: Yale University Press, 2013], 220). For an authoritative discussion on the problem of retroactivity, see William A. Schabas, "Retroactive Application of the Genocide Convention," *University of St. Thomas Journal of Law and Public Policy* 2, vol. 4 (Spring 2010): 36–59.

15. Varga's statement, October 28, 1956, AJA, 60/4/4.

16. Scott Lucas, *Freedom's War: The US Crusade Against the Soviet Union, 1945–46* (Manchester, UK: Manchester University Press, 1999), 254–260; Ilya Gaiduk, *Divided Together: The United States and the Soviet Union in the United Nations, 1945–1965* (Washington, DC: Woodrow Wilson Center Press, 2012), 218–221; Brian McCauley, "Hungary and Suez, 1956: The Limits of Soviet and American Power," *Journal of Contemporary History* 4, vol. 16 (October 1981): 779–794; Tony Judt, *Postwar: A History of Europe Since 1945* (New York: Penguin, 2005), 297–298, 314–319.

17. UN doc. A/PV.587.

18. Jennifer Amos, "Embracing and Contesting: The Soviet Union and the Universal Declaration of Human Rights, 1948–1958" in *Human Rights in the Twentieth Century*, ed. Stefan Ludwig Hoffmann (Cambridge, UK: Cambridge University Press, 2010), 157.

19. "Svet i teni v zale Generalnoi Assamblei," *Pravda*, November 19, 1956. See also Al. Romanov, "Otkrytyi vopros," *LG*, December 1, 1956.

20. "Protiv popytok ispolzovania OON dlia vmeshatelstva vo vnutrennie dela Vengrii," *Pravda*, November 20, 1956; "Debate in U.N. Assembly on Bid to Condemn Soviet and Hungary for Deportations," *NYT*, November 20, 1956.

21. Paul W. Ward, "Israel Willing to Pull Back Its Troops; U.N. Delays Any Action on Hungary Case," *Baltimore Sun*, November 9, 1956; Michael James, "U.N. to Consider Genocide Charge Against Russians," *NYT*, November 17, 1956; Henry W. Harris, "Russian Deportations up Before U.N. Today," *Daily Boston Globe*, November 19, 1956.

22. "Cuba Drops Its Charge on Genocide," *Hartford Courant*, November 19, 1956; "Charge Revised on Deportation," *Washington Post and Times Herald*, November 19, 1956; cf. Lemkin, "The Genocide Convention" [1956], AJA, 60/4/7.

23. Michael James, "Deportation Hit: Assembly's Resolution Cites Convention on Genocide," *NYT*, November 22, 1956.

24. According to Paul Lendavai's estimates, 229 Hungarians were executed and 22,000 others sentenced. As part of the "campaign of vengeance," some 13,000 landed in internment camps without legal procedure. The deportation of young insurgents into the Soviet Union was shortly rescinded upon the request of Kádár, who deemed it counterproductive. In April 1960 the Hungarian government declared partial amnesty and abolished the internment camps. See Paul Lendavai, *One Day That Shook the Communist World: The 1956 Hungarian Uprising and Its Legacy* (Princeton, NJ: Princeton University Press, 2008), 185, 214–224.

25. UN doc. A/PV.585. The reference to Khrushchev describing mass deportations from the North Caucasus as "genocide" may be coming from Cyrus L. Sulzberger's article "Khrushchev's Stalin: III—Autocrat and Autocracy" that appeared on June 9, 1956 in *NYT*.

26. "Po povodu nedostoinykh popytok podderzhat antinarodnye sily v Vengrii," *Pravda*, November 22, 1956. For the text of the resolution see UN doc. A/RES/1127 (XI).

27. "Kto narushaet prava cheloveka?" *Pravda*, December 15, 1956.

28. Weiss-Wendt, *The Soviet Union*, 138–140.

29. Cyrus L. Sulzberger, "Khrushchev's Stalin: III—Autocrat and Autocracy," *NYT*, June 9, 1956. During a secret meeting between Khrushchev and Tito in the first days on November 1956, the latter acquiesced in the Soviet use of force in Hungary. See McCauley, "Hungary and Suez, 1956," 791–792; Judt, *Postwar*, 320–321.

30. "Reds Invented Death Camps, Slav Reports," *Chicago Tribune*, February 6, 1965; Mihajlo Mihajlov, "Now It Can Be Told—By the Russians," *NYT*, March 14, 1965.

31. "President Tito Raps Prosecutor," *Baltimore Sun*, March 6, 1965; "Around the World: Writer Arrested," *Washington Post*, March 13, 1965; Anatole Shub, "Slav Writer Loses Post on Trial Eve," *Washington Post*, April 29, 1965.

32. Eric Bourne, "Slander Case Poses Test for Yugoslav Court," *Christian Science Monitor*, May 22, 1965; David Binder, "Voyage of Discovery," *NYT*, January 2, 1966; "Author Mihajlov Denies 'False Rumors' Charge," *Hartford Courant*, September 23, 1966; "Slavs Sentence Foe of System," *Baltimore Sun*, September 24, 1966; David Binder, "Mihajlov, Yugoslav Oppositionist, Sent to Prison," *NYT*, November 13, 1966; "Mihajlov Ends Yugoslav Prison Term," *NYT*, March 5, 1970. See also Richard Byrne, "The Path of Most Resistance," *Chronicle of Higher Education* 9, vol. 54 (October 26, 2007): A56.

33. Michael Dobbs, "Albania Keeps the Pot Boiling," *Guardian*, December 21, 1978.

4. THE STRUGGLE FOR INFLUENCE IN POSTCOLONIAL AFRICA AND THE MIDDLE EAST

1. Soviet Foreign Ministry, draft directive to the USSR delegation at the first session of the General Assembly re: non-self-governing territories, September 18, 1946, AVP RF, 6/8/16/223.

2. Carol Anderson, *Eyes off the Prize: The United Nations and the African American Struggle for Human Rights, 1944–1955* (New York: Cambridge University Press, 2003), 36.

3. DoS report, "USSR Attitude Toward the United Nations and the Specialized Agencies," September 15, 1947, NARA, DoS, Bureau of Int. Organization Affairs, 59/3039E/21.

4. Alexander Rudzinski, "The Influence of the United Nations on Soviet Policy," *International Organization* 2, vol. 5 (May 1950): 297; Gaiduk, *Divided Together*, 251.

5. Sergei Mazov, "The USSR and the Former Italian Colonies, 1945–1950," *Cold War History* 3, vol. 3 (April 2003): 49–78; Vladimir Pechatnov, "'The Allies Are Pressing on You to Break Your Will . . .': Foreign Policy Correspondence Between Stalin and Molotov and Other Politburo Members, September 1945–December 1946," *CWIHP*, Working Paper 26 (September 1999): 3–4, 15–17, 22.

6. See, for example, the exchange between Amazasp Arutiunian and Christopher Mayhew during the 127th and 128th meetings of the ECOSOC, ECOSOC Official Records, Third Year: Sixth Session (4–5 February 1948): 34–45.

7. DoS position paper, "Principal Stresses and Strains Facing the US in the UN (II. The Colonial Question in the United Nations)" [1953], NARA, DoS general records, Assistant Secretaries of State for UN Affairs, 1945–1954, 59/58D33/5.

8. Oles M. Smolansky, *The USSR and Iraq: The Soviet Quest for Influence* (Durham, NC: Duke University Press, 1991), 13.

9. Timothy Johnston, "Peace or Pacifism? The Soviet 'Struggle for Peace in All the World,' 1948–54," *Slavonic and East European Review* 2, vol. 86 (April 2008): 280.

10. Madeleine G. Kalb, *The Congo Cables: The Cold War in Africa—From Eisenhower to Kennedy* (New York: Macmillan, 1982), xiii, xix–xx; Roger E. Kanet, "The Superpower Quest for Empire: The Cold War and Soviet Support for 'Wars of National Liberation,'" *Cold War History* 3, vol. 6 (August 2006): 334.

11. Alvin Z. Rubinstein, "Soviet Policy Toward Under-Developed Areas in the Economic and Social Council," *International Organization* 2, vol. 9 (May 1955): 233–234, 237–238.
12. Smolansky, *The USSR and Iraq*, 14–15.
13. Galia Golan, *Soviet Policies in the Middle East from World War II to Gorbachev* (Cambridge, UK: Cambridge University Press, 1990), 11–23.
14. Odd Arne Westad, *The Global Cold War: Third World Interventions and the Making of Our Times* (Cambridge, UK: Cambridge University Press, 2007), 4–6, 40–60, 66–71.
15. The Arab Information Center in New York, draft report, "Algeria and the United Nations," September 15, 1956, NYPL, ZL-273/3. The Arab and Asian states have occasionally assembled in a caucus since 1949. Between 1956 and 1959 the percentage of member states from these two continents in the United Nations increased from 23.5 to 36.6 (Gaiduk, *Divided Together*, 244–247).
16. Westad, *The Global Cold War*, 89, 105.
17. Louis Begley, "How Wily Mitterrand Transformed France," *New York Review of Books* 10, vol. 61 (June 5–18, 2014), 40. For a concise overview of the Algerian War see Judt, *Postwar*, 285–289.
18. "M. Pineau Defends His Policy: No U.N. Vote Acceptable on Algeria," *Times*, February 5, 1957; "Rebels Insist on Free Algeria: Conference Held in Tunis," *Times*, October 31, 1957. Jean-Paul Sartre mentioned Algeria as one of the examples of what he called neocolonial genocide. See his *On Genocide* (Boston: Beacon Press, 1968), 63–67.
19. Lemkin, draft statement "To Avoid Responsibility for Genocide in Algeria the French Are Destroying the Genocide Convention" [after August 3, 1953], NYPL, ZL-273/3. See also Irvin-Erickson, *Raphaël Lemkin*, 217–220.
20. The Arab Information Center in New York, draft report, "Algeria and the United Nations," September 15, 1956, NYPL, ZL-273/3; Irvin-Erickson, *Raphaël Lemkin*, 217–220.
21. Fabian Klose, *Human Rights in the Shadow of Colonial Violence: The Wars of Independence in Kenya and Algeria* (Philadelphia: University of Pennsylvania Press, 2013), 209–212, 214–218.
22. James J. Martin, *The Man Who Invented "Genocide": The Public Career and Consequences of Raphael Lemkin* (Torrance, CA: Institute for Historical Review, 1984), 249. See also Cooper, *Raphael Lemkin*, 263.
23. Klose, *Human Rights*, 210.
24. "Mir nesomnenno pobedit: Alzhirskii vopros," *Pravda*, January 3, 1958; "Na storone boriushchegosia Alzhira vse miroliubivye narody," *Pravda*, April 6, 1959.
25. "Deklaratsia o predostavlenii nezavisimosti kolonialnym stranam i narodam," *Pravda*, September 24, 1960; "Polozhenie v Alzhire chrezvychaino napriazhennoe," "Zaiavlenie TASS," *Pravda*, December 15, 1960; "Pravoe delo pobedit," *Pravda*, December 16, 1960; "Ikh plany obrecheny na proval," *Pravda*, April 23, 1961; "Ostanovit ruku palachei!" *Pravda*, June 1, 1961; "Mir Alzhiru, otpor fashizmu," *Pravda*, March 15, 1962.
26. Martin Thomas, "France Accused: French North Africa Before the United Nations, 1952–1962," *Contemporary European History* 1, vol. 10 (March 2001): 114.
27. "Mr. Nehru Censures Britain," *Times*, May 30, 1961; "Simpatii Indii na storone Angoly," *Pravda*, June 4, 1961.
28. "Tragedia Kongo ne dolzhna povtoritsia," *Pravda*, June 2, 1961.
29. "Voina nezavisimoi Afriki," *Pravda*, September 2, 1970; "Privetstvennye vystuplenia zarubezhnykh gostei," *Pravda*, April 9, 1971; "Karateli svirepstvuiut," *Pravda*, September 10, 1972; "Osuzhdenie portugalskikh karatelei," *Pravda*, July 23, 1973.
30. Philip Potter, "Portugal Denies Atrocity Charge," *Baltimore Sun*, July 19, 1973.
31. Martin Meredith, *The Fate of Africa: From the Hopes of Freedom to the Heart of Despair* (New York: Public Affairs, 2005), 93–115; Kalb, *The Congo Cables*, xiii, 41–42, 55–58, 62–63, 69–70, 169–172; Gaiduk, *Divided Together*, 256–258, 272f.
32. "Soviet Flouts Demand by Hammarskjöld," *Observer*, September 11, 1960.

33. "Polsha negoduet," *Izvestia*, February 14, 1961. For Soviet reaction to the death of Lumumba see Kalb, *The Congo Cables*, 226–230.

34. "Polsha negoduet," *Izvestia*, February 14, 1961; "Spasti zhizn patriota," *Izvestia*, November 27, 1964.

35. "Zametaiut sledy," *Izvestia*, November 23, 1968.

36. "Na katorgu bez suda," *LG*, February 11, 1969.

37. "Sovmestnoe sovetsko-ganskoe kommiunike," *Pravda*, July 26, 1961; "Solidarnost, druzhba, sotrudnichestvo," *Pravda*, June 14, 1963.

38. "Potvorstvuiut rasistam," *Pravda*, February 23, 1969.

39. Meredith, *The Fate of Africa*, 128–134, 319–321.

40. F. Tarasov, "Kalebasa mistera Smita," *Pravda*, February 23, 1974.

41. "Prizyv k boikotu," *Pravda*, January 9, 1975; "Osuzhdenie politiki rasizma," *Pravda*, May 27, 1977.

42. "Za edinstvo neprisoedinivshikhsia stran," *Pravda*, September 4, 1979.

43. Meredith, *The Fate of Africa*, 193–204. This analysis has been largely upheld by recent research. See a special issue of *Journal of Genocide Research* (2–3, vol. 16 [2014]) on the Biafra War, especially contributions by Douglas Anthony, Roy Doron, Mari-Luce Desgrandchamps, and Brian McNeil.

44. Maxim Matusevich, *No Easy Row for a Russian Hoe: Ideology and Pragmatism in Nigerian-Soviet Relations, 1960–1991* (Trenton, NJ: Africa World Press, 2003), 106–28.

45. *The French African Connection*, documentary series produced by Tambay A. Obenson, broadcast on Al-Jazeera English, April 6, 2014.

46. Guest editorial, "Strange Bedfellows," *Chicago Tribune*, April 25, 1969.

47. D. Lozinov, "Izbityi triuk," *Izvestia*, March 27, 1969.

48. "Investigators See No Sign of Genocide in Biafra," *Washington Post and Times Herald*, October 4, 1968; George Melloan, "Bitter Nigeria," *Wall Street Journal*, February 26, 1969; Iakov Etinger, "Nigeriiskii krizis 1967–1970 godov," *Voprosy istorii* 4 (April 1976): 142.

49. Gary J. Bass, *The Blood Telegram: Nixon, Kissinger, and a Forgotten Genocide* (New York: Alfred A. Knopf, 2013), 84.

50. Kissinger to Nixon, January 28, 1969, https://history.state.gov/historicaldocuments/frus1969–76ve05p1/d25.

51. Cf. white paper by the National Security Council Interdepartmental Group for Africa, February 10, 1969, https://history.state.gov/historicaldocuments/frus1969–76ve05p1/d35; Kissinger to Nixon, July 7, 1969, https://history.state.gov/historicaldocuments/frus1969–76ve05p1/d82; CIA memo, August 5, 1969, https://history.state.gov/historicaldocuments/frus1969–76ve05p1/d100; US Embassy in Nigeria to the State Department, August 5, 1969, https://history.state.gov/historicaldocuments/frus1969–76ve05p1/d99; US Embassy in Nigeria to the State Department, January 10, 1970, https://history.state.gov/historicaldocuments/frus1969–76ve05p1/d156; memo of conversation with Assistant US Secretary of State David D. Newsom, January 17, 1970, https://history.state.gov/historicaldocuments/frus1969–76ve05p1/d169; memo to Kissinger, February 16, 1970, https://history.state.gov/historicaldocuments/frus1969–76ve05p1/d186; National Intelligence Estimate, November 2, 1970, https://history.state.gov/historicaldocuments/frus1969–76ve05p1/d201.

52. "Genocide Is Charged by Biafran Unit Here," *NYT*, January 20, 1970.

53. Robert Morris, "The Genocide Treaty," *Wanderer*, December 3, 1970. See also "The Genocide Convention," *Liberty Lowdown* 87 (May 1970), WAG, 37/3/34.

54. Matusevich, *No Easy Row for a Russian Hoe*, 17.

55. "Konets besslavnoi avantiury," *Izvestia*, January 15, 1970; "Press-konferntsia posla," *Izvestia*, January 20, 1970; N. Alov, "Poslednii reis 'serogo prividenia'," *LG*, January 28, 1970.

56. Meredith, *The Fate of Africa*, 205.

57. Matusevich, *No Easy Row for a Russian Hoe*, 146, 360–361. Even some leaders of the national liberation movements, whenever it fit their agenda, had no scruples comparing white rule in Africa to Soviet control of Eastern Europe.

58. Smolansky, *The USSR and Iraq*, 63, 65.

59. Edgar O'Balance, *The Kurdish Revolt, 1961–1970* (London: Faber and Faber, 1973), 12, 31, 34, 49–51, 56, 63–64, 89–94, 104–108; David McDowall, *The Kurds, a Minority Rights Group Report* (September 1991): 26–28; docs. nos. 67, 78, 80, 84 in *From Encroachment to Involvement: A Documentary Study of Soviet Policy in the Middle East, 1945–1973*, ed. Yaacov Ro'i (New York: John Wiley & Sons, 1974), 315–317, 355–358, 361–363, 403–405.

60. Golan, *Soviet Policies in the Middle East*, 157–164.

61. "Prekratit prestuplenia protiv kurdov!" *Pravda*, June 16, 1963; "Ostanovit prestuplenia v Irake!" *Pravda*, June 20, 1963.

62. "V zashchitu prav kurdskogo naselenia," *Pravda*, July 2, 1963. Mongolia became a party to the Genocide Convention in January 1967. On Mongolia's admission to the United Nations see Gaiduk, *Divided Together*, 213–214.

63. "Soviet Scores Iraq on Kurdish Policy," *NYT*, July 5, 1963; "Prekratit ubiistva," *Pravda*, July 7, 1963.

64. William Korey, "What Hope for the Genocide Convention?" *Vista, the Magazine of the United Nations Association* (November–December 1972): 43–44.

65. "V zashchitu kurdov," *Pravda*, July 9, 1963.

66. "Zaiavlenie sovetskogo pravitelstva pravitelstvu Irana," *Pravda*, July 10, 1963; Henry Tanner, "Soviet Sees Peril in Kurdish Issue," *NYT*, July 10, 1963.

67. "Iraq Hits at Soviet on Kurdish Question," *NYT*, July 11, 1963; "USSR and the Kurds," *NYT*, July 13, 1963.

68. "Sovetskie liudi s vami, bratia kurdy," *Pravda*, July 4, 1963; "Predostavit avtonomiiu Kurdistanu," *Pravda*, August 18, 1963.

69. Louis Fleming, "Red Bloc Retreats on Iraq-Kurd Intervention," *Los Angeles Times*, July 26, 1963.

70. DoS position paper, "Principal Stresses and Strains Facing the US in the UN (V. Bloc Politics in the United Nations)" [1953], NARA, DoS general records, Assistant Secretaries of State for UN Affairs, 1945–1954, 59/58D33/5.

71. O'Balance, *The Kurdish Revolt*, 101–102.

72. Haim Shemesh, *Soviet-Iraqi Relations, 1968–1988: In the Shadow of the Iraq-Iran Conflict* (Boulder, CO: Lynne Rienner, 1992), 5–8.

73. Smolansky, *The USSR and Iraq*, 68–97; Golan, *Soviet Policies in the Middle East*, 164–172, 181; doc. no. 102 in *From Encroachment to Involvement*, 505–509.

74. CIA memo to Kissinger, July 26, 1973, https://history.state.gov/historicaldocuments/frus1969–76v27/d225; US Embassy in Iran to the State Department, June 26, 1974, https://history.state.gov/historicaldocuments/frus1969–76v27/d62; US Embassy in Iran to the State Department, March 23, 1975, https://history.state.gov/historicaldocuments/frus1969–76v27/d283.

75. Smolansky, *The USSR and Iraq*, 243–65; Golan, *Soviet Policies in the Middle East*, 174, 194–196, 281–283. According to Iranian sources, between 1983 and 1988 Iraq used chemical weapons at least 193 times, killing or wounding some 50,000 people in the process. See Power, *"A Problem from Hell,"* 178.

76. Power, *"A Problem from Hell,"* 171–203, 219.

77. Shemesh, *Soviet-Iraqi Relations*, 231–232.

78. Smolansky, *The USSR and Iraq*, 266.

5. SOUTHEAST ASIA AND THE RISE OF COMMUNIST CHINA

1. Clara Hoover to Lemkin, June 7, 1959, NYPL, ZL-273/1.
2. "Tibet and the U.N.," *Manchester Guardian*, July 25, 1959.
3. Howard Tolley, *The International Commission of Jurists: Global Advocates for Human Rights* (Philadelphia: University of Pennsylvania Press, 1994), xiii, 28–39; Yves Dezalay and Bryant G. Garth, *The Internationalization of Palace Wars: Lawyers, Economists, and the Contest to Transform Latin American States* (Chicago, IL: University of Chicago Press, 2002), 63–64.
4. Claude Levenson, "Tibet: A Neo-Colonial Genocide" in *Forgotten Genocides: Oblivion, Denial, and Memory*, ed. René Lemarchand (Philadelphia: University of Pennsylvania Press, 2011), 96–97; David Crowe, *War Crimes, Genocide, and Justice: A Global History* (Basingstoke: Palgrave Macmillan, 2014), 289–291.
5. Samuil Zivs, "Zakonodatelnoe zakreplenie rasovoi diskriminatsii v SShA i stranakh Britanskoi imperii," *SGP* 4 (April 1955): 118. Zivs made a name for himself as a fierce critic of Amnesty International and spokesman for the Soviet Public Anti-Zionist Committee in the 1980s.
6. Levenson, "Tibet," 92, 96.
7. Austin Jersild, *The Sino-Soviet Alliance: An International History* (Chapel Hill, NC: University of North Carolina Press, 2014), 135–136.
8. Anna L. Strong, "Sushchestvuet li 'tibetskii vopros'?" *LG*, October 27, 1959. In her book *When Serfs Stood Up in Tibet*, Strong rejected the claims that Mao had committed genocide by means of flooding Tibet with Han settlers (p. 15). She could not have possibly argued otherwise, since the book was published in 1959 in Beijing.
9. Soviet ambassador to China Pavel Yudin, report on conversation with Deng Xiaoping, June 3, 1959, Wilson Center Digital Archives, doc. 111506.
10. Record of conversation between Khrushchev and top Chinese Communist leaders, October 2, 1959, Wilson Center Digital Archives, doc. 118883. Translated into English, the document may convey too strong a hostility expressed by Khrushchev toward the Dalai Lama. Actually, Khrushchev used the idiomatic expression *v grobu ia ego vidal*, which can be rendered as "I care a damn."
11. "Contentious Problems Await U.N. Assembly: Mr. Khrushchev's Address on Friday," *Times*, September 14, 1959.
12. Korey, "What Hope for the Genocide Convention?" 44.
13. Mikhail Demidenko, "Strategia Mao: voina i golod," *LG*, June 4, 1969. The American press had registered the Soviet change of heart on Mao's policy of terror, specifically in Tibet. See "USSR Says Mao Plans to Establish 'Dictatorship'," *Boston Globe*, March 13, 1969; Frank Starr, "Paper Describes Genocide, War Preparations," *Chicago Tribune*, August 28, 1969.
14. See, for example, "What International Cooperation?" *Chicago Tribune*, January 3, 1965; P. K. Roy, "Genocide in Tibet," *Baltimore Sun*, October 27, 1965; Iona Andronov, "Trevozhnaia granitsa v Gimalaiakh," *LG*, August 11, 1982.
15. Colin Smith, "Russia to Recognize Bangla Desh?" *Observer*, August 8, 1971; "Vizit I. Gandi zakonchen," *Izvestia*, November 7, 1971; "Sessia Generalnoi Assamblei," *Pravda*, December 9, 1971; "Advokaty terrora," *LG*, December 22, 1971; "Osnovnye printsipy," *Izvestia*, January 8, 1972; "Kurs Bangla desh," "Podlinnoe litso maoistov," *Pravda*, January 9, 1972; "Utro Bangladesha," ". . . Vmesti i proigrali," *LG*, January 12, 1972; T. Fedorov, "SShA i vopros o predstavitelstve Kitaia v OON," *Voprosy istorii* 8 (August 1972): 210.
16. "Moscow Sniffs US-Peking Deal to Split World Communism," *Guardian*, February 22, 1972.

17. Bass, *The Blood Telegram*, xiii–xx, 4–5, 12, 60, 77–84, 105, 148, 218–221.
18. M. Yurchenko, "Velikohanskii kurs Pekina," *Izvestia*, February 11, 1972.
19. M. Barnabekov, "Osennie mukhi iz 'Guanmin Zhibao'," *LG*, November 7, 1973.
20. Ernst Henry [Semyon Rostovsky], "Sudba Mongolov v KNR," *LG*, March 14, 1979; "Manevry shovinistov," *Pravda*, August 5, 1979.
21. "Opasnoe skhodstvo," *LG*, August 7, 1974.
22. Jim Gallagher, "Rock Island Runs Monday," *Chicago Tribune*, March 21, 1980.
23. David P. Chandler, *The Tragedy of Cambodian History: Politics, War, and Revolution Since 1945* (New Haven: Yale University Press, 1991), 202–203.
24. Oleg Ignatiev, "Genotsid i Washington," *Pravda*, April 26, 1970; "Vandalism," *Izvestia*, April 27, 1970; M. Ilyinsky, "Pletut intrigi," *Izvestia*, April 28, 1970.
25. DoS, US delegation to the UN to US Secretary of State William P. Rogers, December 4, 1972, NARA, DoS general records, subject numerical files, 1970–1973. Social, 59/1613/3039.
26. "Politika genotsida," *Pravda*, December 3, 1969.
27. "US Mild in Reply to China," *Boston Globe*, June 13, 1972. Cf. Yuri Zhukov, "Pokushenie na klimat," *Pravda*, July 11, 1972. According to the Soviets, *biocide* signified "destruction of all life" and *ecocide* "destruction of the natural environment."
28. Stephen J. Morris, *Why Vietnam Invaded Cambodia: Political Culture and the Causes of War* (Stanford, CA: Stanford University Press, 1999), 75, 88, 201–202, 234.
29. "Protiv lzhi i klevety," *Izvestia*, June 28, 1978; "Po prikazu iz Pekina," *LG*, August 16, 1978; "Litsemerie Pekina," *Pravda*, September 19, 1978; "Polnaia izoliatsia," *Pravda*, October 10, 1978; "Pekinskie eksperimenty na kampuchiiskoi zemle," *Izvestia*, November 1, 1978. In his speech on September 1, 1978, the prime minister of Vietnam described Pol Pot's Cambodia as a "hell on earth, a gigantic concentration camp." While world public opinion has condemned the policy of genocide perpetrated against the Khmer people, he said, China has been using the "counterrevolutionary Pol Pot–Ieng Sary clique" as a tool for territorial expansion, first and foremost on account of Vietnam. Pham Van Dong's speech, September 5, 1978, Wilson Center Digital Archives, doc. 118418.
30. "Peking Makes Fresh Attack on Hanoi," *Guardian*, July 17, 1978.
31. William Safire, "Silence Is Guilt," *NYT*, April 23, 1978. On American responses to the mass crimes committed during the Khmer Rouge rule in 1975–1978 see Elizabeth Becker, *When the War Was Over: The Voices of Cambodia's Revolution and Its People* (New York: Simon and Schuster, 1986), 393–394; Power, *"A Problem from Hell,"* 111–40.
32. "Dissident Says West Duped," *Hartford Courant*, July 1, 1975; Dean Mills, "Solzhenitsyn Talk More Like a Sermon," *Baltimore Sun*, July 2, 1975; Alexander Solzhenitsyn, "Kissinger Surrenders Too Much," *Boston Globe*, December 7, 1975. Shortly before Solzhenitsyn's expulsion from the Soviet Union, William Buckley, rather incomprehensively, speculated in the *Boston Globe* that the Kremlin's attempt to eliminate the outspoken author "would amount to an act of genocide" (Buckley, "Solzhenitsyn and the West," *Boston Globe*, January 19, 1974).
33. Richard P. Mason, "A Staunch Defense of Cambodian Regime," *Boston Globe*, September 24, 1978; Daniel Burstein, "On Cambodia: But, Yet," *NYT*, November 21, 1978.
34. Jimmy Carter, "Statement by the President on Human Rights Violations in Cambodia," April 21, 1978, http://www.presidency.ucsb.edu/ws/?pid=30693.
35. Art Buchwald, "Familiar Sounds from Southeast Asia," *Hartford Courant*, January 11, 1979; cartoon in *Chicago Tribune*, January 14, 1979.
36. "Oproverzhenie klevetnicheskikh izmyshlenii," *Pravda*, January 6, 1979; "Osvobozhdenie Pnompenia," *Pravda*, January 8, 1979.

37. Jamie Frederic Metzl, *Western Responses to Human Rights Abuses in Cambodia, 1975–80* (Basingstoke: Palgrave Macmillan, 1996), 130–133; "Zlodeiania prestupnoi kliki," *Pravda*, January 11, 1979.

38. "Zverstva reaktsionnoi kliki," *Pravda*, January 12, 1979.

39. "Vietnam and Cambodia Exchange Bitter Attacks in Security Council," *Sun*, February 25, 1979.

40. Metzl, *Western Responses*, 144–149, 159.

41. "China Accuses Vietnamese of Genocide," *Guardian*, July 21, 1979.

42. Metzl, *Western Responses*, 141, 150.

43. LeBlanc, *The United States and the Genocide Convention*, 208.

44. "Pol Pot's Men Face Trial for Genocide," *Guardian*, July 30, 1979; "Pol Pot Tribunal Hears List of 'Major Crimes," *Guardian*, August 16, 1979; "Golosa iz proshlogo," *Pravda*, September 16, 1979; "Sud naroda," *Pravda*, October 30, 1979; On the tribunal see Howard J. De Nike et al., *Genocide in Cambodia: Documents from the Trial of Pol Pot and Ieng Sary* (Philadelphia: University of Pennsylvania Press, 2000).

45. Metzl, *Western Responses*, 140.

46. "Za spinoi bespravia," *Pravda*, January 11, 1979; Alexander Serbin, "Primechanie obozrevatelia," *Pravda*, January 16, 1979; "Kampuchii—vseobshchuiu podderzhku," *Pravda*, February 3, 1979; Ros Samay, "Pobeda narodnoi revoliutsii," *Pravda*, March 12, 1979; "Gegemonism Kitaia," *Pravda*, March 19, 1979; "Neblagovidnaia tsel," *Pravda*, August 9, 1981.

47. Fedor Burlatsky, "Protiv magii slov," *LG*, May 23, 1979.

48. Metzl, *Western Responses*, 156–163, 168–169, 172, 180.

49. "Mezhdunarodnoe obozrenie," *Pravda*, December 2, 1979; V. Skvortsov, "Dvulichie," *Pravda*, December 20, 1979.

50. Louis Wiznitzer, "Cambodians: Pawns on the Superpower Chessboard," *Christian Science Monitor*, November 5, 1979.

51. "Ocherednoe svidetelstvo genotsida," *Pravda*, October 2, 1982.

6. (SOVIET) PIGGY IN THE MIDDLE

1. William Korey, "On Banning Genocide: 'We Should Have Been the First'," *World Magazine* (September 26, 1972): unnumbered pages; Michael Galchinsky, *Jews and Human Rights: Dancing at Three Weddings* (Lanham, MD: Rowman & Littlefield, 2007), 94–96. See also Edward S. Goldstein, draft chapter, "German Reparations/Genocide Convention" from an unfinished PhD thesis on the history of the JLC [mid-1970s], WAG, 232/1/6.

2. "The United Nations: Facts and Fallacies," pamphlet distributed by the Church Peace Union [between June 1950 and July 1953], WAG, 25/298/36.

3. Herbert Shapiro, *White Violence and Black Response: From Reconstruction to Montgomery* (Amherst, MA: University of Massachusetts Press, 1988), 398–399.

4. Quoted in Mary L. Dudziak, "Desegregation as a Cold War Imperative," *Stanford Law Review* 41 (November 1988): 116–117. See also George H. Watson's book review: "Mr. Talmadge's Anathema," *Harvard Crimson*, December 6, 1955.

5. Carol Anderson, "Bleached Souls and Red Negroes: The NAACP and Black Communists in the Early Cold War, 1948–1952" in *Window on Freedom: Race, Civil Rights, and Foreign Affairs, 1945–1988*, ed. Brenda Gayle Plummer (Chapel Hill, NC: University of North Carolina Press, 2003), 95.

6. DoS, Office of the President's Special Representative, interoffice memo, June 4, 1962, NARA, DoS decimal files, 1960–1963, 59/949637/570.

7. Louis Shecter, AJC, to Senator Clifford P. Case, February 1, 1962, NARA, DoS decimal files, 1960–1963, 59/949637/570.
8. DoS position paper, "Principal Stresses and Strains Facing the US in the UN (VI. Human Rights)" [1953], NARA, DoS general records, Assistant Secretaries of State for UN Affairs, 1945–1954, 59/58D33/5.
9. Korey, *Genocide Treaty Ratification: Ending an American Embarrassment* (Washington, DC: B'nai B'rith International, November 7, 1988), 12, WAG, 25/138/15.
10. "Zatiagivaiut ratifikatsiiu," *Pravda*, March 13, 1974; Gennady Vasiliev, "Fariseistvo" *Pravda*, August 17, 1978; "Vymysly i realnost" *Pravda*, October 3, 1978; "Na slovakh i na dele," *Pravda*, April 10, 1979; "Potrepannaia mantia," *Pravda*, July 31, 1980; Anatoly Movchan, "Prava cheloveka: slova i dela," *Pravda*, July 24, 1984; Yuri Zhukov, "Neskolko voprosov neproshennym opekunam," *Pravda*, May 5, 1985.
11. "Kogda s nami govoriat iazykom ugroz," *Pravda*, March 17, 1980
12. See, for example, Resolution of the Los Angeles County Federation of Republican Women, March 25, 1970, NARA, DoS general records, subject numerical files, 1970–1973. Social, 59/1613/3042.
13. DoS, John R. Stevenson and Samuel DePalma to Rogers, October 10, 1969, NARA, DoS general records, subject numerical files, 1970–1973. Social, 59/1613/3042.
14. Rogers, memo for the president, February 5, 1970, NARA, DoS general records, subject numerical files, 1970–1973. Social, 59/1613/3042.
15. Schweppe, "A Historical Look at the Genocide Convention," *Human Events*, March 21, 1970.
16. Schweppe to Nixon, March 13, 1970; Stevenson to Schweppe, April 3, 1970, NARA, DoS general records, subject numerical files, 1970–1973. Social, 59/1613/3042.
17. Rogers to Fulbright, "Summary Brief of Arguments on Genocide Convention," March 26, 1970, NARA, DoS general records, subject numerical files, 1970–1973. Social, 59/1613/3042. Former attorney general Nicholas Katzenbach, who voted for US ratification at the ABA's February 1970 meeting, argued that rejection of the treaty might be regarded as proof that the United States had committed genocide in Vietnam (editorial, "The Genocide Hoax," *Chicago Tribune*, February 27, 1970).
18. Jodi Buell, "Ratification of the Genocide Convention? The United States and the United Nations Convention on the Prevention and Punishment of the Crime of Genocide" (Senior thesis: Pacific University, OR, 2004), 22–26.
19. Martin, *The Man Who Invented "Genocide,"* 259–279. See also Hearing Before a Subcommittee of the Committee on Foreign Relations, United States Senate, 91st Congress, 1st Session, the Convention on the Prevention and Punishment of the Crime of Genocide (Washington, DC: US Government Printing Office, 1970), esp. 64–66, 80–84, 165–174.
20. Bricker to Nixon, July 17, 1970, NARA, DoS general records, subject numerical files, 1970–1973. Social, 59/1613/3042.
21. Phillips and Deutsch, "Pitfalls of the Genocide Convention," *ABA Journal* 56 (July 1970): 641–646.
22. Bricker to Harlow, June 26, 1970, NARA, DoS general records, subject numerical files, 1970–1973. Social, 59/1613/3042.
23. "D.A.R. Condemns Genocide Treaty," *NYT*, April 22, 1965.
24. LeBlanc, *The United States and the Genocide Convention*, 152, 164–165.
25. San Diego County Federation of Republican Women's Clubs, Resolution on President Nixon's Request for Ratification of the U.N. Genocide Convention, April 13, 1970, NARA, DoS general records, subject numerical files, 1970–1973. Social, 59/1613/3042.
26. ADL, confidential report, "Organized Opposition to the UN Convention on Genocide," April 1971, WAG, 37/3/34. According to a similar draft document, "Extremist Opposition to

the Proposed Genocide Treaty," the political far right in America boasted some 250,000 active members and several million sympathizers. As of 1971, some 30,000 to 50,000 Americans belonged to identifiable hate groups.

27. Betty Kaye Taylor, Ex. Secretary of CHRGT, memo, June 17, 1971, WAG, 37/3/36.

28. "Genocide Treaty a Communist Hoax," *Emergency Liberty Letter* 26 (June 15, 1970); "Genocide Treaty and Guaranteed Wage Bills Killed!" *Thunderbolt* (October 1970), WAG, 37/3/34.

29. Frank A. Capell, "World Government Trap," *Herald of Freedom* 4, vol. 17 (March 20, 1970), WAG, 37/3/34. Cf. the list of CHRGT member organizations, WAG, 232/2/67.

30. "Nixon Calls for Genocide Treaty: Could Outlaw All Criticism of Radical Minorities," *Thunderbolt* (March 1970); "You Could Be Imprisoned by Genocide Treaty," *Thunderbolt* (April 1970); "Genocide Scheme Threatens White Freedom, Survival," *White Power* (March–April 1970); John J. Synon, "Nixon and the Genocide Treaty," *Independent American* (April–May 1970); "Warning! Warning!" *The Cross and the Flag* (May 1970); "Red 'Genocide,'" *Life Lines*, 77, vol. 12 (July 1, 1970); Liberty Lobby's flyer, "Your President May Be in Danger!" June 15, 1970, WAG, 37/3/34; "The 'Genocide' Plot," pamphlet of the Cinema Educational Guild, 1970, WAG, 37/5/22.

31. Dan Smoot, "Genocide Convention," *Dan Smoot Report*, March 9, 1970; Smoot, "On Surrender by Treaty," *Dan Smoot Report*, April 21, 1971; John B. Gest, "The Genocide Convention," *Wanderer*, March 26, 1970; Robert Morris, "The Genocide Treaty," *Wanderer*, December 3, 1970, WAG, 37/3/34.

32. "Senate to Act on Genocide Treaty: Pact's Possible Passage Perils Patriots," *Liberty Letter* 110 (April 1970), WAG, 37/3/34.

33. "How It Might Happen," *Common Sense*, December 1, 1970, WAG, 37/3/34.

34. Carl M. King, President of Manitoba-Minnesota Mission of the Church of Jesus Christ of Latter-Day Saints, to Nixon, April 27, 1971, NARA, DoS general records, subject numerical files, 1970–1973. Social, 59/1613/3043.

35. Richard E. Woodin, letter to editors, *Monterey Park Californian*, April 29, 1971.

36. Betty Kaye Taylor, Ex. Secretary of CHRGT, memo, February 11, 1974, WAG, 37/3/36. Members of the Foreign Relations Committee and other senators had indicated that the sheer amount of mail from the extremist groups was likely to cause a problem (Taylor to Arnold Forster, Anti-Defamation League, October 8, 1970, WAG, 37/5/22).

37. Holstein to Nixon, January 24, 1972; DoS suggested reply to Holstein, February 2, 1972, NARA, DoS general records, subject numerical files, 1970–1973. Social, 59/1613/3043.

38. "Message from the President of the United States," *United States Senate, 91st Congress, 2nd Session, Executive B, February 19, 1970* (Washington, DC: US Government Printing Office, 1970).

39. Judt, *Postwar*, 501–503.

40. CIA report, "Soviet Objectives and Tactics at the Belgrade Conference," May 1977; Zbigniew Brzezinski, National Security Council, presidential review memo, May 20, 1977; CIA report, "Soviet Foreign Policy at the Crossroads," July 8, 1977; CIA report, "The Evolution of Soviet Reaction to Dissent," July 15, 1977 in Mircea Munteanu and Kristina Terzieva, eds., *From Global Politics to Human Rights: The CSCE Follow Up Meeting, Belgrade, 1977* (a CWIHP document reader), http://www.wilsoncenter.org/sites/default/files/Belgrade-CSCE-PartI-GlobalIssues-5.pdf.

41. Brzezinski to Stuart Eizenstat, President's Assistant for Domestic Affairs and Policy, June 10, 1977, https://history.state.gov/historicaldocuments/frus1977–80v02/d57.

42. Taylor, Ex. Secretary of CHRGT, memos, June 20 and August 8, 1977, WAG, 37/3/36.

43. Goldberg to Carter, November 18, 1977 in *From Global Politics to Human Rights*.

44. Vasili Mitrokhin, "On Human Rights," *A KGB Anthology*, folder 51, Wilson Center Digital Archives, doc. 110120.

45. "Washington litsemerit," *Pravda,* April 13, 1977; "Uvazhat prava cheloveka," *LG,* May 4, 1977; "'Spravedlivost' na eksport," *Pravda,* December 10, 1977.
46. "Litsemernaia kampaniia," *Pravda,* June 17, 1977. Earlier the next year the Publishing House of Political Literature in Moscow printed the Russian translation of the book by CPUSA on the status of human rights in the United States, *Polozhenie v oblasti prav cheloveka v SShA.*
47. William Korey, "Helsinki's Child: Sin of Omission," *Foreign Policy* 39 (Summer 1980): 172–173. Cf. "Otkazalis ratifitsirovat," *Pravda,* August 5, 1977.
48. Mitrokhin, "On Human Rights," *A KGB Anthology,* folder 51, Wilson Center Digital Archives, doc. 110120.
49. "Popranie prav cheloveka," *Pravda,* May 16, 1985.
50. NCRAC chairman Don Lefton, memo, February 22, 1988, WAG, 25/138/15.
51. V. Balashov, "Podygryvaiut reaktsii," *Izvestia,* November 18, 1985. For the main findings of the 1978 and 1985 reports see Matthew Lippman, "A Road Map to the 1948 Convention on the Prevention and Punishment of the Crime of Genocide," *Journal of Genocide Research* 2, vol. 4 (2002): 188–191.
52. Konstantin Rusakov, "Soiuz vo imia mira i sotsializma," *Pravda,* May 15, 1985.
53. "Vo imia gumannoi tseli," *Pravda,* October 5, 1987.

7. MOSCOW TAPS THE NEW LEFT

1. "Iz zhizni liudoedov," *Pravda,* March 27, 1963.
2. Cf. Madeleine Riffaud, "Nichto ikh ne slomit," *Pravda,* January 2, 1965; John D. Bernal, "Prizyv k sovesti vsekh narodov," *Pravda,* March 31, 1965; "Interventy bessilny pered volei naroda," *Pravda,* June 23, 1965; Yuri Zhukov, "Miasnaia lavka McNamary i Co," *Pravda,* August 23, 1965.
3. "Americans Accused of Genocide," *Guardian,* August 27, 1965; Stephen E. Nordlinger, "Russians Accuse U.S. of Genocide," *Baltimore Sun,* August 27, 1965.
4. Yuri Zhukov, "Genotsid," *Pravda,* September 14, 1966. Zhukov served as deputy chairman of the Soviet Peace Committee, an affiliate of the WPC.
5. "Gnevnye demonstratsii u Belogo Doma . . . i u paviliona SShA na 'Ekspo-67'," *Pravda,* April 30, 1967; untitled, *Pravda,* July 11, 1967. That same year George Maciunas in the United States produced his famous poster, which featured an American flag, except that it had the image of death in place of stars, and estimates of victims of genocide in place of stripes. The uppermost line, which gave the name to the poster, read: "U.S.A. surpasses all the genocide records!"
6. Robert H. Estabrook, "Interim Plan on Chinas Put to U.N.," *Washington Post and Times Herald,* November 24, 1966; idem., "Reds' Cold-War Oratory is Classified Three Ways," *Washington Post and Times Herald,* November 27, 1966; Paul Wohl, "Moscow Tells Viets to Beware," *Christian Science Monitor,* April 11, 1967.
7. "Pushki i zakon," *Pravda,* October 16, 1966; Vitaly Korionov, "I eto imenuetsia 'poiskami mira'!" *Pravda,* January 22, 1967; "Zhertvy politiki genotsida," *Pravda,* May 18, 1967.
8. "Prestuplenie genotsida," *Pravda,* June 18, 1967; "Eto pozor Ameriki," *Pravda,* July 26, 1967. Brown was a radical civil rights activist. He served as chairman of the SNCC and was briefly affiliated with the Black Panthers.
9. "Poezd so vzryvchatym gruzom," *Pravda,* July 10, 1970.
10. Alina Koroleva, "Negritianskie vyspuplenia 1960-kh godov v SShA," *Voprosy istorii* 12 (December 1973): 126. Cf. Koroleva, *Dvadtsat millionov protiv Dzhima Krou: negritianskoe dvizhenie v SShA na sovremennom etape* (Moscow: Mysl, 1967).

11. "Politiki genotsida," *Pravda*, February 9, 1972; Oleg Konstantinov, "Politika genotsida," *Pravda*, February 26, 1972.

12. See John Duffett, ed., *Against the Crime of Silence: Proceedings of the International War Crimes Tribunal* (New York: O'Hare Books, 1968); Sartre, *On Genocide*, 4–5, 50–53, 57–58, 67–85. For a critical analysis of the tribunal's findings see Hugo Adam Bedau, "Genocide in Vietnam?" *Boston University Law Review* 3, vol. 53 (May 1973): 588–618. Bedau has pinpointed numerous logical fallacies in Sartre's argument that undercut the thesis of genocide. Helen Fein as well questioned the tribunal's verdict to ultimately conclude that no genocide was committed in Vietnam. Cf. Helen Fein, "Discriminating Genocide from War Crimes: Vietnam and Afghanistan Reexamined," *Denver Journal of International Law and Policy* 1, vol. 22 (Fall 1993): 41–53, 60–61.

13. Arthur Jay Klinghoffer, "International Citizens' Tribunals on Human Rights" in *Genocide, War Crimes, and the West: History and Complicity*, ed. Adam Jones (London: Zed Books, 2004), 346–358.

14. "Varvarstvo," *Pravda*, March 14, 1967.

15. "On Our Great Victory on the Diplomatic Struggle and International Activities Front from Early 1968 to the Present," report presented to the 15 Plenum of the CP of Vietnam Central Committee, August 29, 1968, Wilson Center Digital Archives, doc. 113979. The North Vietnamese delegates attended both the Stockholm and Roskilde sessions and, on occasion, presented tribunal members with rings made from downed American aircraft (Klinghoffer, "International Citizens' Tribunals," 355).

16. "European 'Intellectuals' Plan Alleged War Crimes Show Trial," *Hartford Courant*, April 1, 1967; "'Tribunal' Declares U.S. Guilty," *Christian Science Monitor*, May 11, 1967;

17. "Sartre Terms Invasion by Soviet a War Crime," *NYT*, August 26, 1968.

18. Konstantin Chizhov, "Amerikanskii imperialism—razrushitel mezhdunarodnogo prava," *SGP* 2 (February 1952): 53.

19. Judt, *Postwar*, 222–223.

20. Kenneth J. Campbell, "The International War Crimes Conference, Oslo, June 1971: Excerpts from the Diary of One of the Witnesses" in *Nobody Gets Off the Bus: Viet Nam Generation War Book*, ed. Kali Tal (Chevy Chase, MD: Burning Cities Press, 1994), 148–151.

21. "Gnev i bol Vietnama," *Pravda*, May 25, 1971; S. Timofeieva, "Genotsid v deistvii," *Pravda*, July 17, 1971; "Tsep prestuplenii," *Pravda*, August 17, 1972.

22. Richard H. Shulz, *The Soviet Union and Revolutionary Warfare: Principles, Practices, and Regional Comparisons* (Stanford, CA: Hoover Institution, 1988), 59. Cf. *Folkmord: Rapport från Internationella Kommissionen för undersökning av USAs krigsförbrytelser i Indokina*, ed. Hans Göran Franck and Tomas Rothpfeffer (Stockholm: Rabén & Sjögren, 1971).

23. Peter Weiss, "Istreblenie naroda, akty genotsida," *LG*, August 7, 1968. Cf. Weiss, *Rapporte* (Frankfurt: Suhrkamp, 1968). Weiss's 1968 play *Vietnam-Discourse* drew a parallel between the United States and Nazi Germany.

24. "Istoricheskaia nauka v SSSR: khronikalnye zametki," *Voprosy istorii* 6 (June 1968): 196–197. International Anti-Racism Day has been observed by the United Nations since 1966, commemorating the notorious Sharpeville massacre in South Africa six years earlier.

25. "The Little-Known Background of the Genocide Convention," *Human Events* [1970?], copy in NARA, DoS general records, subject numerical files, 1970–1973. Social, 59/1613/3042.

26. Spencer Rich, "Genocide, Poison Gas Pacts in Peril," *Washington Post*, April 26, 1971. See also *Washington Bulletin*, newsletter of the American Baptist Convention, March 16, 1972, WAG, 37/3/33. For a comprehensive account of Calley's conviction see Michal R. Belknap, *The Vietnam War on Trial: The My Lai Massacre and the Court-Martial of Lieutenant Calley* (Lawrence, KA: University Press of Kansas, 2013).

27. "Genocide Treaty Again Threatens," *Emergency Liberty Letter* 28, April 23, 1971; Dan Smoot, "On Surrender by Treaty," *Dan Smoot Report*, April 21, 1971, WAG, 37/5/22.

28. Vladimir Bolshakov, "Slova i dela," *Pravda*, August 7, 1977.

29. Statement by Senator Strom Thurmond Before the Foreign Relations Committee Reference Opposition to the Genocide Treaty, December 3, 1981, WAG, 37/3/36.

30. "Prekratit agressiu," *Pravda*, August 25, 1971; "Prestupnyi pocherk agressorov," *Izvestia*, March 24, 1972; Michael Parks, "Laos Mired in Fight with Hill Tribesmen," *Sun*, October 31, 1978; Stanley Karnow, "The Meos' Tragedy: America Should Help," *Sun*, August 13, 1979.

31. Editorial, "Handicap on Hungary," *Washington Post and Times Herald*, September 13, 1957.

32. "Race Bias Key Issue in U.N. Debate," *Chicago Daily Defender*, November 5, 1962; "U.S. Sharply Criticizes Soviet Anti-Semitism," *Jewish Advocate*, March 12, 1964. See also Yaacov Ro'i, *The Struggle for Soviet Jewish Emigration, 1948–1967* (Cambridge: Cambridge University Press, 1991), 173.

33. Henry Winston, "Prestuplenie protiv natsii," "Nesmyvaemyi pozor," *Pravda*, October 21, 1963. See also Lentz and Gower, *The Opinions of Mankind*, 171.

34. "Iunost planet, tesnee riady!" *Pravda*, September 26, 1964.

35. "Sovremennye kannibaly," *Izvestia*, September 28, 1963.

36. "Kleimo pozora," *Pravda*, August 28, 1965; "Na povodu u rasistov," *Pravda*, April 24, 1968; Hersey, "Prestuplenie v motele 'Alzhir'," *LG*, July 31, 1968. Cf. Hersey, *Algiers Motel Incident* (Baltimore: John Hopkins University Press, 1997 [1968]), 347–48. On the Soviet coverage of the Watts Riot see Lentz and Gower, *The Opinions of Mankind*, 201.

37. "Instant Cordon Becomes the Verge of Genocide," *Minority Report*, April 10, 1969.

38. Charles H. Martin, "Internationalizing 'the American Dilemma': The Civil Rights Congress and the 1951 Genocide Petition to the United Nations," *Journal of American Ethnic History* 4, vol. 16 (Summer 1997): 55; Gerald Horne, *Black Revolutionary: William Patterson and the Globalization of the African American Freedom Struggle* (Urbana, IL: University of Illinois Press, 2013), 193.

39. Robert G. Weisbord, *Genocide? Birth Control and the Black American* (Westport, CT: Greenwood Press, 1975), 158–82.

40. Horne, *Black Revolutionary*, 11–12.

41. "Patterson Named General Manager of the Weekly Worker," *Arkansas State Press*, February 7, 1958. The reconstituted weekly attempted to fill the void left after the demise of the *Daily Worker*, the organ of the CPUSA whose circulation had drastically fallen.

42. Michael "Cetawayo" Tabor, *Capitalism Plus Dope Equals Genocide* (1969), https://archive.org/details/CapitalismPlusDopeEqualsGenocide_10. Tabor has written that "merciless, murdering scum of the planet, vile capitalists" had deployed "pig police . . . in present-day AmeriKKKa" in a conspiracy to destroy blacks by means of narcotics. The tenor of the pamphlet was colored by the fact that its 23-year-old author was a former heroin addict himself.

43. Horne, *Black Revolutionary*, 13, 191–194, 198–199.

44. Horne, *Black Revolutionary*, 194–197. In September 1968 Newton was convicted of voluntary manslaughter following a shootout a year earlier resulting in the death of a police officer. After three subsequent mistrials, in December 1971 the case against Newton was dropped. Brown took over the SNCC's leadership after the departure of Carmichael. As of early 1970 he was a fugitive from the law, charged with inciting a riot and illegal firearm possession.

45. Frank J. Rafalko, *MH/Chaos: The CIA's Campaign Against the Radical New Left and the Black Panthers* (Annapolis, MD: Naval Institute Press, 2011), 136; "V bratskikh partiakh," *Pravda*, May 21, 1970. Historically, Chicago boasted the largest number of black Communists in the nation. The USSR continued funding the CPUSA throughout the 1970s and 1980s.

While Moscow financed militant left-wing groups in Western Europe such as the Red Brigades in Italy or Action directe in France, no evidence had emerged so far of similar support extended to the Black Panthers Party (Judt, *Postwar*, 477, 495f).

46. Horne, *Black Revolutionary*, 197–198.

47. Lloyd Hogan, "Congressmen Conduct Hampton Killing Probe," *Crusader*, December 26, 1969; "Prizyv k mobilizatsii sil," *Pravda*, March 11, 1970; "Million Signatures Needed for Genocide Petition," *Milwaukee Star*, November 7, 1970; "Protest protiv genotsida," *Pravda*, November 18, 1970; Boris Orekhov, "Obviniaem v genotside," *Pravda*, December 3, 1970.

48. "Zhizn Andzhely Devis v opasnosti," *Pravda*, December 18, 1970; "Prekratit proizvol," *Izvestia*, December 9, 1970. See also Sophie Lorenz, "'Heldin des anderen Amerikas'. Die DDR-Solidaritätsbewegung für Angela Davis, 1970–1973," *Zeithistorische Forschungen* 1, vol. 10 (2013): 38–60.

49. "U.S.I.A. Drive Seeks to Counter Idea Miss Davis Is Persecuted," *NYT*, March 15, 1972.

50. Horne, *Black Revolutionary*, 203–206.

51. "Protest kanadskoi obshchestvennosti," *Pravda*, January 19, 1970.

52. "The Little-known Background of the Genocide Convention," *Human Events* [1970?], copy in NARA, DoS general records, subject numerical files, 1970–1973. Social, 59/1613/3042. See also Gene Oishi, "U.S. Still Hesitating on '48 Genocide Pact," *Baltimore Sun*, August 2, 1970.

53. Michael T. Kaufman, "2 Sudanese Rebels, Charging Genocide, Seek Help at U.N.," *NYT*, January 5, 1971; Roy Wilkins, "The Minority Within," *New York Post*, January 16, 1971.

54. William E. Dunham, "Correction, Please!" *Review of the News*, December 9, 1970; Robert Welch, "General and Miscellaneous Comments," *John Birch Society Bulletin*, February 1971, WAG, 37/3/34.

55. Toni Morrison, ed., *To Die for the People: Huey Newton* (San Francisco, CA: City Lights Books, 2009), 164–177.

56. Horne, *Black Revolutionary*, 200–203.

57. Dan Berger and Roxanne Dunbar-Ortiz, "'The Struggle Is for Land': Race, Territory and National Liberation" in *The Hidden 1970s: Histories of Radicalism*, ed. Dan Berger (Newark, NJ: Rutgers University Press, 2010), 68.

58. "'My vse eshche raby'," *Pravda*, November 9, 1979.

59. "Tragedia v Filadelfii," *Pravda*, May 18, 1985.

60. "Konchina U. Pattersona," *Pravda*, March 8, 1980.

61. DoS cable to the US Mission in Geneva, March 10, 1970, NARA, DoS general records, subject numerical files, 1970–1973. Social, 59/1613/3043.

62. AJC, Betty Taylor to Sidney Liskofsky, August 25, 1971, WAG, 37/3/33.

63. Michael S. Kogan, "Rites of Spring: The Genocide Treaty," *Ideas* 1, vol. 4 (1973): 12, WAG, 37/5/22.

64. V. Matveiev and Iu. Semenov, "'Teoria' rasizma na vooruzhenii amerikanskoi reaktsii," *Izvestia*, November 19, 1948.

65. Quoted in Paul Rosier, "'They Are Ancestral Homelands': Race, Place, and Politics in Cold War Native America," *Journal of American History* 4, vol. 92 (March 2006): 1313.

66. Review of Charles Ch. Hyde's book, *International Law: Chiefly as Interpreted and Applied by the United States*, in *SGP* 3 (March 1951): 77.

67. Lentz and Gower, *The Opinions of Mankind*, 33–39, quotation at 37.

68. "Svoboda na slovakh, genotsid na dele," *Izvestia*, June 18, 1961.

69. "Pered bronzovoi dveriu," *Pravda*, May 31, 1968.

70. "Fakel Alkatraza," *Izvestia*, August 13, 1971.

71. Claude Lightfoot, "Sovetskii Soiuz osveshchaet put k svobode narodov," *Pravda*, January 28, 1966.

72. Sherry L. Smith, "Indians, the Counterculture, and the New Left" in *Beyond Red Power: American Indian Politics and Activism Since 1900*, ed. Daniel M. Cobb and Loretta Fowler (Santa Fe, NM: School for Advanced Research Press, 2007), 142–145; Paul C. Smith and Robert A. Warrior, *Like a Hurricane: The Indian Movement from Alcatraz to Wounded Knee* (New York: New Press, 1996), 135.

73. Simpson, "Britain and the Genocide Convention," 30.

74. Sabine to the editors of *U.N. Newsletter*, July 13, 1949, NYPL, ZL-273/1.

75. "'My dlia nikh khuzhe sobak . . .'," *Izvestia*, February 14, 1977. See also, "Pozor Ameriki," *Pravda*, March 28, 1978.

76. Vitaly Gan, "Razygrali fars," *Pravda*, September 16, 1984.

77. "Film ob indeitsakh Kanady," *LG*, November 5, 1980; Reuters news, *Izvestia*, June 19, 1981; "S raznykh pozitsyi," *Pravda*, March 22, 1982.

78. "Na iuzhnykh ostrovakh," *Izvestia*, October 23, 1983.

79. "Politika genotsida prodolzhaetsia," *Izvestia*, April 21, 1977. See also "Protiv politiki genotsida," *Pravda*, June 19, 1977. For an authoritative treatment of both the Pine Ridge and the Wounded Knee episodes see Smith and Warrior, *Like a Hurricane*, 194–268.

80. "Za priznanie prav indeitsev," *Pravda*, September 25, 1977.

81. John Kifner, "U.S. Indians Give Complaints to Soviet for Use in Belgrade," *NYT*, June 17, 1977; "Indian Leader Attacks U.S. Before U.N. Conference," *Los Angeles Times*, September 20, 1977. As the main characteristics of the AIM Daniel M. Cobb and Loretta Fowler have identified "militant rhetoric, audacious confrontational strategies, and larger-than-life personalities" (Cobb and Fowler, "Introduction" in *Beyond Red Power*, x).

82. Russell Means, *Where White Men Fear to Tread: The Autobiography of Russell Means* (New York: St. Martin's Griffin, 1995), 365, 372, 549–550.

83. "Zhertvy genotsida," *Pravda*, December 22, 1977; "A umer li Dzho Makkarti?" *Pravda*, May 19, 1980; Kobysh, "Kstati o skalpakh," *LG*, June 20, 1984; Valery Tishkov, "Mir dolzhen priiti nam na pomoshch," *LG*, January 9, 1985 ("cultural genocide" was spelled out by Russell Means in an interview; he specifically charged the Bureau of Indian Affairs with the crime; see Means, *Where White Men Fear to Tread*, 10–11, 19, 21); "Za iskorenenie rasizma," *Pravda*, November 5, 1985.

84. Gennady Vasiliev, "Indeitsy protestuiut," *Pravda*, July 13, 1978; idem., "Protiv politiki genotsida," *Pravda*, July 17, 1978; idem., "Indeitsy u Belogo Doma," *Pravda*, July 28, 1978 .

85. "SShA: v tiskakh krizisa," *Pravda*, June 3, 1980; Vasiliev, "Litso rasizma," *Pravda*, July 14, 1980.

86. Smith and Warrior, *Like a Hurricane*, 269–78; Robert Eric Konigsberg, "Who Killed Anna Mae?" *New York Times Magazine* (April 27, 2014): 34–40, 48.

87. Natalia Larionova, "Sudba indeitsev," *Pravda*, January 30, 1984; "Spasti zhizn Leonarda Peltiera!" *Pravda*, June 14, 1984; Kobysh, "Kstati o skalpakh," *LG*, June 20, 1984; "Nravy belykh rasistov," *Pravda*, June 27, 1984; "Uvertki gosdepartamenta," *Pravda*, June 30, 1984; "Otmenit nespravedlivyi prigovor," *Pravda*, September 20, 1985; "Spravedlivost dolzhna vostorzhestvovat," *Pravda*, October 16, 1985; "V zashchitu 'uznika sovesti,'" *Pravda*, October 13, 1986.

88. Elizabeth A. Dilauro, "U.S. Must Look to Its Own Rights Abuses," *LA Times*, January 20, 1986; Michael Dobbs, "Soviet Peace Committee Gives Hero's Welcome to U.S. Activists," *Washington Post*, May 31, 1988.

89. Kobysh, "Priemy dikogo zapada v raketno-iadernyi vek," *Izvestia*, October 28, 1981.

90. A. Palladin, "I dazhe bez prava na materinstvo," *Izvestia*, October 6, 1984.

91. Natalia Larionova, "Prava i bespravie," *Pravda*, November 3, 1988.

8. SOVIET-TURKISH RELATIONS AND SOCIALIST ARMENIA

1. Richard H. Dekmejian, "Soviet-Turkish Relations and Politics in the Armenian SSR," *Soviet Studies* 4, vol. 19 (April 1968): 510–512. See also Artiom Ulunian, "Soviet Cold War Perceptions of Turkey and Greece," *Cold War History* 2, vol. 3 (January 2003): 36–45; Barın Kayaoğlu, "Strategic Imperatives, Democratic Rhetoric: The United States and Turkey, 1945–52," *Cold War History* 3, vol. 9 (August 2009): 321–345; Thomas de Waal, *Great Catastrophe: Armenians and Turks in the Shadow of Genocide* (Oxford, UK: Oxford University Press, 2015), 113–118.

2. "Istoricheskaia nauka v SSSR: khronikalnye zametki," *Voprosy istorii* 8 (August 1965): 17, 143–147, 183–185. Cf. *Genotsid armian v osmanskoi imperii: Sbornik dokumentov i materialov*, ed. Mkrtich Nersisyan et al. (Yerevan: Academy of Science of the Armenian SSR, 1966); John Kirakosyan, *Zapadnaia Armenia v gody pervoi mirovoi voiny* (Yerevan: Yerevan University Press, 1971), esp. 367–456.

3. Presidium of the Central Committee of the Armenian Communist Party to the CPSU Central Committee, November 13, 1964, reproduced in *Genotsid armian: Otvetstvennost Turtsii i obiazatelstva mirovogo soobshchestva*, vol. 2, pt. 2, *Dokumenty. Dopolnenie k 1-mu i 2-mu tomam sbornika*, ed. Yuri Barsegov (Moscow: Gardariki, 2005), 15–17. According to the 1970s estimates, the Armenian Diaspora of some 2.6 million was as large as the population of Soviet Armenia.

4. Nikita Zarobyan and Armen Grogoryan, "Rubikon-65," *Yerevan* (April 2006): 138.

5. Zaruhi Shushanyan, "Between the Memories and the Present: On the Armenian Genocide" (MA thesis: Institute of Social Studies, The Hague, 2013).

6. Mkrtich Nersisyan and Nikolai Ushakov, "Genotsid—tiagchaishee prestuplenie pered chelovechestvom," *Pravda*, April 24, 1965. The original draft by Nersisyan put emphasis on the mass murder of Armenians but was subsequently watered down by his assigned coauthor (Zarobyan and Grogoryan, "Rubikon-65," 139).

7. "Spasenie Sevana," *Pravda*, June 9, 1968.

8. "Soviet Article Accuses Turks," *NYT*, April 25, 1965. Reportedly, the students forced the Turkish embassy to lower its flag in observance of the Armenian victimhood in 1915.

9. Harutyun Marutyan, "Pamiatnik zhertvam genotsida v kontekste ritualov pamiati armianskogo voprosa," *Etnograficheskoe obozrenie* 3 (2008): 120, 122; Tsypylma Darieva, "'The Road to Golgotha': Representing Loss in Postsocialist Armenia," *Focaal—European Journal of Anthropology* 52 (2008): 96.

10. Transcript of the CPSU Politburo meeting, February 21, 1985, NSA, READD-RADD, doc. R10045.

11. Zarobyan and Grogoryan, "Rubikon-65," 141; de Waal, *Great Catastrophe*, 144.

12. Dekmejian, "Soviet-Turkish Relations," 514–516; Zarobyan and Grogoryan, "Rubikon-65," 141, 143.

13. Rouben P. Adalian, "Armenian Genocide Memorial in Yerevan" in *Encyclopedia of Genocide*, ed. Israel W. Charny, vol. 1 (Santa Barbara, CA: ABC-CLIO, 1999), 102–103; idem., *Historical Dictionary of Armenia* (Lanham, MD: Scarecrow Press, 2010), 57; Darieva, "'The Road to Golgotha,'" 97.

14. Jamil Hasanli, *Stalin and the Turkish Crisis of the Cold War, 1945–1953* (Lanham, MD: Lexington Books, 2011), 389–390.

15. Anton Kochinyan and Badal Muradyan to the CPSU Central Committee, September 30, 1966, reproduced in: *Genotsid armian: Otvetstvennost Turtsii*, 18–19.

16. Dekmejian, "Soviet-Turkish Relations," 513–518.

17. Marutyan, "Can Collective Memory of Genocide Lead to Reconciliation? A View from Yerevan" in *Prospects for Reconciliation: Theory and Practice*, ed. Hranush Kharatyan-Araqelyan

and Leyla Neyzi (Bonn: DVV International, 2011), 26; Darieva, "'The Road to Golgotha,'" 98–99.

18. Transcript of the CPSU Politburo meeting, February 21, 1985, NSA, READD-RADD, doc. R10045.

19. Michael Parks, "Kremlin Counteracts Nationalism in Armenia," *Baltimore Sun*, December 31, 1974.

20. Shushanyan, "Between the Memories and the Present." For further discussion on Paragraph 30 see Schabas, *Genocide in International Law*, 464–465.

21. Cf. UN docs. E/CN.4/Sub.2/L.583 and E/CN.4/Sub.2/416.

22. Victor Ambartsumyan, "Imperialism—vinovnik genotsida," *Pravda*, April 24, 1975.

23. "Slovno feniks iz pepla . . . ," *LG*, September 5, 1979.

24. "Vstrechi v puti," *LG*, June 13, 1979.

25. Ambartsumyan, "Osuzhden chelovechestvom," *Pravda*, April 24, 1985.

26. Transcript of the CPSU Politburo meeting, February 21, 1985, NSA, READD-RADD, doc. R10045. For the Turkish position on the Senate resolutions concerning the Armenian genocide see Sibel Kavuncu, "A Problem in Turkey–US Relations in the 1980's: Armenian Draft Resolutions," *Review of Armenian Studies* 21 (2010): 97–126.

27. Ibid. According to Turkish sources, between 1973 and 1985 the Armenian terrorists had attempted 193 assassinations of Turkish diplomats, forty-five of which were successful (Kavuncu, "A Problem in Turkey-US Relations," 98, 114). The CIA listed 168 attacks for the period 1975–1983, including twelve successful assassinations. The Marxist-leaning Armenian Secret Army was responsible for sixty-four of these attacks. The USSR proved not immune to Armenian terrorism when, on February 1, 1980, bombs simultaneously went off in front of the Soviet Information Bureau in Paris and the Aeroflot office in Brussels. See CIA, research paper, "The Armenian Secret Army for the Liberation of Armenia: A Continuing International Threat," January 1984, http://www.foia.cia.gov/sites/default/files/document_conversions/89801/DOC_0005462031.pdf. Cf. de Waal, *Great Catastrophe*, 151–171.

28. Shavarsh Simonyan, "Notes on the Genocide of Armenians in the Ottoman Turkey (1876–1922) and the Trial of Young Turks," 1986, selectively reproduced in Shushanyan, "Between the Memories and the Present."

29. Golan, *Soviet Policies in the Middle East*, 33, 244–257.

30. On the strategic importance of Turkey in the US policy vis-à-vis the USSR see William M. Arkin, "Playing Chicken in Turkey," *Bulletin of the Atomic Scientists* 9, vol. 41 (October 1985): 4–5.

31. DoS, memo of conversation between Necdet Tezel, Ronald Bettauer, and Jon Greenwalt, June 18, 1970, NARA, DoS general records, subject numerical files, 1970–1973. Social, 59/1613/3042.

32. Richard L. Wentworth, "As Congress Considers Tribute to Armenians, Reagan Assures Key Ally, Turkey," *Christian Science Monitor*, April 24, 1985.

33. Vanakn N. Dadrian, "Those Audacious Armenians," *Christian Science Monitor*, January 10, 1978. See also Hayk Demoyan, *Western Media Coverage of the Nagorno-Karabakh Conflict in 1988–1990* (Yerevan: Tigran Mets, 2008), 33.

34. Demoyan, *Western Media Coverage*, 48–52.

35. Martin Walker, "Armenians Go for Non-Violence in Fight for Disputed Enclave," *Guardian*, March 14, 1988; "Armenians in Moscow Condemn Soviet Press," *Washington Post*, March 14, 1988.

36. Marutyan, "Istoricheskaia pamiat v dialoge mezhdu kulturami," *21-yi vek* 2 (6) (2007): 53–54; idem., "Can Collective Memory of Genocide Lead to Reconciliation?" 27.

37. Roy Medvedev and Giulietto Chiesa, *Time of Change: An Insider's View of Russia's Transformation* (London: I. B. Tauris, 1991), 209.
38. "Zasedanie Presidiuma Verkhovnogo Soveta SSSR," *Pravda*, July 20, 1988.
39. "130 Died, Sakharov Says," *NYT*, November 26, 1988; George Skelton, "Governor Asks Reagan, Bush to Plead Armenia Case with Gorbachev," *Los Angeles Times*, December 4, 1988; no title, *Izvestia*, September 1, 1990.
40. Suren Arutyunyan to Gorbachev [between May 21 and November 22, 1988], reproduced in Shushanyan, "Between the Memories and the Present."
41. A. Sarkisian, "Pamiati zhertv genotsida," *Pravda*, April 25, 1989; "Vystuplenia na s'ezde Narodnykh Deputatov SSSR," *Pravda*, June 2, 1989; Sergei Baruzdin, "Ekstremizmu—net!" *Pravda*, February 24, 1990.
42. Caroline Cox's statement, January 1, 1992; Cox to Yeltsin, January 14, 1992. Documents deposited in the Andrei Sakharov Archives at Harvard University. When consulted, the records were in the process of systematization at Brandeis University, prior to the archive's move to Harvard in 2004.

9. THE ISRAELI-PALESTINIAN CONFLICT

1. Lewis, *The Birth of the New Justice*, 207.
2. "Geneva Site Wins in U.N. Social Body," *NYT*, February 14, 1948.
3. Correspondence between Acheson and US Ambassador to Israel James G. MacDonald, April 1 and 7, 1949, NARA, DoS decimal files, 1945–1949, 59/760050/2186.
4. The Genocide Convention: Hearings, 279, 303.
5. Golan, *Soviet Policies in the Middle East*, 34–43. See also Laurent Rucker, "Moscow's Surprise: The Soviet-Israeli Alliance of 1947–1949," *Cold War International History Project* 46 (July 2005): 1–37; Gaiduk, *Divided Together*, 132–137; Konstantyn Sawczuk, *The Ukraine in the United Nations Organization: Study in Soviet Foreign Policy, 1944–1950* (New York: Columbia University Press, 1975), 75–83.
6. Fateev, *Obraz vraga*, 187–188.
7. Ibid., 58–94.
8. Richard Reston, "Soviet Press Mounts Anti-Israel Campaign," *Los Angeles Times*, June 17, 1967; "Obuzdat zakhvatchikov," *Pravda*, June 17, 1967; Erik Alexeyev, "Prestuplenie genotsida," *Pravda*, June 18, 1967; "Otpor avantiuristam," *Pravda*, June 19, 1967; B. Strelnikov, "Agressory u pozornogo stolba," *Pravda*, June 29, 1967; Alexander Bukharov, "Daian—zakhvatchik," *LG*, July 5, 1967.
9. "We Cannot Stand Idly By . . ."; "Fedorenko Remark Protested," *NYT*, June 18, 1967.
10. "Kto usugubliaet blizhnevostochnyi krizis?" *Pravda*, December 18, 1969.
11. L. Kuznetsov, "Krai goria i slez," *Pravda*, February 11, 1970; "Reaktsionnoe nutro sionizma," *Pravda*, March 10, 1970.
12. "Provokatsionnye vylazki sionistov," *Pravda*, November 3, 1971.
13. Robert H. Estabrook, "Soviets Call U.S. Genocidal at U.N.," *Washington Post*, December 11, 1970.
14. Nora Levin, *The Jews of the Soviet Union Since 1917: Paradox of Survival*, vol. 2 (New York: New York University Press, 1988), 694–695.
15. Borovik, "Neostorozhnye otkrovenia mistera Shvartsa," *LG*, February 24, 1971.
16. "Jewish Students Disrupt Washington performance of Moscow Orchestra," *Jewish Advocate*, January 22, 1970; "USSR Dancers Greeted by Demonstrators," *Jewish Advocate*, September 24, 1970.
17. "Pokonchit s provokatsiiami sionistov!" *Pravda*, January 15, 1971.

18. Golan, *Soviet Policies in the Middle East*, 110–120; docs. nos. 95, 116 in *From Encroachment to Involvement*, 461f, 588f.

19. "Mezhdunarodnaia obshchestvennost vozmushchena zlodeianiiami izrailskoi voenshchiny," *Pravda*, September 15, 1972; "Novyi akt agressii izrailskoi voenshchiny," *Pravda*, September 17, 1972.

20. "K polozheniiu na Blizhnem Bostoke," *Pravda*, March 24, 1978.

21. S. Svistunov, "Beschinstva okkupantov," *Pravda*, April 12, 1979; "Osuzhdenie deistvii zakhvatchikov," *Pravda*, February 10, 1979.

22. "Egypt Calls Israeli Attack on Palestinians 'Genocide'," *Los Angeles Times*, March 15, 1978; Flora Lewis, "Lybian Leader Vows to Back Revolts in Arab States," *NYT*, June 20, 1978; Robert Levey, "Castro Says the Rich Nations Should Give the Poor $300b," *Boston Globe*, October 13, 1979.

23. "Soviet, in U.N., Charges Israeli 'Genocide'," *NYT*, May 11, 1976; "Soviet's U.N. Charge Rebuffed by Israel," *NYT*, May 13, 1976.

24. "Rabota UNESCO," *Izvestia*, October 22, 1980.

25. R. Moseev, "Nepreklonnaia volia palestintsev," *Pravda*, December 31, 1981.

26. "Edinodushnoe osuzhdenie," *Pravda*, June 12, 1982; "Moshchnaia podderzhka," *Pravda*, June 16, 1982.

27. Golan, *Soviet Policies in the Middle East*, 124–137.

28. "Moscow Says Israel Seeks 'Extermination' of Palestinian People," *Washington Post*, June 7, 1982.

29. Hisham Sharabi, "Israel's War on the Palestinians: Lebanon Invasion Is Part of a Pattern That Includes Genocide," *Los Angeles Times*, June 11, 1982.

30. Bernard D. Nossiter, "Gromyko Says Israel Commits Genocide," *NYT*, June 22, 1982.

31. "'Prekratit agressiiu!'—govoriat sovetskie liudi," *Pravda*, June 26, 1982; "Solidarnost sovetskikh liudei," *Pravda*, June 27, 1982; "Golos solidarnosti i protesta," *Pravda*, June 28, 1982; "Gnev i vozmushchenie," *Pravda*, July 7, 1982; "Gnevnyi protest sovetskikh liudei," *Pravda*, July 10, 1982; "Gnevnoe osuzhdenie," *Pravda*, July 11, 1982; "Protest," *Pravda*, July 14, 1982; "Ostanovit palachei," *Pravda*, July 15, 1982; "Pozor agressoram," *Pravda*, July 18, 1982; "Mir—Blizhnemu Vostoku," *Pravda*, July 19, 1982; "Prekratit agressiiu," *Pravda*, July 25, 1982; "Golos solidarnosti," *Pravda*, July 29, 1982; "Prestupnikov—k otvetu," *Pravda*, August 4, 1982.

32. "Mir—Blizhnemu Vostoku," *Pravda*, July 30, 1982; "Gnevnyi protest," *Pravda*, August 6, 1982.

33. "Agressora k otvetu," July 17, 1982; A. Tolkunov, "Souchastniki genotsida," *Pravda*, August 2, 1982.

34. "Obviniaiutsia v genotside," *Pravda*, July 5, 1982.

35. "Otvety L. I. Brezhneva na voprosy gazety 'Pravda'," *Pravda*, July 21, 1982; "Obuzdat agressorov," *Pravda*, August 6, 1982.

36. See, for example, V. Bolshakov, "Eksportery genotsida," *Pravda*, August 14, 1982.

37. "Livan: tragedia prodolzhaetsia," *Pravda*, July 30, 1982.

38. "Livan: prestuplenia agressora," *Pravda*, July 16, 1982; "Koltso blokady szhimaetsia," *Pravda*, August 4, 1982; "Gnevnoe osuzhdenie agressora," *Pravda*, August 19, 1982.

39. Irina Lediakh, "Rasizm i ideologiia fashizma i mezhdunarodnogo imperializma," *SGP* 1 (January 1984): 96.

40. "Obviniaiutsia v genotside," *Pravda*, August 31, 1982; "Pered sudom narodov," *Pravda*, September 22, 1982. The findings and conclusions of the Platts-Mills commission are available at http://www.abbc.net/lebanon/occupation/encyclopedia_palestine_problem_ch30–3.htm.

41. "Vinovny v genotside," *Pravda*, October 26, 1982.

42. "Livan: aggressor ne unimaetsia," *Pravda*, July 26, 1982; "V bratskikh partiakh," *Pravda*, August 11, 1982; "Livan: Sokhraniaetsia napriazhennaia obstanovka," *Pravda*, August 25, 1982; "OOP: borba ne okonchena," *Pravda*, August 29, 1982; "V bratskikh partiakh," *Pravda*, September 10, 1982; "Tragedia Livana prodolzhaetsia," *Pravda*, September 18, 1982.
43. "Mir vozmushchen," *Pravda*, September 20, 1982; "Polozhit konets genotsidu," *Pravda*, September 22, 1982; "Osuzhdenie genotsida," *Pravda*, September 29, 1982.
44. Robert Rozett and Shmuel Spector, eds., *Encyclopedia of the Holocaust* (Milton Park, UK: Routledge, 2013), 234.
45. Norman Podhoretz, "The Massacre: Who Was Responsible?" *Washington Post*, September 24, 1982.
46. Bernard D. Nossiter, "General Assembly Condemns Massacre and Calls for a Security Council Investigation," *NYT*, September 25, 1982.
47. Schabas, *Genocide in International Law*, 454–455.
48. Cf. Palestine Arab Delegation, *An Indictment of Israeli Political and Military Leaders for Genocide, Crimes Against Humanity and War Crimes Against the Palestinians in the West Bank and Gaza* (New York: Palestine Arab Delegation, 1984).
49. Stanley Meisler, "Summit Veteran Gromyko Not Even a Spectator Now," *Los Angeles Times*, November 20, 1985.
50. "Za vyzhivanie i razvitie," *Pravda*, January 16, 1988.
51. Yuri Tyssovskii, *Prestuplenie bez nakazaniia: Chto proizoshlo v Livane* (Moscow: Progress, 1983), 82; Taras Klimenko, *Sionizm—genotsid v deitsvii* (Drepropetrovsk: Promin, 1986), 181.
52. Vladimir Peresada, "Mnenie obozrevatelia," *Pravda*, January 21, 1988.
53. Will Lissner, "Soviet Is Accused of Abusing Jews," *NYT*, March 22, 1951. See also Martin, *The Man Who Invented "Genocide,"* 228.
54. "Rassenmord als Waffe," *Aufbau*, June 8, 1951.
55. DoS, Assistant Secretary Jack K. McVall to Benton, June 1, 1951, NARA, DoS decimal files, 1950–54, 59/862915/1341.
56. NCRAC, resolution on genocide, June 17–20, 1954, NYPL, ZL-273/1.
57. Harry Schwartz, "Retreat from Stalin Policy," *NYT*, August 23, 1961; Arnold Beichman, "Anti-Semitism Probe Asked," *Christian Science Monitor*, October 22, 1962; "Soviet Attacks on Jews Seen as 'Genocide'," *Los Angeles Times*, April 7, 1964; "Red Pressure on Jews Told to Encino Club," *Los Angeles Times*, October 7, 1964; "Cultural Genocide," *Chicago Tribune*, February 5, 1971.
58. "Genocide Charged," *Chicago Tribune*, January 17, 1972; "Izvestia Attacks Congressmen on Tour for 'Hostile' Actions," *Los Angeles Times*, January 17, 1972.
59. "The Jews in Russia," *Chicago Daily Defender*, October 9, 1963. This particular case was cited five months later by the American delegate in the CHR when she accused the USSR of "cultural or even ethnic genocide" of the Jews.
60. "Councils Invite Public to See Movie, 'Price of Silence,' on Russian Jews," *American Israelite*, February 18, 1965.
61. "Book Claims 'Genocide' by Russia," *Los Angeles Times*, June 28, 1970.
62. "Rally Protests 'Cultural' Killing," *Hartford Courant*, August 10, 1970.
63. Quoted in Bass, *The Blood Telegram*, 339.
64. AJC, draft statement, "Genocide," 1971, WAG, 37/3/33.
65. Anne M. Foss, "The Genocide Convention: American Ratification," *Analysis*, publication of the Synagogue Council of America, 38 (June 1, 1973): 4, WAG, 37/3/33.
66. Magruder to Proxmire, July 11 and September 5, 1973; Proxmire to Magruder, July 24, 1973; Stanton D. Anderson, DoS Acting Assistant Secretary for Congressional Relations

to Proxmire, August 8, 1973, NARA, DoS general records, subject numerical files, 1970–73. Social, 59/1613/3043.

67. Korey, "The Anniversary of a 'Secret' Soviet Crime," *NYT*, August 12, 1972.

68. "Soviet 'Intellectual Genocide'," *Jewish Advocate*, June 25, 1981.

69. Alexei Grigoriev, "Krugovaia oborona," *Izvestia*, August 22, 1979. The documentary series went off the air following the Soviet invasion of Afghanistan.

70. "Rai, obernuvshiisia adom," *LG*, May 23, 1984. On the history of the Anti-Zionist Committee see William Korey, "The Soviet Public Anti-Zionist Committee: An Analysis" in *Soviet Jewry in the 1980s: The Politics of Anti-Semitism and Emigration and the Dynamics of Resettlement*, ed. Robert O. Freedman (Durham, NC: Duke University Press, 1989), 26–50.

71. "Zionism-Nazism: zloveshchee rukopozhatie," *LG*, October 17, 1984

72. Cesar Solodar, "Obyknovennyi sionizm," *LG*, April 3, 1985; "Zionism Is Equated with Nazism in New Wave of Soviet Propaganda," *American Israelite*, October 13, 1977. See also Solodar's book, *Dikaia polyn* (Moscow: Sovetskaia Rossia, 1977).

73. Karen Khachaturov, "Pokhititeli razuma," *Izvestia*, January 13, 1985.

74. Vladimir Abarinov, "Paguba i nadezhda," *LG*, October 12, 1988.

75. "Miting obshchestvennosti," *Pravda*, September 26, 1988.

76. "Soviet Rally Commemorates Nazi Massacre of Jews," *Chicago Tribune*, September 26, 1988.

77. "Reagan Challenges Soviets at Holocaust Memorial Site," *Los Angeles Times*, October 5, 1988.

78. "'Mesie Nenavist'," *Pravda*, September 14, 1988.

79. "Mir za nedeliu," *Pravda*, November 13, 1988.

80. Yuri Glukhov, "Bezmolvnyi krik," *Pravda*, May 3, 1990; "Massovye rasstrely nevinnykh liudei," *Pravda*, August 8, 1991.

10. AN UNCERTAIN END TO THE COLD WAR AND THE REACTIVATION OF THE GENOCIDE TREATY

1. Darius S. Jhabvaia, "Afghanistan Accuses Pakistan of Genocide," *Boston Globe*, October 12, 1974.

2. Mark Galeotti, *Afghanistan: The Soviet Union's Last War* (London: Frank Cass, 1995), 10–13; David W. Lesch, *1979: The Year That Shaped the Modern Middle East* (Boulder, CO: Westview Press, 2001), 53–56. See also Douglas J. MacEachin, *Predicting the Soviet Invasion of Afghanistan: The Intelligence Community's Record* (Washington, DC: Center for the Study of Intelligence, CIA, 2002).

3. Arthur Unger, "Dan Rather: More Soviet Killing Looms in Afghanistan," *Christian Science Monitor*, April 3, 1980; Ben Bradlee, "Russia's Vietnam?" *Boston Globe*, May 11, 1980.

4. "TASS Attacks Rather for CBS Afghan Report," *Washington Post*, April 6, 1980; "Soviet Paper Finds Anchor Switch Sinister," *Baltimore Sun*, May 1, 1980.

5. V. Volodin, "Anatomia lzhi," *Izvestia*, July 11, 1980.

6. Alexander Prokhanov, "Soldaty revoliutsii," *LG*, April 16, 1980; "Babrak Karmal: my uvereny v svoei pobede," *LG*, July 23, 1980.

7. Evan Maxwell, "Germ Warfare Charge Hailed by Refugees," *Los Angeles Times*, September 15, 1981; Alex Brummer, "US Accuses Moscow of a Campaign of Genocide," *Guardian*, March 23, 1982; Stuart J. D. Schwartzstein, "Chemical Warfare in Afghanistan: An Independent Assessment," *World Affairs* 3, vol. 145 (Winter 1982/83): 267–272; Milton Leitenberg and Raymond A. Zilinskas, *The Soviet Biological Weapons Program: A History* (Cambridge, MA: Harvard University Press, 2012), 450–451, 457.

8. Communication from Mark Galeotti, June 11, 2013. See also Edgar O'Balance, *Afghan Wars: Battles in a Hostile Land, 1839 to the Present* (London: Brassey's, 2002), 114.
9. Cf. Crowe, *War Crimes*, 330–331. The total population of Afghanistan was estimated at 15 million.
10. Edward Giradet, "Afghanistan: Soviet 'Migratory Genocide' and Failed UN Talks," *Christian Science Monitor*, December 6, 1983.
11. "U.N. Gets Report on Afghan War," *Washington Post*, October 28, 1985; "Afghanistan: This Is Genocide," *Washington Post*, December 15, 1985.
12. V. Baikov, "U linii Diuranda," *Pravda*, December 27, 1985 "Boi v raione perevala," *Izvestia*, December 30, 1985; "Pugaiut genotsidom," "Reshitelnyi protest," *Izvestia*, January 7, 1986; "press-konferentsia v Moskve," *Pravda*, January 11, 1986; "Presech genotsid," *Pravda*, February 9, 1986.
13. "Soviet Media Takes Up Pashtun Cause," *New Straits Times*, January 4, 1986; "Gnevnoe osuzhdenie repressii," *Izvestia*, February 4, 1986; V. Kuznetsov, "Tanki derzhat nas pod pritselom," *Izvestia*, March 19, 1986; A. Kapralov, "U genotsida odno litso," *Izvestia*, June 14, 1986.
14. "West German Accuses Soviet of Genocide," *NYT*, January 12, 1985; "Meese Accuses the Soviets of Atrocities in Afghanistan," *Christian Science Monitor*, March 27, 1986; "Meese Anger at Moscow 'Torture'," *Guardian*, March 27, 1986; Elaine Sciolino, "U.N. Speakers Tackle Drugs, Terror and War," *NYT*, September 30, 1986; Yitzhak Rabi, "U.S. Disappoints Israel in UN Vote," *Jewish Advocate*, December 11, 1986; "Excerpts from the Reagan Interview with 4 Correspondents," *NYT*, December 4, 1987.
15. Theodore B. Olson, Assistant Attorney General, memo for Attorney General William French Smith, June 2, 1982, NARA, Department of Justice general records, subject files of the Assistant to the Attorney General, 60/1402143/546. See also testimony by Proxmire in *Congressional Record: Proceedings and Debates of the 95th Congress, First Session* (May 24, 1977): 1; Betty Kaye Taylor, "The Genocide Convention," *Free Trade Union News* 9, vol. 32 (September 1977): 15, WAG, 37/6/35.
16. DoS Legal Adviser John R. Stevenson to Edwin A. Kujawa, President of San Diego County Federation of Republican Women's Clubs, May 25, 1970, NARA, DoS general records, subject numerical files, 1970–1973. Social, 59/1613/3042.
17. Olson, memo for Attorney General William French Smith, June 2, 1982, NARA, Department of Justice general records, subject files of the Assistant to the Attorney General, 60/1402143/546.
18. Department of Justice, [Kenneth O. Simon?], handwritten meeting notes, December 19, 1983, NARA, Department of Justice general records, subject files of the Assistant to the Attorney General, 60/1402143/546.
19. Simon to French Smith, December 22, 1983, NARA, Department of Justice general records, subject files of the Assistant to the Attorney General, 60/1402143/546.
20. Riley to French Smith, June 4, 1984, NARA, Department of Justice general records, subject files of the Assistant to the Attorney General, 60/1402143/546. Riley explicitly used the word *Holocaust*. For contemporaneous examples of Soviet allegations of US hypocrisy see Anatoly Movchan, "Prava cheloveka: slova i dela," *Pravda*, July 24, 1984; Vitaly Gan, "Razygrali fars," *Pravda*, September 16, 1984; A. Palladin, "I dazhe bez prava na materinstvo," *Izvestia*, October 6, 1984.
21. Korey, *Genocide Treaty Ratification*, 15–16, WAG, 25/138/15. See also Miles Harvey, "Compromise Efforts Fail on Genocide Treaty," *Los Angeles Times*, September 14, 1984.
22. LeBlanc, *The United States and the Genocide Convention*, 170.
23. Lawrence J. LeBlanc, "The United States and the Genocide Convention: The Sovereignty Package in Perspective" in *The Genocide Convention: The Legacy of 60 Years*, 178. The Soviet

Union welcomed *Nicaragua vs. USA* as a victory for international law, while continuing not to recognize the ICJ's jurisdiction. See Lauri Mälksoo, *Russian Approaches to International Law* (Oxford, UK: Oxford University Press, 2015), 154.

24. "Satiricheskaia kolonka: Shkola genotsida," *Izvestia*, June 26, 1970.

25. "Ostanovit ruku palachei!" *Pravda*, February 27, 1974; Volodia Teitelboim, "Patriot Luis Korvalan," *Pravda*, September 28, 1974; "'Chili–dlinnaia i uzkaia tiurma'," *Pravda*, October 22, 1974; "Reshitelnoe osuzhdenie," *Pravda*, September 18, 1975. Both Teitelboim and Corvalán eventually received political asylum in the Soviet Union where they stayed until 1988.

26. "Zaiavlenie pravitelstva Kuby," *Pravda*, September 11, 1978; "Borba narastaet," Vitaly Kobysh, "Genotsid v Nicaragua," *Pravda*, September 23, 1978; "Vyrazhenie solidarnosti," *Pravda*, June 29, 1979.

27. Guenter Grass, "Revolution in the Shadow of the Superpowers," *Guardian*, January 29, 1983. Several Miskito groups joined the antigovernment guerrillas. In retaliation for killing several Sandinista soldiers, governmental forces executed some thirty Miskito and forced the rest over the border into Honduras.

28. "Vooruzhennaia borba," *Pravda*, July 10, 1980; "Genotsid pod zavesoi lzhi," *Pravda*, February 14, 1981.

29. V. Terentiev, "Genotsid," Izvestia, March 23, 1968; V. Spassky, "Grabiteli v sutanakh," *Izvestia*, August 19, 1984; "Genotsid po-amerikanski," *Izvestia*, October 25, 1984; "Genotsid po-amerikanski," *Pravda*, October 26, 1984. For a scholarly analysis see works by Philip M. Fearnside, especially his article "Environmental Impacts of Brazil's Tucuruí Dam: Unlearned Lessons for Hydroelectric Development in Amazonia," *Environmental Management* 3, vol. 27 (March 2001): 386–387.

30. Kobysh, "Snova ob indeitsakh i genotside," *LG*, October 31, 1984.

31. Terry Atlas, "Reagan Backs Treaty on Genocide," *Chicago Tribune*, September 6, 1984; "A Surprise on Genocide," *Chicago Tribune*, September 13, 1984; George F. Will, "Genocide Treaty Only Rhetoric," *Hartford Courant*, September 20, 1984.

32. Martin Tolchin, "Committee Backs Genocide Treaty," *NYT*, September 20, 1984.

33. Orrin G. Hatch, "Reject the Genocide Convention," *NYT*, April 23, 1985.

34. David Hoffman, "Bergen-Belsen Put on Trip Itinerary," *Washington Post*, April 20, 1985; op-ed: "Reagan's German Blunder Feeds Soviet Propaganda," *Philadelphia Tribune*, May 10, 1985.

35. "Senators Push Genocide Pact," *Washington Post*, October 15, 1985; "Reagan Presses for Genocide Pact," *NYT*, October 17, 1985.

36. "Soviets Escalate Their 'PR Wars'," *Chicago Tribune*, November 16, 1985; "Soviet Accuse U.S. of Violating American Indians' Human Rights," *Los Angeles Times*, November 20, 1985; "Soviet Delegate Hits U.S. Over 'Cultural Genocide'," *Los Angeles Times*, November 25, 1985; "Human Rights Issue Splits Culture Forum," *Los Angeles Times*, November 26, 1985. "Stupid remarks" were indeed hard to die. As the US president on June 12, 1987 famously challenged Gorbachev at the Brandenburg Gate in West Berlin to "tear down this wall," tens of thousands of protesters marched through the city shouting anti-Reagan chants and carrying banners with such slogans as "USA, International Genocide Headquarters" ("Reagan Demands 'Gate Open'," *Hartford Courant*, June 12, 1987).

37. Hearing Before the Committee on Foreign Relations, United States Senate, 99th Congress, 1st Session, on the Prevention and Punishment of the Crime of Genocide, March 5, 1985 (Washington, DC: US Government Printing Office, 1985), 8, 13, 65–66, 71–72, 89, 111, 115–146. Cf. Martin, *The Man Who Invented "Genocide,"* 287–301. See also David Silverberg, "1985 Political 'Solutions' Create Problems of 1986: Analysis," *Jewish Exponent*, January 3, 1986.

38. Rowland Evans and Robert Novak, "Dole's Dilemma," *Washington Post*, February 19, 1986.

39. David Lightman, "Genocide Pact, Stalled 37 Years, Is Ratified," *Hartford Courant*, February 20, 1986; David Friedman, "Senate Ratifies Genocide Convention," *Jewish Advocate*, February 27, 1986; David Friedman, "Proxmire Honored for Genocide Treaty Support," *Jewish Advocate*, May 1, 1986.

40. LeBlanc, *The United States and the Genocide Convention*, 69–70, 83.

41. Lou Cannon, "Reagan, Noting Holocaust, Vows to Sign Anti-Genocide Pact," *Washington Post*, October 31, 1988.

42. Thomas Neumann, Ex. Vice President of the B'nai B'rith International, memo, November 7, 1988, WAG, 25/138/15.

43. "Verit li 'Amnistii'?" *Pravda*, October 21, 1988.

44. Mikhail Gorbachev, "Politicheskii doklad Tsentralnogo Komiteta KPSS XXVII s'ezdu Kommunisticheskoi Partii Sovetskogo Soiuza," *Pravda*, February 26, 1986.

45. Excerpts of Address by Mikhail Gorbachev at the 43rd UN General Assembly Session, December 7, 1988, Wilson Center Digital Archives, doc. 116224.

46. Minutes of the CPSU Central Committee's meeting, December 27–28, 1988, Wilson Center Digital Archives, doc. 112478.

47. UN doc. A/44/171 (March 9, 1989); P. Golub, "Otdaem prioritet pravu," *Izvestia*, March 9, 1989; "Soviets to Abide by World Court in Rights Cases," *Los Angeles Times*, March 9, 1989; "Official Documents: Soviet Union Accepts Compulsory Jurisdiction of ICJ for Six Human Rights Conventions," *American Journal of International Law* 2, vol. 83 (April 1989): 457.

48. Joseph Rothschild and Nancy M. Wingfield, *Return to Diversity: A Political History of East Central Europe Since World War II* (New York: Oxford University Press, 2000), 246–248.

49. "K sobytiiam v Rumynii," *Pravda*, December 26, 1989. See also David L. Nersessian, *Genocide and Political Groups* (Oxford: Oxford University Press, 2010), 117–118.

50. Holly Cartner, "Trials in Romania," *News from Helsinki Watch* 6, vol. 2 (1990): 1–5; V. Vedrashko, "Neobkhodimo doverie," *Pravda*, January 28, 1990; "Anatomia diktatury," *LG*, February 21, 1990. The persons in question were Interior Minister Tudor Postelnicu and members of the Political Executive Committee, Ion Dincă, Manea Mănescu, and Emil Bobu.

51. "Tak i ostaetsia zagadkoi," *Pravda*, July 26, 1990; "Den za dnem," *Pravda*, October 14, 1990. Despite the gravity of the imputed offense, both individuals ended up serving just a few years in jail. In fact, Nicu Ceauşescu was eventually sentenced on charges of embezzlement.

52. A. Cherniak and A. Chernenko, "SSSR—nash obshchii dom," *Pravda*, April 3, 1989.

53. Vasil Bykov, "Khleb i dostoinstvo," *LG*, June 27, 1990; Boris Oleinik, "Khochu sberech svoiu partiiu," *LG*, July 18, 1990; Alexandra Goujon, "'Genozid': A Rallying Cry in Belarus. A Rhetoric Analysis of Some Belarusian Nationalist Texts," *Journal of Genocide Research* 3, vol. 1 (November 1999): 356–357.

54. "Russkoiazychnoe naselenie prosit o pomoshchi," *Izvestia*, February 6, 1991. See also James Forsyth, *The Caucasus: A History* (Cambridge, UK: Cambridge University Press, 2013), 687, 810. Elena Bonner, in an undated communication, endorsed the opinion that Georgians were carrying out genocide in South Ossetia.

55. Vladimir Zarubin, "Obrezanie konsensusa," *Molodaia gvardiia* 7 (July 1991): 25–32.

56. Nikolai Potapov, "Idoly i zhupely," *Pravda*, March 31, 1989.

57. Victor Kozhemiako, "Plata za zhizn," *Pravda*, June 17, 1990.

58. B. Pipia, "Zastoi, pokaianie, doroga k khramu," *Pravda*, June 29, 1990.

59. David A. Harris, "Finish the Job on the Genocide Convention Treaty," *Washington Jewish Week*, March 17, 1988; Nicolas C. McBride, "After 40 Years, US Appears Ready to Ratify UN Genocide Treaty," *Christian Science Monitor*, May 10, 1988.

CONCLUSION

1. Iu. Kolosov, "Otvetstvennost za prava cheloveka," *Izvestia*, December 9, 1968.
2. "Kazhdyi sam po sebe," *Pravda*, March 7, 1969.
3. "Mirror of Opinion: Radio Free Europe," *Christian Science Monitor*, April 3, 1972.
4. The United Nations has periodically commissioned reviews of the Genocide Convention (e.g., the 1985 Whitaker Report). Improvements proposed by the UN rapporteurs have never been followed up for fear of a political stalemate not unlike that of the early years of the Cold War. The unanswered calls for expansion of the UN Security Council and/or the elimination of the veto power belong in the same category.
5. Martin, *The Man Who Invented "Genocide,"* 286.

AFTERWORD

1. Russian Ministry of Justice, "Federalnyi spisok ekstremistskikh materialov: 3151," (2015), http://minjust.ru/extremist-materials?field_extremist_content_value=%D0%BB%D0%B5%D0%BC%D0%BA%D0%B8%D0%BD. Further publications in both Russian and Ukrainian about the famine listed as "extremist" include Vladimir Vasilenko's *The 1932–33 Holodomor in Ukraine as Genocide: A Legal Assessment* (2009) and Vasyl Morochko's *Genocide of the Ukrainians: The Holodomor of 1932–33* (2007).
2. Foreign Power: Excerpts from Lithuanian Laws on Communism, Occupation, Resistance (Vilnius: Lithuanian Parliament, 2000), passim.
3. Allan Jaarma, "Investigation and Prosecution of War Crimes and Crimes Against Humanity Committed in Soviet-Occupied Estonia in the 1940s and 1950s," lecture delivered at the Estonian National Library in Tallinn on April 24, 2001.
4. Norman M. Naimark, *Stalin's Genocides* (Princeton, NJ: Princeton University Press, 2010), 24–29. Naimark pays lip service to both logic and legal complexity when he talks approvingly of the genocide trials in the Baltic states.
5. On the problematic nature of fitting individual cases of collaboration in the Holocaust under the heading of genocide see Anton Weiss-Wendt and Uğur Ümit Üngör, "Collaboration in Genocide: The Ottoman Empire 1915–1916, the German-Occupied Baltic 1941–1944, and Rwanda 1944," *Holocaust and Genocide Studies* 3, vol. 25 (Winter 2011): 405–410, 424–428.
6. Rokas M. Tracevskis, "Law Opens Way for Genocide Home Trials," *Baltic Times*, March 16, 2000; Lev Krichevsky, "Lithuania May Indict Jews for Genocide," *Jewish News of Greater Phoenix*, December 11, 1997.
7. Mumin Shakirov, "Eto plevok v litso," *Radio Liberty*, April 10, 2017.
8. David Satter, *It Was a Long Time Ago, and It Never Happened Anyway: Russia and the Communist Past* (New Haven: Yale University Press, 2012), 221–226, 247–250.
9. Mathew Kupfer and Thomas de Waal, "Crying Genocide: Use and Abuse of Political Rhetoric in Russia and Ukraine," Carnegie Endowment for International Peace, July 28, 2014.
10. See, for example, O. Antipova et al., eds., *Golod v SSSR, 1930–1934* (Moscow: Federal Archival Agency of the Russian Federation, 2009), 6–8; Victor Kondrashin, *Golod 1932–1933 godov: Tragediia rossiiskoi derevni* (Moscow: Rosspen, 2008), 10–35; Alexander Diukov, *Mif o genotside: Repressii sovetskikh vlastei v Estonii (1940–1953)* (Moscow: Foundation Historical Memory, 2007).
11. Robert D. Kaplan, "Geopolitics of the New World Order," *Time Magazine*, March 20, 2014. Ukraine's decision to cut off gas to the separatist-held areas "smacks of genocide," according to Putin. See "Putin Warns Gas Supplies to Ukraine, Europe Could Be Disrupted," *Reuters*, February 25, 2015.

12. "Russia Investigates Ukrainian Top Brass Over 'Genocide'," *Moscow Times*, October 2, 2014.

13. "Russian Throws Rights Accusations Back at U.S. with Ferguson Unrest," *Reuters*, November 26, 2014.

14. "Bastryrkin: Chislo postradvshikh ot voennykh prestuplenii kievskogo rezhima prevysilo 22000 chelovek," *Russnext.ru* (January 29, 2016), http://rusnext.ru/news/1454064729.

15. "Bastyrkin: Sledstvie raspologaet iavnymi priznakami genotsida v Iuzhnoi Ossetii," *Regnum.ru* (December 23, 2008), https://regnum.ru/news/1103513.html. On the application of the term *genocide* to the South Ossetia War see Mälksoo, *Russian Approaches to International Law*, 180, 185, 189.

16. Mälksoo, *Russian Approaches to International Law*, 80–81, 112–115, 121, 133–134, 137–139, 155, 172–173, 180–182, 187, 192.

17. See Erickson, "'Russia Will Not Be Trifled With'," 242–268.

18. Rodney Muhumuza, "Burundi's President Signs Bill on Withdrawal from the ICC," *Washington Post*, October 18, 2016; Simon Allison, "South Africa Begins Process to Exit International Criminal Court," *Daily Maverick*, October 21, 2016; "Gambia Announces Withdrawal from International Criminal Court," *Reuters*, October 26, 2016. The newly elected president of Gambia in February 2017 reversed the decision to leave the ICC.

19. Alexandra Sims, "Vladimir Putin Signs Law Allowing Russia to Ignore International Human Rights Rulings," *Independent*, December 15, 2015.

20. "Philippines President Rodrigo Duterte Announces His 'Separation' from the US," *Telegraph*, October 20, 2016; "Duterte to Critics: Stop Threatening About ICC," *ABS-CBN News*, October 16, 2016.

21. "Philippines' Duterte Says May Follow Russia's Withdrawal from 'Useless' ICC," *Reuters*, November 17, 2016.

22. "John Kerry: ISIS Is Committing Genocide in Syria and Iraq," *Guardian*, March 17, 2016.

BIBLIOGRAPHY

PRIMARY SOURCES

American Jewish Archives (AJA), Cincinnati

60 Raphael Lemkin Papers

American Jewish Historical Society (AJHS), New York City

154 Raphael Lemkin Collection

Foreign Policy Archives of the Russian Foreign Ministry (AVP RF), Moscow

6 Secretariat of Vyacheslav Molotov

Foreign Relations of the United States (FRUS), published online at: https://history.state.gov/historicaldocuments

1969–1976 Nixon Administration

1977–1980 Carter Administration

National Archives (NA), London, England

FO-1110 Foreign Office, Information Research Department

National Archives and Records Administration (NARA), College Park, MD

59 Department of State

60 Department of Justice

9999 Ronald Reagan Presidential Library

National Security Archives at George Washington University (NSA), Washington, DC

READD-RADD Russian and East European Collection

New York Public Library (NYPL), New York City

ZL-273 Raphael Lemkin Papers, 1947–1959

Russian State Archives of Social and Political History (RGASPI), Moscow

82 Vyacheslav Molotov

Select records from the central Russian archives published online by the Alexander N. Yakovlev Foundation at: http://www.alexanderyakovlev.org/db-docs

6 (AVP RF) Secretariat of Vyacheslav Molotov

17 (RGASPI) CPSU Central Committee

129 (AVP RF) Relations with the United States

9401 (GARF) Secretariat of the NKVD/MVD

9414 (GARF) GULAG (1930–1960)

Tamiment Library & Robert F. Wagner Labor Archives (WAG), New York City

25 Jewish Labor Committee

37 Ad Hoc Committee on the Human Rights and Genocide Treaties

23 Edward S. Goldstein Papers

United Nations official records

ECOSOC

General Assembly

International Law Commission

Sixth Committee

Woodrow Wilson Digital Archives

Mitrokhin Archive

Sino-Soviet Relations

United States–Soviet Relations
Vietnam War

JOURNALS

American Bar Association Journal
American Journal of International Law
American Slavic and East European Review
Baltic Worlds
Boston University Law Review
Bulletin of the Atomic Scientists
Case Western Reserve Journal of International Law
Cold War History
Cold War International History Project Bulletin
Contemporary European History
The Cross and the Flag (Los Angeles, CA)
Denver Journal of International Law and Policy
Environmental Management
Etnograficheskoe obozrenie
Focaal—European Journal of Anthropology
Historical Journal
Ideas (New York City)
The Intermarium: Bulletin of the Central European Federal Clubs in Paris and in Rome
International Organization
Journal of American History
Journal of Contemporary History
Journal of Genocide Research
Molodaia gvardiia
News from Helsinki Watch
New York Review of Books
New York University Journal of International Law & Politics
Novoe vremia
Review of Armenian Studies (Ankara, Turkey)
Review of Politics
Review of the News (Belmont, MA)
Sovetskoe gosudarstvo i pravo
Soviet Studies
University of Chicago Law Review
University of St. Thomas Journal of Law and Public Policy
Vista, the Magazine of the United Nations Association
Voprosy istorii
World Magazine
World Affairs
Yerevan (Yerevan, Armenia)
Zeithistorische Forschungen

NEWSPAPERS AND NEWSLETTERS

American Israelite (Cincinnati, OH)
Analysis (Washington, DC)

Arizona Republic (Phoenix, AZ)
Arkansas State Press (Little Rock, AR)
Aufbau (New York City)
Baltimore Sun
Bergens Tidene (Bergen, Norway)
Boston Globe
Chicago Daily Defender
Chicago Daily Tribune
Chicago Tribune
Christian Crusade Weekly (Tulsa, OK)
Christian Science Monitor
Chronicle of Higher Education
Cinema Educational Guild (Hollywood, CA)
Common Sense (Union Township, NJ)
Conservative Viewpoint (Sterling, VA)
Councilor (Shreveport, LA)
Crusader (Rockford, IL)
Daily Boston Globe
Dan Smoot Report (Dallas, TX)
Fiery Cross (Swartz, LA)
Free Trade Union News
Hartford Courant
Herald of Freedom (Zarephath, NJ)
Human Events (Washington, DC)
Independent American (New Orleans, LA)
Izvestia
Jewish Advocate (Boston, MA)
Jewish Exponent (Philadelphia, PA)
John Birch Society Bulletin (Belmont, MA)
Liberty Letter (Washington, DC)
Liberty Lowdown (Washington, DC)
Life Lines (Dallas, TX)
Literaturnaia Gazeta
Los Angeles Times
Manchester Guardian
Manion Forum (South Bend, IN)
Milwaukee Star
Minority Report (Dayton, OH)
Monterey Park Californian
New Straits Times (Kuala Lumpur, Malaysia)
New York Post
New York Times
New York Times Magazine
Observer
Philadelphia Tribune
Pravda
Red Line (St. Louis, MO)
Thunderbolt (Savannah, GA)
Truth Seeker (San Diego, CA)
Twin Circle (Denver, CO)

Wall Street Journal
Wanderer (St. Paul, MN)
Washington Jewish Week
Washington Post
Washington Post and Times Herald (1954–1959)

PUBLISHED SOURCES

Abramcyk, Mikola, *I Accuse the Kremlin of Genocide of My Nation: Based on the Secret Documents of the Military Persecutors and N.K.V.D. of the U.S.S.R.* (Toronto: Byelorussian Alliance of Canada, 1950).

Abrams, Bradley, "Hope Died Last: The Czechoslovak Road to Stalinism" in *Stalinism Revisited: The Establishment of Communist Regimes in East-Central Europe*, ed. Vladimir Tismaneanu (Budapest: Central European University Press, 2009): 345–365.

Adalian, P. Rouben, *Historical Dictionary of Armenia* (Lanham, MD: Scarecrow Press, 2010).

Amos, Jennifer, "Embracing and Contesting: The Soviet Union and the Universal Declaration of Human Rights, 1948–1958" in *Human Rights in the Twentieth Century*, ed. Stefan Ludwig Hoffmann (Cambridge, UK: Cambridge University Press, 2010), 147–165.

Anderson, Carol, "Bleached Souls and Red Negroes: The NAACP and Black Communists in the Early Cold War, 1948–1952" in *Window on Freedom: Race, Civil Rights, and Foreign Affairs, 1945–1988*, ed. Brenda Gayle Plummer (Chapel Hill, NC: University of North Carolina Press, 2003), 93–112.

Anderson, *Eyes off the Prize: The United Nations and the African American Struggle for Human Rights, 1944–1955* (New York: Cambridge University Press, 2003).

Andriukhin, Mikhail, *Genotsid—prestuplenie protiv chelovechestva* (Moscow: Moscow Law Institute, 1954).

Andriukhin, *Genotsid—tiagchaishee prestuplenie protiv chelovechestva* (Moscow: Gosiurizdat, 1961).

Andriukhin, *Genotsid v politike imperialisticheskikh gosudarstv* (Moscow: Znanie, 1967).

Angster, Julia, "'The Finest Labour Network in Europe': American Labour and the Cold War" in *The US Government, Citizen Groups and the Cold War: The State-Private Network*, ed. Helen Laville and Hugh Wilford (Abingdon, UK: Routledge, 2006), 100–115.

Appeal to the United Nations on Genocide (Reutlingen: Supreme Lithuanian Committee of Liberation, 1951).

Applebaum, Anne, *Gulag: A History* (New York: Doubleday, 2003).

Arkin, M. William, "Playing Chicken in Turkey," *Bulletin of the Atomic Scientists* 9, vol. 41 (October 1985): 4–5.

Avtorkhanov, Abdurakhman, *Narodoubiistvo v SSSR: Ubiistvo chechenskogo naroda* (Munich: "Free Caucasus," 1952).

Barnes, A. Steven, *Death and Redemption: The Gulag and the Shaping of Soviet Society* (Princeton, NJ: Princeton University Press, 2011).

Barsegov, Yuri, ed., *Genotsid armian: Otvetstvennost Turtsii i obiazatelstva mirovogo soobshchestva*, vol. 2, pt. 2, *Dokumenty. Dopolnenie k 1-mu i 2-mu tomam Sbornika* (Moscow: Gardariki, 2005).

Bartman, Christi Scott, *Lawfare: Use of the Definition of Aggressive War by the Soviet and Russian Federation Governments* (Newcastle: Cambridge Scholars Publishing, 2010).

Bass, J. Gary, *The Blood Telegram: Nixon, Kissinger, and a Forgotten Genocide* (New York: Alfred A. Knopf, 2013).

Bassiouni, M. Cherif, "Enslavement as an International Crime," *New York University Journal of International Law & Politics* 23 (1991): 445–517.

Becker, Elizabeth, *When the War Was Over: The Voices of Cambodia's Revolution and Its People* (New York: Simon and Schuster, 1986).

Bedau, A. Hugo, "Genocide in Vietnam?" *Boston University Law Review* 3, vol. 53 (May 1973): 574–622.

Begley, Louis, "How Wily Mitterrand Transformed France," *New York Review of Books* 10, vol. 61 (June 5–18, 2014).

Black, Allida, ed., *The Eleanor Roosevelt Papers: The Human Rights Years, 1945–1948* (Charlottesville, VA: University of Virginia Press, 2010).

Bogdanov, Oleg, "Amerikanskaia mezhdunarodno-pravovaia doktrina na sluzhbe imperialisticheskoi ekspansii," *SGP* 5 (May 1952): 70–73.

Brauer, Birgit, "Chechens and the Survival of Their Cultural Identity in Exile," *Journal of Genocide Research* 3, vol. 4 (2002): 387–400.

Buell, Jodi, "Ratification of the Genocide Convention? The United States and the United Nations Convention on the Prevention and Punishment of the Crime of Genocide" (Senior thesis: Pacific University, OR, 2004).

Campbell, J. Kenneth, "The International War Crimes Conference, Oslo, June 1971: Excerpts from the Diary of One of the Witnesses" in *Nobody Gets Off the Bus: Viet Nam Generation War Book*, ed. Kali Tal (Chevy Chase, MD: Burning Cities Press, 1994), 148–151.

Camus, Albert, *Algerian Chronicles* (Cambridge, MA: Belknap Press, 2013).

Carruthers, L. Susan, *Cold War Captives: Imprisonment, Escape, and Brainwashing* (Berkeley, CA: University of California Press, 2009).

Cartner, Holly, "Trials in Romania," *News from Helsinki Watch* 6, vol. 2 (1990): 1–5.

Chandler, P. David, *The Tragedy of Cambodian History: Politics, War, and Revolution since 1945* (New Haven: Yale University Press, 1991).

The Crimes of Khrushchev, pt. 1–7, Committee on Un-American Activities, House of Representatives, 86th Congress, 1st Session (Washington, DC: Government Printing Office, 1959).

Crowe, David, *War Crimes, Genocide, and Justice: A Global History* (Basingstoke: Palgrave Macmillan, 2014).

Dallin, Alexander, *The Soviet Union at the United Nations* (London: Methuen, 1962).

Dallin, David, *The Economics of Slave Labor* (Chicago: Henry Regnery, 1949).

Dallin and Boris I. Nicolaevsky, *Forced Labor in Soviet Russia* (New Haven: Yale University Press, 1947).

Darieva, Tsypylma, "'The Road to Golgotha': Representing Loss in Postsocialist Armenia," *Focaal—European Journal of Anthropology* 52 (2008): 92–108.

Deker, Nikolai, and Andrei Lebed, eds., *Genocide in the USSR: Studies in Group Destruction* (Munich: Institut zur Erforschung der UdSSR, 1958).

Dekmejian, H. Richard, "Soviet-Turkish Relations and Politics in the Armenian SSR," *Soviet Studies*, 4, vol. 19 (April 1968): 510–525.

Demoyan, Hayk, *Western Media Coverage of the Nagorno-Karabakh Conflict in 1988–1990* (Yerevan: Tigran Mets, 2008).

De Nike, Howard J., et al., eds., *Genocide in Cambodia: Documents from the Trial of Pol Pot and Ieng Sary* (Philadelphia: University of Pennsylvania Press, 2000).

Dezalay, Yves, and Bryant G. Garth, *The Internationalization of Palace Wars: Lawyers, Economists, and the Contest to Transform Latin American States* (Chicago: University of Chicago Press, 2002).

Dmitriev, E., "Amerikanskie 'gosudarstvovedy'—prisluzhniki reaktsii i fashizma," *SGP* 7 (July 1952): 59–62.

Dudziak, L. Mary, "Desegregation as a Cold War Imperative," *Stanford Law Review* 41 (November 1988): 61–120.

Duffett, John, ed., *Against the Crime of Silence: Proceedings of the International War Crimes Tribunal* (New York: O'Hare Books, 1968).

Engerman, A. David, *Know Your Enemy: The Rise and Fall of America's Soviet Experts* (Oxford: Oxford University Press, 2009).

Erickson, John, "'Russia Will Not Be Trifled With': Geopolitical Facts and Fantasies" in *Geopolitics, Geography and Strategy*, ed. Collin S. Gray and Geoffrey Sloan (London: Frank Cass, 1999): 242–268.

Fateev, Andrei, *Obraz vraga v sovetskoi propagande, 1945–1954 gg.* (Moscow: IRI RAN, 1999).

Fearnside, M. Philip, "Environmental Impacts of Brazil's Tucuruí Dam: Unlearned Lessons for Hydroelectric Development in Amazonia," *Environmental Management* 3, vol. 27 (March 2001): 377–96.

Fein, Helen, "Discriminating Genocide from War Crimes: Vietnam and Afghanistan Reexamined," *Denver Journal of International Law and Policy* 1, vol. 22 (Fall 1993): 29–62.

Foreign Power: Excerpts from Lithuanian Laws on Communism, Occupation, Resistance (Vilnius: Lithuanian Parliament, 2000).

Forsyth, James, *The Caucasus: A History* (Cambridge, UK: Cambridge University Press, 2013).

Gaiduk, Ilya, *Divided Together: The United States and the Soviet Union in the United Nations, 1945–1965* (Washington, DC: Woodrow Wilson Center Press, 2012).

Galchinsky, Michael, *Jews and Human Rights: Dancing at Three Weddings* (Lanham, MD: Rowman & Littlefield, 2007).

Galeotti, Mark, *Afghanistan: The Soviet Union's Last War* (London: Frank Cass, 1995).

Galkin, Alexander, ed., *Genocide* (Moscow: Progress Publishers, 1985).

Genocide by Deportation: An Appeal to the United Nations to Enforce the Law (New York: Hungarian National Council, 1951).

Golan, Galia, *Soviet Policies in the Middle East from World War II to Gorbachev* (Cambridge, UK: Cambridge University Press, 1990).

Gorny, Serge, "American Criminal Law as It Is Taught in Russia: A Translation from a Soviet Textbook," *American Bar Association Journal* 36 (July 1950): 542–545.

Goujon, Alexandra, "'Genozid': A Rallying Cry in Belarus. A Rhetoric Analysis of Some Belarusian Nationalist Texts," *Journal of Genocide Research* 3, vol. 1 (November 1999): 353–366.

Hammer, P. Darrell, "Legal Education in the USSR," *Soviet Studies* 1, vol. 9 (July 1957): 20–27.

Hasanli, Jamil, *Stalin and the Turkish Crisis of the Cold War, 1945–1953* (Lanham, MD: Lexington Books, 2011).

Hazard, N. John, "Law Practice in Russia: The Organized Bar in the U.S.S.R.," *American Bar Association Journal* 35 (March 1949): 177–180, 264–275.

Hearing Before the Committee on Foreign Relations, United States Senate, 99th Congress, 1st Session, on the Prevention and Punishment of the Crime of Genocide, March 5, 1985 (Washington, DC: US Government Printing Office, 1985).

Hearing Before a Subcommittee of the Committee on Foreign Relations, United States Senate, 91st Congress, 1st Session, on the Convention on the Prevention and Punishment of the Crime of Genocide (Washington, DC: US Government Printing Office, 1970).

Herling, K. Albert, *The Soviet Slave Empire* (New York: Wilfred Funk, 1951).

Hersey, John, *Algiers Motel Incident* (Baltimore: Johns Hopkins University Press, 1997 [1968]).

Hohenberg, John, "The Crusade That Changed the U.N.," *Saturday Review* (November 9, 1968): 86–87.

Horne, Gerald, *Black Revolutionary: William Patterson and the Globalization of the African American Freedom Struggle* (Urbana, IL: University of Illinois Press, 2013).

Investigation of Communist Take-Over and Occupation of Hungary, Fifth Interim Report of Hearings Before the Subcommittee on Hungary of the Select Committee on Communist Aggression, House of Representatives, 83rd Congress, 2nd Session (Washington, DC: Government Printing Office, 1954).

Irvin-Erickson, Douglas, *Raphaël Lemkin and the Concept of Genocide* (Philadelphia: University of Pennsylvania Press, 2016).

Ivanov, F., "Chetvertaia sessiia Komissii mezhdunarodnogo prava OON," *SGP* 11 (November 1952): 72–79.

Jersild, Austin, *The Sino-Soviet Alliance: An International History* (Chapel Hill, NC: University of North Carolina Press, 2014).

Johnston, Timothy, "Peace or Pacifism? The Soviet 'Struggle for Peace in All the World,' 1948–54," *Slavonic and East European Review* 2, vol. 86 (April 2008): 259–282.

Judt, Tony, *Postwar: A History of Europe Since 1945* (New York: Penguin, 2005).

Kádár Lynn, Katalin, "At War While at Peace: United States Cold War Policy and the National Committee for a Free Europe, Inc." in *The Inauguration of Organized Political Warfare: Cold War Organizations Sponsored by the National Committee for a Free Europe/Free Europe Committee*, ed. Kádár Lynn (Saint Helena, CA: Helena History Press, 2013), 7–70.

Kádár Lynn, "The Hungarian National Council/Hungarian National Committee" in *The Inauguration of Organized Political Warfare: Cold War Organizations Sponsored by the National Committee for a Free Europe/Free Europe Committee*, ed. Katalin Kádár Lynn (Saint Helena, CA: Helena History Press, 2013), 237–308.

Kaelas, Aleksander, *Human Rights and Genocide in the Baltic States: A Statement Submitted to the Delegations to the United Nations General Assembly, September 1950* (Stockholm: Estonian Information Center, 1950).

Kalb, G. Madeleine, *The Congo Cables: The Cold War in Africa—From Eisenhower to Kennedy* (New York: Macmillan, 1982).

Kalme, Albert, *Total Terror: An Exposé of Genocide in the Baltics* (New York: Appleton-Century-Crofts, 1951).

Kanet, E. Roger, "The Superpower Quest for Empire: The Cold War and Soviet Support for 'Wars of National Liberation,'" *Cold War History* 3, vol. 6 (August 2006): 331–352.

Kavuncu, Sibel, "A Problem in Turkey-US Relations in the 1980's: Armenian Draft Resolutions," *Review of Armenian Studies* 21 (2010): 97–126.

Kayaoğlu, Barın, "Strategic Imperatives, Democratic Rhetoric: The United States and Turkey, 1945–52," *Cold War History* 3, vol. 9 (August 2009): 321–345.

Klimenko, Taras, *Sionizm—genotsid v deitsvii* (Drepropetrovsk: Promin, 1986).

Klinghoffer, Arthur Jay, "International Citizens' Tribunals on Human Rights" in *Genocide, War Crimes, and the West: History and Complicity*, ed. Adam Jones (London: Zed Books, 2004), 346–360.

Klose, Fabian, *Human Rights in the Shadow of Colonial Violence: The Wars of Independence in Kenya and Algeria* (Philadelphia: University of Pennsylvania Press, 2013).

Konigsberg, Robert Eric, "Who Killed Anna Mae?" *New York Times Magazine* (April 27, 2014): 34–40, 48.

Korey, William, "America's Shame: The Unratified Genocide Treaty" in *Genocide and Human Rights: A Global Anthology*, ed. Jack N. Porter (Lanham, MD: University Press of America, 1982), 280–296.

Korey, *Genocide Treaty Ratification: Ending an American Embarrassment* (Washington, DC: B'nai B'rith International, November 7, 1988), WAG, 25/138/15.

Korey, "Helsinki's Child: Sin of Omission," *Foreign Policy* 39 (Summer 1980): 172–175.

Korey, "On Banning Genocide: 'We Should Have Been the First'," *World Magazine* (September 26, 1972): unnumbered pages.

Korey, "The Soviet Public Anti-Zionist Committee: An Analysis" in *Soviet Jewry in the 1980s: The Politics of Anti-Semitism and Emigration and the Dynamics of Resettlement*, ed. Robert O. Freedman (Durham, NC: Duke University Press, 1989), 26–50.

Korey, "What Hope for the Genocide Convention?" *Vista, the Magazine of the United Nations Association* (November–December 1972): 43–45, 51.

Kravchenko, Victor, *I Chose Freedom: The Personal and Political Life of a Soviet Official* (Garden City, NY: Garden City Publishing, 1947).

Kulski, W. Władysław, "Present Trends in Soviet International Law," *Proceedings of the American Society of International Law at Its Annual Meeting* 47 (April 23–25, 1953): 59–89.

Kulski, "The Soviet Attitude Towards International Law and International Relations," *AJIL* 3, vol. 47 (July 1953): 485–491.

Kulski, "Soviet Comments on International Law," *AJIL* 2, vol. 45 (April 1951): 347–353.

Kulski, "Soviet Comments on International Law," *AJIL* 4, vol. 45 (October 1951): 762–770.

Kulski, "Soviet Comments on International Law and International Relations," *AJIL* 3, vol. 45 (July 1951): 556–564.

Kulski, "Soviet Comments on International Law and International Relations," *AJIL* 1, vol. 47 (January 1953): 125–134.

Kulski, "Soviet Comments on International Law and International Relations," *AJIL* 2, vol. 48 (April 1954): 307–313.

Lasswell, D. Harold, "The Prospects of Cooperation in a Bipolar World," *University of Chicago Law Review* 4, vol. 15 (Summer 1948): 877, 887.

LeBlanc, J. Lawrence, *The United States and the Genocide Convention* (Durham, NC: Duke University Press, 1991).

LeBlanc, "The United States and the Genocide Convention: The Sovereignty Package in Perspective" in *The Genocide Convention: The Legacy of 60 Years*, ed. H. G. van der Wilt et al. (Leiden: Martinus Nijhoff, 2012), 173–186.

Lediakh, Irina, "Rasizm i ideologiia fashizma i mezhdunarodnogo imperializma," *SGP* 1 (January 1984): 92–97.

Leitenberg, Milton, and Raymond A. Zilinskas, *The Soviet Biological Weapons Program: A History* (Cambridge, MA: Harvard University Press, 2012).

Lendavai, Paul, *One Day That Shook the Communist World: The 1956 Hungarian Uprising and Its Legacy* (Princeton, NJ: Princeton University Press, 2008).

Lentz, Richard, and Karla K. Gower, *The Opinions of Mankind: Racial Issues, Press, and Propaganda in the Cold War* (Columbia, MO: University of Missouri Press, 2010).

Lepeshkin, Alexei, "Fashizatsia mestnykh organov upravleniia SShA," *SGP* 8 (August 1953): 66–77.

Lesch, W. David, *1979: The Year That Shaped the Modern Middle East* (Boulder, CO: Westview Press, 2001).

Levenson, Claude, "Tibet: A Neo-Colonial Genocide" in *Forgotten Genocides: Oblivion, Denial, and Memory*, ed. René Lemarchand (Philadelphia: University of Pennsylvania Press, 2011).

Levin, David, "'Mezhdunarodnoe pravo' amerikanskikh imperialisticheskikh razboinikov," *SGP* 3 (March 1951): 77–81.

Levin, Josif, "Fashizatsiia gosudarstvennogo stroia SShA," *SGP* 4 (April 1951): 69–79.

Levin, Nora, *The Jews of the Soviet Union Since 1917: Paradox of Survival*, vol. 2 (New York: New York University Press, 1988).

Lewis, Mark, *The Birth of the New Justice: The Internationalization of Crime and Punishment, 1919–1950* (Oxford, UK: Oxford University Press, 2014).

Lippman, Mathew, "The Drafting and Development of the 1948 Convention on Genocide and the Politics of International Law" in *The Genocide Convention: The Legacy of 60 Years*, ed. H. G. van der Wilt et al. (Leiden: Martinus Nijhoff, 2012), 15–25.

Lippman, "A Road Map to the 1948 Convention on the Prevention and Punishment of the Crime of Genocide," *Journal of Genocide Research* 2, vol. 4 (2002): 177–195.

Lissitzyn, J. Oliver, "Recent Soviet Literature on International Law," *American Slavic and East European Review* 4, vol. 11 (December 1952): 257–273.

Lorenz, Sophie, "'Heldin des anderen Amerikas.' Die DDR-Solidaritätsbewegung für Angela Davis, 1970–1973," *Zeithistorische Forschungen* 1, vol. 10 (2013): 38–60.

Lucas, Scott, *Freedom's War: The US Crusade Against the Soviet Union, 1945–46* (Manchester, UK: Manchester University Press, 1999).

Mälksoo, Lauri, *Russian Approaches to International Law* (Oxford, UK: Oxford University Press, 2015).

Martin, J. James, *The Man Who Invented "Genocide": The Public Career and Consequences of Raphael Lemkin* (Torrance, CA: Institute for Historical Review, 1984).

Marutyan, Harutyun, "Can Collective Memory of Genocide Lead to Reconciliation? A View from Yerevan" in *Prospects for Reconciliation: Theory and Practice*, ed. Hranush Kharatyan-Araqelyan and Leyla Neyzi (Bonn: DVV International, 2011): 24–38.

Marutyan, "Istoricheskaia pamiat v dialoge mezhdu kulturami," *21-yi vek* 2 (6) (2007): 44–59.

Marutyan, "Pamiatnik zhertvam genotsida v kontekste ritualov pamiati armianskogo voprosa," *Etnograficheskoe obozrenie* 3 (2008): 119–128.

Matusevich, Maxim, *No Easy Row for a Russian Hoe: Ideology and Pragmatism in Nigerian-Soviet Relations, 1960–1991* (Trenton, NJ: Africa World Press, 2003).

Mazov, Sergei, "The USSR and the Former Italian Colonies, 1945–1950," *Cold War History* 3, vol. 3 (April 2003): 49–78.

Mazower, Mark, *No Enchanted Palace: The End of Empire and the Ideological Origins of the United Nations* (Princeton, NJ: Princeton University Press, 2009).

Mazower, "The Strange Triumph of Human Rights, 1933–1950," *Historical Journal* 2, vol. 47 (2004): 379–398.

McCauley, Brian, "Hungary and Suez, 1956: The Limits of Soviet and American Power," *Journal of Contemporary History* 4, vol. 16 (October 1981): 779–794.

McDowall, David, *The Kurds*, a Minority Rights Group Report (September 1991): 1–32.

Means, Russell, *Where White Men Fear to Tread: The Autobiography of Russell Means* (New York: St. Martin's Griffin, 1995).

Medvedev, Roy, and Giulietto Chiesa, *Time of Change: An Insider's View of Russia's Transformation* (London: I. B. Tauris, 1991).

Meredith, Martin, *The Fate of Africa: From the Hopes of Freedom to the Heart of Despair* (New York: Public Affairs, 2005).

Metzl, F. Jamie, *Western Responses to Human Rights Abuses in Cambodia, 1975–80* (Basingstoke: Palgrave Macmillan, 1996).

Modzhorian, Lydia, "Reaktsionyye iuristy na sluzhbe amerikanskikh agressorov," *SGP* 10 (October 1952): 85–90.

Morris, J. Stephen, *Why Vietnam Invaded Cambodia: Political Culture and the Causes of War* (Stanford, CA: Stanford University Press, 1999).

Morrison, Toni, ed., *To Die for the People: Huey Newton* (San Francisco, CA: City Lights Books, 2009).

Naimark, M. Norman, *Stalin's Genocides* (Princeton, NJ: Princeton University Press, 2010).

Nersessian, L. David, *Genocide and Political Groups* (Oxford: Oxford University Press, 2010).

O'Balance, Edgar, *Afghan Wars: Battles in a Hostile Land, 1839 to the Present* (London: Brassey's, 2002).

O'Balance, *The Kurdish Revolt, 1961–1970* (London: Faber and Faber, 1973).

Ó Tuathail, Gearóid, *Critical Geopolitics* (Minneapolis: University of Minnesota Press, 1996).

Palestine Arab Delegation, *An Indictment of Israeli Political and Military Leaders for Genocide, Crimes Against Humanity and War Crimes Against the Palestinians in the West Bank and Gaza* (New York: Palestine Arab Delegation, 1984).

Pechatnov, Vladimir, "'The Allies Are Pressing on You to Break Your Will . . .': Foreign Policy Correspondence Between Stalin and Molotov and Other Politburo Members, September 1945–December 1946," *CWIHP*, Working Paper 26 (September 1999): 1–25.

Pelékis, K. [Bronius Kviklys], *Genocide: Lithuania's Threefold Tragedy* (Bielefeld: Venta, 1949).

Pohl, Michaela, "'It Cannot Be That Our Graves Will Be Here': The Survival of Chechen and Ingush Deportees in Kazakhstan, 1944–1957," *Journal of Genocide Research* 3, vol. 4 (2002): 401–430.

Power, Samantha, *"A Problem from Hell": America and the Age of Genocide* (New York: Basic Books, 2002).

Rafalko, J. Frank, *MH/Chaos: The CIA's Campaign Against the Radical New Left and the Black Panthers* (Annapolis, MD: Naval Institute Press, 2011).

Richardson, Curtis, "Stalinist Terror and the Kalmyks' National Revival: A Cultural and Historical Perspective," *Journal of Genocide Research* 3, vol. 4 (2002): 441–451.

Ro'i, Yaacov, ed., *From Encroachment to Involvement: A Documentary Study of Soviet Policy in the Middle East, 1945–1973* (New York: John Wiley & Sons, 1974).

Ro'i, *The Struggle for Soviet Jewish Emigration, 1948–1967* (Cambridge: Cambridge University Press, 1991).

Rosier, Paul, "'They Are Ancestral Homelands': Race, Place, and Politics in Cold War Native America," *Journal of American History* 4, vol. 92 (March 2006): 1300–1326.

Rosser, F. Richard, "Soviet Opposition to Racial Discrimination in the United Nations," *Russian Review* 1, vol. 21 (January 1962): 25–37.

Rothschild, Joseph, and Nancy M. Wingfield, *Return to Diversity: A Political History of East Central Europe Since World War II* (New York: Oxford University Press, 2000).

Rubinstein, Z. Alvin, "Soviet Policy Toward Under-Developed Areas in the Economic and Social Council," *International Organization* 2, vol. 9 (May 1955): 232–243.

Rucker, Laurent, "Moscow's Surprise: The Soviet-Israeli Alliance of 1947–1949," *Cold War International History Project* 46 (July 2005): 1–37.

Rudzinski, Alexander, "The Influence of the United Nations on Soviet Policy," *International Organization* 2, vol. 5 (May 1950): 282–299.

Samuelson, Lennart, "A Pathbreaker: Robert Conquest and Soviet Studies During the Cold War," *Baltic Worlds* 1, vol. 2 (April 2009): 47–51.

Sartre, Jean-Paul, *On Genocide* (Boston: Beacon Press, 1968).

Satter, David, *It Was a Long Time Ago, and It Never Happened Anyway: Russia and the Communist Past* (New Haven: Yale University Press, 2012).

Sawczuk, Konstantyn, *The Ukraine in the United Nations Organization: Study in Soviet Foreign Policy, 1944–1950* (New York: Columbia University Press, 1975).

Schabas, A. William, "Genocide and Crimes Against Humanity: Clarifying the Relationship" in *The Genocide Convention: The Legacy of 60 Years*, ed. H. G. van der Wilt et al. (Leiden: Martinus Nijhoff, 2012), 3–14.

Schabas, *Genocide in International Law: The Crimes of Crimes* (Cambridge, UK: Cambridge University Press, 2000).

Schabas, "Retroactive Application of the Genocide Convention," *University of St. Thomas Journal of Law and Public Policy* 2, vol. 4 (Spring 2010): 36–59.

Schwartzstein, J. D. Stuart, "Chemical Warfare in Afghanistan: An Independent Assessment," *World Affairs* 3, vol. 145 (Winter 1982/83): 267–272.

Shabad, Boris, "Fashizatsia gosudarstva SShA," *SGP* 1 (January 1951): 38–45.

Shapiro, Herbert, *White Violence and Black Response: From Reconstruction to Montgomery* (Amherst, MA: University of Massachusetts Press, 1988).

Shemesh, Haim, *Soviet-Iraqi Relations, 1968–1988: In the Shadow of the Iraq-Iran Conflict* (Boulder, CO: Lynne Rienner, 1992).

Shulz, H. Richard, *The Soviet Union and Revolutionary Warfare: Principles, Practices, and Regional Comparisons* (Stanford, CA: Hoover Institution, 1988).

Shushanyan, Zaruhi, "Between the Memories and the Present: On the Armenian Genocide" (MA thesis: Institute of Social Studies, The Hague, 2013).

Smele, D. Jonathan, *The Russian Revolution and Civil War, 1917–1921: An Annotated Bibliography* (London: Continuum, 2002).

Smith, E. Karen, *Genocide and the Europeans* (Cambridge, UK: Cambridge University Press, 2010).

Smith, C. Paul, and Robert A. Warrior, *Like a Hurricane: The Indian Movement from Alcatraz to Wounded Knee* (New York: New Press, 1996).

Smith, L. Sherry, "Indians, the Counterculture, and the New Left" in *Beyond Red Power: American Indian Politics and Activism Since 1900*, ed. Daniel M. Cobb and Loretta Fowler (Santa Fe, NM: School for Advanced Research Press, 2007): 142–160.

Smolansky, M. Oles, *The USSR and Iraq: The Soviet Quest for Influence* (Durham, NC: Duke University Press, 1991).

Szeftel, Marc, review of Dallin and Nicolaevsky's book in *American Historical Review* 3, vol. 54 (April 1949): 603–605.

Szyszkowski, Wacław, "Should the Genocide Convention Remain a Dead Letter?" *The Intermarium: Bulletin of the Central European Federal Clubs in Paris and in Rome* 15, vol. 7 (May 1951): 12–14.

Tabor, Michael, *Capitalism Plus Dope Equals Genocide* (1969), https://archive.org/details/CapitalismPlusDopeEqualsGenocide_10.

Thomas, Martin, "France Accused: French North Africa Before the United Nations, 1952–1962," *Contemporary European History* 1, vol. 10 (March 2001): 91–121.

Tikhvinsky, Sergei, "Itogi i perspektivy issledovanii sovetskikh istorikov," *Voprosy istorii* 7 (July 1985): 3–13.

Tismaneanu, Vladimir, "Diabolical Pedagogy and the (Il)logic of Stalinism in Eastern Europe" in *Stalinism Revisited: The Establishment of Communist Regimes in East-Central Europe*, ed. Vladimir Tismaneanu (Budapest: CEU Press, 2009): 25–49.

Tolley, Howard, *The International Commission of Jurists: Global Advocates for Human Rights* (Philadelphia: University of Pennsylvania Press, 1994).

Trainin, Aron, *Bor'ba progressivnykh sil protiv unichtozheniia natsional'nykh grupp i ras (Konferentsia v N'iu-Iorke po bor'be s genotsidom)* (Moscow: Pravda, 1948).

Trainin, "Bor'ba s genotsidom kak mezhdunarodnym prestupleniem," *SGP* 5 (May 1948): 1–16.

Trainin, *Izbrannye proizvedeniia: Zashchita mira i ugolovnyi zakon* (Moscow: Nauka, [1956] 1969).

Trainin, *Ugolovnaia interventsiia* (Moscow: OGIZ, 1935).

Trainin, *Ugolovnaia otvetstvennost gitlerovtsev* (Moscow: Iiurizdat, 1944).

Tyssovski, Yuri, *Prestuplenie bez nakazaniia: Chto proizoshlo v Livane* (Moscow: Progress, 1983).

Ulunian, Artiom, "Soviet Cold War Perceptions of Turkey and Greece," *Cold War History* 2, vol. 3 (January 2003): 36–45.

Urquhart, Brian, "Finding the Hidden UN," *New York Review of Books* 9, vol. 57 (May 27–June 9, 2010).

Volchkov, Alexander, and Arkady Poltorak, "Printsipy Niurnbergskogo prigovora i mezhdunarodnoe pravo," *SGP* 1 (January 1957): 27–37.

Volodin, S., "Konventsiia o preduprezhdenii prestupleniia genotsida i nakazaniia za nego," *SGP* 7 (December 1954): 125–128.

de Waal, Thomas, *Great Catastrophe: Armenians and Turks in the Shadow of Genocide* (Oxford, UK: Oxford University Press, 2015).

Weigert, W. Hans, et al., *Principles of Political Geography* (New York: Appleton-Century-Crofts, 1957).

Weisbord, G. Robert, *Genocide? Birth Control and the Black American* (Westport, CT: Greenwood Press, 1975).

Weiss-Wendt, Anton, *The Soviet Union and the Gutting of the UN Genocide Convention* (Madison, WI: University of Wisconsin Press, 2017).

Weiss-Wendt, Anton, and Uğur Ümit Üngör, "Collaboration in Genocide: The Ottoman Empire 1915–1916, the German-Occupied Baltic 1941–1944, and Rwanda 1944," *Holocaust and Genocide Studies* 3, vol. 25 (Winter 2011): 404–437.

Werth, Nicolas, "A State Against Its People: Violence, Repression, and Terror in the Soviet Union" in *The Black Book of Communism: Crimes, Terror, Repression*, ed. Stéphane Courtois et al. (Cambridge, MA: Harvard University Press, 1999), 33–268.

Westad, Odd Arne, *The Global Cold War: Third World Interventions and the Making of Our Times* (Cambridge, UK: Cambridge University Press, 2007).

Williams, Brian Glyn, "Hidden Ethnocide in the Soviet Muslim Borderlands: The Ethnic Cleansing of the Crimean Tartars," *Journal of Genocide Research* 3, vol. 4 (2002): 357–373.

Zadorozhnyi, Grigory, "Amerikanskaia pravovaia doktrina—zleishii vrag mezhdunarodnogo prava," *SGP* 1 (January 1953): 66–74.

Zadorozhnyi, "'Amerikanskii zhurnal mezhdunarodnogo prava'—propovednik mezhdunarodnogo razboia i bespraviia," *SGP* 12 (December 1952): 80–87.

Zarobyan, Nikita, and Armen Grogoryan, "Rubikon-65," *Yerevan* (April 2006): 135–143.

Zivs, Samuil, "Zakonodatelnoe zakreplenie rasovoi diskriminatsii v SShA i stranakh Britanskoi imperii," *SGP* 4 (April 1955): 109–118.

INDEX

ABOUT THE AUTHOR

ANTON WEISS-WENDT is Research Professor at the Norwegian Holocaust Center in Oslo. He is the author and/or editor of eight books, including *Murder Without Hatred: Estonians and the Holocaust* and *The Soviet Union and the Gutting of the UN Genocide Convention.*